PROFESSIONAL
XMPP PROGRAMMING
WITH JAVASCRIPT AND JQUERY

PROFESSIONAL

XMPP Programming with JavaScript® and jQuery

PROFESSIONAL

XMPP Programming with JavaScript® and jQuery

Jack Moffitt

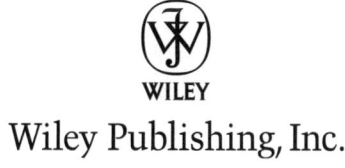

WILEY

Wiley Publishing, Inc.

Professional XMPP Programming with JavaScript® and jQuery

Published by
Wiley Publishing, Inc.
10475 Crosspoint Boulevard
Indianapolis, IN 46256
www.wiley.com

Copyright © 2010 by Wiley Publishing, Inc., Indianapolis, Indiana

Published simultaneously in Canada

ISBN: 978-0-470-54071-8

Manufactured in the United States of America

10 9 8 7 6 5 4 3 2 1

For general information on our other products and services please contact our Customer Care Department within the United States at (877) 762-2974, outside the United States at (317) 572-3993 or fax (317) 572-4002.

Wiley also publishes its books in a variety of electronic formats. Some content that appears in print may not be available in electronic books.

Library of Congress Control Number: 2009900000

Dedicated to my wife Kimberly and our son Jasper, whose loves, hugs, and smiles make every day the best day ever.

CREDITS

EXECUTIVE EDITOR
Carol Long

PROJECT EDITOR
Ed Connor

TECHNICAL EDITOR
Dave Cridland

PRODUCTION EDITOR
Kathleen Wisor

COPY EDITOR
Kim Cofer

EDITORIAL DIRECTOR
Robyn B. Siesky

EDITORIAL MANAGER
Mary Beth Wakefield

MARKETING MANAGER
David Mayhew

PRODUCTION MANAGER
Tim Tate

**VICE PRESIDENT AND
EXECUTIVE GROUP PUBLISHER**
Richard Swadley

VICE PRESIDENT AND EXECUTIVE PUBLISHER
Barry Pruett

ASSOCIATE PUBLISHER
Jim Minatel

PROJECT COORDINATOR, COVER
Lynsey Stanford

COMPOSITOR
Craig Johnson, Happenstance Type-O-Rama

PROOFREADER
Carrie Hunter, Word One

INDEXER
Robert Swanson

COVER DESIGNER
Michael E. Trent

COVER IMAGE
© Punchstock/Glowimages

ABOUT THE AUTHOR

 **JACK MOFFITT** is a hacker and entrepreneur based in Albuquerque, New Mexico. He has founded several startups built on XMPP technology including Chesspark, a real-time, multi-user gaming platform, and Collecta, a real-time search engine for the Web.

He has started and contributed to numerous XMPP related open source and free software projects including the Strophe XMPP client libraries, the Punjab XMPP connection manager, the Palaver multi-user chat component, the Speeqe group chat application.

He also has served several terms on both the XSF Board of Directors and the XSF Council. Previous to his XMPP work, he created the Icecast streaming media server, managed the Ogg, Vorbis, and Theora codec projects, and co-founded the Xiph.org Foundation, a standards organization for royalty-free multimedia technologies for the Internet. He is passionate about free software and open source, open standards, and Internet technology. His favorite programming languages include JavaScript, Erlang, and Python. You can find him at `http://metajack.im`, blogging about start-ups and code, as @metajack on Twitter and Identica, or often spreading the word of XMPP at technology conferences.

ACKNOWLEDGMENTS

WE ALL STAND ON THE SHOULDERS OF GIANTS, and I am fortunate to have stood on many friendly ones throughout my career and while writing this book. Thanks to Carol Long and Ed Connor for the encouragement, handholding, reminders, and patience that every author needs. Thanks also to Jason Salas who not only encouraged me on this project but made the appropriate introductions. Thanks to Dave Cridland for his work ensuring the technical quality of this book and his tireless humor. I'm hugely indebted to Peter Saint-Andre, patron saint of XMPP, and the rest of the XMPP Standards Foundation members for their advice, criticism, and friendship over the years. My colleagues at Collecta and Chesspark also deserve credit for all their friendship, support, and advice, without which I could not have written this book. Finally, the biggest thanks of all to my wife; not only did she encourage me in this project and put up with my long hours and absence, she also worked hard as my first reader and made many helpful suggestions to the text.

CONTENTS

PART II: THE APPLICATIONS

CHAPTER 3: SAYING HELLO: THE FIRST APPLICATION

CHAPTER 4: EXPLORING THE XMPP PROTOCOL: A DEBUGGING CONSOLE

INTRODUCTION

XMPP POWERS A WIDE RANGE OF APPLICATIONS including instant messaging, multi-user chat, voice and video conferencing, collaborative spaces, real-time gaming, data synchronization, and even search. Although XMPP started its life as an open, standardized alternative to proprietary instant messaging systems like ICQ and AOL Instant Messenger, it has matured into an extremely robust protocol for all kinds of exciting creations.

Facebook uses XMPP technology as part of its chat system. Google uses XMPP to power Google Talk and its exciting new Google Wave protocol. Collecta has built a real-time search engine based extensively on XMPP's publish-subscribe system. Several web browsers are experimenting with XMPP as the basis of their synchronization and sharing systems. Dozens of other companies have XMPP-enabled their web applications to provide enhanced user experiences and real-time interaction.

The core of XMPP is the exchange of small, structured chunks of information. Like HTTP, XMPP is a client-server protocol, but it differs from HTTP by allowing either side to send data to the other asynchronously. XMPP connections are long lived, and data is pushed instead of pulled.

Because of XMPP's differences, it provides an excellent companion protocol to HTTP. XMPP-powered web applications are to AJAX what AJAX was to the static web site; they are the next level of interactivity and dynamism. Where JavaScript and dynamic HTML have brought desktop application features to the web browser, XMPP brings new communications possibilities to the Web.

XMPP has many common social web features built in, due to its instant messaging heritage. Contact lists and subscriptions create social graphs, presence updates help users keep track of who is doing what, and private messaging makes communication among users trivial. XMPP also has nearly 300 extensions, providing a broad and useful range of tools on which to build sophisticated applications. With only a handful of these, along with the core protocol, amazing things can be built

This book teaches you to harness the promise of XMPP in your own applications, enabling you to build applications that are social, collaborative, real time, or all of the above. You will develop a series of increasingly sophisticated XMPP applications, starting from "Hello, World!" and finishing with a collaborative text editor, a shared sketch pad, and a real-time, multi-player game. By the end, you will have all the tools you need to build the next generation of applications using XMPP or to add new real-time, push, or social features to your current applications.

WHO THIS BOOK IS FOR

This book is written for developers interested in making XMPP applications. You need not have any previous experience with XMPP, although it will certainly be helpful if you do. The book starts from the assumption that you've heard great things about XMPP and are looking to dive right in.

The JavaScript language is used to develop all the applications in the book because it is an easy language to understand, is familiar to a large number of programmers, and comes on every computer with a web browser. Even though this book uses JavaScript, all the concepts and applications could be developed in any language; most of the "hard parts" are not related to the programming language, the libraries used, or the web browser. You do not need to be a JavaScript expert to understand and work with the code in this book.

It is assumed that you understand the basic front-end web technologies, CSS and HTML. If you've ever written a little HTML from scratch and changed a few CSS styling properties, you should be fine.

This book also makes use of two libraries, jQuery and Strophe. It is helpful if you have used jQuery before, but if you haven't, a short primer is included in Appendix A. The Strophe library is explained fully as the applications are developed.

WHAT THIS BOOK COVERS

The XMPP protocol and its extensions cover a lot of ground. This book focuses on the pieces of XMPP in wide use. The following topics receive much attention:

➤ XMPP's instant messaging features like rosters, presence and subscriptions, and private chats

➤ XMPP stanzas, stanza errors, and client protocol syntax and semantics

➤ Extending XMPP stanzas

➤ Service discovery (XEP-0030)

➤ Data Forms (XEP-0004)

➤ Multi-User Chat (XEP-0045)

➤ Publish-Subscribe (XEP-0060)

Although these topics are all approached from the client side, almost all of it is equally applicable to XMPP bots or server components and plug-ins.

The book also covers XMPP programming related topics such as application design, event handling, and combining simple protocol elements into a greater whole. Along the way, a few web programming topics are also discussed such as the Canvas API.

XMPP is now more than 10 years old and quite mature. This book covers the 1.0 version of the core protocol. The XMPP protocol parts of this book should work unchanged in future versions of the protocol, just as HTTP 1.0 clients can easily communicate with HTTP 1.1 servers.

XMPP has many extensions and several of these are also covered. For the most part, the book concentrates on extensions that are in a stable, mature state. For each extension used, the document number is always given, and if in doubt, you can always check the latest version of the extension to see if it has been changed or superseded.

The book was written with the 1.3 series versions of jQuery and the 1.7 series versions of jQuery UI. These libraries generally remain backward compatible to a large degree. Version 1.0 of the Strophe library is used, but future 1.X versions should also work fine.

HOW THIS BOOK IS STRUCTURED

This book is primarily organized as a walkthrough tutorial of a series of example XMPP applications. Each application increases in difficulty and teaches you one or more useful parts of the XMPP protocol and its extensions. These applications are stripped down for clarity, but they are examples of the kinds of applications XMPP developers create every day.

This book is divided into three parts.

The first part is an introduction to the XMPP protocol, its uses, and XMPP application design. Chapter 1 covers the use cases for XMPP, the history of the protocol, and its component parts. Chapter 2 explains when XMPP is a good choice for the job and goes into detail about how XMPP applications work, particularly for the Web.

The second part is the meat of the book and contains nine XMPP applications that solve a variety of problems. Each application is more complex than the last and builds on the concepts of the previous ones. Chapter 3 starts with a simple "Hello, World!" type example, and by Chapter 11 you build a real-time, multi-player game.

The last part covers a few advanced but important topics. Chapter 12 discusses attached sessions, a useful trick for security, optimization, and persistence. Chapter 13 goes into detail about how best to deploy and scale XMPP-based applications. Chapter 14 explains how to use Strophe's plug-in system and how to create your own plug-ins.

WHAT YOU NEED TO USE THIS BOOK

This book makes use of web technologies and therefore requires almost no special tools. You can use, build, and run the applications in this book on virtually any platform. The libraries needed for the applications are explained in Chapter 3, and most can be used without downloading any code.

You will need some way to serve web pages such as a local web server or a hosting account somewhere. If you don't have these readily available, you can use the Tape program to serve the files; Tape is a simple web server and is explained in Appendix B. It is an unfortunate requirement of browser security policy that you can't easily run these applications directly from your local file system.

You will need an XMPP account (or multiple accounts in some cases if you want to test the code by yourself) to run the applications. You can avail yourself of any of the public XMPP servers for this purpose, although you will need to ensure that the server has support for publish-subscribe and multi-user chat; most do. You can also download and run your own XMPP server instead, although this is not covered in the book.

Chapter 12 requires some server-side assistance. The example uses the Python programming language along with the Django framework to provide this. This chapter is an advanced topic and is not needed for the normal applications in the book.

CONVENTIONS

To help you get the most from the text and keep track of what's happening, we've used a number of conventions throughout the book.

 Boxes like this one hold important, not-to-be forgotten information that is directly relevant to the surrounding text.

 Notes, tips, hints, tricks, and asides to the current discussion are offset and placed in italics like this.

As for styles in the text:

➤ We *highlight* new terms and important words when we introduce them.

➤ We show keyboard strokes like this: Ctrl+A.

➤ We show file names, URLs, and code within the text like so: `persistence.properties`.

➤ We present code in two different ways:

```
We use a monofont type with no highlighting for most code examples.
We use boldface highlighting to emphasize code that is of particularly
importance in the present context.
```

SOURCE CODE

As you work through the examples in this book, you may choose either to type in all the code manually or to use the source code files that accompany the book. All of the source code used in this book is available for download at `http://www.wrox.com`. Once at the site, simply locate the book's title (either by using the Search box or by using one of the title lists) and click the Download Code link on the book's detail page to obtain all the source code for the book.

Because many books have similar titles, you may find it easiest to search by ISBN; this book's ISBN is 978-0-470-54071-8.

Once you download the code, just decompress it with your favorite compression tool. Alternatively, you can go to the main Wrox code download page at `http://www.wrox.com/dynamic/books/download.aspx` to see the code available for this book and all other Wrox books.

ERRATA

We make every effort to ensure that there are no errors in the text or in the code. However, no one is perfect, and mistakes do occur. If you find an error in one of our books, like a spelling mistake or faulty piece of code, we would be very grateful for your feedback. By sending in errata, you may save another reader hours of frustration and at the same time you will be helping us provide even higher quality information.

To find the errata page for this book, go to `http://www.wrox.com` and locate the title using the Search box or one of the title lists. Then, on the book details page, click the Book Errata link. On this page you can view all errata that has been submitted for this book and posted by Wrox editors. A complete book list including links to each book's errata is also available at `www.wrox.com/misc-pages/booklist.shtml`.

If you don't spot "your" error on the Book Errata page, go to `www.wrox.com/contact/techsupport.shtml` and complete the form there to send us the error you have found. We'll check the information and, if appropriate, post a message to the book's errata page and fix the problem in subsequent editions of the book.

P2P.WROX.COM

For author and peer discussion, join the P2P forums at `p2p.wrox.com`. The forums are a web-based system for you to post messages relating to Wrox books and related technologies and interact with other readers and technology users. The forums offer a subscription feature to e-mail you topics of interest of your choosing when new posts are made to the forums. Wrox authors, editors, other industry experts, and your fellow readers are present on these forums.

At `http://p2p.wrox.com` you will find a number of different forums that will help you not only as you read this book, but also as you develop your own applications. To join the forums, just follow these steps:

1. Go to `p2p.wrox.com` and click the Register link.

2. Read the terms of use and click Agree.

3. Complete the required information to join as well as any optional information you wish to provide and click Submit.

4. You will receive an e-mail with information describing how to verify your account and complete the joining process.

 You can read messages in the forums without joining P2P but in order to post your own messages, you must join.

Once you join, you can post new messages and respond to messages other users post. You can read messages at any time on the Web. If you would like to have new messages from a particular forum e-mailed to you, click the Subscribe to this Forum icon by the forum name in the forum listing.

For more information about how to use the Wrox P2P, be sure to read the P2P FAQs for answers to questions about how the forum software works as well as many common questions specific to P2P and Wrox books. To read the FAQs, click the FAQ link on any P2P page.

PART I
XMPP Protocol and Architecture

1
Getting to Know XMPP

WHAT'S IN THIS CHAPTER?

➤ The history of XMPP

➤ XMPP networks and connections

➤ XMPP's three building block stanzas

The eXtensible Messaging and Presence Protocol (XMPP) is, at its most basic level, a protocol for moving small, structured pieces of data between two places. From this humble basis, it has been used to build large-scale instant messaging systems, Internet gaming platforms, search engines, collaboration spaces, and voice and video conferencing systems. More unique applications appear every day, further demonstrating how versatile and powerful XMPP can be.

XMPP is made of a few small building blocks, and on top of these primitives many larger constructions have been made. Within XMPP are systems for building publish-subscribe services, multi-user chat, form retrieval and processing, service discovery, real-time data transfer, privacy control, and remote procedure calls. Often, XMPP programmers create their own, unique constructions that are fitted exactly for the problem at hand.

Most social media constructs that have propelled web sites like Facebook, MySpace, and Twitter into the forefront are also baked into XMPP. Within XMPP, you'll find rosters full of contacts that create a social graph with directed or undirected edges. Presence notifications are sent automatically when contacts come online and go offline, and private and public messages are the bread and butter application of XMPP systems. Developers will sometimes choose XMPP as the underlying technology layer simply because it gives them many social features for free, leaving them to concentrate on the unique pieces of their application.

The possibilities are vast, but before you can begin, you need to know about XMPP's different pieces and how they fit together into a cohesive whole.

WHAT IS XMPP?

XMPP, like all protocols, defines a format for moving data between two or more communicating entities. In XMPP's case, the entities are normally a client and a server, although it also allows for peer-to-peer communication between two servers or two clients. Many XMPP servers exist on the Internet, accessible to all, and form a federated network of interconnected systems.

Data exchanged over XMPP is in XML, giving the communication a rich, extensible structure. Many modern protocols forgo the bandwidth savings of a binary encoding for the more practical feature of being human readable and therefore easily debugged. XMPP's choice to piggyback on XML means that it can take advantage of the large amount of knowledge and supporting software for dealing with XML.

One major feature XMPP gets by using XML is XML's extensibility. It is extremely easy to add new features to the protocol that are both backward and forward compatible. This extensibility is put to great use in the more than 200 protocol extensions registered with the XMPP Standards Foundation and has provided developers with a rich and practically unlimited set of tools.

XML is known primarily as a document format, but in XMPP, XML data is organized as a pair of streams, one stream for each direction of communication. Each XML stream consists of an opening element, followed by XMPP stanzas and other top-level elements, and then a closing element. Each XMPP stanza is a first-level child element of the stream with all its descendent elements and attributes. At the end of an XMPP connection, the two streams form a pair of valid XML documents.

XMPP stanzas make up the core part of the protocol, and XMPP applications are concerned with sending and responding to various kinds of stanzas. Stanzas may contain information about other entities' availability on the network, personal messages similar to e-mail, or structured communication intended for computer processing. An example stanza is shown here:

```
<message to='elizabeth@longbourn.lit'
         from='darcy@pemberley.lit/dance'
         type='chat'>
  <body>What think you of books?</body>
</message>
```

In a typical client-server XMPP session, a stanza such as this one from Elizabeth to Mr. Darcy will travel from Elizabeth's client to her server. Her server will notice that it is addressed to an entity on a remote server and will establish an XMPP connection with the remote server and forward the message there. This communication between servers resembles the e-mail network, but unlike e-mail servers, XMPP servers always communicate directly with each other and not through intermediate servers.

This direct communication eliminates some common vectors for spam and unauthorized messages. This is just one of the many ways in which XMPP is designed for security. It also supports encrypted communications between endpoints through use of Transport Layer Security (TLS) and strong authentication mechanisms via Simple Authentication and Security Layers (SASL).

XMPP is designed for the exchange of small bits of information, not large blobs of binary data. XMPP can, however, be used to negotiate and set up out-of-band or in-band transports, which can move large blocks from point to point. For these kinds of transfers, XMPP functions as a signaling layer.

The focus on small, structured bits of data gives the XMPP protocol extremely low latency and makes it extremely useful for real-time applications. These applications, which include collaborative spaces, games, and synchronization, are driving XMPP's growth in popularity as developers experiment with the real-time Web.

You will see how easy it is to make real-time web applications through this book's examples. By the end of the book you should have a thorough understanding of why so many people are excited about XMPP's power and promise.

A BRIEF HISTORY OF XMPP

The XMPP protocol is now more than 10 years old, and it has come a long way from its humble beginnings. Much of XMPP's design is due to the environment in which XMPP was created, and the history of XMPP provides an interesting case study in how open protocols foster adoption and innovation.

In 1996, Mirabilis released ICQ, which popularized rapid, personal communication among Internet users. Its use spread rapidly, and before long other companies were releasing similar products. In 1997, AOL launched AOL Instant Messenger. Yahoo followed suit in 1998 with Yahoo Pager (eventually renamed Yahoo Messenger), and in 1999 Microsoft finally joined the competition with MSN Messenger (now Windows Live Messenger).

Each of these instant messaging applications was tied to a proprietary protocol and network run by the companies that made them. Users of ICQ could not talk to Yahoo users and vice versa. It became common for users to run more than one of these applications to be able to talk to all of their contacts because no single vendor claimed 100% market share.

It didn't take long before developers desired to write their own clients for these proprietary IM networks. Some wished to make multiprotocol clients that could unite two or more of the IM networks, and others wanted to bring these applications to operating systems other than Microsoft Windows and Apple's Mac OS. These developers ran into many roadblocks; they had to reverse-engineer undocumented protocols, and the IM networks aggressively changed the protocol to thwart third-party developers.

It was in this climate that the idea for an open, decentralized IM network and protocol was born.

Jeremie Miller announced the Jabber project in January of 1999. Jabber was a decentralized instant messaging protocol based on XML and a server implementation called jabberd. A community immediately formed around the protocol and implementations spawning more clients and more ideas. By May of 2000, the core protocols were stabilized and jabberd reached a production release.

The Jabber Software Foundation (JSF) was founded in 2001 to coordinate the efforts around the Jabber protocol and its implementations. By late 2002, the JSF had submitted the core protocol specifications to the IETF process, and an IETF working group was formed. In October 2004, this standards process produced improved versions of the Jabber protocols, renamed XMPP, documented as RFCs 3920, 3921, 3922, and 3923.

During the protocol's early life, developers continued to expand its possibilities by submitting protocol extensions to the JSF. These extensions were called Jabber Extension Proposals (JEPs).

Eventually the JSF and the extensions followed the naming change from Jabber to XMPP and became the XMPP Standards Foundation (XSF) and XMPP Extension Proposals (XEPs).

By 2005, large-scale deployments of XMPP technology were well underway, highlighted by the launch of Google Talk, Google's own XMPP-based IM service.

Today, the XMPP ecosystem is quite large. Nearly 300 extensions have been accepted as XEPs, and dozens of client and server implementations have been created — both commercial and open source. Software developers of virtually any programming language can find a library to speed their XMPP application development efforts.

XMPP applications started out very IM-centric, reflecting its origins, but developers have found XMPP to be quite capable for a number of applications that weren't originally foreseen including search engines and synchronization software. This utility is a testament to the power of an open system and open standardization process.

Most recently, the IETF has formed a new XMPP working group to prepare the next versions of the XMPP specifications, incorporating all the knowledge gained since the original RFCs were published. XMPP continues to be refined and extended so that application developers and Internet users will always have an open, decentralized communications protocol.

THE XMPP NETWORK

Any XMPP network is composed of a number of actors. These actors can be categorized as servers, clients, components, and server plug-ins. An XMPP developer will write code to create or modify one of these types of actors. Each actor has its place on the XMPP network's stage.

Servers

XMPP servers, or more accurately, XMPP entities speaking the server-to-server protocol or the server end of the client-to-server protocol, are the circulatory system of any XMPP network. A server's job is to route stanzas, whether they are internal from one user to another or from a local user to a user on a remote server.

The set of XMPP servers that can mutually communicate forms an XMPP network. The set of public XMPP servers forms the global, federated XMPP network. If a server does not speak the server-to-server protocol, it becomes an island, unable to communicate with external servers.

An XMPP server will usually allow users to connect to it. It is, however, also possible to write applications or services that speak the server-to-server protocol directly in order to improve efficiency by eliminating routing overhead.

Anyone can run an XMPP server, and full-featured servers are available for nearly every platform. Ejabberd, Openfire, and Tigase are three popular open source choices that will work on Windows, Mac OS X, or Linux systems. Several commercial XMPP servers are available as well, including M-Link and Jabber XCP.

Clients

The majority of XMPP entities are clients, which connect to XMPP servers via the client-to-server protocol. Many of these entities are human-driven, traditional IM users, but there are also automated services running as *bots*.

Clients must authenticate to an XMPP server somewhere. The server routes all stanzas the client sends to the appropriate destination. The server also manages several aspects of the clients' sessions, including their roster and their bare address, which you see more of shortly.

All of the applications in this book are written as client applications. This is typically the starting point of most XMPP development. For applications without a user focus or with demanding needs, it is often preferable to create a different kind of entity, such as a server component.

Components

Clients are not the only things that may connect to XMPP servers; most servers also support external server *components*. These components augment the behavior of the server by adding some new service. These components have their own identity and address within the server, but run externally and communicate over a component protocol.

The component protocol (defined in XEP-0114) enables developers to create server extensions in a server-agnostic way. Any component using the protocol can run on any server that speaks the component protocol (assuming it doesn't use some special feature specific to a particular server). A multi-user chat service is a typical example of something that is often implemented as a component.

Components also authenticate to the server, but this authentication is simpler than the full SASL authentication for clients. Typically authentication is done with a simple password.

Each component becomes a separately addressable entity within the server and appears to the outside world as a sub-server. XMPP servers do not manage anything beyond basic stanza routing on behalf of connected components. This allows great freedom to component developers to do things exactly as they want, but places greater responsibility on them when they need functionality such as rosters and presence management.

The server also allows a component to internally route or manage stanzas for itself. A component can therefore create separately addressable pieces to be used as rooms, users, or whatever the developer requires. This is something that a client session cannot do and can be used to create really elegant services.

Finally, because components do not have resources managed for them, services that operate with many users or with a high amount of traffic can manage their own resources in a way that makes sense for their purpose. Developers often create services as client bots, only to discover later that the server's roster management capabilities often do not scale well to thousands upon thousands of contacts. Components can manage rosters, if they have them at all, in whichever way makes sense for the task and scale required.

Plug-ins

Many XMPP servers can also be extended via *plug-ins*. These plug-ins are usually written in the same programming language as the server itself and run inside the server's processes. Their purpose overlaps to a large degree with external components, but plug-ins may also access internal server data structures and change core server behavior.

The virtually limitless abilities afforded to server plug-ins come with a cost; plug-ins are not portable between different servers. A different server may be written in a completely different language, and its internal data structures may differ radically. This cost aside, plug-ins are sometimes the only way to get a particular job done.

Plug-ins have reduced overhead compared to components because they do not need to communicate over a network socket. They also need not parse or serialize XML and can, instead, work directly with internal server representations of stanzas. This can lead to much needed performance improvements when the application must scale.

XMPP ADDRESSING

Every entity on an XMPP network will have one or more addresses, or *JIDs*. JIDs (short for jabber identifiers) can take a variety of forms, but they normally look just like e-mail addresses. `darcy@pemberley.lit` and `elizabeth@longbourn.lit` are two examples of JIDs.

Each JID is made up of up to three pieces, the *local part*, the *domain*, and the *resource*. The domain portion is always required, but the other two pieces are optional, depending on their context.

The domain is the resolvable DNS name of the entity — a server, component, or plug-in. A JID consisting of just a domain is valid and addresses a server. Stanzas addressed to a domain are handled by the server itself and potentially routed to a component or plug-in.

The local part usually identifies a particular user at a domain. It appears at the beginning of a JID, before the domain, and it is separated from the rest of the JID by the @ character, just like the local part of an e-mail address. The local part can also be used to identify other objects; a multi-user chat service will expose each room as a JID where the local part references the room.

A JID's resource part most often identifies a particular XMPP connection of a client. For XMPP clients, each connection is assigned a resource. If Mr. Darcy, whose JID is `darcy@pemberley.lit`, is connected both from his study and his library, his connections will be addressable as `darcy@pemberley.lit/study` and `darcy@pemberley.lit/library`. Like the local part, a resource can be used to identify other things; on a multi-user chat service, the resource part of the JID is used to identify a particular user of a chat room.

JIDs are divided into two categories, *bare JIDs* and *full JIDs*. The full JID is always the most specific address for a particular entity, and the bare JID is simply the full JID with any resource part removed. For example, if a client's full JID is `darcy@pemberley.lit/library`, its bare JID would be `darcy@pemberley.lit`. In some cases, the bare JID and the full JID are the same, such as when addressing a server or a specific multi-user chat room.

Bare JIDs for clients are somewhat special, because the server itself will handle stanzas addressed to a client's bare JID. For example, a message sent to a client's bare JID will be forwarded to one or more connected resources of the user, or if the user is offline, stored for later delivery. Stanzas sent to full JIDs, however, are usually routed directly to the client's connection for that resource. You can think of bare JIDs as addressing the user's account as opposed to addressing one of the user's connected clients.

XMPP STANZAS

Work is accomplished in XMPP by the sending and receiving of XMPP stanzas over an XMPP stream. Three basic stanzas make up the core XMPP toolset. These stanzas are `<presence>`, `<message>`, and `<iq>`. Each type of stanza has its place and purpose, and by composing the right kinds of quantities of these stanzas, sophisticated behaviors can be achieved.

Remember that an XMPP stream is a set of two XML documents, one for each direction of communication. These documents have a root `<stream:stream>` element. The children of this `<stream:stream>` element consist of routable *stanzas* and stream related top-level children.

Each stanza is an XML element, including its children. The end points of XMPP communication process input and generate output on a stanza-by-stanza basis. The following example shows a simplified and short XMPP session:

```
<stream:stream>
  <iq type='get'>
    <query xmlns='jabber:iq:roster'/>
  </iq>

  <presence/>

  <message to='darcy@pemberley.lit'
           from='elizabaeth@longbourn.lit/ballroom'
           type='chat'>
    <body>I cannot talk of books in a ball-room; my head is always full of
      something else.</body>
  </message>

  <presence type='unavailable'/>
</stream:stream>
```

In this example, Elizabeth created an XMPP stream by sending the opening `<stream:stream>` tag. With the stream open, she sent her first stanza, an `<iq>` element. This `<iq>` element requested Elizabeth's roster, the list of all her stored contacts. Next, she notified the server that she was online and available with a `<presence>` stanza. After noticing that Mr. Darcy was online, she sent him a short `<message>` stanza, thwarting his attempt at small talk. Finally, Elizabeth sent another `<presence>` stanza to inform the server she was unavailable and closed the `<stream:stream>` element, ending the session.

You have now seen an example of each kind of XMPP stanza in action. Each of these is explained in more detail, but first, you should learn about what properties they all share.

Common Attributes

All three stanzas support a set of common attributes. Whether they are attributes of `<presence>`, `<message>`, or `<iq>` elements, the following attributes all mean the same thing.

from

Stanzas almost always have a `from` attribute. This attribute identifies the JID of the stanza's origin. Setting the `from` attribute on outgoing stanzas is not recommended; the server adds the correct `from` attribute to all stanzas as they pass through, and if you set the `from` attribute incorrectly, the server may reject your stanza altogether.

If the `from` attribute is missing on a received stanza in a client-to-server stream, this is interpreted to mean that the stanza originated from the server itself. In the server-to-server protocol, a missing `from` attribute is an error.

Note that the example stanzas in this book often include the `from` attribute. This is done for clarity and disambiguation.

to

XMPP servers route your stanzas to the JID supplied in the `to` attribute. Similarly to the `from` attribute, if the `to` attribute is missing in a client-to-server stream, the server assumes it is a message intended for the server itself. It is recommended that you omit the `to` attribute when you address the server itself.

If the JID specified in the `to` attribute is a user, the server potentially handles the stanza on the user's behalf. If the destination is a bare JID, the server handles the stanza. This behavior is different for the three stanza types, and is explained alongside each type. If a full JID is specified as the destination, the server routes the stanza directly to the user.

type

The `type` attribute specifies the specific kind of `<presence>`, `<message>`, or `<iq>` stanza. Each of the three basic stanzas has several possible values for the `type` attribute, and these are explained when each stanza is covered in detail.

All three stanzas may have their `type` attribute set to a value of `error`. This indicates that the stanza is an error response to a received stanza of the same kind. You must not respond to a stanza with an `error` type, to avoid feedback loops on the network.

id

Stanzas may be given an `id` attribute to aid in identifying responses. For `<iq>` stanzas, this attribute is required, but for the other two it is optional. If a stanza is generated in reply to a stanza with an `id` attribute, the reply stanza must contain an `id` attribute with the same value.

The `id` attribute needs to be unique enough that the stanza's sender can use it to disambiguate responses. Often, it is easiest just to make these unique in a given stream to avoid any ambiguity.

Reply stanzas for `<message>` and `<presence>` stanzas are generally limited to reporting errors. Reply stanzas for `<iq>` can signal successful operations, acknowledge a command, or return requested data. In all these cases, the client uses the `id` attribute of the reply stanza to identify which request stanza it is associated with. In cases where many stanzas of the same type are sent in a short time frame, this capability is essential because the replies may be delivered out of order.

Presence Stanzas

The `<presence>` stanza controls and reports the availability of an entity. This availability can range from simple online and offline to the more complex away and do not disturb. In addition, `<presence>` stanzas are used to establish and terminate presence subscriptions to other entities.

In traditional instant messaging systems, presence notifications are the main source of traffic. To enable instant communication, it is necessary to know when the other party is available to communicate. When you send an e-mail, you have no idea if the recipient is currently checking and responding to e-mail, but with instant messages and presence notifications, you know before the message is sent if the recipient is around.

For applications in other domains, presence notifications can be used to signal similar kinds of information. For example, some developers have written bots that set their presence to do not disturb when they are too busy to accept more work. The basic online and offline states can let applications know whether a service is currently functioning or down for maintenance.

Normal Presence Stanzas

A normal `<presence>` stanza contains no `type` attribute or a `type` attribute that has the value `unavailable` or `error`. These stanzas set or indicate an entity's presence or availability for communication.

There is no `available` value for the `type` attribute because this is indicated instead by the lack of a `type` attribute.

Users manipulate their own presence status by sending `<presence>` stanzas without a `to` attribute, addressing the server directly. You've seen two short examples of this already, and these are included along with some longer examples here:

```
<presence/>

<presence type='unavailable'/>

<presence>
  <show>away</show>
  <status>at the ball</status>
</presence>

<presence>
  <status>touring the countryside</status>
  <priority>10</priority>
</presence>

<presence>
  <priority>10</priority>
</presence>
```

The first two stanzas set a user's presence status to online or offline, respectively. These are also typically the first and last presence stanzas sent during an XMPP session.

The next two examples both show extra presence information in the form of `<show>`, `<status>`, and `<priority>` children.

The `<show>` element is used to communicate the nature of the user's availability. The element is named "show" because it requests that the recipient's client use this information to update a visual indicator of the sender's presence. Only one `<show>` child is allowed in a `<presence>` stanza, and this element may only contain the following possible values: `away`, `chat`, `dnd`, and `xa`. These values communicate that a user is away, is interested in chatting, does not wish to be disturbed, or is away for an extended period.

A `<status>` element is a human-readable string that the user can set to any value in order to communicate presence information. This string is generally displayed next to the contact's name in the recipient's chat client.

Each connected resource of a user has a priority between –128 and 127. This priority is set to zero by default, but can be manipulated by including a `<priority>` element in `<presence>` stanzas. Users with multiple simultaneous connections may use this to indicate which resource should receive chat messages addressed to their bare JID. The server will deliver such messages to the resource with the highest priority. A negative priority has a special meaning; resources with a negative priority will never have messages delivered to them that were addressed to the bare JID. Negative priorities are extremely useful for automated applications that run on the same JID as a human is using for regular chat.

Extending Presence Stanzas

It is tempting for developers to want to extend `<presence>` stanzas to include more detailed information such as the song the user is currently listening to or the person's mood. Because `<presence>` stanzas are broadcast to all contacts (even those that may not have an interest in the information) and constitute a large share of the network traffic in the XMPP network, this practice is discouraged. These kinds of extensions are handled by protocols that more tightly focus delivery of this extra information.

Presence Subscriptions

The user's server automatically broadcasts presence information to contacts that have a presence subscription to the user. Similarly, users receive presence updates from all contacts for which they have a presence subscription. Presence subscriptions are established and controlled by use of `<presence>` stanzas.

Unlike some social network and IM systems, presence subscriptions in XMPP are directional. If Elizabeth has a subscription to Mr. Darcy's presence information, this does not imply that Mr. Darcy has a subscription to Elizabeth. If a bidirectional subscription is desired, a subscription must be separately established in both directions. Bidirectional subscriptions are often the norm for human communicators, but many services (and even some users) are interested in only one of the directions.

Presence subscription stanzas can be identified by a `type` attribute that has a value of `subscribe`, `unsubscribe`, `subscribed`, or `unsubscribed`. The first two values request that a new presence subscription be established or an existing subscription be removed, and the other two are the answers to such requests.

The following example shows Elizabeth and Mr. Darcy establishing a mutual presence subscription:

```
<presence from='elizabeth@longbourn.lit/outside'
          to='darcy@pemberley.lit'
          type='subscribe'/>

<presence from='darcy@pemberley.lit/library'
          to='elizabeth@longbourn.lit/outside'
          type='subscribed'/>

<presence from='darcy@pemberley.lit/library'
          to='elizabeth@longbourn.lit'
          type='subscribe'/>

<presence from='elizabeth@longbourn.lit/outside'
          to='darcy@pemberley.lit/library'
          type='subscribed'/>
```

After this exchange of stanzas, both Elizabeth and Mr. Darcy will find each other in their rosters and be notified of each other's presence updates.

Chapter 6 explores a fairly traditional IM application with the ability to establish and remove subscriptions as well as showing contacts' presence statuses.

Directed Presence

The final kind of `<presence>` stanza is *directed presence*. A directed presence stanza is a normal `<presence>` stanza addressed directly to another user or some other entity. These can be used to communicate presence to entities that do not have a presence subscription, usually because the presence information is needed only temporarily.

One important feature of directed presence is that the recipient of the presence information is automatically notified when the sender becomes unavailable even if the sender forgets to notify the recipient explicitly. Services can use directed presence to establish temporary knowledge of a user's availability that won't accidentally get out of date.

You see directed presence in action in Chapter 8 because it is quite important for multi-user chat.

Message Stanzas

As their name implies, `<message>` stanzas are used to send messages from one entity to another. These messages may be simple chat messages that you are familiar with from other IM systems, but they can also be used to transport any kind of structured information. For example, the SketchCast application in Chapter 9 uses `<message>` stanzas to transport drawing instructions, and in Chapter 11 `<message>` stanzas are used to communicate game state and new game moves.

A `<message>` stanza is fire and forget; there is no built in reliability, similar to e-mail messages. Once the message has been sent, the sender has no information on whether it was delivered or when it was received. In some cases, such as when sending to a non-existent server, the sender may receive an error stanza alerting them to the problem. Reliable delivery can be achieved by layering acknowledgments into your application's protocol (see Message Receipts in XEP-0184 for an example of this).

Here are some example `<message>` stanzas:

```
<message from='bingley@netherfield.lit/drawing_room'
         to='darcy@pemberley.lit'
         type='chat'>
  <body>Come, Darcy, I must have you dance.</body>
  <thread>4fd61b376fbc4950b9433f031a5595ab</thread>
</message>

<message from='bennets@chat.meryton.lit/mrs.bennet'
         to='mr.bennet@longbourn.lit/study'
         type='groupchat'>
  <body>We have had a most delightful evening, a most excellent ball.</body>
</message>
```

The first example shows a typical `<message>` stanza for a private chat, including a thread identifier. The second example is a multi-user chat message that Mrs. Bennet has sent to the bennets@chat.meryton.lit room, received by Mr. Bennet.

Message Types

Several different types of `<message>` stanzas exist. These types are indicated with the `type` attribute, and this attribute can have the value `chat`, `error`, `normal`, `groupchat`, or `headline`. Sometimes the message's type is used to inform a user's client how best to present the message, but some XMPP extensions, multi-user chat being a prime example, use the `type` attribute to disambiguate context.

The `type` attribute of a `<message>` stanza is optional, but it is recommended that applications provide one. Also, any reply `<message>` stanza should mirror the `type` attribute received. If no `type` attribute is specified, the `<message>` stanza is interpreted as if it had a `type` attribute set to `normal`.

Messages of type `chat` are sent in the context of a one-to-one chat conversation. This type is the most common in IM applications, which are primarily concerned with private, one-to-one communication.

The `error` type is used in reply to a message that generated an error. These are commonly seen in response to malformed addressing; sending a `<message>` stanza to a non-existent domain or user results in a reply stanza with the `type` attribute set to `error`.

A `<message>` stanza with a type of `normal` has been sent outside the context of a one-to-one chat. This type is rarely used in practice.

The `groupchat` type is used for messages sent from multi-user chats. It is used to disambiguate direct, private messages from a multi-user chat participant from the broadcast messages that participant sends to everyone in the room. A private message has the `type` attribute set to `chat`, whereas a message sent to everyone in the room contains a `type` attribute set to `groupchat`.

The last `<message>` stanza type is `headline`. These types of messages are used mostly by automated services that do not expect or support replies. If automatically generated e-mail had a `type` attribute, it would use a value of `headline`.

Message Contents

Though `<message>` stanzas are allowed to contain arbitrary extension elements, the `<body>` and `<thread>` elements are the normal mechanisms provided for adding content to messages. Both of these child elements are optional.

The `<body>` element contains the human-readable contents of the message. More than one `<body>` element can be included as long as each of them contains a distinct `xml:lang` attribute, and this allows for `<message>` stanzas to be sent with content in multiple languages.

Conversations, like e-mail, can form *threads*, where each message in a thread is related to the same conversation. Threads are created by adding a `<thread>` element to a `<message>` stanza. The content of the `<thread>` element is some unique identifier that distinguishes the thread. A reply stanza should contain the same `<thread>` element as the one it is a reply to.

In IM contexts, among others, there are a few commonly used extensions to the message contents. XHTML-IM, defined in XEP-0071, is used to provide formatting, hyperlinking, and rich media in messages. Chapter 5's microblogging client, Arthur, uses XHTML-IM to provide enhanced message bodies. Another extension, Chat State Notifications (XEP-0085), allows users to notify each other of when they are composing a message or have gone idle. The Gab application in Chapter 6 uses these notifications to provide a nice user experience when one party is typing for a long time; the recipient will have some indication that the other party is still actively engaged in the conversation.

IQ Stanzas

The `<iq>` stanza stands for Info/Query and provides a request and response mechanism for XMPP communication. It is very similar to the basic workings of the HTTP protocol, allowing both get and set queries, similar to the GET and POST actions of HTTP.

Each `<iq>` stanza is required to have a response, and, as mentioned previously, the stanza's required `id` attribute is used to associate a response with the request that caused it. The `<iq>` stanza comes in four flavors differentiated by the stanza's `type` attribute. There are two types of `<iq>` stanza requests, `get` and `set`, and two types of responses, `result` and `error`. Throughout the book these are often abbreviated as *IQ-get*, *IQ-set*, *IQ-result*, and *IQ-error*.

Every IQ-get or IQ-set must receive a response IQ-result or IQ-error. The following examples show some common `<iq>` stanzas and their possible responses. Note that unlike `<message>` and `<presence>` stanzas, which have defined children elements, `<iq>` stanzas typically contain only extension elements relating to their function. Also, each pair of `<iq>` stanzas has a matching `id` attribute.

```
<iq from='jane@longbourn.lit/garden'
    type='get'
    id='roster1'>
  <query xmlns='jabber:iq:roster'/>
</iq>

<iq to='jane@longbourn.lit/garden'
```

```
      type='error'
      id='roster1'>
  <query xmlns='jabber:iq:roster'/>
  <error type='cancel'>
    <feature-not-implemented xmlns='urn:ietf:params:xml:ns:xmpp-stanzas'/>
  </error>
</iq>
```

Jane sent a malformed roster retrieval request to her server. The server replied with an error. Error stanzas are covered in detail later.

```
<iq from='jane@longbourn.lit/garden'
    type='get'
    id='roster2'>
  <query xmlns='jabber:iq:roster'/>
</iq>

<iq to='jane@longbourn.lit/garden'
    type='result'
    id='roster2'>
  <query xmlns='jabber:iq:roster'>
    <item jid='elizabeth@longbourn.lit' name='Elizabeth'/>
    <item jid='bingley@netherfield.lit' name='Bingley'/>
  </query>
</iq>
```

After resending a corrected request, the server replied to Jane with her small roster. You can see that Elizabeth and Bingley are both in Jane's contact list.

```
<iq from='jane@longbourn.lit/garden'
    type='set'
    id='roster3'>
  <query xmlns='jabber:iq:roster'>
    <item jid='darcy@pemberley.lit' name='Mr. Darcy'/>
  </query>
</iq>

<iq to='jane@longbourn.lit/garden'
    type='result'
    id='roster3'/>
```

Jane attempts to add Mr. Darcy to her roster, and the server indicates success with a blank IQ-result. In the cases where the response is simply an acknowledgment of success, the IQ-result stanza will often be empty.

The `<iq>` stanza is quite useful in any case where result data or simple acknowledgment is required. Most XMPP extension protocols use a mix of `<iq>` and `<message>` stanzas to accomplish their goals. The `<iq>` stanzas are used for things like configuration and state changes, whereas `<message>` stanzas are used for regular communication. In some cases `<iq>` stanzas are used for communication because stanza acknowledgment can be used for rate limiting.

Error Stanzas

All three of the XMPP stanzas have an error type, and the contents of each type of error stanza are arranged in the same pattern. Error stanzas have a well-defined structure, often including the contents of the original, offending stanza, the generic error information, and, optionally, an application-specific error condition and information.

All error stanzas must have a `type` attribute set to `error` and one `<error>` child element. Many error stanzas also include the original stanza's contents, but this is not required and, in some cases, not desirable.

The `<error>` child has a required `type` attribute of its own, which can be one of `cancel`, `continue`, `modify`, `auth`, or `wait`. The `cancel` value signifies that the action should not be retried, because it will always fail. A value of `continue` generally indicates a warning and is not frequently encountered. An error type of `modify` communicates that the data sent needs some change in order to be accepted. An `auth` error informs the entity that the action should be retried after authenticating in some way. Finally, the `wait` value reports that the server is temporarily having some problem, and the original stanza should be resent unmodified after a short time.

An `<error>` child is also required to contain an error condition from a list of defined conditions as a child element. It may also contain a `<text>` element giving further details about the error. An application-specific error condition can also be specified in a child element of the `<error>` element under its own namespace.

Table 1-1 lists the most common defined error conditions. For more information on these, please refer to Section 3.9.2 of RFC 3920. Note that each of these condition elements must be under the `urn:ietf:params:xml:ns:xmpp-stanzas` namespace.

TABLE 1-1: Common Defined Error Conditions

CONDITION ELEMENT	DESCRIPTION
`<bad-request/>`	The request was malformed or includes unexpected data.
`<conflict/>`	Another resource or session exists with the same name.
`<feature-not-implemented/>`	The feature requested is not implemented by the service.
`<forbidden/>`	The client does not have authorization to make the request.
`<internal-server-error/>`	The server had an undefined internal error that prevented it from processing the request.
`<item-not-found/>`	The item involved in the request does not exist. This error is equivalent to the HTTP 404 error.
`<recipient-unavailable/>`	The intended recipient is temporarily unavailable.
`<remote-server-not-found/>`	The remote server does not exist or could not be reached.
`<remote-server-timeout/>`	Communication with the remote server has been interrupted.
`<service-unavailable/>`	The requested service is not provided.

The following example IQ-error stanza shows a fully constructed error response to a publish-subscribe related `<iq>` stanza:

```
<iq from='pubsub.pemberley.lit'
    to='elizabeth@longbourn.lit/sitting_room'
    type='error'
    id='subscribe1'>
  <pubsub xmlns='http://jabber.org/protocol/pubsub'>
    <subscribe node='latest_books'
               jid='elizabeth@longbourn.lit'/>
  </pubsub>
  <error type='cancel'>
    <not-allowed xmlns='urn:ietf:params:xml:ns:xmpp-stanzas'/>
    <closed-node xmlns='http://jabber.org/protocol/pubsub#errors'/>
    <text xmlns='urn:ietf:params:xml:ns:xmpp-stanzas'>
      You must be on the whitelist to subscribe to this node.
    </text>
  </error>
</iq>
```

The error's type is `cancel`, indicating that this action should not be retried and the condition `<not-allowed/>` indicates the general failure. The `<text/>` child contains a description of the problem. Finally, the application condition element, `<closed-node/>`, gives the exact application error.

THE CONNECTION LIFE CYCLE

The three stanzas you've learned about can accomplish virtually any task in XMPP when combined properly. However, sending stanzas usually requires an authenticated XMPP session be established. This section describes the other portions of an XMPP connection's life cycle — connection, stream set up, authentication, and disconnection.

Connection

Before any stanzas are sent, an XMPP stream is necessary. Before an XMPP stream can exist, a connection must be made to an XMPP server. XMPP includes some sophisticated support for establishing connections to the right servers.

Typically clients and servers utilize the domain name system (DNS) to resolve a server's domain name into an address they can connect to. E-mail services in particular use mail exchange (MX) records to provide a list of servers that handle mail for a given domain so that one well-known server address does not have to handle every service. E-mail, being an early Internet application, got special treatment in DNS. These days, service records (SRV) are used to provide a similar function for arbitrary services.

The first thing an XMPP client or server does when connecting to another XMPP server is to query the appropriate SRV record at the server's domain. The response may include multiple SRV records, which can be used to load balance connections across multiple servers.

If an appropriate SRV record cannot be found, the application tries to connect to the given domain directly as a fallback. Most libraries also allow you to specify a server to connect to explicitly.

Stream Set Up

Once a connection is established to a given XMPP server, an XMPP stream is started. An XMPP stream is opened by sending the opening `<stream:stream>` element to the server. The server responds by sending the response stream's opening `<stream:stream>` tag.

Once XMPP streams are open in both directions, elements can be sent back and forth. At this stage of the connection life cycle, these elements will be related to the stream and the stream's features.

The server first sends a `<stream:features>` element, which details all the supported features on the XMPP stream. These mostly relate to encryption and authentication options that are available. For example, the server will specify if encryption (TLS) is available and whether or not anonymous logins are allowed.

You don't normally need to know much detail about this stage of an XMPP connection as the many libraries for XMPP development handle this work for you, but the following example shows a typical exchange of `<stream:stream>` elements as well as the server's feature list.

First, the client sends the opening element to the server:

```
<?xml version='1.0'?>
<stream:stream xmlns='jabber:client'
               xmlns:stream='http://etherx.jabber.org/streams'
               version='1.0'
               to='pemberley.lit'>
```

The server replies:

```
<?xml version='1.0'?>
<stream:stream xmlns='jabber:client'
               xmlns:stream='http://etherx.jabber.org/streams'
               version='1.0'
               from='pemberley.lit'
               id='893ca401f5ff2ec29499984e9b7e8afc'
               xml:lang='en'>
  <stream:features>
    <stream:features>
      <starttls xmlns='urn:ietf:params:xml:ns:xmpp-tls'/>
      <compression xmlns='http://jabber.org/features/compress'>
        <method>zlib</method>
      </compression>
      <mechanisms xmlns='urn:ietf:params:xml:ns:xmpp-sasl'>
        <mechanism>DIGEST-MD5</mechanism>
        <mechanism>PLAIN</mechanism>
      </mechanisms>
    </stream:features>
  </stream:features>
```

From this exchange, you know that the pemberley.org server supports TLS, stream compression via zlib, and several authentication mechanisms.

The XMPP streams set up between two servers look identical except that the top-level namespace is `jabber:server` instead of `jabber:client`.

Authentication

XMPP allows for Transport Layer Security (TLS) encryption, and most clients use this by default. Once TLS support is advertised by the server, the client starts the TLS connection and upgrades the current socket to an encrypted one without disconnecting. Once TLS encryption is established, a new pair of XMPP streams is created.

Authentication in XMPP uses the Simple Authentication and Security Layers (SASL) protocol, and depending on the server involved, can support a number of authentication mechanisms. Normally servers provide plain text authentication and MD5 digest-based authentication, but some servers support authenticating via Kerberos or special tokens.

These same encryption and authentication technologies are also used in many other protocols — e-mail and LDAP are two examples — and common libraries exist for supporting TLS and SASL that can be used equally well for XMPP.

Once authentication is complete, a client must bind a resource for the connection and start a session. If you are watching XMPP traffic on the wire, you will see <bind> and <session> elements — inside <iq> stanzas — being sent to do these jobs. If the client does not provide a resource to bind, the server chooses one for it, usually randomly. Also, the server may alter the user's chosen resource even if the client provides one.

When two servers connect to each other, the authentication steps are slightly different. The servers exchange and verify TLS certificates, or the recipient server uses a *dialback* protocol to verify the sender's identity via DNS.

Disconnection

When users are done with their XMPP sessions, they terminate the sessions and disconnect. The most polite way to terminate a session is to first send unavailable presence and then close the <stream:stream> element.

By sending a final unavailable presence, the user's contacts can be informed about the reasons for the user's departure. Closing the stream explicitly allows any in-flight stanzas to arrive safely.

A polite disconnection would look like this:

```
    <presence type='unavailable'/>
</stream:stream>
```

The server then terminates its stream to the client.

SUMMARY

In this chapter, you met the XMPP protocol and learned about its history, use cases, addressing, vocabulary, and the connection life cycle. You've also seen several example XMPP stanzas and learned about the different entities composing an XMPP network.

You should now understand:

- ➤ XMPP is an open, standardized protocol, originally developed to replace proprietary IM networks.

- ➤ The XMPP protocol is more than a decade old and quite mature.

- ➤ XMPP is great for writing IM applications, but it also excels at any task that benefits from exchanging structured messages.

- ➤ Servers, clients, components, and plug-ins are all parts of XMPP networks and have their special uses.

- ➤ XMPP addresses, called JIDs, resemble e-mail addresses and decompose into three parts: the local part, the domain, and the resource.

- ➤ Full JIDs are the most specific addresses for an entity; for example, darcy@pemberley.lit/library.

- ➤ Bare JIDs are the same as full JIDs without the resource; for example, darcy@pemberley.lit.

- ➤ Servers will handle stanzas to a client's bare JID, potentially routing them to one or more connected resources.

- ➤ Stanzas addressed to a full JID are delivered directly to the given resource.

- ➤ There are three stanzas in the main XMPP vocabulary: `<message>`, `<presence>`, and `<iq>`.

- ➤ The `<message>` stanza is used for fire-and-forget messages between two entities.

- ➤ `<presence>` stanzas communicate presence status changes and are used to manipulate presence subscriptions.

- ➤ The `<iq>` stanza provides request-response semantics very similar to the GET and POST operations of the HTTP protocol.

- ➤ Every XMPP session has a life cycle consisting of several phases: connection, stream set up, authentication, the session body, and disconnection.

The basic concepts and protocol syntax of XMPP are only once piece of the puzzle. You learn about how to use these ideas to design XMPP applications in the next chapter.

2

Designing XMPP Applications

WHAT'S IN THIS CHAPTER?

➤ Differences between HTTP and XMPP

➤ Using BOSH to bridge XMPP and HTTP

➤ Application architecture and protocol design

No matter how wonderful any protocol appears, it can never be the best solution for every problem. Many problems can be solved with XMPP that would be difficult in other protocols, but even XMPP has its sweet spot, outside of which it often makes sense to use other technologies. To make the best XMPP applications possible, you must first understand what problems XMPP is good at, and how you can design your application to leverage XMPP to its fullest.

XMPP's sweet spot is real-time communication, collaboration, and data exchange. Where other protocols pull data, XMPP pushes it, allowing more efficient notification and faster responses to new information. XMPP has native support for social features found in many of today's most popular applications, making it easy for developers to add and build upon people's relationships and communication. The rich, extensible vocabulary of XML stanzas provides a robust and varied set of tools for building many common patterns or composing into your own protocols.

Although XMPP applications can be developed in many contexts, both on the backend and the front-end, this book's applications use the web browser as their environment and web technologies as their implementation. Because web browsers don't speak XMPP natively, only HTTP, you will also discover how XMPP and HTTP be made to work together to create amazing, interactive applications.

LEARNING FROM OTHERS

It's always nice to get a little inspiration before starting a project, and many great XMPP applications out there provide inspiration and insight into what is possible. The following applications are just scratching the surface of XMPP's potential, but they serve as good examples of what you can do with a little help from XMPP, even in the context of an existing application.

Just as XMPP started as a protocol for better instant messaging, the first application is an IM client. Figure 2-1 shows a screenshot of the Adium client (http://adium.im) running on Mac OS X. This client supports XMPP as well as a number of other IM protocols. Comparable clients exist for every platform imaginable.

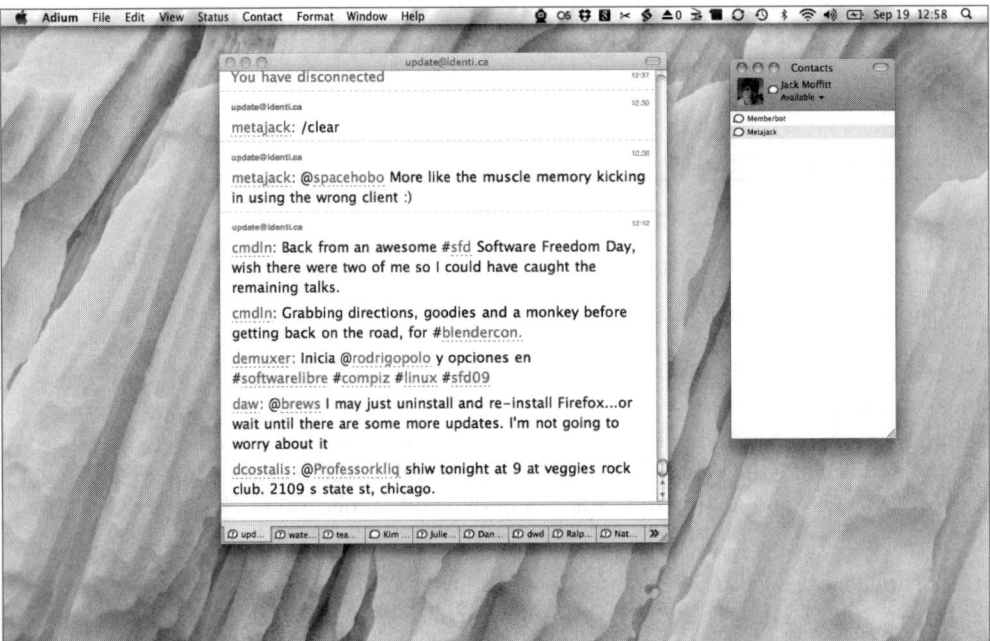

FIGURE 2-1

Google has made huge investments in XMPP technology. It started with the Google Talk service, which it has improved over the years. Google Talk provides IM services to anyone with a Gmail account, as well as to all its Google Apps for Domains customers. Google also did the initial work on Jingle, the XMPP extension that enables voice and video conferencing. Its upcoming Wave protocol is an XMPP extension itself, and its cloud computing platform, AppEngine, is also XMPP enabled. Figure 2-2 shows the Gmail client (http://gmail.com), which also includes a simple, web-based IM client.

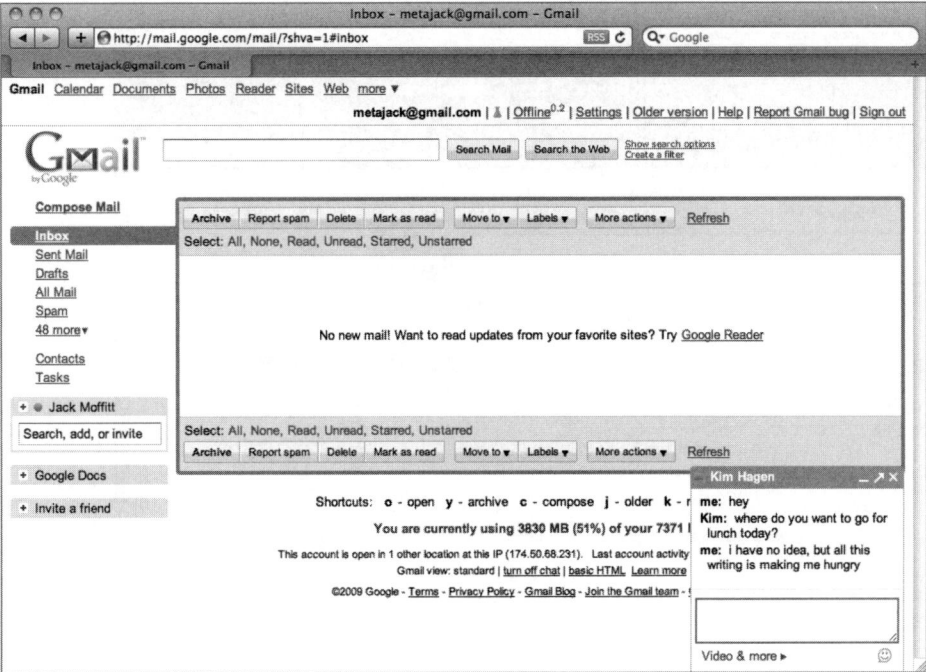

FIGURE 2-2

With the advent of Twitter, the rise of microblogging is at hand, even in the corporate environment. Services like Socialcast, Yammer, and Presently all offer private microblogging services to companies to improve the companies' internal communications. Because low-latency communication is quite desirable, it is no surprise that many of these companies turn to XMPP as a solution. Figure 2-3 shows the Presently application (`http://presentlyapp.com`) allowing users to keep in touch with their co-workers. Presently is using the Strophe library to handle XMPP communication, just like the applications in this book. They also use XMPP to power their backend infrastructure.

XMPP is great at enabling communication and collaboration, supporting features like group chat and file sharing. Drop.io (`http://drop.io`) has turned XMPP's multi-user chat rooms into rich, collaborative spaces capable of sharing audio, video, chat, and images. Figure 2-4 shows an example of one of these collaborative spaces in chat mode. The Strophe library also powers the Drop.io application.

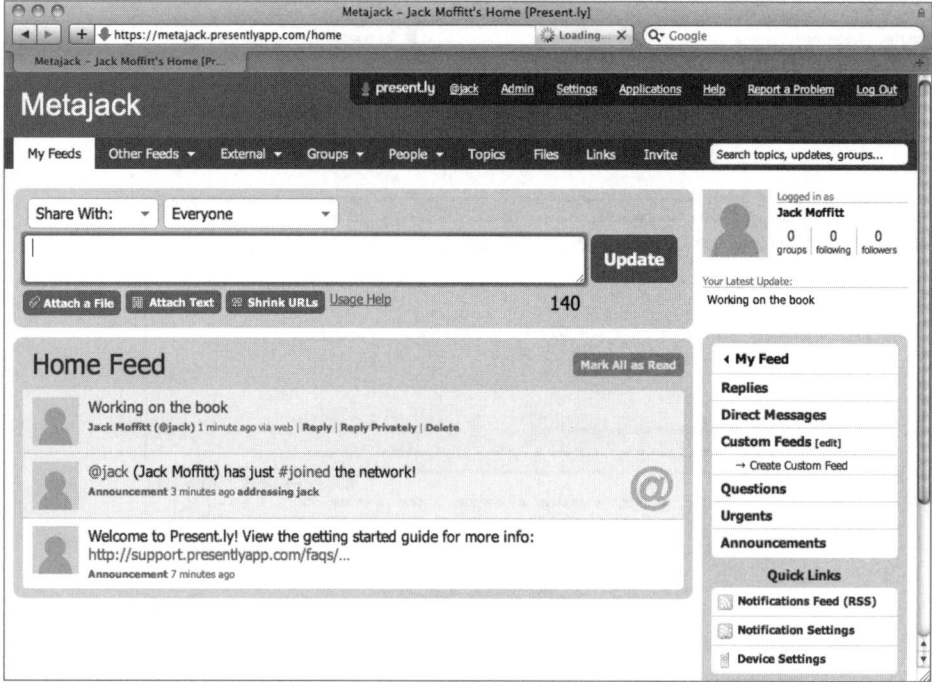

FIGURE 2-3

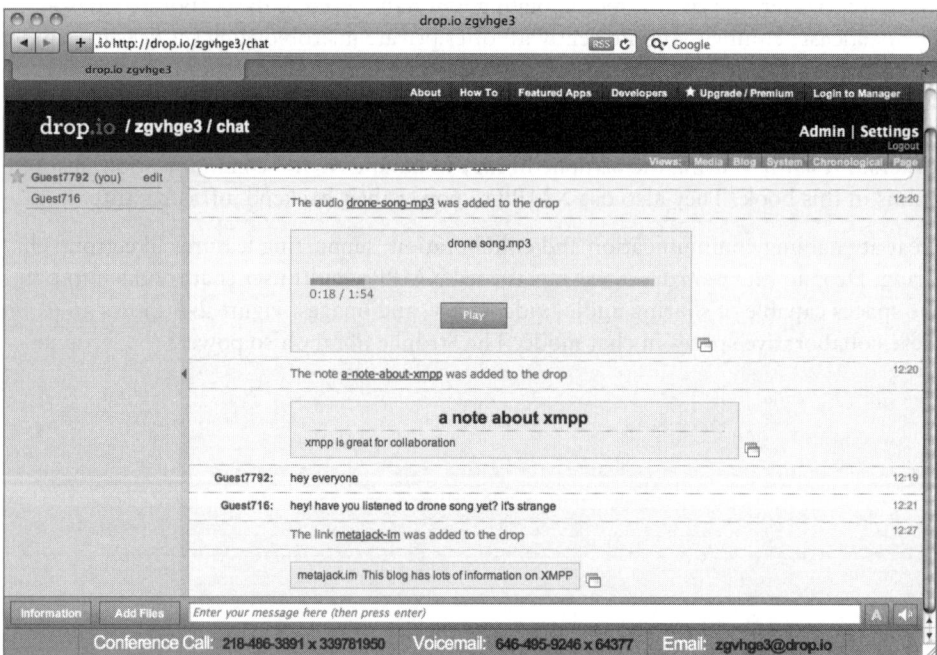

FIGURE 2-4

Strophe was actually born from the desire to create a web-based, multi-player game system on top of XMPP. Finding no suitable implementations of XMPP over HTTP, my team set about creating one on top of which to build our application. Today, Chesspark enables players from all around the world to play chess with each other in real time, whether the games are slow and thoughtful or at lightning speed. Without XMPP and Strophe, the work would have been immensely more challenging. Figure 2-5 shows Chesspark (`http://chesspark.com`) in action.

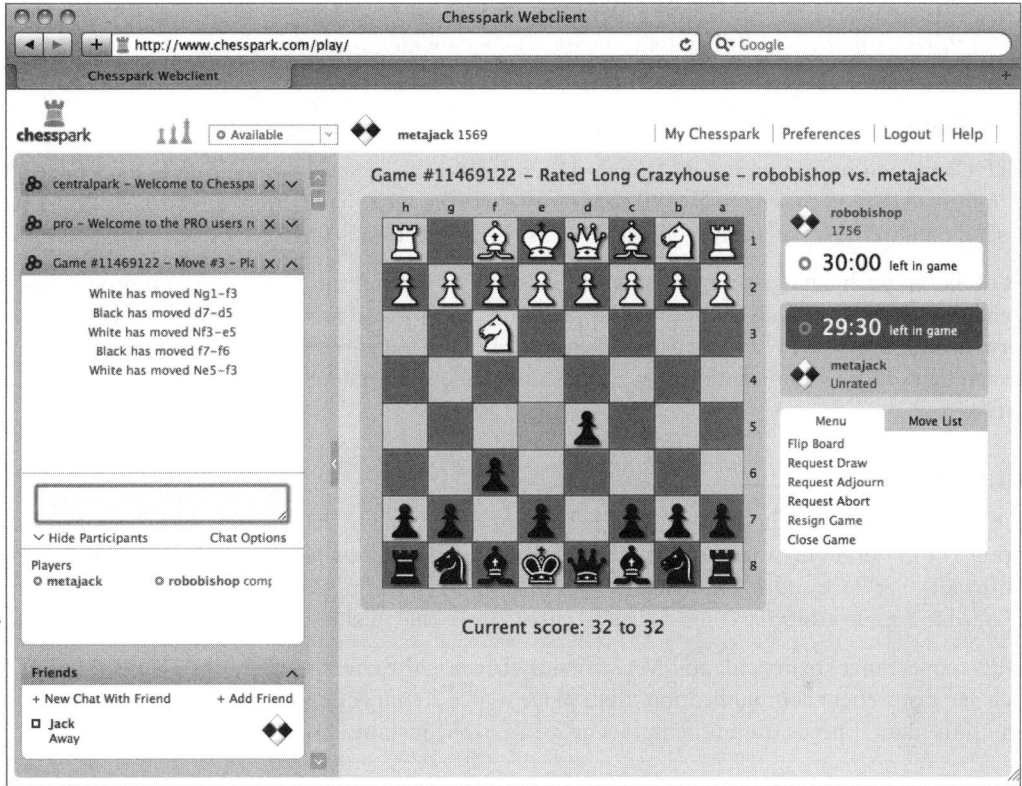

FIGURE 2-5

XMPP VERSUS HTTP

Every project benefits when the right tools are chosen to complete it. Therefore, it is important to know when XMPP best meets the needs of your application. You probably have some idea that XMPP might better suit your needs or are interested in exploring the protocol's possibilities. This section attempts to point out where XMPP is most useful in comparison to the Web's native protocol, HTTP.

Advantages of XMPP

XMPP has the following advantages over HTTP, each of which are explored in detail:

- ➤ Enables pushing data, not just pulling
- ➤ Firewall friendly
- ➤ Strong authentication and security
- ➤ Provides many out-of-the-box tools for solving a wide range of problems

Pushing Data

HTTP clients can only request data from a server. Unless the server is responding to a client request, it cannot send data to the client. XMPP connections, on the other hand, are bidirectional. Either party can send data to the other at any time, as long as the connection is open.

This ability to push data greatly expands the possibilities for web applications and protocol design. Instead of inefficient polling for updates, applications can instead receive notifications when new information is available. Not only does this result in many fewer requests, it also makes the latency between the time new information is available and the time the client is aware of this information nearly zero.

Pleasing Firewalls

Some web applications support the use of HTTP callbacks, where the web server makes requests to another HTTP server in order to send data. This would be a handy feature to push data if it weren't for firewalls, network address translation (NAT), and other realities of the Internet. In practice it is very hard to enable arbitrary connections to clients from the outside world.

XMPP connections are firewall and NAT friendly because the client initiates the connection on which server-to-client communication takes place. Once a connection is established, the server can push all the data it needs to the client, just as it can in the response to an HTTP request.

Improving Security

XMPP is built on top of TLS and SASL technologies, which provide robust encryption and security for XMPP connections. Though HTTP uses SSL, the HTTP authentication mechanisms did not see much implementation or use by developers. Instead, the Web is full of sites that have implemented their own authentication schemes, often badly.

A Bigger Toolbox

HTTP is limited to simple request-response semantics and provides support for only a handful of operations — GET, PUT, POST, DELETE, and so on. XMPP includes three different low-level tools, <presence>, <message>, and <iq> stanzas, and almost 300 extensions that compose these tools into sophisticated protocols.

It's certainly possible to build many of the same constructs on top of HTTP, but protocol design is non-trivial. The extensions and protocols of XMPP are robust and widely reviewed; comparable HTTP extensions tend to be incompatible with each other, brittle, or primitive.

Many XMPP tools rely on and take advantage of the ability to push data. Any HTTP solution to similar problems would need to re-invent much of XMPP.

Disadvantages of XMPP

Every protocol is a bag of both features and problems. In many cases XMPP is not the best tool for the job or suffers from some limitation. XMPP's drawbacks include:

- ➤ Stateful protocol
- ➤ Community and deployments are not as broad as HTTP
- ➤ More overhead than HTTP for simple chores
- ➤ Specialized implementations still needed

Statefulness

HTTP is a stateless protocol; XMPP is stateful. Stateless protocols are easier to scale because each server does not need to know the entire state in order to serve a request. This drawback of XMPP is less onerous in practice because most non-trivial web applications make extensive use of cookies, backend databases, and many other forms of stored state.

Many of the same tools used to scale HTTP-based applications can also be used to scale XMPP-based ones, although the number and diversity of such tools is more limited, due to XMPP's younger age and lesser popularity.

Smaller Ecosystem

HTTP is nearly twice as old as XMPP, and as the foundation of the Web, has become extremely popular and well understood. HTTP's ecosystem is bigger than XMPP's in almost every respect as a result of this. There are more HTTP libraries, more HTTP servers, and more engineers who understand HTTP than there are for nearly every other protocol in existence, including XMPP.

That said, the same situation exists for the C and Java programming languages compared to Python, Ruby, Perl, Objective-C, and others. These less popular languages are no less capable of doing great things, and often are a better solution to many tasks. Many companies find using the most powerful tool gives them a competitive advantage over those companies using only the most popular tools.

Sometimes when developing XMPP applications you will come across a piece that is not implemented well or in a different way than you require. It is generally very easy to build solutions to these problems, because the protocols and interactions are already defined and documented. It is also the case that custom implementations of XMPP extensions, should they be required for your project, need not implement the entire specification, only the parts they depend on.

More Overhead

XMPP is not optimized for short-lived sessions or simple requests. These are both areas where HTTP is a clear winner. It takes some resources to set up, maintain, and destroy XMPP sessions. It is perfectly capable of serving static documents, but unless this is in a larger context where XMPP is used, this use is outside of XMPP's sweet spot.

For longer connections or more sophisticated interactions, the XMPP overhead is negligible compared to an HTTP solution. Any HTTP solution would also need to support state, push notifications, and the other features that make XMPP so interesting. HTTP-based solutions for similar problems are starting to appear, but the XMPP ones tend to be more mature and more optimized.

Specialized Implementations

It used to be that the Apache web server was all anyone needed to build web applications. These days, companies are building their own specialized systems to process web requests in order to eke out performance improvements and lower response times.

XMPP is just entering its golden age of applications and development, and companies haven't had as much time to spend building specialized XMPP servers and libraries for specific needs. Most XMPP servers are designed around traditional IM use cases, although many can be stripped down and put to other uses.

Most of the time your application will not be so demanding as to need specialized implementations to power it. Over time, the community of application developers pushing XMPP to its limits will follow the HTTP community's example and develop specialized tools focused on performance and massive scale.

BRIDGING XMPP AND THE WEB

Even though several browsers are experimenting with features that use XMPP, none of the major browsers currently provides built-in support for the XMPP protocol. However, by using some clever programming and a little server-side help, you can tunnel XMPP sessions over HTTP connections efficiently and effectively.

The technology that enables this efficient tunneling is called HTTP long polling. Coupled with a simple HTTP-based management protocol and an XMPP connection manager, it is possible to bring XMPP, and all its charms, into HTTP-speaking applications.

Long Polling

Early web pages that wanted to provide access to live, changing data used page refreshes at set intervals. This blunt method works reasonably well when the data is constantly changing; for example, many news sites use timed refreshes for live blogging major events.

Microsoft eventually released an API within Internet Explorer called XMLHttpRequest, which allowed JavaScript code in web pages to make requests and process the data returned without reloading the page. This API eventually found its way into all major browsers, and programmers began to pick up and make use of this handy tool. This technique was eventually given the name AJAX, for Asynchronous JavaScript and XML.

With AJAX, it is possible to update data without refreshing the entire page. This increase in efficiency paid dividends, and nearly everything became more dynamic and responsive.

Even with AJAX, data was still being requested, or *polled*, at timed intervals. If you've ever worked under an overbearing boss asking "is the software done yet?," you have experienced polling. Though servers cannot get annoyed or angry, they can be crippled if too many clients poll too fast; you get less done if someone is constantly distracting you. However, to get quick updates, the polling interval needs to be quite small; the lowest latency possible is the length of the polling interval.

Another issue with polling is that most poll requests do not receive new data. In order to see changes within a reasonable time frame of when they occur, the polling interval must be quite short, but the actual data may not change very often. Just as with your (hopefully fictional) overbearing employer, the server's answer to "is the software done yet?" is usually "not yet."

Some clever folks discovered a neat trick to solve this problem. Instead of answering the request immediately, they can hang on to it for some period of time if no new data is ready.

For example, if there is new data ready on the server, the server answers immediately. If there is not new data, the server keeps the connection open, holding any reply. Once new data arrives, it finally responds to the request. If no new data arrives after some period of time, the server can send back an empty reply, so as not to hold too many open connections at once. Once a request is returned, the client immediately sends a new one, and the whole process starts over.

Because each polling request is potentially open for a long period of time, this technique is called *long polling*. It has many advantages over normal polling.

The client receives new data the moment it becomes available, because it always has at least one connection open and waiting for an update from the server. By setting the length of the poll to something high, the total number of requests the server has to handle remains reasonable, even though the latency of the updates is minimized. Users see instant changes in data, and server operators don't go broke trying to scale out their systems; everybody wins.

The only real change is that instead of the *client* waiting to resend the request, the *server* waits until it has something to say before it responds.

Multiple libraries and protocols have been designed to take advantage of long polling, but XMPP's is one of the oldest implementations. In XMPP, this bridge is called BOSH, for Bidirectional streams Over Synchronous HTTP. You may also have heard of Comet or reverse HTTP, which are protocols built on the same technique.

One drawback is that the server needs to be a little smarter in order to deal with these long polling requests, and that is where a connection manager comes in.

Managing the Connection

XMPP connections live for arbitrarily long periods of time, but HTTP requests are quite short lived. A connection manager maintains an XMPP connection for a third party and provides access to the connection via the HTTP long polling technique.

The browser and the connection manager communicate over HTTP using a simple protocol called BOSH. Essentially, BOSH helps an HTTP client establish a new XMPP session, then transports stanzas back and forth over HTTP wrapped in a special <body> element. It also provides some security features to make sure that XMPP sessions can't be easily hijacked. The connection manager communicates with an XMPP server as if it were a normal client.

In this way, an HTTP application can control a real XMPP session. Because of the efficiency and low latency afforded by the long polling technique, the end result performs quite well, rivaling native connections.

It may seem like a lot of effort to get XMPP into a browser, but not only does this work well in practice, it turns out this technique even has some advantages over direct XMPP connections:

> Interactions with the connection manager are request by request, which allows the client to move from network to network. The managed connection stays available even if the end user's IP address changes several times.

> Because one failing request doesn't terminate the managed connection, these managed sessions are extremely robust and tolerant of temporary network failure.

> Because connection managers cache and resend data for a request, you don't have to worry about losing data when your connection is interrupted.

> HTTP is extremely firewall friendly, and because most connection managers run on standard HTTP ports, managed connections still work even in limited network environments that don't allow anything but HTTP.

These advantages make managed connections a perfect fit for some scenarios, even when direct XMPP communication is possible.

Making JavaScript Speak XMPP

With HTTP long polling, you have the technology for low-latency data updates from a server. Combining this with a connection manager gives you a way to send and receive XMPP data over a series of HTTP requests. The last piece of the puzzle is making this easy to do from JavaScript, the Web's native programming language.

The Strophe library was created to make programming XMPP applications in JavaScript as easy as in any other language, hiding all the gory details of the managed connection. As far as Strophe's users are concerned, it appears as if they are working with a native XMPP connection just as they would in any other environment.

Long polling applications have some special requirements compared to normal AJAX applications. Most AJAX libraries do very little error handling because the number of AJAX requests that fail is a small percentage. Unfortunately for XMPP applications, any failed request can result in a huge increase in latency and a tarnished user experience. For this reason, Strophe handles as many errors as it can gracefully and uses early timeouts to detect problems before they would otherwise be discovered.

These features make Strophe quite reliable and high-performance, even in the face of unavoidable, occasional errors. Strophe's users have frequently reported their applications can live for days without being disconnected.

MAKING XMPP APPLICATIONS

The XMPP protocol is a good choice for a variety of application domains, and you've seen some technical details on how XMPP can be used from the Web. Now it's time to learn a few details about making XMPP applications before you embark on your first application in the next chapter.

The Browser Platform

The web browser is probably the most deployed and most used application platform that has ever existed. Web browsers exist on every kind of computer and even many mobile phones, and more importantly, the users of these devices tend to be very familiar with the browser and web applications.

As more and more sophistication has been demanded of web applications, new technologies and abstractions have been created to evolve the platform. XMPP brings yet another new set of technologies and abstractions, but with it comes enormous potential for real-time, interactive, and collaborative applications. The rise of the social Web has given rise to social applications, and if developers want to take more steps toward connecting the human race, technologies like XMPP will help them do it.

For XMPP developers, targeting the web browser as a platform makes enormous sense. Web applications are cross-platform, easily deployable, and come with a large user base already familiar with them. More than that, web technologies make heavy use of HTML, and it is often the case that tools for manipulating HTML work very well on XML, and therefore, on XMPP.

One such tool, familiar to many web developers, is the jQuery library. jQuery makes many mundane manipulations of HTML and CSS easy and fun. This power is also almost equally applicable to XML data, because it shares a very similar structure. This book's applications use jQuery to process and manipulate both the user interface, a combination of HTML and CSS, and the incoming XMPP data.

Web technologies have their warts, but from a practical standpoint, both web developers and XMPP developers could scarcely ask for a better platform on which to create new and wonderful things.

Basic Infrastructure

Just as web applications often need a web server and an application server or framework, XMPP applications require some basic infrastructure. An XMPP connection requires an XMPP server and, often, an account on that server. An XMPP application also needs to communicate with a connection manager, because browsers don't yet speak XMPP natively. Finally, any services the application uses will need to be provided by the XMPP server.

The XMPP server requirement is not a very difficult one. It is quite easy to download, install, and run an XMPP server on nearly any platform, and there are several to choose from. You can also make use of public XMPP servers that a user may already have an account on, although this depends on the amount of data your application uses; many public XMPP servers are optimized for IM traffic and will limit high-throughput clients.

Many users already have XMPP accounts, thanks to the efforts of Google, LiveJournal, forward-thinking ISPs, and other large organizations. If you run your own server and require users to register there, it is generally easy to programmatically create XMPP accounts from a normal web application back end.

All the major XMPP servers come with built-in support for HTTP-managed connections, or BOSH support. It is usually a matter of altering a configuration file slightly to turn this on, if it is not enabled by default. If you want to allow users to connect to arbitrary XMPP servers, you will need a standalone connection manager. Please see Appendix B for more information on using and configuring connection managers.

Each XMPP server supports a core set of functionality as well as a number of XMPP extensions. Generally the extensions are documented at the XMPP server's web site. Most servers support the mature and popular extensions such as multi-user chat and publish-subscribe. If your application makes use of XMPP extensions, be sure to check that your server supports these extensions.

Many XMPP applications can be realized without any special web application servers or other infrastructure. The applications in this book are all self-contained and designed to be run on publicly available XMPP servers. A connection manager is also provided for your development purposes, so you need not set one up while you work through the applications in the book.

Protocol Design

Unless you are creating a new and better version of an existing XMPP service, like multi-user chat or the traditional IM functions, you will probably be doing some protocol design to realize your vision. XMPP provides a lot of tools to build on, and often the simple composition of these tools is enough to satisfy the needs of most applications. The following guidelines have influenced the applications in this book and may help you in your own protocol designs.

Compose Existing Protocols

If your application can be implemented with the composition of existing protocol extensions, it is often best to do so. With almost 300 such published extensions, there is usually a good starting point available already.

Even if the particular extensions used do not have implementations, it is far easier to implement a protocol than to design one from scratch. The extension's authors have already been thinking about the problem domain with enough gusto to drive them to document a solution. Furthermore, XMPP extensions are a community effort, and your feedback will help improve the extension for everyone.

For a concrete example, consider the game developed in Chapter 11. One possible solution is to create a new protocol for all game interaction. Instead, the application layers game semantics on top of multi-user chat rooms. This involves a small amount of protocol design to handle the game-specific content, but reuses a large amount of work from a well-tested, existing extension.

Using protocol composition saves work, and it makes new protocols much easier to understand by others. To understand your new protocol, they need only understand how the pieces fit together and possibly a few small, new things.

Keep It Simple

Keeping it simple is excellent advice in nearly every domain, and it applies equally to XMPP protocol design. If you do have to create something completely new, try to do it as simply as possible.

Not only will your protocol be easier to understand, the lack of complexity will result in fewer bugs and less development time. Usually a complex protocol is a sign that a simpler path has been overlooked.

Many XMPP extensions are themselves extended later to address new use cases. It is not necessary, nor is it desirable, to pack every feature that may be needed into the protocols at the beginning. In fact, many of the more complex extensions end up getting split into a core part and several related extensions once they get large.

Avoid Extending Presence

The `<presence>` stanza can often be the largest factor in a server's traffic. Most `<presence>` stanza extensions are not applicable to the general case. Instead of extending `<presence>` stanzas directly, it is a best practice to make use of the Personal Eventing Protocol, or PEP, defined in XEP-0163, which allows users to subscribe to the extra data they are interested in.

The PEP extension, along with Entity Capabilities (XEP-0114) and Service Discovery (XEP-0015), make providing extended presence-type information efficient and opt-in.

Other stanzas do not require similar optimizations, because they are not normally broadcast to many people at once.

Participate in the Community

The XMPP community contains numerous individuals with protocol design experience, and they are generally quite friendly. You may also want to document and submit your new protocol as an XMPP extension if you think it would be generally useful. Even if your extension is not intended to be useful beyond your own applications, it can be very helpful to get the community's feedback on your designs.

Protocol design discussions normally take place on the *standards list*, which you can subscribe to by visiting the discussions page at the XSF web site, `http://xmpp.org/about/discuss.shtml`. Feel free to ask questions, share your protocol ideas, and contribute to the discussion and feedback of other protocols. The community always welcomes new members.

Should you want to submit your protocol as an official extension, you will want to document it in the XEP format using the template and guidelines provided at the extension submission page, `http://xmpp.org/extensions/submit.shtml`. New extensions will be considered by the XSF

Council for acceptance. The requirements for acceptance are simply that the extension be generally useful and not already covered by existing work.

You can also join the XSF as a member; the XSF is an open organization, run by its membership. Elections are held every quarter, and the XSF is always looking for new members, whether they are developers or just enthusiasts. See the membership page, `http://xmpp.org/xsf/members/`, for more information.

SUMMARY

In this chapter, you learned why XMPP is often the best tool for the job and how it is different from HTTP. You also discovered how XMPP can be made to work in the HTTP-only world of web browsers and how XMPP applications are built.

Along the way, the following topics were covered:

- ➤ Inspiring examples of the XMPP applications of others
- ➤ The pros and cons of XMPP versus HTTP
- ➤ HTTP long polling
- ➤ Managed XMPP connections (BOSH)
- ➤ The Strophe library
- ➤ Required infrastructure for XMPP applications
- ➤ How to design XMPP protocols

In the next chapter, you finally begin your XMPP development career by creating your first application.

PART II
The Applications

3

Saying Hello:
The First Application

WHAT'S IN THIS CHAPTER?

- ➤ Creating and organizing an XMPP project

- ➤ Making connections to XMPP servers

- ➤ Building and manipulating XMPP stanzas

- ➤ Sending data to the server

- ➤ Handling XMPP events

XMPP started as an open, federated protocol for instant messaging, but has become a powerful protocol for building many kinds of applications. The bulk of this book walks you through building various interesting applications as you explore the XMPP protocol and its numerous possibilities. These applications are all built with JavaScript, HTML, and CSS, and, though simple, show off how easy it is to make powerful programs with XMPP.

The first application you write is the XMPP equivalent of the famous "Hello, World" example. It sends a message to your XMPP server and displays the response. It sounds simple, and it is, but there is a lot to cover with setting up the user interface, getting the required libraries, and learning about the Strophe library.

By the end of this chapter, you'll be ready to start building much more interesting applications. By the end of the book, you'll have built some compelling projects that would have been difficult without XMPP.

This chapter may be one of the toughest in the book simply because it is filled with lots of things that will be brand new.

The applications in this book assume some knowledge of the jQuery library. If you are not yet familiar with jQuery, there is a brief tutorial in Appendix A.

APPLICATION PREVIEW

Before you start on each application, there will be a few preview screenshots of what the final result will look like.

Figure 3-1 and Figure 3-2 show a glimpse into the future of your XMPP programming career. These screenshots let you see what the final application will look like, and they also provide a reference point that you can compare your own work against.

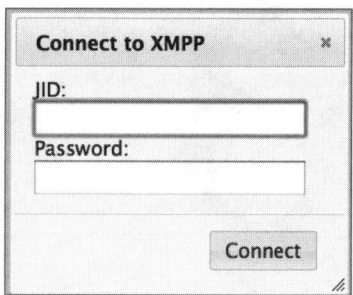

FIGURE 3-1

The login dialog box shown in Figure 3-1 opens when the application first starts and accepts the user's XMPP address and password. Once the application has sent a message to the server, the server's response is displayed similarly to Figure 3-2.

Hello

Connection established.

Sending ping to jabber.org.

Received pong from server in 4029ms.

Connection terminated.

FIGURE 3-2

The user interfaces are kept deliberately simple to let you concentrate on the XMPP protocol and the JavaScript code.

HELLO DESIGN

Every application is composed of small pieces that fit together in a particular way. These pieces may be user interface elements, XMPP protocol handlers, or implementations of a certain process. In each chapter, you first learn about the various pieces involved in the chapter's application and how they fit together to form a cohesive whole.

The first application is called Hello, and you've already seen the two main visible pieces in Figure 3-1 and Figure 3-2: the login dialog box and the server response screen. There are a few pieces you can't see as well: the XMPP connection handling, XMPP stanza generation, and the event handling.

When a user first opens the application, they are presented with the login dialog box in order to enter their XMPP username and password. When the user then clicks Connect, Hello must initiate a connection to the XMPP server and authenticate the user.

Once connected, Hello's task is to send a simple stanza to the user's server and wait for the server's reply. The Strophe library provides the ability to attach *handlers* to a connection in order to respond to specific stanzas. You will see that these handlers make dealing with incoming requests and responses very easy.

Finally, Hello displays a more human-readable version of the server's reply and disconnects.

Hello is not an ambitious application, but as you see throughout the book, the same XMPP tools used here are repeated in every application.

PREPARING THE WAY

Before you can get started writing code, you must first collect a few JavaScript libraries that you will use to build the applications. You need the following pieces:

➤ **jQuery:** The jQuery library makes dealing with HTML and CSS a breeze, and it is also extremely handy for manipulating XML, and therefore, XMPP stanzas.

➤ **jQuery UI:** The jQuery UI library provides some common user interface building blocks that you will need, including dialog boxes and tabs.

➤ **Strophe:** The Strophe library makes writing XMPP client applications extremely simple and is available in multiple programming languages. You'll be using the JavaScript version of course!

➤ **flXHR:** Strophe can make use of flXHR, a Flash replacement for the standard XMLHttpRequest API, to make dealing with JavaScript's *same origin policy* easier. Normally, a JavaScript application cannot talk to external servers, but with the help of Flash and flXHR, Strophe can overcome this restriction.

Additionally, if you do not already have an XMPP account on a public server, you need to create one.

SAME ORIGIN POLICY

JavaScript code runs in a sandboxed environment for security reasons. Though web applications can load JavaScript code from anywhere, all the code must restrict its communication to the server that hosts the web application. This restriction is called the same origin policy.

In recent times, it has become common to find workarounds to this policy so that more interesting applications can be built. Most web application libraries, including jQuery, already provide some methods for making cross-domain requests. Unfortunately, the normal workarounds for HTTP GET operations do not work for XMPP, which must use HTTP POST instead.

This book uses the flXHR library to enable cross-domain requests, but other solutions are possible. The most common alternative is to use reverse HTTP proxies to make the BOSH connection manager appear local to the application's home server. This alternative is discussed in Appendix B.

jQuery and jQuery UI

The jQuery and jQuery UI libraries are available from `http://jquery.com` and `http://ui.jquery.com` respectively. The version used in the book's examples is 1.3.2 for jQuery and 1.7.2 for jQuery UI. Later versions of these libraries should also work.

The jQuery libraries, like many JavaScript libraries, come in normal or minified versions. Either will work, but during development, it is recommended that you use the normal version, because minified JavaScript can hinder debugging.

Google has made many JavaScript libraries, including jQuery and jQuery UI, available via its AJAX Library API. This means that you don't even have to download the libraries if you are developing from an Internet-connected computer; you can just link directly to the ones on Google's super fast servers.

The sample code in this book uses the Google-hosted versions. To include jQuery, jQuery UI, and the UI theme CSS in your HTML, put the following lines in the `<head>` element:

```
<link rel='stylesheet' href='http://ajax.googleapis.com/ajax/libs/jqueryui/1.7.2/th
emes/cupertino/jquery-ui.css'>
<script src='http://ajax.googleapis.com/ajax/libs/jquery/1.3.2/jquery.js'></script>
<script src='http://ajax.googleapis.com/ajax/libs/jqueryui/1.7.2/jquery-ui.js'>
</script>
```

If you want to use the minified versions of the libraries, you need only to change the `js` extension to `min.js`.

If you have downloaded the libraries yourself and want to use local copies, the following lines should work assuming that jQuery and jQuery UI are installed in the `scripts` subdirectory of your application and the jQuery UI themes are installed under `styles/themes`:

```
<link rel='stylesheet' href='styles/themes/cupertino/jquery-ui-1.7.2.custom.css'>
<script src='scripts/jquery-1.3.2.js'></script>
<script src='scripts/jquery-ui-1.7.2.custom.js'></script>
```

jQuery UI comes with dozens of themes, and any of these themes can be used with the book's applications. The example code and the screenshots both use the `cupertino` theme. You can browse all the available themes at the jQuery UI web site and substitute your preferred one wherever you see `cupertino`.

Strophe

You can find the Strophe library at `http://code.stanziq.com/strophe`. You'll want to make sure to download the latest version for JavaScript. Be sure not to accidentally download libstrophe, which is a C library, unless of course you want to write some XMPP code in C.

Throughout the book, it is assumed that the `strophe.js` file, as well as any Strophe plug-in files, are placed under the `scripts` directory. They can then be included in the HTML file with the following line:

```
<script src='scripts/strophe.js'></script>
```

flXHR

The flXHR library is located at `http://flxhr.flensed.com`. This library provides cross-domain request support for Strophe and is enabled via a special Strophe plug-in. You will need at least version 1.0.4 of flXHR, but a later version should work just fine.

Once you've downloaded flXHR and uncompressed it, you can place the contents of the `flensed-1.0/deploy` directory into the `scripts` directory inside your application's directory.

Enabling flXHR in your application is as easy as loading two additional JavaScript files:

```
<script src='scripts/flXHR.js'></script>
<script src='scripts/strophe.flxhr.js'></script>
```

The first script, `flXHR.js`, loads the flXHR library. The second script is a special Strophe plug-in that enables Strophe to use flXHR for cross-domain requests.

XMPP Accounts

If you don't already have an XMPP account, you can create one at one of the many public XMPP servers. There is a long list of these public XMPP services at `http://xmpp.org/services/`. The jabber.org server is always a popular choice, and you can create an account there by visiting `http://register.jabber.org`.

Please note that if you have an existing XMPP account, most XMPP accounts are normally provided for typical instant messaging use. Each server may have different sets of features enabled, so you will need to make sure your server supports the features needed for the application you are building. The jabber.org server supports all the functionality needed in this book, for example.

You should now have all the libraries you need to start building XMPP applications as well as an XMPP account to use with these applications. It's time to start building something!

STARTING YOUR FIRST APPLICATION

All the applications in this book consist of an HTML file, a CSS file, and one or more JavaScript files in addition to the required libraries discussed in the previous section. The HTML and CSS files make up the user interface of the application and include the dialog boxes used, the various controls the user interacts with, and the styling information for making those elements attractive. The main focus of your attention will be on the JavaScript files, which contain all the application's code.

User Interface

Each chapter begins with the basic HTML and CSS layouts for the application. During a chapter, new things may be added to these files, but for the most part, the initial HTML and CSS are also the final versions.

For this first application, a more detailed explanation is provided for the HTML and CSS used, but if you are already well versed in Web technologies, feel free to skim the code and skip to the next section.

The HTML for the Hello application is shown in Listing 3-1.

In the `<head>` section, aside from the necessary libraries, it loads the `hello.css` and `hello.js` files, which are the CSS styling and JavaScript code for the application.

Toward the end of the `<body>` section you will see the login dialog box. jQuery UI dialog boxes are created from normal `<div>` elements by calling jQuery UI's `dialog()` function on the specific `<div>` element that you want to become a dialog box. Because the dialog box will be created, shown, and hidden by JavaScript code, its `<div>` element is given the `hidden` class so that it appears only when needed.

The empty `<div>` with the `id` attribute of `log` is used to show the server's response as well as status updates as the application is running. This enables you to follow along with what is happening very easily and see exactly what the code you are writing is doing.

LISTING 3-1: hello.html

```html
<!DOCTYPE HTML PUBLIC "-//W3C//DTD HTML 4.01//EN"
            "http://www.w3.org/TR/html4/strict.dtd">
<html>
  <head>
    <title>Hello - Chapter 3</title>

    <link rel='stylesheet'href='http://ajax.googleapis.com/ajax/libs/j
query/1.7.2/themes/cupertino/jquery-ui.css'>
    <script src='http://ajax.googleapis.com/ajax/libs/jquery/1.3.2/jque
ry.js'></script>
    <script src='http://ajax.googleapis.com/ajax/libs/jqueryui/1.7.2/jq
uery-ui.js'></script>
    <script src='scripts/strophe.js'></script>
    <script src='scripts/flXHR.js'></script>
    <script src='scripts/strophe.flxhr.js'></script>

    <link rel='stylesheet' href='hello.css'>
    <script src='hello.js'></script>
  </head>
  <body>
    <h1>Hello</h1>

    <div id='log'>
    </div>

    <!-- login dialog -->
    <div id='login_dialog' class='hidden'>
      <label>JID:</label><input type='text' id='jid'>
      <label>Password:</label><input type='password' id='password'>
    </div>
  </body>
</html>
```

The CSS styles for Hello are shown in Listing 3-2. This file contains a few styles to make the application prettier.

LISTING 3-2: hello.css

```css
body {
    font-family: Helvetica;
}

h1 {
    text-align: center;
}

.hidden {
    display: none;
}

#log {
    padding: 10px;
}
```

With the HTML and CSS files covered, you can get started on the code.

Application Code

The JavaScript code in this book is structured into three basic sections. First, there is the application's namespace object, where all of the application's state and functions are defined. Following the namespace object is the document ready handler, which initializes the application once the browser is ready. Finally come the custom event handlers, which handle internal events that are not triggered by elements or user interactions.

Namespacing

The namespace object is used to avoid the use of global variables as much as possible. One can never trust that every third-party library will keep to itself, but you can ensure a minimum of problems by putting your own application state and global variables inside a single object, the namespace object.

Instead of defining your variables and functions like this:

```js
var some_global = 0;
var another_global = true;

function my_adder(x, y) {
    return x + y;
}
```

you can put the same code into a global MyNamespace object:

```js
var MyNamespace = {
    some_global: 0,
```

```
        another_global: true,

    my_adder: function (x, y) {
        return x + y;
    }
};
```

The syntax used is slightly different, because each symbol becomes a property of the `MyNamespace` object, which is defined as an object literal using the `{}` syntax. Now if another library also defines `some_global`, your code will not be affected.

You can access the attributes of the namespace object just like any other object's attributes. Writing `MyNamespace.some_global` would access the `some_global` attribute, and calling `MyNamespace.my_adder(1, 2)` would return 3.

The only caveat to namespace objects is that you must take care that the last attribute does not have a trailing comma. If you forget this little detail, the code will not load correctly in Internet Explorer. The following code will fail:

```
var MyNamespace = {
    some_global: 0,
};
```

The comma after the 0 will signal to the interpreter that another attribute definition will follow, but none exists. These extra commas are often allowed in other languages, and most browsers will ignore them in JavaScript as well, but Internet Explorer is quite picky about this.

Document Ready Handler

The *document ready event* is fired as soon as the document object model (DOM) is available for use by JavaScript code. This event fires before the entire page's content is loaded, unlike the *document load event*, which fires once all the CSS, scripts, and images are fetched and ready. It is generally best to put initialization code here, because the DOM will be available, and the ready event is fired early enough that the user won't have to wait long for initialization to start.

The jQuery library makes it extremely easy to write functions that will be executed when the document ready event is fired. You create a document ready event handler function using the jQuery's `ready()` method. The following code alerts the user as soon as the document ready event fires:

```
$(document).ready(function () {
    alert("document ready");
});
```

Notice that the initialization function doesn't have a name, and the function is passed directly into the `ready()` function. Functions like this are called anonymous functions, and they are quite common when using callback-based libraries like jQuery and Strophe.

The applications in this book will often have some initialization code in the document ready handler to do things like create dialog boxes and set up interaction event handlers. When the text says to add something to the document ready handler, you can simply place the relevant code at the end of this initialization function.

Custom Event Handlers

The jQuery library makes it easy to create and use your own custom events. These custom events are often used to make code easier to read and to reduce coupling between components. For example, instead of placing all the code for connecting to an XMPP server inside the function that handles the user's click on the Connect button, you can have the `click` event handler trigger a custom event called `connect` and place the connection code in the `connect` event handler.

Using custom events makes it easy to extend the code later without having to change the flow in multiple locations. If more things needed to happen in response to the `connect` event just described, you can simply add another handler for that event containing the new logic; there is no need to add more complexity to the login dialog box's code.

To fire custom events, you call:

```
$(document).trigger('event_name', event_data);
```

The event's name can be anything you want, although it is wise not to use the same names as normal DOM events like `click` and `keypress`. The `event_data` parameter can be set to anything you'd like to pass to the event handler, or if you don't need to pass anything extra, you can omit it entirely.

You create a handler for these events using `bind()`:

```
$(document).bind('event_name', function (e, data) {
    var event_data = data;
});
```

This sets up the function provided as a handler for the `event_name` event. The first parameter passed is the event object, similar to the one that gets passed for normal DOM events. The second parameter is the same `event_data` passed into `trigger()`.

You see shortly how namespace objects, the document ready handler, and custom event handlers interact as you develop the initial code for Hello.

MAKING CONNECTIONS

Before Hello can send any data to the server, it must first establish a connection. You will need to gather the XMPP credentials from the user and then use Strophe to connect to the XMPP server. Once a connection is established, Strophe uses the credentials provided to authenticate and create a session, allowing data to be sent and received over XMPP.

The Connection Life Cycle

XMPP connections are created, destroyed, and go through a number of phases during their lifetimes, as discussed in Chapter 1. It is important to understand these phases, because the phase transitions are generally where important application logic will be found. For example, if your application needs to be connected to do anything useful, it will be waiting for the transition to the *connected* phase.

When you ask Strophe to connect to a server, you also provide it a *callback function*, which Strophe invokes every time the connection phase changes. This allows your application to handle events like the connection starting, authentication failing, or disconnection.

The full list of these phase changes or statuses is shown in Table 3-1. The status names correspond to constants defined in the `Strophe.Status` object. For example, the CONNECTED status is `Strophe .Status.CONNECTED`.

TABLE 3-1: Strophe Connection Statuses

STATUS	DESCRIPTION
CONNECTING	Strophe has started its attempt to make a connection to the XMPP server.
AUTHENTICATING	The connection has been established, and Strophe is now attempting to authenticate and create a session.
CONNECTED	A session has been established, and user data may now flow freely.
DISCONNECTING	Termination of the connection has started.
DISCONNECTED	The connection is fully terminated.
CONNFAIL	Strophe encountered a problem trying to establish the connection.
AUTHFAIL	An error occurred during the authentication process.

A normal XMPP connection will progress through the first five phases, and your application will be concerned mostly with CONNECTED and DISCONNECTED. Errors in the connection can be handled by watching for the CONNFAIL and AUTHFAIL statuses. The -ING statuses are not often used, except to provide visible updates in the UI so that users know what is happening while they wait.

Creating a Connection

XMPP connections are managed through the `Strophe.Connection` object. In Chapter 2 you learned that a BOSH connection manager provides the bridge between the worlds of HTTP and XMPP. BOSH connection managers are exposed to HTTP clients as URLs, and the `Strophe.Connection` object you create needs to know about one of these URLs.

Many XMPP servers come with support for BOSH built in, and they typically expose the service at `http://example.com:5280/http-bind` or `http://example.com:5280/xmpp-httpbind`. Some BOSH connection managers can handle communications for arbitrary XMPP servers, but generally the built-in connection managers can talk only to the server they run on.

For developing the applications in this book, you are free to use the BOSH connection manager at `http://bosh.metajack.im:5280/xmpp-httpbind`. This BOSH connection manager is able to speak to any public XMPP server. This server is provided specifically for readers of this book to use during development to avoid everyone having to set up their own BOSH service.

You can create a new `Strophe.Connection` object just as you would any other JavaScript object, by using the `new` keyword:

```
var conn = new Strophe.Connection("http://bosh.metajack.im:5280/xmpp-httpbind");
```

Once you have a connection object, you can call `connect()` and `disconnect()` to start and end communication with the server:

```
// starting a connection to example.com
conn.connect("user@example.com", "mypassword", my_callback);

// disconnecting
conn.disconnect();
```

The first two parameters to `connect()` are the JID and password to use to authenticate the session, and the last parameter is the callback function discussed earlier. The callback function will be called with a single parameter that is set to one of the statuses described in the previous section. A simple callback function that disconnects once the connection reaches the CONNECTED phase is shown here:

```
function my_callback(status) {
    if (status === Strophe.Status.CONNECTED) {
        conn.disconnect();
    }
}
```

Every time the connection changes its status, this callback function is executed. The `my_callback()` function simply ignores any status but the CONNECTED status, and disconnects once the connection has reached that status.

There's not much work involved to start and stop connections. You can use this new knowledge to implement the login dialog box for Hello.

Connecting Hello

To establish a connection, you must first gather the user's credentials. The login dialog box exists for this purpose, but it is initially hidden and needs to be created and shown. You can use jQuery UI's `dialog()` function to show and hide this dialog box and use custom events to start the connection using Strophe.

The `dialog()` function is called on the elements that you want to convert into dialog boxes and takes a list of properties defining how the dialog boxes should behave. Most of the properties used won't be fully explained here, but their functions are fairly obvious from their names. All the properties are fully explained in the jQuery UI documentation at `http://ui.jquery.com/`.

Create the `hello.js` file and add the following code to it:

Available for download on Wrox.com

```
$(document).ready(function () {
    $('#login_dialog').dialog({
        autoOpen: true,
        draggable: false,
        modal: true,
        title: 'Connect to XMPP',
```

```
        buttons: {
            "Connect": function () {
                $(document).trigger('connect', {
                    jid: $('#jid').val(),
                    password: $('#password').val()
                });

                $('#password').val('');
                $(this).dialog('close');
            }
        }
    });
});
```

code snippet hello.js

The most important property is `buttons`, which defines the dialog box's buttons and the actions to take when those buttons are clicked. A single button is defined here called Connect. When the Connect button is clicked, a custom event called `connect` is triggered, and the JID and password are passed along to the event's handlers. Once the event has triggered, the password field is cleared and the dialog box is closed. When the function defined for the Connect button is executed, the `this` object will be set to the dialog box's main element, `#login_dialog`. You can wrap `this` with jQuery to easily access the dialog box's other methods, like `close`, as is done in the preceding code.

Next, you will need to create a handler for the `connect` event that creates a new `Strophe.Connection` object and calls the `connect()` method. You will also need to provide a callback that can respond to changes in the connection status.

Add the following custom event handlers to the document ready function you wrote earlier:

```
$(document).bind('connect', function (ev, data) {
    var conn = new Strophe.Connection(
        "http://bosh.metajack.im:5280/xmpp-httpbind");
    conn.connect(data.jid, data.password, function (status) {
        if (status === Strophe.Status.CONNECTED) {
            $(document).trigger('connected');
        } else if (status === Strophe.Status.DISCONNECTED) {
            $(document).trigger('disconnected');
        }
    });
});

$(document).bind('connected', function () {
    // nothing here yet
});

$(document).bind('disconnected', function () {
    // nothing here yet
});
```

code snippet hello.js

The handler for the `connect` event creates a new connection object and calls `connect()` with a callback function that merely triggers new custom events. The `connected` event is fired whenever Strophe notifies the callback function of the `CONNECTED` status, and the `disconnected` event is fired for the `DISCONNECTED` status.

The next two event handlers are bound to these new custom events but don't yet do anything.

This connection event design is a pattern used throughout this book's applications. The custom events have made it trivial to separate out the various parts of the connection process, and you can modify any of the handlers without affecting the others.

There is one last set of additions to make before you move on to the next section of Hello. The logging area is used for notifying the user of what is happening as the application runs, so you should create a function to write messages to this area and log whenever the `connected` and `disconnected` events are triggered.

First, create a namespace object for Hello and add a `connection` property and the `log()` function. The `connection` property will store the active connection object so that it can be accessed later. The `log()` function simply updates the logging area with a message. The following code can go before the document ready handler at the top of the file:

```
var Hello = {
    connection: null,

    log: function (msg) {
        $('#log').append("<p>" + msg + "</p>");
    }
};
```

code snippet hello.js

The `connection` property is initialized to `null`, but you'll need to assign the created connection object to it and set it back to `null` when the connection is terminated. You should also add the logging message to the `connected` event handler. The modified event handlers are shown here, with their modified lines highlighted:

```
$(document).bind('connect', function (ev, data) {
    var conn = new Strophe.Connection(
        "http://bosh.metajack.im:5280/xmpp-httpbind");
    conn.connect(data.jid, data.password, function (status) {
        if (status === Strophe.Status.CONNECTED) {
            $(document).trigger('connected');
        } else if (status === Strophe.Status.DISCONNECTED) {
            $(document).trigger('disconnected');
        }
    });

    Hello.connection = conn;
});

$(document).bind('connected', function () {
    // inform the user
    Hello.log("Connection established.");
```

```
    });

    $(document).bind('disconnected', function () {
        Hello.log("Connection terminated.");

        // remove dead connection object
        Hello.connection = null;
    });
```

code snippet hello.js

Hello doesn't do too much yet, but it should be ready for its first test run. If you need to verify that all the code is in the right spot, the full `hello.js` file built so far is shown in Listing 3-3.

LISTING 3-3: hello.js (initial version)

```
var Hello = {
    connection: null,

    log: function (msg) {
        $('#log').append("<p>" + msg + "</p>");
    }
};

$(document).ready(function () {
    $('#login_dialog').dialog({
        autoOpen: true,
        draggable: false,
        modal: true,
        title: 'Connect to XMPP',
        buttons: {
            "Connect": function () {
                $(document).trigger('connect', {
                    jid: $('#jid').val(),
                    password: $('#password').val()
                });

                $('#password').val('');
                $(this).dialog('close');
            }
        }
    });
});

$(document).bind('connect', function (ev, data) {
    var conn = new Strophe.Connection(
        "http://bosh.metajack.im:5280/xmpp-httpbind");
    conn.connect(data.jid, data.password, function (status) {
        if (status === Strophe.Status.CONNECTED) {
            $(document).trigger('connected');
        } else if (status === Strophe.Status.DISCONNECTED) {
```

```
                $(document).trigger('disconnected');
            }
        });

        Hello.connection = conn;
    });

    $(document).bind('connected', function () {
        // inform the user
        Hello.log("Connection established.");
    });

    $(document).bind('disconnected', function () {
        Hello.log("Connection terminated.");
        // remove dead connection object
        Hello.connection = null;
    });
```

Running the Application

Because Hello is a web application consisting only of HTML, CSS, and JavaScript it is fairly easy to run and test. Unfortunately, although the flXHR library allows you to do cross-domain requests with no server setup, it doesn't allow you to run applications from `file://` URLs that make requests to `http://` URLs. This means you will need to use a web server to serve Hello over HTTP, and point your browser to the `http://` URL.

You don't need anything fancy; any web server will work, and any cheap hosting service should work fine as well. Simple-to-install web servers exist for every platform imaginable, and some operating systems have them built in. You can also use the Tape program to serve the files; Tape is described in Appendix B.

Once you have a web server running or have uploaded your code to your favorite web host, you can point your browser to the URL for `hello.html` on that server and try to log in. You should see a log message that says "Connection established."

If something goes wrong, check your web browser's error console to make sure the code is not throwing an error you aren't seeing. Also, make sure you have all the dependencies installed and in the correct locations.

CREATING STANZAS

Building XMPP stanzas is one of the most important parts of writing an XMPP application. Even if you can use plug-ins to handle most of your protocol work with XMPP, you will probably have to create some of your own stanzas too. Strophe comes with some powerful stanza-building tools to make this as painless as possible.

XMPP stanzas are just partial XML documents. You can certainly use the browser's own DOM manipulation functions to build stanzas, but the DOM API can be quite tedious, and varies slightly from browser to browser. Strophe abstracts these APIs, in much the same way jQuery abstracts you from the same APIs, so that you can focus on creating the stanzas you need without worrying about all the details.

Strophe Builders

Constructing XMPP stanzas is the job of `Strophe.Builder` objects. These objects were inspired by jQuery and make building stanzas extremely fast and easy. Strophe then goes above and beyond by providing several shortcut functions to accomplish common construction operations.

A builder is created with two parameters: an element name and a set of attributes. The first line of the following code creates the stanza `<presence/>` and the second line creates the stanza `<presence to='example.com'/>`:

```
var pres1 = new Strophe.Builder("presence");
var pres2 = new Strophe.Builder("presence", {to: "example.com"});
```

Because building stanzas is such a common operation and typing "`new Strophe.Builder`" is rather long, Strophe provides four global aliases for stanza creation: `$build()`, `$msg()`, `$pres()`, and `$iq()`. The code for these functions just creates `Strophe.Builder` objects exactly like the examples shown. The function `$build()` takes the same two arguments as the constructor for `Strophe.Builder`. The other three functions create `<message/>`, `<presence/>`, and `<iq/>` stanzas, respectively, and take an optional argument of the desired attributes.

You can shorten the preceding code using either `$build()` or `$pres()`, although the latter is most often used:

```
var pres1 = $build("presence");
var pres2 = $build("presence", {to: "example.com"});
var pres3 = $pres();
var pres4 = $pres({to: "example.com"});
```

Building more complex stanzas is accomplished via *chaining* function calls. Just like jQuery, Strophe's building shortcut methods return the builder object when they are called. Most of the methods on the builder object, which you see shortly, also return the builder object. This means that you can keep calling methods in a chain, just like in jQuery. Don't worry if this sounds confusing; you will see plenty of examples.

All the builder object's methods have shortened names to save typing. The chainable methods that return the builder object are `c()`, `cnode()`, `t()`, `attrs()`, and `up()`. There are also two methods that do not return the builder object, `toString()` and `tree()`.

The `toString()` method serializes the stanza to text. This can be very handy for debugging purposes. For example, `$pres().toString()` returns the string "`<presence/>`". The method `tree()` does a similar job, but returns the DOM element at the top of the stanza's element tree. This isn't normally used, but if you need access to the DOM elements created inside a builder object, it is there.

You add a new child element to the stanza with `c()` and `cnode()`. The former takes the same parameters as `$build()` and appends a new child element to current element. The latter method does the same job, but takes a single DOM element as input. Most of the time `c()` will be more than sufficient, but occasionally `cnode()` is useful for copying or reusing already built pieces of stanzas.

Because these methods return the builder object, they can be easily chained:

```
var stanza = $build("foo").c("bar").c("baz");
```

Calling `stanza.toString()` would result in:

```
<foo><bar><baz/></bar></foo>
```

Each time you add a child, the current element in the builder changes to the new child. If you want to create multiple children on the same element, you must walk back up the tree one level after calling `c()`. You can do this with the `up()` method.

The `up()` method can be added to the previous example to build a slightly different stanza:

```
var stanza = $build("foo").c("bar").up().c("baz");
```

The XML produced by this would be:

```
<foo><bar/><baz/></foo>
```

Text children are added with the `t()` method. Unlike the similar `c()` method, `t()` does not change the current element.

A typical XMPP message can be created with `$msg()` and the `c()` and `t()` methods as in the following example:

```
var message = $msg({to: "darcy@pemberley.lit", type: "chat"})
    .c("body").t("How do you do?");
```

The XML produced by this builder is:

```
<message to='darcy@pemberley.lit'
         type='chat'>
  <body>How do you do?</body>
</message>
```

The last method of the builder object is `attrs()`, which takes an attribute set and uses it to augment the current element's attribute set. This is useful when partial stanzas are built by other pieces of code and you need to add some final attributes before sending it across the connection. It's not used often, but it can be quite handy for abstracting stanza building functionality.

The following code shows several builders that are a little more elaborate as well as the stanzas they produce:

```
var iq = $iq({to: "pemberley.lit", type: "get", id: "disco1"})
    .c("query", {xmlns: "http://jabber.org/protocol/disco#info"});

// produces:
//
// <iq to='pemberley.lit'
//     type='get'
```

```
//        id='disco1'>
//     <query xmlns='http://jabber.org/protocol/disco#info'/>
//  </iq>

var presence = $pres().c("show").t("away").up()
    .c("status").t("Off to Meryton");

// produces
//
// <presence>
//     <show>away</show>
//     <status>Off to Meryton</status>
// </presence>
```

Saying Hello

The Hello application needs to send a stanza to the server to say "hello," and you can do this by using the Strophe builder functions. The "hello" stanza will be an IQ-get stanza containing a ping request.

As soon as the connection is ready to accept data, the connection's callback function is called with a status of CONNECTED. This triggers the connected event and calls your attached handler. This is the perfect place to send the ping request to the server.

The modified event handler is shown here:

```
$(document).bind('connected', function () {
    // inform the user
    Hello.log("Connection established.");

    var domain = Strophe.getDomainFromJid(Hello.connection.jid);

    Hello.send_ping(domain);
});
```

code snippet hello.js

You need to add the send_ping() function to the Hello namespace object as well:

```
send_ping: function (to) {
    var ping = $iq({
        to: to,
        type: "get",
        id: "ping1"}).c("ping", {xmlns: "urn:xmpp:ping"});

    Hello.connection.send(ping);
}
```

code snippet hello.js

Some new things are used here that you haven't seen before. The send() method of the connection object sends a stanza to the server. The jid attribute of the connection object contains the full JID associated with the connection. The Strophe object contains several methods to make dealing with JIDs easier: getUserFromJid(), getDomainFromJid(), getResourceFromJid(), and getBareJidFromJid().

The JID helper functions return various portions of the JID. The following code shows how these functions are used and what they return:

```
Strophe.getUserFromJid("darcy@pemberley.lit/library"); // "darcy"
Strophe.getDomainFromJid("darcy@pemberley.lit/library"); // "pemberley.lit"
Strophe.getResourceFromJid("darcy@pemberley.lit/library"); // "library"
Strophe.getBareJidFromJid("darcy@pemberley.lit/library"); // "darcy@pemberley.lit"
```

Hello now sends a ping to the user's server, but it does not yet do anything with the server's response. The last piece of the puzzle is handling incoming stanzas.

HANDLING EVENTS

Most XMPP applications are event driven. Some events are triggered by user interactions like clicking the mouse or pressing a key, and others are triggered by incoming stanzas. For example, when a message is received the application handles it by displaying it to the user. Handling incoming stanzas is probably the most important part of any XMPP application, and Strophe makes doing so quite simple.

Adding and Removing Handlers

New stanza handlers can be added with `addHandler()` and removed with `deleteHandler()`. The following code shows the basics of using these functions:

```
var ref = conn.addHandler(my_handler_function, null, "message");
// once the handler is no longer needed:
connection.deleteHandler(ref);
```

The `addHandler()` function returns a handler reference. This reference is only used for passing to `deleteHandler()` to identify the specific handler to remove.

The `deleteHandler()` function is not often used since handler functions have a way of removing themselves when they are no longer needed. In some cases, the knowledge of when to remove a handler is not available within the handler, and `deleteHandler()` does the job in these situations.

Stanza Matching

The `addHandler()` function takes one or more parameters. The first parameter is the function that is invoked when a matching stanza is received. The rest of the parameters are matching criteria. The full list of these parameters is shown in this abbreviated function definition from the Strophe source code:

```
addHandler: function (handler, ns, name, type, id, from) {
    // implementation omitted
}
```

If any of the criteria are null or undefined, any stanza will match. Otherwise, stanzas will match only if they satisfy the criteria by string equality in a particular part of the stanza. The last four criteria — name, `type`, `id`, and `from` — specify filters on the stanza's element name and the `type`, `id`, and `from` attributes. These four criteria are checked only on the top-level element, not on any of the element's descendants. The first criterion, ns, is slightly different, and it is checked for the top-level element as well as its immediate children. You see why shortly.

The name criterion will almost always be null, to match any stanza, or one of message, presence, or iq. The addHandler() example set up a handler that would be called for any <message> stanza received.

The type, id, and from criteria match the main attributes of <message>, <presence> and <iq> stanzas. You can use type to differentiate between regular chat messages and group chat messages or to separate out IQ-result stanzas from IQ-error stanzas. The id criterion is often used to handle replies to specific requests, like the IQ-result associated with a particular IQ-get request. Matching on the from attribute limits the handler to dealing with messages that come from a specific JID. You should use from with care, because you may not always know which resource another user or service will use to communicate with you. A bare JID supplied as a from criterion will not match any full JID; the match must be exact.

Matching on the ns (for namespace) criterion is mostly done with IQ stanzas. IQ stanzas generally contain a single child element that is namespaced according to the type of function it serves. For example, the ping stanza you sent earlier was an IQ-get stanza with a <ping/> child under the urn:xmpp:ping namespace. Setting up a handler to catch all incoming ping requests could be done with the following code:

```
conn.addHandler(my_ping_handler, "urn:xmpp:ping", "iq");
```

The function my_ping_handler() would be called anytime the connection received an IQ stanza with a child under the urn:xmpp:ping namespace. It would get all of these stanzas, regardless of their type, id, or from attributes, because those criteria were left unspecified.

Stanza Handler Functions

Whenever a matching stanza is found for a handler, the handler function is invoked and passed the stanza as its argument. Unless the function returns true or some expression that evaluates to true, the handler function will be removed once it finishes.

The following example stanza handler is called a one-shot handler, because it returns false. After this handler is finished with the first stanza, it will be deleted and will not be called again unless it is explicitly re-added by another call to addHandler().

```
function my_ping_handler(iq) {
    // do something interesting
    return false;
}
```

If the function doesn't use the return statement at all, it returns undefined, which results in the same outcome as returning false. If you find that your handlers stop working, be sure to check their return value.

The next example shows a handler that returns true and is therefore able to process as many stanzas as are received. The handle_incoming_ping() function responds with a pong to some incoming ping request.

```
function handle_incoming_ping(iq) {
    // conn is assumed to be a global pointing to a valid
    // Strophe.Connection object
    var pong = $iq({to: $(iq).attr('from'), type: "result", id: $(iq).attr('id')});
    conn.send(pong);

    return true;
}
```

Handling Responses in Hello

The last piece required for Hello is to handle the server's reply to the ping request. You can use your new knowledge of stanza handlers to implement this. As with most pings, it is interesting and fun to measure how long it takes to receive a response, so you can add some timing code to Hello as well.

Typically, handlers should be added for responses before you send the initial requests. This helps to avoid race conditions when the server generates a response so fast that the handler isn't added in time to catch it.

Modify the connected event handler to match the one shown here:

```
$(document).bind('connected', function () {
    // inform the user
    Hello.log("Connection established.");

    Hello.connection.addHandler(Hello.handle_pong, null, "iq", null, "ping1");

    var domain = Strophe.getDomainFromJid(Hello.connection.jid);

    Hello.send_ping(domain);
});
```

code snippet hello.js

The `send_ping()` function also needs the following changes:

```
send_ping: function (to) {
    var ping = $iq({
        to: to,
        type: "get",
        id: "ping1"}).c("ping", {xmlns: "urn:xmpp:ping"});

    Hello.log("Sending ping to " + to + ".");

    Hello.start_time = (new Date()).getTime();
    Hello.connection.send(ping);
}
```

code snippet hello.js

The handler function is added before the code sends the stanza, and the time the request was sent is kept in the `start_time` property of the Hello namespace object. This new version also adds another message to the log so the user sees what is happening.

You'll also need to add the new property and the `handle_pong()` function to the Hello namespace object. These additions are shown in the following code:

```
start_time: null,

handle_pong: function (iq) {
    var elapsed = (new Date()).getTime() - Hello.start_time;
    Hello.log("Received pong from server in " + elapsed + "ms");

    Hello.connection.disconnect();

    return false;
}
```

code snippet hello.js

With these final additions, Hello should be fully functional. Point your browser to `hello.html` and give it a whirl! How fast is your server's response? The final version of `hello.js` appears in Listing 3-4.

LISTING 3-4: hello.js (final)

```
var Hello = {
    connection: null,
    start_time: null,

    log: function (msg) {
        $('#log').append("<p>" + msg + "</p>");
    },

    send_ping: function (to) {
        var ping = $iq({
            to: to,
            type: "get",
            id: "ping1"}).c("ping", {xmlns: "urn:xmpp:ping"});

        Hello.log("Sending ping to " + to + ".");

        Hello.start_time = (new Date()).getTime();
        Hello.connection.send(ping);
    },

    handle_pong: function (iq) {
        var elapsed = (new Date()).getTime() - Hello.start_time;
        Hello.log("Received pong from server in " + elapsed + "ms.");

        Hello.connection.disconnect();

        return false;
    }
};

$(document).ready(function () {
    $('#login_dialog').dialog({
```

```
                autoOpen: true,
                draggable: false,
                modal: true,
                title: 'Connect to XMPP',
                buttons: {
                    "Connect": function () {
                        $(document).trigger('connect', {
                            jid: $('#jid').val(),
                            password: $('#password').val()
                        });

                        $('#password').val('');
                        $(this).dialog('close');
                    }
                }
        });
});

$(document).bind('connect', function (ev, data) {
    var conn = new Strophe.Connection(
        "http://bosh.metajack.im:5280/xmpp-httpbind");
    conn.connect(data.jid, data.password, function (status) {
        if (status === Strophe.Status.CONNECTED) {
            $(document).trigger('connected');
        } else if (status === Strophe.Status.DISCONNECTED) {
            $(document).trigger('disconnected');
        }
    });

    Hello.connection = conn;
});

$(document).bind('connected', function () {
    // inform the user
    Hello.log("Connection established.");

    Hello.connection.addHandler(Hello.handle_pong,
                                null, "iq", null, "ping1");

    var domain = Strophe.getDomainFromJid(Hello.connection.jid);

    Hello.send_ping(domain);
});

$(document).bind('disconnected', function () {
    Hello.log("Connection terminated.");

    // remove dead connection object
    Hello.connection = null;
});
```

MORE HELLOS

The best thing about simple applications is that they are the easiest to improve. Try adding the following things to Hello:

➤ A single measurement is often not representative; modify Hello to do several pings and measure the average response time.

➤ If you used a serial approach to the previous task, try a parallel one; if you already created a parallel version, try making it run serially.

SUMMARY

Congratulations, you've now written your first Strophe application and quite possibly your first XMPP application. As you've seen, using XMPP with Strophe and jQuery is pretty simple. You've learned:

➤ How to get everything required for a Strophe-based XMPP application.

➤ How to test and run XMPP applications.

➤ How to make and terminate connections.

➤ How to send data to the server.

➤ How to handle incoming stanzas.

➤ How to use custom events in jQuery.

With the basics under your belt, you can move on to making your first *useful* XMPP application in the next chapter.

Exploring the XMPP Protocol: A Debugging Console

WHAT'S IN THIS CHAPTER?

➤ Hooking into Strophe's logging facilities

➤ Parsing XML

➤ Manipulating your presence

➤ Querying for software versions

➤ Dealing with XMPP errors

Developers have always enjoyed crafting and refining their tools. In your journey through XMPP applications, you will need a tool to aid exploration and to inspect protocol traffic. Few web developers could live without the view source command or the ability to easily craft URLs to test functionality of remote sites. In the world of XMPP stanzas, such a tool would allow you to inspect protocol traffic and easily create stanzas to send. You'll build a protocol debugging console named Peek over the course of this chapter, and, afterwards, you will use it to investigate a few XMPP services and typical protocol situations.

Peek will be useful throughout this book. Whenever you encounter an example stanza, you can load Peek, type in the stanza, and watch what happens in response. In this way, you can play with various XMPP features even before you start building applications.

Many of the parts required to build Peek have already been introduced: establishing connections, sending stanzas, and setting up basic handlers for incoming traffic. However, Peek will need some new features of Strophe, and once Peek is built, you'll use it to explore a few new XMPP concepts.

APPLICATION PREVIEW

The finished application — shown in Figure 4-1 — is reminiscent of color terminals and code editors with fancy highlighting.

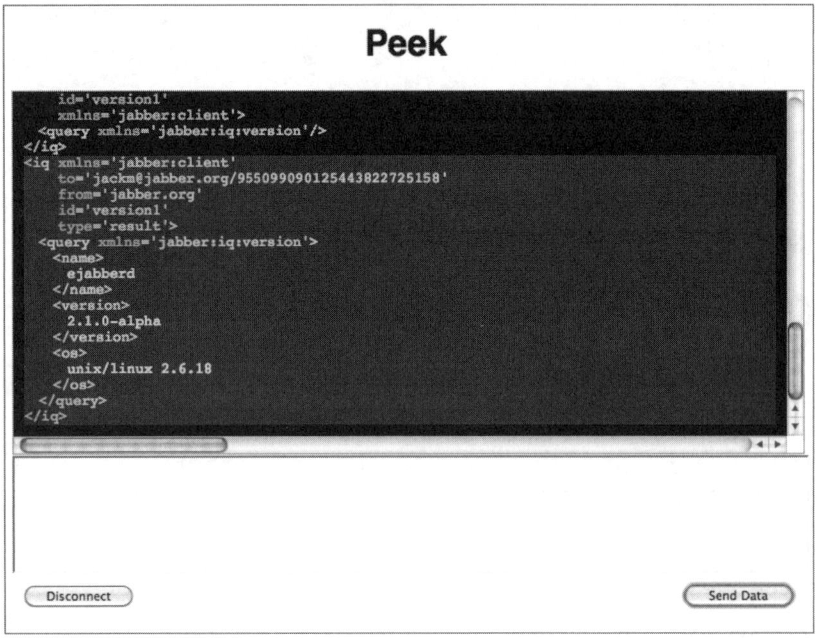

```
        id='version1'
        xmlns='jabber:client'>
    <query xmlns='jabber:iq:version'/>
</iq>
<iq xmlns='jabber:client'
    to='jackm@jabber.org/9550990901254438822725158'
    from='jabber.org'
    id='version1'
    type='result'>
  <query xmlns='jabber:iq:version'>
    <name>
      ejabberd
    </name>
    <version>
      2.1.0-alpha
    </version>
    <os>
      unix/linux 2.6.18
    </os>
  </query>
</iq>
```

Disconnect   Send Data

FIGURE 4-1

The top area with the black background is where all the stanzas appear that were sent to or received from the server. The input area below accepts either XML input or Strophe's stanza building commands.

PEEK DESIGN

The debugging console is one of the simplest things you can build with XMPP. Peek needs to be able to send traffic and display traffic, but it doesn't need any traffic processing logic beyond those humble requirements. Making the user interface look nice constitutes the bulk of the work.

Every connection in Strophe has some special functions for hooking into the protocol data that is being sent and received. These functions come in two forms: `xmlInput()` and `xmlOuptut()` for structured traffic and `rawInput()` and `rawOutput()` for the actual character data. Normally these functions do nothing, but Peek will override them to get a view of the data flowing in and out of the connection.

When a connection is first established, Strophe sends and receives several stanzas behind the scenes to handle authentication and session setup. The CONNECTED status is achieved only when a session has been successfully started. You'll first handle traffic display so that you can see these setup stanzas as they happen.

The XMPP streams carry data in XML, but that XML is not formatted for display. In fact, most XMPP servers, clients, and libraries will send XML that is stripped of unnecessary whitespace. Stanzas viewed on the wire will look mostly like one giant string of text. Following is an example stanza with pleasant formatting, followed by the same stanza as it would typically appear:

```
<message to='darcy@pemberley.lit/meryton'
         from='bingley@netherfield.lit/meryton'
         type='chat'>
  <body>Come, Darcy, I must have you dance. I hate to see you standing about by
    yourself in this stupid manner. You had much better dance.</body>
</message>

<message to='darcy@pemberley.lit/meryton' from='bingley@netherfield.lit/meryton'
type='chat'><body>Come, Darcy, I must have you dance. I hate to see you standing
about by yourself in this stupid manner. You had much better dance.</body></mess
age>
```

For short stanzas this difference is not great, but for longer stanzas and within large groups of stanzas, the latter is almost unreadable.

You will be using `xmlInput()` and `xmlOutput()` to get structured traffic, and then wrapping this in HTML and CSS to display the traffic using syntax highlighting and extra whitespace. We won't be covering this display translation code in much detail because it is orthogonal to your objective, but the code is easy to understand and modify if you're curious.

With your console set up and receiving protocol traffic, your attentions will turn to handling user input. You start by allowing the user to input XML stanzas by hand. Because Strophe only accepts actual XML data for sending across the connection, you must parse this input text into XML and then send it over the connection. You'll use the web browser's native XML parsing abilities to accomplish this.

Typing out XML is fairly tedious, so you'll add the ability for users to use Strophe's own stanza building commands like `$msg()`, `$pres()`, and `$iq()`. Peek will use JavaScript's `eval()` to execute this code.

If it sounds simple, it is. However, Peek will be extremely useful in experimenting with and debugging your applications and the servers with which you interact.

BUILDING THE CONSOLE

Peek will use the same application structure as the Hello application from Chapter 3. You will first need to create the user interface by building `peek.html` and `peek.css`, and then you'll create the application logic in JavaScript. The final source code is included at the end of the section in case you get stuck.

User Interface

Peek's user interface is extremely simple. It consists of an area to display the protocol traffic, a text area input for the user to create outgoing stanzas, and a few buttons. A login dialog box is included as well, but it is initially hidden just like in Chapter 3. These elements appear in the initial version of the HTML code shown in Listing 4-1.

LISTING 4-1: peek.html

```
<!DOCTYPE HTML PUBLIC "-//W3C//DTD HTML 4.01//EN"
          "http://www.w3.org/TR/html4/strict.dtd">
<html>
  <head>
    <meta http-equiv="Content-type" content="text/html;charset=UTF-8" />
    <title>Peek - Chapter 4</title>

    <link rel='stylesheet' href='http://ajax.googleapis.com/ajax/libs/j
          queryui/1.7.2/themes/cupertino/jquery-ui.css'>
    <script src='http://ajax.googleapis.com/ajax/libs/jquery/1.3.2/jque
          ry.js'></script>
    <script src='http://ajax.googleapis.com/ajax/libs/jqueryui/1.7.2/jq
          uery-ui.js'></script>
    <script src='scripts/strophe.js'></script>
    <script src='scripts/flXHR.js'></script>
    <script src='scripts/strophe.flxhr.js'></script>

    <link rel='stylesheet' type='text/css' href='peek.css'>
    <script type='text/javascript' src='peek.js'></script>
  </head>
  <body>
    <h1>Peek</h1>

    <div id='console'></div>
    <textarea id='input' class='disabled'
              disabled='disabled'></textarea>

    <div id='buttonbar'>
      <input id='send_button' type='submit' value='Send Data'
          disabled='disabled' class='button'>
      <input id='disconnect_button' type='submit' value='Disconnect'
          disabled='disabled' class='button'>
    </div>

    <!-- login dialog -->
    <div id='login_dialog' class='hidden'>
      <label>JID:</label><input type='text' id='jid'>
      <label>Password:</label><input type='password' id='password'>
    </div>
  </body>
</html>
```

The initial CSS code appears in Listing 4-2. The only style that is not immediately obvious is .incoming, which you will use to distinguish incoming traffic from outgoing in the console.

LISTING 4-2: peek.css

```css
body {
    font-family: Helvetica;
}

h1 {
    text-align: center;
}

#console {
    padding: 10px;
    height: 300px;
    border: solid 1px #aaa;

    background-color: #000;
    color: #eee;
    font-family: monospace;

    overflow: auto;
}

#input {
    width: 100%;
    height: 100px;
    font-family: monospace;
}

.incoming {
    background-color: #111;
}

textarea.disabled {
    background-color: #bbb;
}

#buttonbar {
    margin: 10px;
}

#disconnect_button {
    float: left;
    width: 100px;
}

#send_button {
    float: right;
    width: 100px;
}
```

You add a few new styles to peek.css later in this section.

Displaying Traffic

Now that you've built a simple user interface, it is time to wire up the login dialog box and hook into Strophe's logging functions to make stanzas appear in the console.

First, you'll need to create the login dialog box and have it open when the page loads. This can be done in response to the document ready event just like you did in Chapter 3. Place the following code into a file called `peek.js`:

```javascript
$(document).ready(function () {
    $('#login_dialog').dialog({
        autoOpen: true,
        draggable: false,
        modal: true,
        title: 'Connect to XMPP',
        buttons: {
            "Connect": function () {
                $(document).trigger('connect', {
                    jid: $('#jid').val(),
                    password: $('#password').val()
                });

                $('#password').val('');
                $(this).dialog('close');
            }
        }
    });
});
```

code snippet peek.js

jQuery UI's `dialog()` function converts your `<div>` into a modal dialog box that opens automatically. A Connect button is added that will fire the `connect` event and then close the dialog.

Add the following handler after the document ready handler:

```javascript
$(document).bind('connect', function (ev, data) {
    var conn = new Strophe.Connection(
        'http://bosh.metajack.im:5280/xmpp-httpbind');

    conn.xmlInput = function (body) {
        Peek.show_traffic(body, 'incoming');
    };
    conn.xmlOutput = function (body) {
        Peek.show_traffic(body, 'outgoing');
    };

    conn.connect(data.jid, data.password, function (status) {
        if (status === Strophe.Status.CONNECTED) {
            $(document).trigger('connected');
        } else if (status === Strophe.Status.DISCONNECTED) {
            $(document).trigger('disconnected');
        }
    }
```

```
        });
        Peek.connection = conn;
    });
```

code snippet peek.js

Much of this code you've seen before in Chapter 3. The highlighted lines are new, and they overwrite the blank, do-nothing default logging functions of the connection object with your own versions. Instead of pointing to two functions that would be almost identical, inline functions are used that will call `show_traffic()` with the correct parameters.

Add the following implementation of the `Peek` object, including the `show_traffic()` and `xml2html()` function, after the document ready handler:

```
var Peek = {
    connection: null,

    show_traffic: function (body, type) {
        if (body.childNodes.length > 0) {
            var console = $('#console').get(0);
            var at_bottom = console.scrollTop >= console.scrollHeight -
                console.clientHeight;;

            $.each(body.childNodes, function () {
                $('#console').append("<div class='" + type + "'>" +
                                    Peek.xml2html(Strophe.serialize(this)) +
                                    "</div>");
            });

            if (at_bottom) {
                console.scrollTop = console.scrollHeight;
            }

        }
    },

    xml2html: function (s) {
        return s.replace(/&/g, "&amp;")
            .replace(/</g, "&lt;")
            .replace(/>/g, "&gt;");
    }
};
```

code snippet peek.js

The `Peek` object serves as a namespace container for all application code and state. This is good programming practice, and isolates your code from other applications. Currently, the only application state the application has is the `connection` variable.

Web browsers do not speak XMPP natively (at least not yet) so XMPP connections must be tunneled through HTTP requests. A side effect of this tunneling is that stanzas are delivered in a <body>

wrapper, which contains some metadata about the request. The details of this tunneling, called BOSH, are the subject of XEP-0124 and XEP-0206 and were touched on in Chapter 2. The `show_traffic()` function ignores this `<body>` wrapper and deals with its children, which are the stanzas themselves.

Each stanza is converted from XML to text (this is referred to as serialization) using a new Strophe function, `Strophe.serialize()`. The XML string produced by Strophe's `serialize()` function must first be escaped before insertion into the HTML document, or the XML elements will be interpreted as HTML ones. The escaping is done by the `xml2html()` function, which replaces the special characters with their escaped versions. Then the text is appended to the console's content as a `<div>`. Incoming stanzas are given a CSS class of `incoming`, and outgoing stanzas receive the class `outgoing`. These are typical uses of jQuery.

The console should scroll to the bottom when new data comes in, so the `scrollTop` attribute of the element is set equal to its `scrollHeight`. However, it would be frustrating if it moved to the bottom while you were scrolled up to read something at the top. The code checks to see if the console is currently all the way at the bottom before changing the scroll position. If the user is looking at something old, the window will not jump to the bottom when something new comes in. When the user returns to the bottom, the auto-scrolling behavior will kick in again.

Finally, you should add some logic to make the Disconnect button functional. Once Peek is connected, you'll want to enable the Disconnect button, and when Peek disconnects, you'll want to disable the button. You can do this by binding the `connected` and `disconnected` events, which your connection callback fires when those states are reported by Strophe. Add the following handlers at the end of `peek.js`:

Available for download on Wrox.com

```
$(document).bind('connected', function () {
    $('#disconnect_button').removeAttr('disabled');
});

$(document).bind('disconnected', function () {
    $('#disconnect_button').attr('disabled', 'disabled');
});
```

code snippet peek.js

To make the button do something, you must handle its click event. Add the following code to the document ready event handler:

Available for download on Wrox.com

```
$('#disconnect_button').click(function () {
    Peek.connection.disconnect();
});
```

code snippet peek.js

If you load the application in a web browser and log in to your favorite XMPP server, you'll see the stanzas that are sent during authentication appear in the console. The only problem is that they are shown as long strings without any formatting. It's time for you to make them prettier and easier to read.

Making XML Pretty

Looking at long strings of text gets old pretty fast, so you'll want to reformat the XML to produce a more pleasing and readable display. A typical way to do this is via indentation. Each child element should appear indented under its parent, with its children similarly indented. Attributes can also be indented so that they line up with all the other attributes, each on its own line. Finally, you can assign different colors to all the different pieces: punctuation, tag names, attributes, attribute values, and content.

First, you'll want to add some appropriate CSS styles for the transformation to use. Add the following styles to `peek.css`:

```css
.xml_punc { color: #888; }
.xml_tag { color: #e77; }
.xml_aname { color: #55d; }
.xml_avalue { color: #77f; }
.xml_text { color: #aaa }
.xml_level0 { padding-left: 0; }
.xml_level1 { padding-left: 1em; }
.xml_level2 { padding-left: 2em; }
.xml_level3 { padding-left: 3em; }
.xml_level4 { padding-left: 4em; }
.xml_level5 { padding-left: 5em; }
.xml_level6 { padding-left: 6em; }
.xml_level7 { padding-left: 7em; }
.xml_level8 { padding-left: 8em; }
.xml_level9 { padding-left: 9em; }
```

code snippet peek.css

Each level of children will be indented 1 em, up to nine levels of children. The other styles are explained in Table 4-1.

TABLE 4-1: XML Styles

CSS CLASS	USED FOR
`.xml_punc`	Tag punctuation such as <, >, /, =
`.xml_tag`	Element tag names
`.xml_aname`	Attribute names
`.xml_avalue`	Attribute values
`.xml_text`	Text children of an element

Next, you'll need to modify `show_traffic()` to use something besides `Strophe.serialize()` to generate the representation. In the following code, `Peek.pretty_xml()` has replaced the old serialization code on the highlighted line:

Available for download on Wrox.com

```
show_traffic: function (body, type) {
    if (body.childNodes.length > 0) {
        var console = $('#console').get(0);
        var at_bottom = console.scrollTop >= console.scrollHeight -
            console.clientHeight;;

        $.each(body.childNodes, function () {
            $('#console').append("<div class='" + type + "'>" +
                          Peek.pretty_xml(this) +
                          "</div>");
        });
    }
}
```

code snippet peek.js

Finally, you'll need to implement `pretty_xml()`. The implementation in Listing 4-3 is recursive. First it styles the opening tag and its attributes; then the function calls itself for each child tag; and finally, it styles the closing tag. There are a few extra cases to handle the text children and empty tags as well. Each line of the output is in its own `<div>` element, and the text children are in their own, potentially multiline `<div>`.

You might wonder why the code puts all the strings, part by part, into an array instead of concatenating them all together with +. Using an array to hold parts of a larger string and then joining it all together at once is a common optimization pattern in JavaScript. Because JavaScript strings are immutable, a new string must be created when two strings are joined. Waiting until all the small strings are created to do the final concatenation saves a lot of intermediate string creation work by the interpreter. Similar string concatenation optimization patterns exist for other programming languages with immutable strings like Python and Java.

Available for download on Wrox.com

LISTING 4-3: The pretty_xml() function in peek.js

```
pretty_xml: function (xml, level) {
    var i, j;
    var result = [];
    if (!level) {
        level = 0;
    }

    result.push("<div class='xml_level" + level + "'>");
    result.push("<span class='xml_punc'>&lt;</span>");
    result.push("<span class='xml_tag'>");
    result.push(xml.tagName);
    result.push("</span>");

    // attributes
    var attrs = xml.attributes;
```

```
        var attr_lead = []
        for (i = 0; i < xml.tagName.length + 1; i++) {
            attr_lead.push(" ");
        }
        attr_lead = attr_lead.join("");

        for (i = 0; i < attrs.length; i++) {
            result.push(" <span class='xml_aname'>");
            result.push(attrs[i].nodeName);
            result.push("</span><span class='xml_punc'>='</span>");
            result.push("<span class='xml_avalue'>");
            result.push(attrs[i].nodeValue);
            result.push("</span><span class='xml_punc'>'</span>");

            if (i !== attrs.length - 1) {
                result.push("</div><div class='xml_level" + level + "'>");
                result.push(attr_lead);
            }
        }

        if (xml.childNodes.length === 0) {
            result.push("<span class='xml_punc'>/&gt;</span></div>");
        } else {
            result.push("<span class='xml_punc'>&gt;</span></div>");

            // children
            $.each(xml.childNodes, function () {
                if (this.nodeType === 1) {
                    result.push(Peek.pretty_xml(this, level + 1));
                } else if (this.nodeType === 3) {
                    result.push("<div class='xml_text xml_level" +
                                (level + 1) + "'>");
                    result.push(this.nodeValue);
                    result.push("</div>");
                }
            });

            result.push("<div class='xml xml_level" + level + "'>");
            result.push("<span class='xml_punc'>&lt;/</span>");
            result.push("<span class='xml_tag'>");
            result.push(xml.tagName);
            result.push("</span>");
            result.push("<span class='xml_punc'>&gt;</span></div>");
        }

        return result.join("");
    }
```

If you load the Peek application again with these changes, you'll see pretty XML output just like in Figure 4-1 at the beginning of the chapter.

Dealing with XML Input

The console now shows beautiful, colorized XML stanzas, but unfortunately, once the initial authentication and session setup is complete, there are no more stanzas to render. It's time to add user input to Peek so that you can interact with the console.

First, you'll need to enable the input field and the Send button once the connection is ready to accept stanzas. You already did this for the Disconnect button in the `connected` and `disconnected` event handlers. Because both buttons have the `button` class, you can handle both buttons at the same time. For the text area, you'll also need to remove the `disabled` class, which was used to alter the background color. The new handlers are shown here with the changed lines highlighted:

```javascript
$(document).bind('connected', function () {
    $('.button').removeAttr('disabled');
    $('#input').removeClass('disabled').removeAttr('disabled');
});

$(document).bind('disconnected', function () {
    $('.button').attr('disabled', 'disabled');
    $('#input').addClass('disabled').attr('disabled', 'disabled');
});
```

code snippet peek.js

The user can now type in XML in the text area whenever an established connection exists. You just need to do something when the user clicks Send.

Strophe's `send()` function only accepts valid XML DOM objects or Strophe.Builder objects. This makes it difficult to send invalid XML over the XMPP connection. Sending invalid XML would cause the server to terminate the connection immediately. Users can only input text, however, so you must first create a function that parses text into XML. Fortunately, web browsers all come with built-in XML parsers. Add the following `text_to_xml()` function to the Peek object:

```javascript
text_to_xml: function (text) {
    var doc = null;
    if (window['DOMParser']) {
        var parser = new DOMParser();
        doc = parser.parseFromString(text, 'text/xml');
    } else if (window['ActiveXObject']) {
        var doc = new ActiveXObject("MSXML2.DOMDocument");
        doc.async = false;
        doc.loadXML(text);
    } else {
        throw {
            type: 'PeekError',
            message: 'No DOMParser object found.'
        };
    }

    var elem = doc.documentElement;
    if ($(elem).filter('parsererror').length > 0) {
```

```
        return null;
    }
    return elem;
}
```

The `text_to_xml()` function creates an XML parser and parses the string. Internet Explorer 6 does not have the `DOMParser` class, so you must use an ActiveX object instead. Firefox, Safari, and Opera, however, all implement `DOMParser`. The ActiveX object differs slightly from the `DOMParser` API, but for Peek's needs, the changes required are very minor.

Some `DOMParser` objects will produce XML documents for invalid input, and these error documents will have a top-level `<parsererror>` element. You must check for this so that you don't accidentally send these error documents as XMPP stanzas.

All that is left is to wire up the Send button to the `text_to_xml()` function and send the result. You can add the following code to the document ready event handler to achieve this:

```
$('#send_button').click(function () {
    var xml = Peek.text_to_xml($('#input').val());
    if (xml) {
        Peek.connection.send(xml);
        $('#input').val('');
    }
});
```

Notice that you don't need to add the XML to the console. Strophe automatically passes the stanza to the `xmlInput()` and `rawInput()` logging functions, and these already take care of adding pretty XML data to the console.

There is one last thing to do — handle input errors. Currently if the user types something invalid, like `<<presence/>`, clicking Send does nothing. It would be nice to give the user some feedback. jQuery makes it extremely easy to do this. The modified Send button click event handler animates the background fading to red when an input error is detected:

```
$('#send_button').click(function () {
    var xml = Peek.text_to_xml($('#input').val());
    if (xml) {
        Peek.connection.send(xml);
        $('#input').val('');
    } else {
        $('#input').animate({backgroundColor: "#faa"}, 200);
    }
});
```

Now you must also reset the background color once the user starts to correct his mistake. You can use a keypress event handler to do this. The following code should be added to the document ready handler:

```
$('#input').keypress(function () {
    $(this).css({backgroundColor: '#fff'});
});
```

code snippet peek.js

Peek is now a working XMPP debugger!

Making Input Easier

Typing out all the XML by hand can be a little tiresome. Strophe compensates for this by having the easy-to-use `Builder` object and its helper functions, `$msg()`, `$pres()`, and `$iq()`. It's easy to extend Peek to allow users to input code as well as XML, making their life much easier if they know a little JavaScript.

First, you must detect if the input is code or XML. The easiest way to do this is to look at the first character. If it is <, then it looks a lot like XML; if it is $ it looks a lot like one of the three `Builder` object helper functions. If the user's input looks like code, you can use JavaScript's `eval()` function to execute it. You can replace the Send button click event handler with this new logic:

```
$('#send_button').click(function () {
    var input = $('#input').val();
    var error = false;
    if (input.length > 0) {
        if (input[0] === '<') {
            var xml = Peek.text_to_xml(input);
            if (xml) {
                Peek.connection.send(xml);
                $('#input').val('');
            } else {
                error = true;
            }
        } else if (input[0] === '$') {
            try {
                var builder = eval(input);
                Peek.connection.send(builder);
                $('#input').val('');
            } catch (e) {
                error = true;
            }
        } else {
            error = true;
        }
    }

    if (error) {
        $('#input').animate({backgroundColor: "#faa"});
    }
});
```

code snippet peek.js

For the case where the first character is <, the logic is exactly the same. When the first character is $, however, Peek evaluates the input as code, and if there are no errors, attempts to send this as a stanza. If the code throws an exception (for example, if the code contains a syntax error or does not produce a `Builder` object), an error is flagged.

Peek is now ready to help you explore the depths of XMPP. The completed `peek.js` file appears in Listing 4-4.

LISTING 4-4: peek.js (final)

```javascript
var Peek = {
    connection: null,

    show_traffic: function (body, type) {
        if (body.childNodes.length > 0) {
            var console = $('#console').get(0);
            var at_bottom = console.scrollTop >= console.scrollHeight -
                console.clientHeight;;

            $.each(body.childNodes, function () {
                $('#console').append("<div class='" + type + "'>" +
                                     Peek.pretty_xml(this) +
                                     "</div>");
            });

            if (at_bottom) {
                console.scrollTop = console.scrollHeight;
            }
        }
    },

    pretty_xml: function (xml, level) {
        var i, j;
        var result = [];
        if (!level) {
            level = 0;
        }

        result.push("<div class='xml_level" + level + "'>");
        result.push("<span class='xml_punc'>&lt;</span>");
        result.push("<span class='xml_tag'>");
        result.push(xml.tagName);
        result.push("</span>");

        // attributes
        var attrs = xml.attributes;
        var attr_lead = []
        for (i = 0; i < xml.tagName.length + 1; i++) {
            attr_lead.push(" ");
        }
        attr_lead = attr_lead.join("");

        for (i = 0; i < attrs.length; i++) {
```

continues

LISTING 4-4 *(continued)*

```javascript
            result.push(" <span class='xml_aname'>");
            result.push(attrs[i].nodeName);
            result.push("</span><span class='xml_punc'>='</span>");
            result.push("<span class='xml_avalue'>");
            result.push(attrs[i].nodeValue);
            result.push("</span><span class='xml_punc'>'</span>");

            if (i !== attrs.length - 1) {
                result.push("</div><div class='xml_level" + level + "'>");
                result.push(attr_lead);
            }
        }

        if (xml.childNodes.length === 0) {
            result.push("<span class='xml_punc'>/&gt;</span></div>");
        } else {
            result.push("<span class='xml_punc'>&gt;</span></div>");

            // children
            $.each(xml.childNodes, function () {
                if (this.nodeType === 1) {
                    result.push(Peek.pretty_xml(this, level + 1));
                } else if (this.nodeType === 3) {
                    result.push("<div class='xml_text xml_level" +
                                (level + 1) + "'>");
                    result.push(this.nodeValue);
                    result.push("</div>");
                }
            });

            result.push("<div class='xml xml_level" + level + "'>");
            result.push("<span class='xml_punc'>&lt;/</span>");
            result.push("<span class='xml_tag'>");
            result.push(xml.tagName);
            result.push("</span>");
            result.push("<span class='xml_punc'>&gt;</span></div>");
        }

        return result.join("");
    },

    text_to_xml: function (text) {
        var doc = null;
        if (window['DOMParser']) {
            var parser = new DOMParser();
            doc = parser.parseFromString(text, 'text/xml');
        } else if (window['ActiveXObject']) {
            var doc = new ActiveXObject("MSXML2.DOMDocument");
            doc.async = false;
            doc.loadXML(text);
        } else {
            throw {
```

```
                    type: 'PeekError',
                    message: 'No DOMParser object found.'
                };
            }

        var elem = doc.documentElement;
        if ($(elem).filter('parsererror').length > 0) {
            return null;
        }
        return elem;
    }
};

$(document).ready(function () {
    $('#login_dialog').dialog({
        autoOpen: true,
        draggable: false,
        modal: true,
        title: 'Connect to XMPP',
        buttons: {
            "Connect": function () {
                $(document).trigger('connect', {
                    jid: $('#jid').val(),
                    password: $('#password').val()
                });

                $('#password').val('');
                $(this).dialog('close');
            }
        }
    });

    $('#disconnect_button').click(function () {
        Peek.connection.disconnect();
    });

    $('#send_button').click(function () {
        var input = $('#input').val();
        var error = false;
        if (input.length > 0) {
            if (input[0] === '<') {
                var xml = Peek.text_to_xml(input);
                if (xml) {
                    Peek.connection.send(xml);
                    $('#input').val('');
                } else {
                    error = true;
                }
            } else if (input[0] === '$') {
                try {
                    var builder = eval(input);
                    Peek.connection.send(builder);
                    $('#input').val('');
                } catch (e) {
```

continues

LISTING 4-4 *(continued)*

```
                    console.log(e);
                    error = true;
                }
            } else {
                error = true;
            }
        }

        if (error) {
            $('#input').animate({backgroundColor: "#faa"});
        }
    });

    $('#input').keypress(function () {
        $(this).css({backgroundColor: '#fff'});
    });
});

$(document).bind('connect', function (ev, data) {
    var conn = new Strophe.Connection(
        "http://bosh.metajack.im:5280/xmpp-httpbind");

    conn.xmlInput = function (body) {
        Peek.show_traffic(body, 'incoming');
    };
    conn.xmlOutput = function (body) {
        Peek.show_traffic(body, 'outgoing');
    };

    conn.connect(data.jid, data.password, function (status) {
        if (status === Strophe.Status.CONNECTED) {
            $(document).trigger('connected');
        } else if (status === Strophe.Status.DISCONNECTED) {
            $(document).trigger('disconnected');
        }
    });
    Peek.connection = conn;
});

$(document).bind('connected', function () {
    $('.button').removeAttr('disabled');
    $('#input').removeClass('disabled').removeAttr('disabled');
});

$(document).bind('disconnected', function () {
    $('.button').attr('disabled', 'disabled');
    $('#input').addClass('disabled').attr('disabled', 'disabled');
});
```

EXPLORING XMPP

Peek is quite useful at helping you investigate how something works or why something is not doing what you expect. You can cut and paste the stanza building code from your application and see exactly what the server's response is. If you are unfamiliar with a particular protocol extension, you can type in the examples to see how the server responds to various inputs.

This book is filled with examples that you can try out in Peek. Be sure to adjust the server names and JIDs appropriately; the examples in this book use imaginary server domains and JIDs of fictional characters. You see what happens if you try to use these made-up examples in the section "Dealing with Errors."

Controlling Presence

As you learned in Chapter 1, presence information and presence control are some of the basic features of XMPP. Presence is also one of the simplest parts of the protocol.

Open up the Peek application, log in to your favorite XMPP server, type the following line, and click Send:

```
<presence/>
```

This first `<presence>` element sent on an XMPP connection is called *initial presence*. Normally the server will broadcast your presence to all the connected resources for your JID and all users subscribed to your presence notifications. The initial presence will also cause the server to send presence probes to all the users in your roster with whom you have a presence subscription. The initial presence enables the reception of incoming presence stanzas from your contacts.

If your roster is empty, you'll only see a slightly modified version of your stanza reflected back at you in response. If your roster has other people in it, you'll likely receive presence notifications from them almost immediately. As long as the server considers you online, you will continue to receive presence updates from your contacts as their presence status changes.

Because you didn't specify any attributes on the `<presence>` element, it signals to the server that you are online. Try typing the following input into Peek to set your presence status to away:

```
$pres().c('show').t("away").up().c('status').t("reading");
```

Probing Versions

Most XMPP clients, and even servers, support the Software Version extension (XEP-0092). This simple extension asks an entity to report its software and version number. Servers and XMPP services often use this protocol extension for gathering statistics, and you can use Peek to experiment with requesting software versions.

To request the software version of your server, send an IQ-get stanza with a `<query>` element using the `jabber:iq:version` namespace. You can input either of the following into Peek to ask the Jabber.org server what software it runs:

```
$iq({type: "get", id: "version1", to: "jabber.org"})
    .c("query", {xmlns: "jabber:iq:version"})
```

or

```
<iq type='get' id='version1' to='jabber.org'><query xmlns='jabber:iq:version'/></iq>
```

The server will respond with something similar to the following stanza. Because the Jabber.org server software may have been upgraded by the time you read this book, the response you receive may be different.

```
<iq xmlns='jabber:client'
    from='jabber.org'
    to='darcy@pemberley.lit/library'
    id='version1'
    type='result'>
  <query xmlns='jabber:iq:version'>
    <name>ejabberd</name>
    <version>2.1.0-alpha</version>
    <os>unix/linux 2.6.18</os>
  </query>
</iq>
```

Try probing some of your contacts or other servers to see what software they use.

Dealing with Errors

Handling errors is an important part of any application. The XMPP protocol has a uniform error reporting mechanism used by the core protocol and nearly every extension. IQ-error stanzas were talked about in Chapter 1, but you can use Peek to investigate these and other error situations in more detail.

IQ Stanza Errors

IQ-get and IQ-set stanzas that you send should always receive a reply of IQ-result or IQ-error. You should try building some bad stanzas to see how different entities respond.

The Google Talk service at gmail.com does not support the Software Version extension discussed earlier. Send gmail.com a request for its software version:

```
$iq({type: "get", id: "version2", to: "gmail.com"})
    .c("query", {xmlns: "jabber:iq:version"})
```

The server should respond immediately with an error:

```
<iq from='gmail.com'
    to='darcy@pemberley.lit/library'
    id='version1'
    type='error'>
```

```
    <query xmlns='jabber:iq:version'/>
    <error code='503' type='cancel'>
      <service-unavailable xmlns='urn:ietf:params:xml:ns:xmpp-stanzas'/>
    </error>
</iq>
```

This IQ-error stanza contains the contents of your original request as the first child. Many error stanzas you'll receive will include the original request's contents, although in some cases, this may be omitted if the stanza is quite large or contains sensitive information. The `<error>` element is required, and it should contain a `<text>` element and exactly one other child with the `urn:ietf:params:xml:ns:xmpp-stanzas` namespace. The preceding error stanza did not contain a `<text>` child—it's optional—but you see an example of this in the next section. The latter type of child's name tells you the kind of error that happened. In this case it was `service-unavailable`. This is exactly the error that was expected, because gmail.com does not support this extension.

Notice, also, that the `<error>` element's `type` attribute is `cancel`. This means that you should not try to continue this operation. Some errors will have `type` attributes of `modify`, which means that your application should try again with the input corrected. Other error types are also possible and include `continue`, `auth`, and `wait`. You can send the following stanza to a non-existent room on a multi-user chat service to induce an error:

```
<iq type='get' to='bad-room-123@conference.jabber.org' id='info1'>
  <query xmlns='http://jabber.org/protocol/disco#info'/>
</iq>
```

You should receive a response similar to the following one. Note that the server has supplied a human-readable `<text>` element as well as the normal error condition element.

```
<iq to='darcy@pemberley.lit/library'
    from='bad-room-123@conference.jabber.org'
    id='info1'
    type='error'>
  <query xmlns='http://jabber.org/protocol/disco#info'/>
  <error code='404'
         type='cancel'>
    <item-not-found xmlns='urn:ietf:params:xml:ns:xmpp-stanzas'/>
    <text xmlns='urn:ietf:params:xml:ns:xmpp-stanzas'>
      Conference room does not exist
    </text>
  </error>
</iq>
```

The `<error>` element may also contain an application-specific error condition, which will have a namespace specific to the service. You can find more information on the `<error>` element and IQ-error stanzas in RFC 3920 section 9.3.

Message Stanza Errors

`<message>` stanzas can also result in errors, and these are structured very similarly to IQ-error stanzas. Just like IQ-error stanzas, `<message>` stanza errors will have a `type` attribute of `error`, usually contain the original message, and also contain the same `<error>` elements.

One of the most common message errors is failed delivery to a user. For example, try sending a message to a made-up user on a made-up server:

```
$msg({to: elizabeth@longbourn.lit', type: 'chat'}).c('body')
    .t('What think you of books?')
```

Because the domain longbourn.lit does not exist, the server will respond with a message error like the following:

```
<message to='darcy@pemberley.lit'
         from='elizabeth@longbourn.lit'
         type='error'>
  <body>What think you of books?</body>
  <error code='404'
         type='cancel'>
    <remote-server-not-found xmlns='urn:ietf:params:xml:ns:xmpp-stanzas'/>
  </error>
</message>
```

These kinds of delivery errors are quite common; users often mistype addresses or have contacts that have changed servers.

Presence Stanza Errors

Like message errors, `<presence>` stanza errors generally occur when remote servers are unreachable either because they don't exist or some network link is offline. They occasionally crop up in other places as well. Just like IQ-error and message errors, presence errors have a `type` attribute of `error` and contain the `<error>` element.

Often you will see these as a result of server presence probes. Your XMPP server sends a probe to all your contacts when you send initial presence, and if any of those contacts' servers cannot be reached, this generates a presence error that gets delivered to you. An example of this type of error is included here:

```
<presence to=darcy@pemberley.lit/library'
          from='elizabeth@longbourn.lit'
          type='error'>
  <error code='404'
         type='cancel'>
    <remote-server-not-found xmlns='urn:ietf:params:xml:ns:xmpp-stanzas'/>
  </error>
</presence>
```

For some reason, the longbourn.lit server was not reachable by the pemberley.lit server where Darcy's XMPP account is, and a presence error is returned as a result of the presence probe.

Each type of stanza has a matching error stanza, and they all work the same way. The errors that your application must pay attention to are dependent on the application and the significance of the failure. For instance, clients usually ignore these presence errors because the state of the contact is the same from the user's perspective whether the contact is on an unreachable server or offline. However, presence errors received when trying to join a multi-user chat room (see Chapter 8) indicate real problems that the user should be notified about.

BETTER DEBUGGING

Peek is already extremely useful, but it could be even better. Try adding some extra features:

➤   Make stanzas in the console foldable — clicking on an element hides and shows children.

➤   Often users will want to run the same commands again; add support for command history.

SUMMARY

In this chapter, you built an application to inspect protocol traffic and aid in exploration and debugging of XMPP applications and services. Along the way you:

➤   Hooked into Strophe's structured logging facilities

➤   Parsed XML input from the user

➤   Rendered XML as nicely formatted HTML

➤   Evaluated user input as JavaScript code

Once Peek was built, it was used to explore some common pieces of the XMPP protocol:

➤   Manipulating your own presence information

➤   Retrieving software version information from other entities

➤   Dealing with various common stanza errors

Throughout the rest of the book, you should find Peek useful in diagnosing problems and exploring the XMPP protocol.

In the next chapter, you build a simple messaging client for use with the Identi.ca microblogging service.

5

Microblogging in Real Time: An Identica Client

WHAT'S IN THIS CHAPTER?

➤ Using XMPP `<message>` stanzas

➤ Using the Identica XMPP API

➤ Improving messages with XHTML-IM

➤ Dealing with stored offline messages

Millions of users communicate with friends and the world on Twitter, Identica, Jaiku, and other microblogging services. These services ask users to answer a simple question: "What are you doing?" The resulting stream of users' updates is very similar to a dynamic, global chat room, where each user defines the room they see by the people they are interested in.

Like chat systems, microblogging systems typically have low latencies, facilitating real-time communication among participants. Unfortunately, this low-latency channel is hampered by traditional, high-latency user interfaces. Many power users of microblogging services interact with these systems using third-party clients that make the experience faster.

One such service, Identica, has full support for XMPP clients. In this chapter, you build a real-time microblogging client for the Identica system. You will start to see how XMPP-powered web applications result in a more dynamic, low-latency, real-time experience.

In the previous two chapters, you learned the basics of the Strophe library and built a simple application to facilitate experimentation and debugging. The fun stuff starts in this chapter, in which you make useful software using XMPP that would be challenging to create using other methods.

APPLICATION PREVIEW

Updates on the Identica service are called *dents*. The application you build in this chapter is called Arthur — a reference to Arthur Dent, the protagonist of *The Hitchhiker's Guide to the Galaxy*. Figure 5-1 shows Arthur in action.

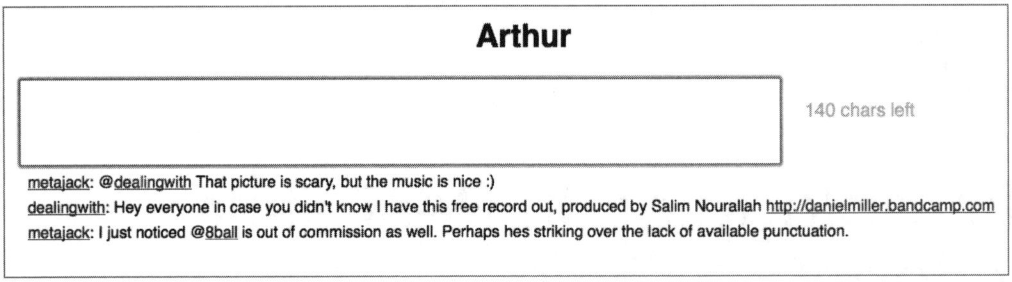

FIGURE 5-1

The input area appears at the top of the application. Users type and send their dents here. Below the input area, incoming messages are displayed in reverse chronological order. These messages often contain clickable links, because they are delivered in XHTML format.

ARTHUR DESIGN

Identica's XMPP API uses XMPP `<message>` stanzas for interacting with the system. The user's dents are sent as messages to update@identi.ca, and the same address sends incoming updates from followed users as they occur. This is exactly how normal one-to-one communication works in XMPP.

Although this API is a little clumsy for user actions aside from new dents, it does have the advantage that any XMPP client can use it without modification. XMPP clients all support one-to-one chats and are therefore capable of basic Identica integration.

Arthur mimics this basic one-to-one chat integration in a web application. Arthur's requirements are much simpler than a full chat client because it needs only to support chatting with a single entity. Because the other end is a computer program, not a human, Arthur doesn't need to support things like typing notification or presence updates. On the other hand, because of the application's narrower focus, the resulting user experience should be a bit nicer because it is designed specifically for microblogging.

Arthur will need to handle incoming messages from the Identica system and display them appropriately. These messages also come with XHTML markup that can be used to improve their display significantly. New dents from the user will need to be sent off to Identica as well. Finally, Arthur must deal with messages that were sent while the user was offline.

MICROBLOGGING WITH IDENTICA

Identica is one among many microblogging services, but it has some important properties that make it one of the best to work with, not the least of which is its XMPP support. Though Twitter is the most well known of these services, its early experiments with XMPP support were abandoned when its priorities shifted mainly toward keeping the site available. Twitter is also a *walled garden*, which is to say that it does not interoperate with other microblogging services.

Identica is the most well known system built on the StatusNet microblogging framework. StatusNet is an open source, federated microblogging platform that anyone can run. In fact, StatusNet is more than just open source; it is a Free Network Service (see `http://autonomo.us/2008/07/franklin-street-statement/`) — a service built on free software but with the added emphasis of giving users control over their data.

Unlike Twitter and other walled garden microblogging services, StatusNet systems form a network of microblogs that are capable of communicating with each other. This federation is very similar to the XMPP network discussed in Chapter 1 or the network of Internet e-mail servers. Any StatusNet site can receive and send updates to other microblogging sites using the Open Microblogging Protocol (OMB).

OPEN MICROBLOGGING PROTOCOL OR OMB

The OMB protocol was created by Evan Prodromou to address the need for an open, federated world of microblogging. Evan also leads the StatusNet project, which is the most well known software that implements OMB.

The current version of OMB is 0.1 and you can find it at:

`http://openmicroblogging.org/protocol/0.1/`

OMB is currently only defined over HTTP transports, but many in the OMB community are hoping to see an XMPP transport added in the next version. If you are interested in participating or reading more about OMB, you can join the mailing list or follow the OMB blog at the following URLs:

`http://lists.openmicroblogging.org/mailman/listinfo/omb`
`http://openmicroblogging.org/`

The philosophy of OMB and the StatusNet project match well with the philosophy of the Internet in general. That many StatusNet sites, including Identica, have great support for XMPP is just an added bonus. The XMPP support also makes it easy for you to build real-time applications on top of StatusNet servers.

Creating Your Account

If you don't already have an Identica account, or an account on another XMPP-enabled StatusNet service, you should create one now, because you will need it to test Arthur. Just visit Identica at `http://identi.ca` (or your favorite XMPP-enabled StatusNet system) and sign up for an account.

My account is `http://identi.ca/metajack` if you are looking for someone to follow with your new account.

Once you have your own account, you'll need to set it up for XMPP notifications.

Turning on XMPP

To configure your Identica account for XMPP support, follow these steps:

1. On any Identica page, click the Connect link in the navigation bar at the top right of the page.

2. Select the IM tab.

3. In the IM Address field, type your Jabber ID and click Add.

4. Make sure the Send Me Notices through Jabber/Gtalk option is enabled. You might also want to enable Send Me Replies through Jabber/GTalk from People I'm Not Subscribed To.

5. Click Save.

6. Identica will send a confirmation message to your XMPP account. Click the confirmation link it provides to complete the setup.

Now your XMPP account should receive messages whenever someone you follow posts an update.

You can test that this is working by sending an update to 8ball. 8ball is an Identica bot that generates random yes or no responses to questions, just like the well known Magic 8-ball toys. Send 8ball a message such as "@8ball Is it working?" Remember, if you didn't enable replies from people you aren't subscribed to, you'll need to subscribe to 8ball first by visiting `http://identi.ca/8ball` and clicking Subscribe.

If all is well, 8ball's random response will appear in your chat client, and you're ready to start building Arthur.

BUILDING ARTHUR

Identica has already started delivering notifications to your XMPP account. These are probably appearing in your favorite chat client looking much like regular private chat messages from your normal contacts. Your first goal is to write enough code that Arthur can connect to your XMPP account, receive updates from Identica, and display them. With that accomplished, you can spend some effort making the incoming messages prettier by using the XHTML-IM extension. Finally, you will need to enable the users to send their updates to Identica.

Getting Started

The HTML and CSS needed follow the same pattern as the previous two chapters. The HTML is shown in Listing 5-1 and the CSS is shown in Listing 5-2.

LISTING 5-1: arthur.html

```html
<!DOCTYPE HTML PUBLIC "-//W3C//DTD HTML 4.01//EN"
        "http://www.w3.org/TR/html4/strict.dtd">
<html>
  <head>
    <meta http-equiv="Content-type" content="text/html;charset=UTF-8">
    <title>Arthur - Chapter 5</title>

    <link rel='stylesheet' href='http://ajax.googleapis.com/ajax/libs/jqueryui/1.7.2/themes/cupertino/jquery-ui.css'>
    <script src='http://ajax.googleapis.com/ajax/libs/jquery/1.3.2/jquery.js'></script>
    <script src='http://ajax.googleapis.com/ajax/libs/jqueryui/1.7.2/jquery-ui.js'></script>
    <script src='scripts/strophe.js'></script>
    <script src='scripts/flXHR.js'></script>
    <script src='scripts/strophe.flxhr.js'></script>

    <link rel='stylesheet' type='text/css' href='arthur.css'>
    <script type='text/javascript' src='arthur.js'></script>
  </head>
  <body>
    <h1>Arthur</h1>

    <textarea id='input' rows='3'></textarea>
    <div id='counter'><span class='count'>140</span> chars left</div>
    <div id='stream'>
    </div>

    <!-- login dialog -->
    <div id='login_dialog' class='hidden'>
      <label>JID:</label><input type='text' id='jid'>
      <label>Password:</label><input type='password' id='password'>
    </div>
  </body>
</html>
```

LISTING 5-2: arthur.css

```css
body {
    font-family: Helvetica;
}

h1 {
    text-align: center;
```

continues

LISTING 5-2 *(continued)*

```
}

#input {
    width: 75%;
    font-size: 16pt;
}

#counter {
    width: 20%;
    float: right;
    padding: 25px;
    font-size: 14pt;
    color: #bbb;
}

.hidden {
    display: none;
}
```

The UI consists of a text area for input along with a character counter. Like Twitter, Identica limits updates to 140 characters. You'll want to let users know how many characters they have left so they don't try and send too many. Below the input area is a <div>, which will be filled with incoming updates. The hidden login dialog box is placed at the end.

Just as in the previous chapters, you'll need to enable the login dialog box and set up the connection flow events. Add the following code to a new file called `arthur.js`:

```
var Arthur = {
    connection: null
};

$(document).ready(function () {
    $('#login_dialog').dialog({
        autoOpen: true,
        draggable: false,
        modal: true,
        title: 'Connect to XMPP',
        buttons: {
            "Connect": function () {
                $(document).trigger('connect', {
                    jid: $('#jid').val(),
                    password: $('#password').val()
                });

                $('#password').val('');
                $(this).dialog('close');
            }
        }
    });
```

```
    });

    $(document).bind('connect', function (ev, data) {
        var conn = new Strophe.Connection(
            'http://bosh.metajack.im:5280/xmpp-httpbind');

        conn.connect(data.jid, data.password, function (status) {
            if (status === Strophe.Status.CONNECTED) {
                $(document).trigger('connected');
            } else if (status === Strophe.Status.DISCONNECTED) {
                $(document).trigger('disconnected');
            }
        });
        Arthur.connection = conn;
    });

    $(document).bind('connected', function () {
        // nothing here yet
    });

    $(document).bind('disconnected', function () {
        // nothing here yet
    });
```

code snippet arthur.js

Users of Arthur should now be able to log in to their XMPP accounts.

Receiving Messages

In Chapter 1 you learned that <message> stanzas are delivered to one or more resources based on each resource's availability and priority. Before Arthur will receive any messages from the server, it must first send an initial <presence> stanza to mark itself as available. Once available, the resource will begin to receive messages sent to the user's bare JID, assuming it has the highest priority or happens to be the only connected resource, or to the full JID of Arthur's connection.

Arthur is only interested in <message> stanzas, so you will want to set up a handler for them so that they get delivered to the appropriate function for display. Be careful to set up your handler *before* sending the initial presence, otherwise you may create a race condition where messages might go by unnoticed between the time presence is sent and the handler is set up.

The following new lines in the connected event handler set up the message handler, send the initial presence, and direct incoming messages to the handle_message() function, which will be implemented shortly:

```
    $(document).bind('connected', function () {
        Arthur.connection.addHandler(Arthur.handle_message,
                                null, "message", "chat");
        Arthur.connection.send($pres());
    });
```

code snippet arthur.js

The handler is set up to look for `<message>` stanzas with a `type` attribute of `chat`. As you learned in Chapter 1, the `chat` type is used for normal, private messages in the XMPP protocol.

Now you must implement the `handle_message()` function. This function needs to extract the body of the message and insert it at the top of the `<div>` used to display the updates. jQuery makes this all too easy. Take care to check that the sender of the message is who you think they are, otherwise you might show the wrong messages!

```
handle_message: function (message) {
    if ($(message).attr('from').match(/^update@identi.ca/)) {
        var body = $(message).children('body').text();
        $('#stream').prepend("<div>" + body + "</div>");
    }

    return true;
}
```

code snippet arthur.js

The code uses `children()` to find only the `<body>` element that is an immediate child of the `<message>` stanza. As you see shortly, Identica messages have an extra `<body>` element, and the code needs to be more specific in this case to find the correct one.

Arthur should now be receiving updates and displaying them.

XHTML-IM

It didn't take long for the XMPP community to get bored with plain text messages. XHTML-IM (XEP-0071) was created to reuse XHTML's existing formatting and inline CSS styling to make messages more structured as well as more visually pleasing. Many XMPP clients support sending and receiving XHTML-IM messages, and XMPP services like Identica often use XHTML-IM to add structure to message contents.

XHTML-IM is a stripped-down version of XHTML designed to be appropriate to the use case of small chat messages. Embedded objects, scripts, style sheets, and content transformations are all removed, leaving a basic set of markup and inline styles. Following is an example `<message>` stanza using XHTML-IM. Notice that both a normal `<body>` element and an XHTML-IM namespaced `<html>` element are provided, allowing for graceful fallback if XHTML-IM is unsupported.

```
<message from='bingley@netherfield.lit'
         to='jane@longbourn.lit'
         type='chat'>
  <body>I hope my dear friends will join me at Netherfield for a ball
  this Tuesday.</body>
  <html xmlns='http://jabber.org/protocol/xhtml-im'>
    <p style='font-weight: bold'>I hope my dear friends will join me at Netherfield
    for a ball this Tuesday.</p>
  </html>
</message>
```

XMPP EXTENSION PROPOSALS OR XEPS

XMPP is defined in the IETF RFCs (Request for Comments documents) 3920 and 3921. These documents cover the basic semantics of XMPP streams, the workings of XMPP federation, and the details on the main stanza types. Anything that is not considered a core part of XMPP but is accepted as a generally useful addition is documented in an XMPP Extension Proposal, or XEP.

Anyone can propose a new XEP by submitting it to the XMPP Standards Foundation (XSF). The XSF Council reviews all new proposed XEPs and votes on whether to accept them into the standardization process. Once accepted, XEPs are assigned numbers and a status of *experimental*. Over time, as people refine and implement the XEP, it may move to a status of *draft* and perhaps eventually to *final*. XEPs in *draft* or *final* status are considered well reviewed and ready for wide implementation and deployment. In some cases, XEPs become *deprecated* or *historical* when they are superseded or fall out of general use.

Some XEPs are very tiny, like Software Version (XEP-0092), and a few are quite large, like Publish-Subscribe (XEP-0060, which you see in detail in Chapter 9). Over the first decade of XMPP's existence nearly 300 XEPs were accepted, and they cover a wide range of functionality from remote commands to publishing song information. Each April 1st, the XSF even publishes a humorous XEP (my favorite of these is XEP-0239).

Several important XEPs are covered throughout this book, and you can find the full list of XEPs and their specifications at:

```
http://xmpp.org/extensions/
```

Adding XHTML-IM to Arthur

If you were to use Peek, the debugging console from the previous chapter, and inspect the incoming messages from Identica, you would see that the service appends an XHTML-IM payload to each update message. These structured payloads will turn usernames, hashtags, groups, and reply references into clickable links. If users see an update in Arthur referencing someone they've never heard of, they can easily click to find out more information.

Because Arthur is a web application, it is extremely easy to render the XHTML-IM message. You can use jQuery's `contents()` method to get all the XHTML children and then insert these into the appropriate place. Since the application uses HTML DOM and the XMPP connection uses XML DOM, you must use `importNode()` to transfer the elements between documents. Unfortunately, IE doesn't support `importNode()`, so for this browser you must use the `xml` property to get the raw text. These changes are highlighted here in the modified `handle_message()`:

```
handle_message: function (message) {
    if ($(message).attr('from').match(/^update@identi.ca/)) {
        var body = $(message).find('html > body').contents();

        var div = $("<div></div>");

        body.each(function () {
            if (document.importNode) {
                $(document.importNode(this, true)).appendTo(div);
            } else {
                // IE workaround
                div.append(this.xml);
            }
        });

        div.prependTo("#stream");
    }

    return true;
}
```

code snippet arthur.js

Please note Arthur does not santize the XHTML it receives. It is possible that someone could inject `<script>` elements and other unwanted things into the message body. If this were a real application, you would want to make sure this possibility is accounted for.

Arthur should now be displaying nicely formatted HTML messages instead of plain text. All that is left is to enable the users to send their own updates back to Identica.

Sending Messages

Sending messages to Identica is done via normal XMPP messages, as you might expect. You don't need to worry about sending XHTML-IM content or dealing with links in the message because the Identica system will translate your input and link all of the appropriate items before delivering it to your subscribers. Before you send the message, you should hook up the character counter so that Arthur can give loquacious users some warning before Identica rejects their long messages.

Counting characters is trivial in JavaScript, because the `String` object supports the `length` property just like arrays. The only challenge is when to measure the length of the text and then update the counter.

Whenever someone types in an input field or text box, the browser triggers the `keydown`, `keypress`, and `keyup` events in that order. The trouble is that the `keypress` event, which is the most obvious choice for where to put the count logic, is triggered before the value of the input field is modified. When the first `keypress` event is triggered, the value of the field will still be blank. Fortunately, the field is modified before the `keyup` event is called, so you can place the appropriate logic there to update the counter.

You can add the following `keyup` event handler to the document ready function, right after the login dialog box initialization code:

```
$('#input').keyup(function () {
    var left = 140 - $(this).val().length;
    $('#counter .count').text('' + left);
});
```

Now Arthur will update the input count while the user is typing.

Once the users are satisfied with their updates, they can hit Enter to submit them. To send these events to Identica, you need only to wrap them in normal `<message>` stanzas to update@identi.ca. This time, you will want to use the `keypress` event so that the Enter key is not part of the messages. Add the following code to the document ready handler:

```
$('#input').keypress(function (ev) {
    if (ev.which === 13) {
        ev.preventDefault();

        var text = $(this).val();
        $(this).val('');
        var msg = $msg({to: 'update@identi.ca', type: 'chat'})
            .c('body').t(text);
        Arthur.connection.send(msg);
    }
});
```

The event object passed into the handler contains a `which` attribute that holds the pressed key's ASCII code, and the code for the Enter key is 13. The handler uses `preventDefault()` to stop the default handler from processing the Enter key, which would add it to the field's value. The handler then sends a `<message>` stanza to update@identi.ca.

You don't have to worry about displaying the update to the user. Identica will notify the users of their own updates as well, so a hyperlinked version of the update will appear in the stream all by itself.

Arthur is now a fully functional microblogging client!

OFFLINE MESSAGES

Before you ship Arthur to your users, there is still one last feature to add — support for offline messages.

Since the early days of XMPP (back then it was still called Jabber), servers have stored messages sent to offline users for later delivery. This feature, though simple, is still not implemented on some proprietary networks! Oddly, this feature wasn't specified in an XEP for three years after XMPP was created. Delayed delivery was finally written down in XEP-0091, which was later replaced by the current Delayed Delivery (XEP-0203).

The sender of a message doesn't need to do anything special to support offline messages. If a message is received for an offline user, a typical server will queue that message for when the user next comes online. Little is required from the recipient as well. When the recipients of offline messages next send initial presence, the server will deliver all pending offline messages to them. If no special attention is paid to these messages, they will appear to have been sent just then, but on closer inspection, they contain extra metadata inserted by the server about when they were originally sent.

Take a look at the following example traffic. First, Jane sends her initial presence, informing the server that she is now available. Next, the server delivers several messages to her; all but the final message were sent before she came online.

```
    JANE: <presence/>

  SERVER: <message from='elizabeth@longbourn.lit/bedroom'
                  to='jane@longbourn.lit/bedroom'
                  type='chat'>
            <body>Miss Bingley sees that her brother is in love with you, and
              wants himto marry Miss Darcy.</body>
            <delay xmlns='urn:xmpp:delay'
                   from='longbourn.lit'
                   stamp='1809-09-22T12:44:13Z'>Offline storage</delay>
          </message>

          <message from='elizabeth@longbourn.lit/bedroom'
                  to='jane@longbourn.lit/bedroom'
                  type='chat'>
            <body>She follows him to town in the hope of keeping him there, and tries
              to persuade you that he does not care about you.</body>
            <delay xmlns='urn:xmpp:delay'
                   from='longbourn.lit'
                   stamp='1809-09-22T12:44:24Z'>Offline storage</delay>
          </message>

          <message from='elizabeth@longbourn.lit/bedroom'
                  to='jane@longbourn.lit/bedroom'
                  type='chat'>
            <body>No one who has ever seen you together, can doubt his
              affection.</body>
          </message>
```

Notice the extra `<delay>` element in the messages that were received while Jane was offline. These extra elements are a delayed delivery marker and indicate that the messages have been delivered some period of time after they were originally received. The `stamp` attribute indicates the time when Jane's server originally received the message.

You can indicate which messages in the stream happened while the user was offline by giving them a special color in the user interface. You do this by assigning an extra CSS class in `handle_message()` when a `<message>` stanza is processed containing a `<delay>` element.

First, add the following CSS class to arthur.css:

```css
.delayed {
    color: #a99;
}
```

Next, the following highlighted lines show the changes that need to be made to handle_message():

```javascript
handle_message: function (message) {
    if ($(message).attr('from').match(/^update@identi.ca/)) {
        var delayed = $(message).find('delay').length > 0;
        var body = $(message).find('html > body').contents();

        var div = $("<div></div>");

        if (delayed) {
            div.addClass('delayed');
        }

        body.each(function () {
            if (document.importNode) {
                $(document.importNode(this, true)).appendTo(div);
            } else {
                // IE workaround
                div.append(this.xml);
            }
        });

        div.prependTo('#stream');
    }

    return true;
}
```

Arthur will show the delayed messages in a pink color so that the users will know what they missed while they were offline.

With that final feature, Arthur is ready for some real users. The final JavaScript code appears in Listing 5-3.

LISTING 5-3: arthur.js

```javascript
var Arthur = {
    connection: null,

    handle_message: function (message) {
        if ($(message).attr('from').match(/^update@identi.ca/)) {
```

continues

LISTING 5-3 *(continued)*

```
        var delayed = $(message).find('delay').length > 0;
        var body = $(message).find('html > body').contents();

        var div = $("<div></div>");

        if (delayed) {
            div.addClass('delayed');
        }

        body.each(function () {
            if (document.importNode) {
                $(document.importNode(this, true)).appendTo(div);
            } else {
                // IE workaround
                div.append(this.xml);
            }
        });

        div.prependTo('#stream');
    }

    return true;
  }
};

$(document).ready(function () {
    $('#login_dialog').dialog({
        autoOpen: true,
        draggable: false,
        modal: true,
        title: 'Connect to XMPP',
        buttons: {
            "Connect": function () {
                $(document).trigger('connect', {
                    jid: $('#jid').val(),
                    password: $('#password').val()
                });

                $('#password').val('');
                $(this).dialog('close');
            }
        }
    });

    $('#input').keyup(function () {
        var left = 140 - $(this).val().length;
        $('#counter .count').text('' + left);
    });

    $('#input').keypress(function (ev) {
        if (ev.which === 13) {
```

```
                ev.preventDefault();

                var text = $(this).val();
                $(this).val('');

                var msg = $msg({to: 'update@identi.ca', type: 'chat'})
                    .c('body').t(text);
                Arthur.connection.send(msg);
            }
        });
    });

    $(document).bind('connect', function (ev, data) {
        var conn = new Strophe.Connection(
            'http://bosh.metajack.im:5280/xmpp-httpbind');

        conn.connect(data.jid, data.password, function (status) {
            if (status === Strophe.Status.CONNECTED) {
                $(document).trigger('connected');
            } else if (status === Strophe.Status.DISCONNECTED) {
                $(document).trigger('disconnected');
            }
        });
        Arthur.connection = conn;
    });

    $(document).bind('connected', function () {
        Arthur.connection.addHandler(Arthur.handle_message,
                                     null, "message", "chat");
        Arthur.connection.send($pres());
    });

    $(document).bind('disconnected', function () {
        // nothing here yet
    });
```

CREATING A BETTER MICROBLOGGER

Identica's XMPP API also supports many other functions — direct messages, favoriting, subscribing to and unsubscribing from users, and viewing profile information. You can send the message "help" to get a complete list of available commands.

Try adding the following to Arthur:

➤ Show the current list of the user's subscriptions.

➤ Translate user's names into their real names by using information from their profile.

➤ Add a button next to each dent to allow users to mark it as a favorite.

SUMMARY

In this chapter, you moved beyond the basic setup of Strophe applications and beyond simply looking at and crafting traffic in a debugger. You created a real-time microblogging client called Arthur, which made keeping up with friends on Identica very easy.

In creating Arthur, you:

> ➤ Learned about Identica, StatusNet, and the Open Microblogging standard.

> ➤ Used the Identica XMPP API to interact with the microblogging service.

> ➤ Created a `<message>` stanza handler to process incoming dents.

> ➤ Added XHTML-IM support to the application.

> ➤ Discovered offline messages and how to detect and deal with them.

Arthur is a very simple example of handling private, one-to-one chats with XMPP. In the next chapter you extend these ideas to a general chat client focused on private messaging with multiple people. You create an even more complex application for group chat in Chapter 8.

Talking with Friends: One-on-One Chat

WHAT'S IN THIS CHAPTER?

➤ Presence subscriptions

➤ Managing rosters and contacts

➤ Message routing

➤ Best practices for one-on-one communication

➤ Chat state notifications

For many years, XMPP was used primarily for its original purpose of instant messaging. The other uses of the protocol, many of which you will see in upcoming chapters, were just the experiments of a few creative hackers. Today, the instant messaging pieces aren't as fashionable as publish-subscribe, group chat, and collaborative applications, but the IM foundations of XMPP remain extremely important.

Instant messaging systems are first class social networks. Each member has a social graph, their roster, and can communicate and participate with others. These social tools are baked into XMPP at a low level, and they make building social applications quite easy. Unlike many popular social networks, the XMPP network is also federated, connecting many disparate communities together.

Social and community aspects of applications are becoming increasingly important, and therefore it is imperative that you gain an understanding of XMPP's basic social tools. The chat application in this chapter, called Gab, may not be on the cutting edge of software, but its parts can be used to add important social features onto nearly any kind of application. Indeed, many users will expect to see these features as they have grown accustomed to them in other tools.

Instant messaging is the oldest use of XMPP, and in this chapter, you build your own basic messaging application for chatting and keeping tabs on friends. Each feature will seem familiar if you've ever used instant messaging applications before and forms a solid basis for developing social software.

APPLICATION PREVIEW

The interface for this chapter's application is quite a bit more complex than the ones you've built in previous chapters. Figure 6-1 shows what the finished application will look like.

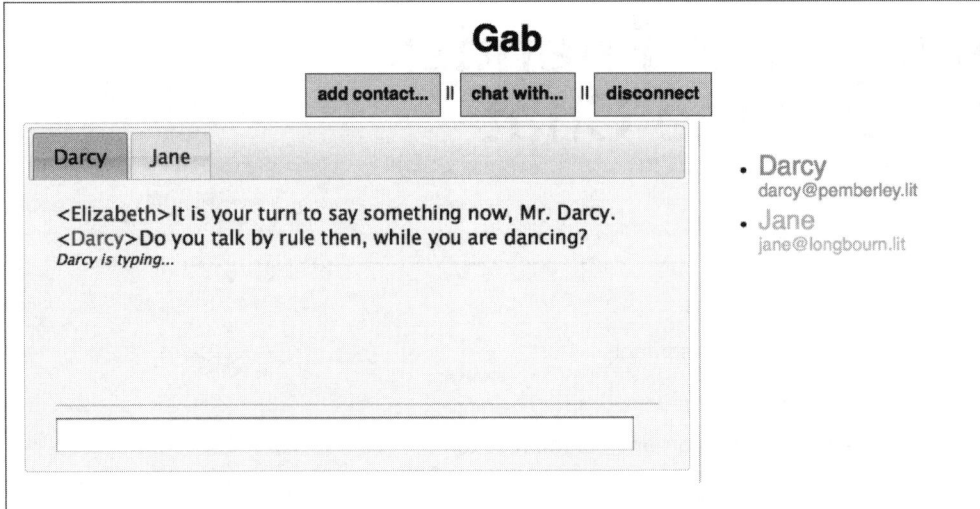

FIGURE 6-1

The chat area is located on the left side. Each chat appears in a separate tab in the interface, allowing the user to keep track of many conversations at once. The roster appears on the right side and shows the name and status for each of the user's contacts. Just above these areas are buttons for common functions.

This interface has a lot going on — multiple tabs, multiple controls, and multiple new pieces of the XMPP protocol.

GAB DESIGN

Instant messaging in XMPP relies heavily on the use of the <message> and <presence> stanzas. A <message> stanza is sent whenever a user communicates with another. You saw a basic example of these stanzas in action in the previous chapter; the Identica API is just a computer program mimicking a user. <presence> stanzas are sent whenever contacts come online, change status to away, or go offline.

These two stanzas go hand in hand. The `<presence>` stanza communicates a user's availability for chat. If a user is offline or away, it may not be the best time to attempt a conversation. An online user, however, is probably happy to talk. Once a user has decided to communicate, `<message>` stanzas do the work of moving pieces of the conversation between its participants.

Presence

XMPP's designers were quite sensitive to privacy issues, so presence information is controlled through subscriptions. In order for Elizabeth to receive presence updates from Wickham, she must first subscribe to those updates. Furthermore, Wickham must approve her subscription request.

Presence subscriptions are asymmetric. If Elizabeth has a subscription to Wickham's presence, it does not necessarily mean that Wickham is subscribed to Elizabeth's. In most cases, a user will send a subscription request to someone, and automatically approve the subscription request coming from that same person.

You see presence subscriptions in detail when you build Gab's roster area functionality.

Messages

As you saw in the previous chapter, messages are usually quite simple. They do have some special delivery semantics that you, as an XMPP programmer, must take into account. These semantics center on addressing and whether a message is addressed to a contact's bare JID (elizabeth@longbourn.lit) or to a full JID (elizabeth@longbourn.lit/library).

Messages can also contain more than just the message's text. They can carry formatting information (as in the previous chapter's use of XHTML-IM), metadata, or application-specific payloads. As you see a little bit later, activity notifications sometimes appear in messages containing no message text at all!

Gab has two major centers of functionality, the chat area and the roster area, as well as a button bar for common functions. Each area deals with one type of stanza. The chat area handles the `<message>` stanzas and the roster area handles `<presence>`.

Chat Area

Gab must support chats with multiple contacts simultaneously. A tab for each chat creates separation between all the conversations as well as making it easy for users to navigate to the one they want.

Each incoming message is stamped with the address of the person who sent it. Each tab handles the incoming messages from a particular sender. An input area for outgoing messages appears at the bottom of every tab.

New chat tabs are created when a new message is received from a contact who does not already have an open tab. Tabs can also be created by pressing the New Chat With button in the action bar above the chat area or by clicking a contact's name in the roster area.

Each chat will need to display messages, status changes, and activity notifications for the associated user.

Roster Area

The roster area displays all the user's contacts as well as their current presence status. This list should be sorted so that the available contacts appear at the top of the list, followed by the ones who are away. Offline contacts appear at the very bottom of the list.

Incoming presence information should update the roster area so that the user is always aware of the latest status for each contact.

Clicking the New Contact button in the action bar adds new contacts to the roster and requests a presence subscription. You must also handle the case when the new contact requests a subscription to the user's own presence so that the user can decide whether to approve or deny the subscription.

With the basic design laid out, it's time to start working on Gab.

MAKING THE INTERFACE

The HTML for Gab's interface appears in Listing 6-1. It contains the action bar, followed by the chat-area `<div>` and the roster-area `<div>`. Below these are several dialog boxes that Gab needs — the login dialog box you've seen in previous chapters, the contact dialog box for adding new contacts to the roster, the chat dialog box for starting new chats, and the approval dialog box for handling incoming presence subscription requests.

Available for download on Wrox.com

LISTING 6-1: gab.html

```
<!DOCTYPE HTML PUBLIC "-//W3C//DTD HTML 4.01//EN"
        "http://www.w3.org/TR/html4/strict.dtd">
<html>
  <head>
    <meta http-equiv="Content-type" content="text/html;charset=UTF-8">
    <title>Gab - Chapter 6</title>

    <link rel='stylesheet' href='http://ajax.googleapis.com/ajax/libs/jqueryu
i/1.7.2/themes/cupertino/jquery-ui.css'>
    <script src='http://ajax.googleapis.com/ajax/libs/jquery/1.3.2/jquery.js'>
    </script>
    <script src='http://ajax.googleapis.com/ajax/libs/jqueryui/1.7.2/jquery-u
i.js'></script>
    <script src='scripts/strophe.js'></script>
    <script src='scripts/flXHR.js'></script>
    <script src='scripts/strophe.flxhr.js'></script>

    <link rel='stylesheet' type='text/css' href='gab.css'>
    <script type='text/javascript' src='gab.js'></script>
  </head>
  <body>
```

```
    <h1>Gab</h1>

    <div id='toolbar'>
      <span class='button' id='new-contact'>add contact..</span> ||
      <span class='button' id='new-chat'>chat with..</span> ||
      <span class='button' id='disconnect'>disconnect</span>
    </div>

    <div id='chat-area'>
      <ul></ul>
    </div>

    <div id='roster-area'>
      <ul></ul>
    </div>

    <!-- login dialog -->
    <div id='login_dialog' class='hidden'>
      <label>JID:</label><input type='text' id='jid'>
      <label>Password:</label><input type='password' id='password'>
    </div>

    <!-- contact dialog -->
    <div id='contact_dialog' class='hidden'>
      <label>JID:</label><input type='text' id='contact-jid'>
      <label>Name:</label><input type='text' id='contact-name'>
    </div>

    <!-- chat dialog -->
    <div id='chat_dialog' class='hidden'>
      <label>JID:</label><input type='text' id='chat-jid'>
    </div>

    <!-- approval dialog -->
    <div id='approve_dialog' class='hidden'>
      <p><span id='approve-jid'></span> has requested a subscription
        to your presence.  Approve or deny?</p>
    </div>
  </body>
</html>
```

The chat area contains a single `<ul>` element, which will become the tab bar. Each visible tab will correspond to an `<li>` child of this element containing the tab's name. The contents of each tab will be inserted as a `<div>` after the `<ul>` element. The jQuery UI `tabs()` function will do the hard work of converting this simple HTML structure into a fully functioning set of chat tabs.

The roster area starts off with an empty list as well. This list will be filled dynamically with roster contacts once Gab has fetched this information from the server.

Listing 6-2 contains the CSS for Gab. The styling is very simple, but goes a long way to making Gab's interface visually appealing.

LISTING 6-2: gab.css

```css
body {
    font-family: Helvetica;
}

h1 {
    text-align: center;
}

.hidden {
    display: none;
}

.button {
    padding: 10px;
    background-color: #ddd;
    border: solid 1px #666;
    font-weight: bold;
}

.button:hover {
    background-color: #ddf;
}

#toolbar {
    text-align: center;
    margin-bottom: 15px;
}

#chat-area {
    float: left;
    width: 600px;
    height: 300px;
}

.chat-messages {
    height: 180px;
    border-bottom: solid 2px #ddd;
    overflow: auto;
}

#chat-area input {
    margin-top: 10px;
    width: 95%;
}

#roster-area {
    float: right;
    border-left: solid 2px #ddd;
    padding: 10px;
    width: 250px;
    height: 300px;
```

```
    }

    .chat-name {
        color: #c33;
    }

    .chat-message .me {
        color: #33c;
    }

    .chat-event {
        font-style: italic;
        font-size: 75%;
    }

    .roster-contact {
        padding: 3px;
    }

    .roster-contact:hover {
        background-color: #aaa;
        color: white;
    }

    .roster-name {
        font-size: 150%;
    }

    .online {
        color: #3c3;
    }

    .away {
        color: #c33;
    }

    .offline {
        color: #ccc;
    }
```

This interface's layout and styling are relatively simple, but it doesn't take much to have a big impact with powerful tools like HTML and CSS.

Now that the interface is created, you should start hooking up the code for the roster area.

BUILDING THE ROSTER

XMPP chat clients generally perform the following actions when they start:

1. Connect and authenticate to the server.

2. Request the roster.

3. Send initial presence.

The last step causes the server to send presence probes to contacts for whom the user has a presence subscription. These probes will result in a `<presence>` stanza being sent back to the user for each contact that is online.

Gab will need to replicate this sequence of actions and handle the resulting roster data and presence updates. First, you will hook up the login dialog box, just as you did in previous chapters, as well as build the basic connection event handling. Create a file called `gab.js` and insert the following code, which should be familiar from the previous chapters:

```javascript
var Gab = {
    connection: null
};

$(document).ready(function () {
    $('#login_dialog').dialog({
        autoOpen: true,
        draggable: false,
        modal: true,
        title: 'Connect to XMPP',
        buttons: {
            "Connect": function () {
                $(document).trigger('connect', {
                    jid: $('#jid').val(),
                    password: $('#password').val()
                });

                $('#password').val('');
                $(this).dialog('close');
            }
        }
    });
});

$(document).bind('connect', function (ev, data) {
    var conn = new Strophe.Connection(
        'http://bosh.metajack.im:5280/xmpp-httpbind');

    conn.connect(data.jid, data.password, function (status) {
        if (status === Strophe.Status.CONNECTED) {
            $(document).trigger('connected');
        } else if (status === Strophe.Status.DISCONNECTED) {
            $(document).trigger('disconnected');
        }
    });
    Gab.connection = conn;
});

$(document).bind('connected', function () {
    // nothing here yet
});

$(document).bind('disconnected', function () {
    // nothing here yet
});
```

code snippet gab.js

Once the user clicks the Connect button, the code starts connecting to the XMPP server. Successful connections fire the `connected` event, and any disconnection (or connection failure) fires `disconnected`.

Now you can request the roster in the `connected` event handler.

Requesting Rosters

Rosters are manipulated with IQ-get and IQ-set stanzas that contain a `<query>` element under the `jabber:iq:roster` namespace. Rosters can be retrieved and contacts modified and deleted using these simple stanzas. You see addition of new contacts soon, but for now, you can focus just on retrieval.

The following stanza requests Elizabeth's roster from her server:

```
<iq from='elizabeth@longbourn.lit/library'
    type='get'
    id='roster1'>
  <query xmlns='jabber:iq:roster'/>
</iq>
```

Her server will reply with something similar to the following:

```
<iq to='elizabeth@longbourn.lit/library'
    type='result'
    id='roster1'>
  <query xmlns='jabber:iq:roster'>
    <item jid='darcy@pemberley.lit' name='Mr. Darcy' subscription='both'/>
    <item jid='jane@longbourn.lit' name='Jane' subscription='both'/>
  </query>
</iq>
```

This roster contains two contacts. The `jid` attribute is the address of the contact, and the `name` attribute is a user-assignable nickname for the contact. The `subscription` attribute is set based on the presence subscription status of the contact. It can have the value `both` if there is a subscription in each direction, `to` if Elizabeth has a subscription but the other party does not, and `from` if Elizabeth is not subscribed to the contact's presence but the other user has a subscription to her presence. Generally, the user will only want to see contacts in the roster for which the subscription value is `both` or `to`.

Add the following JavaScript code to the `connected` event handler to retrieve the roster:

```
$(document).bind('connected', function () {
    var iq = $iq({type: 'get'}).c('query', {xmlns: 'jabber:iq:roster'});
    Gab.connection.sendIQ(iq, Gab.on_roster);
});
```

code snippet gab.js

Next, add the implementation of `on_roster()` to the `Gab` object:

```
on_roster: function (iq) {
    $(iq).find('item').each(function () {
        var jid = $(this).attr('jid');
        var name = $(this).attr('name') || jid;

        // transform jid into an id
        var jid_id = Gab.jid_to_id(jid);

        var contact = $("<li id='" + jid_id + "'>" +
                        "<div class='roster-contact offline'>" +
                        "<div class='roster-name'>" +
                        name +
                        "</div><div class='roster-jid'>" +
                        jid +
                        "</div></div></li>");

        Gab.insert_contact(contact);
    });
}
```

code snippet gab.js

You've probably noticed that there is a new Strophe library function in the preceding event handler — `sendIQ()`. This function handles most of the common ways to deal with IQ stanzas, and it is described more fully in the next section.

The `on_roster()` function traverses the roster items, each one in its own `<item>` element, and calls `insert_contact()` with the appropriate HTML. To find the contact later, it is necessary to give its element an `id` attribute. The code uses a slightly transformed version of the contact's bare JID as the id. The `jid_to_id()` function is shown here and should be added to the `Gab` object:

```
jid_to_id: function (jid) {
    return Strophe.getBareJidFromJid(jid)
        .replace("@", "-")
        .replace(".", "-");
}
```

code snippet gab.js

The `insert_contact()` function is used to keep the contact list sorted correctly. The more available a contact, the higher in the roster they will appear. If two contacts have the same availability then they are sorted by their JID. The following implementations of `insert_contact()` and its helper function `presence_value()` should be added to the `Gab` object:

```
presence_value: function (elem) {
    if (elem.hasClass('online')) {
        return 2;
    } else if (elem.hasClass('away')) {
        return 1;
```

```
        }

        return 0;
    },

    insert_contact: function (elem) {
        var jid = elem.find('.roster-jid').text();
        var pres = Gab.presence_value(elem.find('.roster-contact'));

        var contacts = $('#roster-area li');

        if (contacts.length > 0) {
            var inserted = false;
            contacts.each(function () {
                var cmp_pres = Gab.presence_value(
                    $(this).find('.roster-contact'));
                var cmp_jid = $(this).find('.roster-jid').text();

                if (pres > cmp_pres) {
                    $(this).before(elem);
                    inserted = true;
                    return false;
                } else {
                    if (jid < cmp_jid) {
                        $(this).before(elem);
                        inserted = true;
                        return false;
                    }
                }
            });

            if (!inserted) {
                $('#roster-area ul').append(elem);
            }
        } else {
            $('#roster-area ul').append(elem);
        }
    }
```

code snippet gab.js

If you give Gab a spin in its current form, you should be able to log in to a server and see your roster displayed and sorted.

Handling IQs

<iq> stanzas are special in XMPP in that they are the only stanzas required to have a response. Every IQ-get or IQ-set stanza must receive a corresponding IQ-result or IQ-error stanza, just as any GET or POST request must receive a response in the HTTP protocol. All <iq> stanzas must also contain an id attribute that is unique enough to identify them within a session. The reason for this is that the same id attribute will be used to tag the response so that the code knows to which IQ-get or IQ-set stanza a particular IQ-result or IQ-error stanza corresponds.

Each time you send an IQ-get or IQ-set stanza, you usually want to handle the success and error responses. This means that you must set up a stanza handler for each IQ-get or IQ-set you send. Also, you'll need to take care that your `id` attributes are unique so that incoming responses are not ambiguous.

The `sendIQ()` function wraps all these requirements and the associated behavior in an easy-to-use interface. Instead of creating a unique `id` value, setting up success and error handlers, and then sending out the `<iq>` stanza, `sendIQ()` accepts an `<iq>` stanza, ensures it has a unique `id`, automatically sets up handlers with the success and error callbacks you provide, and ensures the handlers are properly cleaned up after your callbacks are executed.

Calls to `sendIQ()` look like this:

```
Connection.sendIQ(iq_stanza, success_callback, error_callback);
```

The success and error callbacks are both optional. The success callback fires if an IQ-result is received, and the error callback fires on an IQ-error. Both callbacks are passed a single parameter — the response stanza.

In addition, `sendIQ()` accepts a timeout value as an optional fourth parameter. If a response to the IQ-get or IQ-set stanza is not received within the timeout period, the error callback is automatically triggered. This timeout can be very useful for making your code robust in the presence of network or service errors that cause responses to be delayed or unsent.

`sendIQ()` makes dealing with IQ stanzas extremely easy, and you see a lot more of it in later chapters.

Updating Presence Status

After the roster is retrieved, the code should send initial presence to kick off the presence probes and presence updates from the user's contacts. In order not to miss any updates, you should always set up the appropriate handler before you send a stanza that will trigger events of interest. Modify the `on_roster()` handler by adding the following highlighted code:

Available for download on Wrox.com

```
on_roster: function (iq) {
    $(iq).find('item').each(function () {
        var jid = $(this).attr('jid');
        var name = $(this).attr('name') || jid;

        var jid_id = Gab.jid_to_id(jid);

        var contact = $("<li id='" + jid_id + "'>" +
                        "<div class='roster-contact offline'>" +
                        "<div class='roster-name'>" +
                        name +
                        "</div><div class='roster-jid'>" +
                        jid +
                        "</div></div></li>");

        Gab.insert_contact(contact);
```

```
    });

    // set up presence handler and send initial presence
    Gab.connection.addHandler(Gab.on_presence, null, "presence");
    Gab.connection.send($pres());
}
```

code snippet gab.js

Next, implement the on_presence() function to update the list of contacts accordingly. The following code should be added to the Gab object:

```
on_presence: function (presence) {
    var ptype = $(presence).attr('type');
    var from = $(presence).attr('from');

    if (ptype !== 'error') {
        var contact = $('#roster-area li#' + Gab.jid_to_id(from))
            .removeClass("online")
            .removeClass("away")
            .removeClass("offline");
        if (ptype === 'unavailable') {
            contact.addClass("offline");
        } else {
            var show = $(presence).find("show").text();
            if (show === "" || show === "chat") {
                contact.addClass("online");
            } else {
                contact.addClass("away");
            }
        }

        var li = contact.parent();
        li.remove();
        Gab.insert_contact(li);
    }

    return true;
}
```

code snippet gab.js

The presence stanza handler simply updates the CSS class of the contact in the list, which causes the browser to update the screen, and then removes the contact and reinserts it to keep the list correctly ordered. The on_presence() handler uses the same jid_to_id() transformation as on_roster() to find the correct element to modify.

Test out Gab by using it to log in to your favorite account. You should see your roster load and be able to watch the colors change as your contacts come online, change status, and go offline.

Adding New Contacts

Gab already works well for seeing your current contacts, but you must also add functionality so that users can create new ones. New contacts are created in two ways: users can click Add Contact and enter in the contact's information, or they can receive and accept a presence subscription from someone new.

First, you should set up the new contact dialog box and bind the `click` event on the appropriate button to open the dialog box. Add the following code to the document ready function:

```javascript
$('#contact_dialog').dialog({
    autoOpen: false,
    draggable: false,
    modal: true,
    title: 'Add a Contact',
    buttons: {
        "Add": function () {
            $(document).trigger('contact_added', {
                jid: $('#contact-jid').val(),
                name: $('#contact-name').val()
            });

            $('#contact-jid').val('');
            $('#contact-name').val('');

            $(this).dialog('close');
        }
    }
});

$('#new-contact').click(function (ev) {
    $('#contact_dialog').dialog('open');
});
```

code snippet gab.js

The dialog box will fire the `contact_added` event when the user clicks the Add button. You'll need to handle this event to send the appropriate XML to the server to actually add the contact to the user's roster. The following handler should be added after the other document event bindings at the end of `gab.js`:

```javascript
$(document).bind('contact_added', function (ev, data) {
    var iq = $iq({type: "set"}).c("query", {xmlns: "jabber:iq:roster"})
        .c("item", data);
    Gab.connection.sendIQ(iq);

    var subscribe = $pres({to: data.jid, "type": "subscribe"});
    Gab.connection.send(subscribe);
});
```

code snippet gab.js

The `contact_added` event handler creates a roster add IQ-set stanza and sends it to the server. Then it sends a presence stanza of type `subscribe` to the new contact to request a subscription to the contact's presence updates. Notice that there is no code to update the UI with the new roster state. Instead of handling this here, you will create another handler, which will be notified when the user's roster state changes.

Responding to Roster Changes

Users may connect to their XMPP server multiple times, with each connection being assigned its own resource (see Chapter 1 for more details on client resources). Any of these resources could make changes to the roster. To keep every resource synchronized with respect to the roster, an XMPP server will broadcast roster state changes to all connected resources.

Each connected resource will get notified of roster additions, deletions, and modifications, even the ones the resource itself performed. Some actions, like requesting a presence subscription, may cause the roster to change as a side effect. These changes will also be broadcast in the same manner.

Imagine that Jane has just used Gab's new contact dialog box to add Bingley to her roster. Just like the code you saw earlier, Jane's client would send an IQ-set like the one shown here:

```
<iq from='jane@longbourn.lit/sitting_room'
    type='set'
    id='add1'>
  <query xmlns='jabber:iq:roster'>
    <item jid='bingley@netherfield.lit' name='Mr. Bingley'/>
  </query>
</iq>
```

Her server will respond with the IQ-result acknowledging her request:

```
<iq to='jane@longbourn.lit/sitting_room' type='result' id='add1'/>
```

Her server will also broadcast out the roster state change in a very similar IQ-set stanza:

```
<iq to='jane@longbourn.lit/sitting_room'
    type='set'
    id='changed1'>
  <query xmlns='jabber:iq:roster'>
    <item jid='bingley@netherfield.lit' name='Mr. Bingley' subscription='none'/>
  </query>
</iq>
```

The server's reply may contain attributes that were unspecified in the original IQ-set from Jane, as with the `subscription` attribute in the preceding code. Note that, just as with any other IQ stanza, Jane must respond with an IQ-result or IQ-error stanza:

```
<iq type='result' id='changed1'/>
```

If Jane had been connected from multiple resources, each of those connections would have received the same roster addition notification.

Because the server broadcasts state changes to all resources, many XMPP clients will wait for this notification before updating the UI. This also has the advantage that the roster will not display an inconsistent state; if the roster was updated immediately before the response was received, the UI might reflect the addition when the server has actually rejected the operation.

You can now add support for these roster state changes to Gab, which will not only show the modified roster to the user after they add a new contact, but also show any modifications, as they happen, from the user's other resources. The following highlighted lines show the changes that you must make to the `connected` event handler:

```
$(document).bind('connected', function () {
    var iq = $iq({type: 'get'}).c('query', {xmlns: 'jabber:iq:roster'});
    Gab.connection.sendIQ(iq, Gab.on_roster);

    Gab.connection.addHandler(Gab.on_roster_changed,
                              "jabber:iq:roster", "iq", "set");
});
```

code snippet gab.js

The `on_roster_changed()` function defined in the following code will also need to be added to the Gab object:

```
on_roster_changed: function (iq) {
    $(iq).find('item').each(function () {
        var sub = $(this).attr('subscription');
        var jid = $(this).attr('jid');
        var name = $(this).attr('name') || jid;
        var jid_id = Gab.jid_to_id(jid);

        if (sub === 'remove') {
            // contact is being removed
            $('#' + jid_id).remove();
        } else {
            // contact is being added or modified
            var contact_html = "<li id='" + jid_id + "'>" +
                "<div class='" +
                ($('#' + jid_id).attr('class') || "roster-contact offline") +
                "'>" +
                "<div class='roster-name'>" +
                name +
                "</div><div class='roster-jid'>" +
                jid +
                "</div></div></li>";

            if ($('#' + jid_id).length > 0) {
                $('#' + jid_id).replaceWith(contact_html);
            } else {
                Gab.insert_contact(contact_html);
            }
        }
    }
```

```
    });

    return true;
}
```

code snippet gab.js

This handler is triggered anytime an IQ-set is received for a roster update. If the subscription attribute of the `<item>` child is `remove`, the corresponding roster item is deleted. Otherwise a new roster item is added or an old one replaced. You can find more information on roster manipulations in Chapter 14.

Gab will now keep the roster's state in sync with other clients, show presence updates from contacts, and let users add new contacts.

Dealing with Subscription Requests

Roster additions may also happen as a result of new presence subscription requests being accepted by the user. Recall that in an earlier example you saw Jane add Bingley as a contact. After adding him to the roster, she would send a presence subscription request. Gab takes these same steps in the `contact_added` event handler you saw earlier.

Jane's subscription request to Bingley would appear as shown here:

```
<presence from='jane@longbourn.lit/sitting_room'
          to='bingley@netherfield.lit'
          type='subscribe'/>
```

Bingley can approve or deny her request by replying with a presence stanza containing a type attribute of `subscribed` or `unsubscribed`, respectively. His response, approving Jane's subscription, is shown here:

```
<presence from='bingley@netherfield.lit/parlor'
          to='jane@longbourn.lit/sitting_room'
          type='subscribed'/>
```

If Bingley wanted to deny Jane's subscription request, this stanza would have had a type of `unsubscribed`.

If Bingley had not already had Jane as a contact in his roster, the server would immediately add Jane and send him a roster update including the subscription state.

```
<iq to='bingley@netherfield.lit/parlour'
    type='set'
    id='newcontact1'>
  <query xmlns='jabber:iq:roster'>
    <item jid='elizabeth@longbourn.lit'
          subscription='from'/>
  </query>
</iq>
```

The subscription attribute has a value of from because Bingley does not yet have a subscription to Jane's presence. Normally, he would now request a subscription to her presence, and if Jane approves the request, the final subscription state would be both.

The roster update handler you created earlier will also work for change notifications triggered by approving a subscription request, but you must still handle the request itself. The following code should be added to the document ready handler to enable the approval dialog box:

```
$('#approve_dialog').dialog({
    autoOpen: false,
    draggable: false,
    modal: true,
    title: 'Subscription Request',
    buttons: {
        "Deny": function () {
            Gab.connection.send($pres({
                to: Gab.pending_subscriber,
                "type": "unsubscribed"}));
            Gab.pending_subscriber = null;

            $(this).dialog('close');
        },

        "Approve": function () {
            Gab.connection.send($pres({
                to: Gab.pending_subscriber,
                "type": "subscribed"}));
            Gab.pending_subscriber = null;
            $(this).dialog('close');
        }
    }
});
```

code snippet gab.js

The Approve and Deny buttons send a response <presence> stanza with a type attribute set to either subscribed or unsubscribed, respectively. If the request is approved, the server generates a roster modification; if the request is denied, the sender is notified of the rejection, and the roster will not be changed.

Next, you must modify the presence handler you wrote earlier to handle incoming subscription requests. The following highlighted lines show the needed modifications to the Gab object:

```
pending_subscriber: null,

on_presence: function (presence) {
    var ptype = $(presence).attr('type');
    var from = $(presence).attr('from');

    if (ptype === 'subscribe') {
        // populate pending_subscriber, the approve-jid span, and
        // open the dialog
        Gab.pending_subscriber = from;
```

```
        $('#approve-jid').text(Strophe.getBareJidFromJid(from));
        $('#approve_dialog').dialog('open');
    } else if (ptype !== 'error') {
        var contact = $('#roster-area li#' + Gab.jid_to_id(from))
            .removeClass("online")
            .removeClass("away")
            .removeClass("offline");
        if (ptype === 'unavailable') {
            contact.addClass("offline");
        } else {
            var show = $(presence).find("show").text();
            if (show === "" || show === "chat") {
                contact.addClass("online");
            } else {
                contact.addClass("away");
            }
        }

        var li = contact.parent();
        li.remove();
        Gab.insert_contact(li);
    }

    return true;
}
```

Note that the `pending_subscriber` attribute has been added to the `Gab` object. This is used by the new subscribe request handling code. When the `on_presence()` handler receives a subscribe request, it just populates this attribute and prepares and opens the dialog box. The user's action in the dialog box determines which kind of response is generated.

Gab will now handle the incoming subscription requests, but generally when a request is approved the user will want to send a complementary subscribe request so that the final subscription is bi-directional. Modify the Approve button's action to match the highlighted lines in the following code:

```
"Approve": function () {
    Gab.connection.send($pres({
        to: Gab.pending_subscriber,
        "type": "subscribed"}));

    Gab.connection.send($pres({
        to: Gab.pending_subscriber,
        "type": "subscribe"}));

    Gab.pending_subscriber = null;
}
```

Now, whenever the user approves a subscription request, Gab will send a subscription request back. Gab's roster area is finished for the time being, and it's time to do some work on the chat area.

BUILDING THE CHATS

Chatting is the heart of Gab, and all the action takes place in the chat area. You'll be using jQuery UI's tab controls to make displaying and switching between multiple chats very easy. Each of the chat tabs will represent a conversation with a particular contact, and each tab will also have an input area for sending messages. A new chat tab will appear whenever a new message from a user without an existing tab is received. Clicking a contact in the roster will either select an existing chat tab or create a new one if one doesn't already exist.

Before you begin on the code, you should review the basics of the jQuery UI tab control if you haven't seen it before.

Working with Tabs

jQuery UI's tab control is quite powerful. It provides familiar tabbing functionality that you have probably seen before in a variety of desktop and web applications. It imposes some specific constraints on element ids and structure, and it also has a lot of options.

The tabbed area contains a bar, which holds all of the labeled tabs. This bar appears as a `<ul>` element in the HTML. The Gab application's HTML already contains this element as you can see at the beginning of the chapter in Listing 6-1. Each tab will have an `<li>` child that contains its name as a hyperlink with a special `href` attribute.

Following is an example of the HTML that is needed for a tabbed area containing two tabs:

```
<div id='tab-example'>
  <ul>
    <li><a href='#tab-example-1'>First Tab</a></li>
    <li><a href='#tab-example-2'>Second Tab</a></li>
  </ul>

  <div id='tab-example-1'>
    <p>This is the first tab.  Neat!</p>
  </div>

  <div id='tab-example-2'>
    <p>And here is the second tab.</p>
  </div>
</div>
```

Each tab has an `<li>` entry in the `<ul>` element as well as a corresponding `<div>` containing the tab's content. The `href` attribute and the `<div>` element's `id` attribute must be the same except for the leading # in the `href` attribute.

The tab area can be initialized with a call to `tabs()`. For example, to turn the preceding HTML into a tab control, run:

```
$('#tab-example').tabs();
```

New tabs are added with the `add` subcommand of `tabs()`. You can add a new tab to the preceding ones with:

```
$('#tab-example').tabs('add', '#tab-example-3', 'Third Tab');
$('#tab-example-3').html("<p>Finally, a third tab!</p>");
```

You can also programmatically change the selected tab with the select subcommand. Switch to the second tab with:

```
$('#tab-example').tabs('select', '#tab-example-2');
```

Tabs support a number of other subcommands as well as various options that control their behavior. Please refer to jQuery UI's documentation if you'd like to explore the additional functionality.

You will put your new tabbing knowledge to use in the next section when you create some chat windows.

Creating New Chats

The easiest place to start creating chats is by letting users click contacts in the roster to create or select chat windows. Before you can implement these actions though, you must first initialize the chat area. Add the following code to the document ready handler:

```
$('#chat-area').tabs().find('.ui-tabs-nav').sortable({axis: 'x'});
```

code snippet gab.js

The code initializes the chat area as a tabbed control and then makes the tabs sortable in the tab bar using jQuery UI's `sortable()` function. This allows the user to reorder the tabs after they are created so that they appear exactly where the user prefers.

Now that you have a real tab area, you'll need to respond to click events on the roster contacts. Up to now, you've always used `bind()` or `click()` to set up event handlers, but now you'll have to use `live()`. Like `bind()`, `live()` attaches a handler function to an event, but it will also do this for any elements that are created *after* `live()` is called. Because roster contacts are being added dynamically, you must use `live()` to ensure that any future roster contacts will still get the right event handlers.

Place the following click event handler into Gab's document ready handler:

```
$('.roster-contact').live('click', function () {
    var jid = $(this).find(".roster-jid").text();
    var name = $(this).find(".roster-name").text();
    var jid_id = Gab.jid_to_id(jid);

    if ($('#chat-' + jid_id).length > 0) {
        $('#chat-area').tabs('select', '#chat-' + jid_id);
    } else {
        $('#chat-area').tabs('add', '#chat-' + jid_id, name);
        $('#chat-' + jid_id).append(
            "<div class='chat-messages'></div>" +
            "<input type='text' class='chat-input'>");
```

```
            $('#chat-' + jid_id).data('jid', jid);
        }

        $('#chat-' + jid_id + ' input').focus();
});
```

This click handler first finds the JID and name of the contact. It determines if a chat tab already exists for this contact, and if so, selects it. Otherwise, it creates a new chat tab for the contact and initializes its content. Finally, the text input box is focused so that the user can start typing immediately. Notice that the jQuery `data()` function is used to stash the JID of the contact with the `<div>` element. This JID will be needed by other code later.

These newly created chat tabs aren't very interesting yet. You need to enable the user to send messages and update the content when new messages are received.

Sending Messages

You should send the user's message whenever they hit the Enter key inside the input box. Once again, you can use jQuery's live event handlers to do this:

```
$('.roster-input').live('keypress', function (ev) {
    if (ev.which === 13) {
        ev.preventDefault();

        var body = $(this).val();
        var jid = $(this).parent().data('jid');

        Gab.connection.send($msg({
            to: jid,
            "type": "chat"
        }).c('body').t(body));

        $(this).parent().find('.chat-messages').append(
            "<div class='chat-message'>&lt;" +
            "<span class='chat-name me'>" +
            Strophe.getNodeFromJid(Gab.connection.jid) +
            "</span>&gt;<span class='chat-text'>" +
            body +
            "</span></div>");

        Gab.scroll_chat(Gab.jid_to_id(jid));

        $(this).val('');
    }
});
```

First, the default action of adding the Enter key to the data is prevented. The text of the message and the stashed JID are retrieved, and they are both used to construct the message that is sent. The text is also echoed to the display, and the input box is cleared to make it ready for the user to enter new text.

Now, you must handle incoming messages so that their content can be placed in the appropriate tab. The following highlighted lines show the required modifications to the `connected` event handler to set up a new `<message>` stanza handler:

```
$(document).bind('connected', function () {
    var iq = $iq({type: 'get'}).c('query', {xmlns: 'jabber:iq:roster'});
    Gab.connection.sendIQ(iq, Gab.on_roster);

    Gab.connection.addHandler(Gab.on_roster_changed,
                              "jabber:iq:roster", "iq", "set");

    Gab.connection.addHandler(Gab.on_message,
                              null, "message", "chat");
});
```

code snippet gab.js

Next, you must implement `on_message()` and its helper function `scroll_chat()` in the `Gab` object:

```
on_message: function (message) {
    var jid = Strophe.getBareJidFromJid($(message).attr('from'));
    var jid_id = Gab.jid_to_id(jid);

    if ($('#chat-' + jid_id).length === 0) {
        $('#chat-area').tabs('add', '#chat-' + jid_id, jid);
        $('#chat-' + jid_id).append(
            "<div class='chat-messages'></div>" +
            "<input type='text' class='chat-input'>");
        $('#chat-' + jid_id).data('jid', jid);
    }

    $('#chat-area').tabs('select', '#chat-' + jid_id);
    $('#chat-' + jid_id + ' input').focus();

    var body = $(message).find("html > body");

    if (body.length === 0) {
        body = $(message).find('body');
        if (body.length > 0) {
            body = body.text()
        } else {
            body = null;
        }
    } else {
```

```
            body = body.contents();

            var span = $("<span></span>");
            body.each(function () {
                if (document.importNode) {
                    $(document.importNode(this, true)).appendTo(span);
                } else {
                    // IE workaround
                    span.append(this.xml);
                }
            });

            body = span;
        }

        if (body) {
            // add the new message
            $('#chat-' + jid_id + ' .chat-messages').append(
                "<div class='chat-message'>" +
                "&lt;<span class='chat-name'>" +
                Strophe.getNodeFromJid(jid) +
                "</span>&gt;<span class='chat-text'>" +
                "</span></div>");

            $('#chat-' + jid_id + ' .chat-message:last .chat-text')
                .append(body);

            Gab.scroll_chat(jid_id);
        }

        return true;
    },

    scroll_chat: function (jid_id) {
        var div = $('#chat-' + jid_id + ' .chat-messages').get(0);
        div.scrollTop = div.scrollHeight;
    }
```

code snippet gab.js

The on_message() handler is slightly involved. First, it detects whether an existing chat tab is available for this contact, and if not, creates one. Then it selects the tab and focuses the input box. Once the tab has been properly displayed, it then extracts the body of the message (looking for XHTML-IM payloads like you saw in Chapter 5), creates a new <div> element for the message, and then appends the body. Finally, it returns true so that it will continue to be called for future messages.

Gab is now a simple, but capable, instant messaging client. Take a few minutes to play around with it and make sure it works as expected.

BEST PRACTICES FOR INSTANT MESSAGING

Gab is currently a little too simple, and it doesn't conform to the standard best practices for communication. For example, outgoing messages are always sent to the bare JID of the user, even if a full address is known for them. Messages need to be addressed with care because their delivery is affected by a server's routing rules.

Understanding Message Routing

XMPP `<message>` stanzas sent to connected clients are routed specially by XMPP servers. Particularly, the server will do different things depending on whether the `to` attribute is a bare JID or a full JID.

Messages addressed to a user's bare JID are delivered to the connected resource with the highest priority. If multiple resources are tied for the highest priority, the server may choose to deliver the message to all of them or choose the best one. How a server chooses the best resource for delivery is server dependent. Most servers deliver messages to all tied resources, but you may encounter servers that attempt to guess by estimating the most recently active resource.

Messages addressed to full JIDs are delivered only to that specific resource, or if that resource is offline, potentially to offline storage until the user next comes online.

Because sending a message to a bare JID may result in multiple deliveries, it is best to address messages to the full JID as soon as you receive the full address of the other party.

For example, if you haven't recently been communicating with a user, you should address a message to their bare JID. Once they respond, you will know which resource they are using to talk to you, and you can then use that destination to address future messages to them.

Users may go online and offline or away and back during a chat. Because they may want to receive messages at a different location after these events, it is best to forget the full addresses of users whenever their presence status changes. Once you have their first reply, you can again start addressing messages to the potentially new, full address.

Now that you have a better understanding of message routing, you can update Gab to do the right thing when sending messages.

Addressing Messages Better

Changing Gab to address messages to full JIDs is very easy. The address to send messages to is already stored in the chat tab's `<div>` element, so all that is needed is to replace the bare JID stored there with the user's full JID. Of course, you only want to do this once you know the full address in `on_message()`. Modify the following highlighted lines in your `on_message()` handler:

Available for download on Wrox.com

```
on_message: function (message) {
    var full_jid = $(message).attr('from');
    var jid = Strophe.getBareJidFromJid(full_jid);
    var jid_id = Gab.jid_to_id(jid);

    if ($('#chat-' + jid_id).length === 0) {
        $('#chat-area').tabs('add', '#chat-' + jid_id, jid);
```

```
            $('#chat-' + jid_id).append(
                "<div class='chat-messages'></div>" +
                    "<input type='text' class='chat-input'>");
        }

        $('#chat-' + jid_id).data('jid', full_jid);

        $('#chat-area').tabs('select', '#chat-' + jid_id);
        $('#chat-' + jid_id + ' input').focus();

        var body = $(message).find("html > body");

        if (body.length === 0) {
            body = $(message).find('body');
            if (body.length > 0) {
                body = body.text()
            } else {
                body = null;
            }
        } else {
            body = body.contents();

            var span = $("<span></span>");
            body.each(function () {
                if (document.importNode) {
                    $(document.importNode(this, true)).appendTo(span);
                } else {
                    // IE workaround
                    span.append(this.xml);
                }
            });

            body = span;
        }

        if (body) {
            // add the new message
            $('#chat-' + jid_id + ' .chat-messages').append(
                "<div class='chat-message'>" +
                "&lt;<span class='chat-name'>" +
                Strophe.getNodeFromJid(jid) +
                "</span>&gt;<span class='chat-text'>" +
                "</span></div>");

            $('#chat-' + jid_id + ' .chat-message:last .chat-text')
                .append(body);

            Gab.scroll_chat(jid_id);
        }

        return true;
    }
```

code snippet gab.js

Whenever a message is received from a user, the JID data stashed in the <div> element for that user is updated to the full address. Now all that remains is to switch back to the bare JID whenever a user's presence changes. Make the following highlighted changes to your on_presence() handler:

```javascript
on_presence: function (presence) {
    var ptype = $(presence).attr('type');
    var from = $(presence).attr('from');

    if (ptype === 'subscribe') {
        // populate pending_subscriber, the approve-jid span, and
        // open the dialog
        Gab.pending_subscriber = from;
        $('#approve-jid').text(Strophe.getBareJidFromJid(from));
        $('#approve_dialog').dialog('open');
    } else if (ptype !== 'error') {
        var contact = $('#roster-area li#' + Gab.jid_to_id(from))
            .removeClass("online")
            .removeClass("away")
            .removeClass("offline");
        if (ptype === 'unavailable') {
            contact.addClass("offline");
        } else {
            var show = $(presence).find("show").text();
            if (show === "" || show === "chat") {
                contact.addClass("online");
            } else {
                contact.addClass("away");
            }
        }

        var li = contact.parent();
        li.remove();
        Gab.insert_contact(li);
    }

    // reset addressing for user since their presence changed
    var jid_id = Gab.jid_to_id(from);
    $('#chat-' + jid_id).data('jid', Strophe.getBareJidFromJid(fom));

    return true;
},
```

Gab should now switch between full and bare addressing as the user's presence changes and it learns about their connected resources.

ADDING ACTIVITY NOTIFICATIONS

Many clients support sending and receiving activity notifications. These notifications inform the opposite party when someone is typing, paying attention to the chat, or has left or closed the chat. These events are all defined in Chat State Notifications (XEP-0085). To make Gab more user friendly, you will add support for displaying and sending typing notifications.

Understanding Chat States

Following are the five defined chat states:

- ➤ **Active:** The user is paying attention to the chat.

- ➤ **Inactive:** The user is not paying attention to the chat.

- ➤ **Composing:** The user is typing a message for the chat.

- ➤ **Paused:** The user was typing, but has briefly stopped.

- ➤ **Gone:** The user has closed or left the chat.

Each state can transition to one or more of the other states. For example, a user in the composing state may move to paused or to active, and a user in the gone state can only move to active. You can find the full list of state transitions in XEP-0085.

Some clients may not support activity notifications. Gab assumes that all clients will understand these, which is not optimal, but shouldn't cause any problems because elements that are not understood will be ignored. In a real-world application, you would want to detect support for this feature and disable sending the notifications to the other party if their client couldn't process them. The specification details several ways in which this detection can be done.

Notifications are communicated in `<message>` stanzas. Some states are communicated alongside the message body, but some are sent in their own messages that do not contain bodies. The following example stanzas show a user entering the composing state, and then sending the completed message along with the transition to the active state:

```
<message from='darcy@pemberley.lit/rosings'
         to='elizabeth@longbourn.lit/hunsford'
         type='chat'>
  <composing xmlns='http://jabber.org/protocol/chatstates'/>
</message>

<message from='darcy@pemberley.lit/rosings'
         to='elizabeth@longbourn.lit/hunsford'
         type='chat'>
  <body>In vain have I struggled. It will not do. My feelings will not be repressed.
    You must allow me to tell you how ardently I admire and love you.</body>
  <active xmlns='http://jabber.org/protocol/chatstates'/>
</message>
```

Darcy's client first sends a notification to Elizabeth that he has begun typing. Several seconds later, a normal message is received with the beginnings of his proposal along with a second notification that he is paying attention to this chat. Elizabeth's client can use these notifications to modify her display appropriately.

Sending Notifications

Gab supports only the active and composing states. When the user starts typing, the composing state is communicated to the intended recipient. Upon completion of the message, the active state is sent. This is exactly the series of events shown in the previous example.

First, you should modify the `keypress` event handler of the chat tab input boxes to send the composing notification. It will also need to append the active state notification once the message is sent. The modified handler is shown here:

```javascript
$('.chat-input').live('keypress', function (ev) {
    var jid = $(this).parent().data('jid');

    if (ev.which === 13) {
        ev.preventDefault();

        var body = $(this).val();

        var message = $msg({to: jid,
                            "type": "chat"})
            .c('body').t(body).up()
            .c('active', {xmlns: "http://jabber.org/protocol/chatstates"});
        Gab.connection.send(message);

        $(this).parent().find('.chat-messages').append(
            "<div class='chat-message'>&lt;" +
            "<span class='chat-name me'>" +
            Strophe.getNodeFromJid(Gab.connection.jid) +
            "</span>&gt;<span class='chat-text'>" +
            body +
            "</span></div>");

        Gab.scroll_chat(Gab.jid_to_id(jid));

        $(this).val('');
        $(this).parent().data('composing', false);
    } else {
        var composing = $(this).parent().data('composing');
        if (!composing) {
            var notify = $msg({to: jid, "type": "chat"})
                .c('composing', {xmlns: "http://jabber.org/protocol/chatstates"});
            Gab.connection.send(notify);

            $(this).parent().data('composing', true);
        }
    }
});
```

code snippet gab.js

The user's chat partner will now get typing notifications as the user starts typing. If you run Gab and start a conversation with yourself in another client, you can see this in action.

Receiving Notifications

You'll also want to add support to Gab for incoming typing notifications. You can do this by watching for the composing notification in incoming messages. Add the following highlighted code to the `on_message()` handler:

```
on_message: function (message) {
    var full_jid = $(message).attr('from');
    var jid = Strophe.getBareJidFromJid(full_jid);
    var jid_id = Gab.jid_to_id(jid);

    if ($('#chat-' + jid_id).length === 0) {
        $('#chat-area').tabs('add', '#chat-' + jid_id, jid);
        $('#chat-' + jid_id).append(
            "<div class='chat-messages'></div>" +
                "<input type='text' class='chat-input'>");
    }

    $('#chat-' + jid_id).data('jid', full_jid);

    $('#chat-area').tabs('select', '#chat-' + jid_id);
    $('#chat-' + jid_id + ' input').focus();

    var composing = $(message).find('composing');
    if (composing.length > 0) {
        $('#chat-' + jid_id + ' .chat-messages').append(
            "<div class='chat-event'>" +
                Strophe.getNodeFromJid(jid) +
                " is typing..</div>");

        Gab.scroll_chat(jid_id);
    }

    if (body.length === 0) {
        body = $(message).find('body');
        if (body.length > 0) {
            body = body.text()
        } else {
            body = null;
        }
    } else {
        body = body.contents();

        var span = $("<span></span>");
        body.each(function () {
            if (document.importNode) {
                $(document.importNode(this, true)).appendTo(span);
            } else {
                // IE workaround
                span.append(this.xml);
            }
        }
```

```
        });

        body = span;
    }

    if (body) {
        // remove notifications since user is now active
        $('#chat-' + jid_id + ' .chat-event').remove();

        // add the new message
        $('#chat-' + jid_id + ' .chat-messages').append(
            "<div class='chat-message'>" +
            "&lt;<span class='chat-name'>" +
            Strophe.getNodeFromJid(jid) +
            "</span>&gt;<span class='chat-text'>" +
            "</span></div>");

        $('#chat-' + jid_id + ' .chat-message:last .chat-text')
            .append(body);

        Gab.scroll_chat(jid_id);
    }

    return true;
}
```

code snippet gab.js

Every time the other party starts typing, Gab will now show a small message informing the user of this activity. When the other party finally sends their message, the typing notification will disappear.

FINAL TOUCHES

You still have two small pieces left, the two other buttons in the toolbar.

The Disconnect button is quite simple. Add the following click event handler to the document ready function:

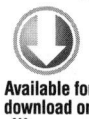

```
$('#disconnect').click(function () {
    Gab.connection.disconnect();
});
```

code snippet gab.js

You must also reset the UI in the `disconnected` event handler. Make the highlighted changes to the handler:

```
$(document).bind('disconnected', function () {
    Gab.connection = null;
    Gab.pending_subscriber = null;

    $('#roster-area ul').empty();
```

```
    $('#chat-area ul').empty();
    $('#chat-area div').remove();

    $('#login_dialog').dialog('open');
});
```

To implement the New Chat dialog box, you must first initialize the dialog box, and then bind the button click to the `dialog('open')` call. Add the following code to the document ready function to do this:

```
$('#chat_dialog').dialog({
    autoOpen: false,
    draggable: false,
    modal: true,
    title: 'Start a Chat',
    buttons: {
        "Start": function () {
            var jid = $('#chat-jid').val();
            var jid_id = Gab.jid_to_id(jid);

            $('#chat-area').tabs('add', '#chat-' + jid_id, jid);
            $('#chat-' + jid_id).append(
                "<div class='chat-messages'></div>" +
                "<input type='text' class='chat-input'>");

            $('#chat-' + jid_id).data('jid', jid);

            $('#chat-area').tabs('select', '#chat-' + jid_id);
            $('#chat-' + jid_id + ' input').focus();


            $('#chat-jid').val('');

            $(this).dialog('close');
        }
    }
});

$('#new-chat').click(function () {
    $('#chat_dialog').dialog('open');
});
```

With these last additions, the application is complete. Gab has become more than just a simple chat client with its support for notifications, sortable tabs, multiple chats, and the roster. The final version of the code appears in Listing 6-3.

LISTING 6-3: gab.js

```js
var Gab = {
    connection: null,

    jid_to_id: function (jid) {
        return Strophe.getBareJidFromJid(jid)
            .replace("@", "-")
            .replace(".", "-");
    },

    on_roster: function (iq) {
        $(iq).find('item').each(function () {
            var jid = $(this).attr('jid');
            var name = $(this).attr('name') || jid;

            // transform jid into an id
            var jid_id = Gab.jid_to_id(jid);

            var contact = $("<li id='" + jid_id + "'>" +
                            "<div class='roster-contact offline'>" +
                            "<div class='roster-name'>" +
                            name +
                            "</div><div class='roster-jid'>" +
                            jid +
                            "</div></div></li>");

            Gab.insert_contact(contact);
        });

        // set up presence handler and send initial presence
        Gab.connection.addHandler(Gab.on_presence, null, "presence");
        Gab.connection.send($pres());
    },

    pending_subscriber: null,

    on_presence: function (presence) {
        var ptype = $(presence).attr('type');
        var from = $(presence).attr('from');
        var jid_id = Gab.jid_to_id(from);

        if (ptype === 'subscribe') {
            // populate pending_subscriber, the approve-jid span, and
            // open the dialog
            Gab.pending_subscriber = from;
            $('#approve-jid').text(Strophe.getBareJidFromJid(from));
            $('#approve_dialog').dialog('open');
        } else if (ptype !== 'error') {
            var contact = $('#roster-area li#' + jid_id + ' .roster-contact')
                .removeClass("online")
                .removeClass("away")
                .removeClass("offline");
            if (ptype === 'unavailable') {
                contact.addClass("offline");
```

continues

LISTING 6-3 *(continued)*

```
        } else {
            var show = $(presence).find("show").text();
            if (show === "" || show === "chat") {
                contact.addClass("online");
            } else {
                contact.addClass("away");
            }
        }

        var li = contact.parent();
        li.remove();
        Gab.insert_contact(li);
    }

    // reset addressing for user since their presence changed
    var jid_id = Gab.jid_to_id(from);
    $('#chat-' + jid_id).data('jid', Strophe.getBareJidFromJid(from));

    return true;
},

on_roster_changed: function (iq) {
    $(iq).find('item').each(function () {
        var sub = $(this).attr('subscription');
        var jid = $(this).attr('jid');
        var name = $(this).attr('name') || jid;
        var jid_id = Gab.jid_to_id(jid);

        if (sub === 'remove') {
            // contact is being removed
            $('#' + jid_id).remove();
        } else {
            // contact is being added or modified
            var contact_html = "<li id='" + jid_id + "'>" +
                "<div class='" +
                ($('#' + jid_id).attr('class') || "roster-contact offline") +
                "'>" +
                "<div class='roster-name'>" +
                name +
                "</div><div class='roster-jid'>" +
                jid +
                "</div></div></li>";

            if ($('#' + jid_id).length > 0) {
                $('#' + jid_id).replaceWith(contact_html);
            } else {
                Gab.insert_contact(contact_html);
            }
        }
    });

    return true;
```

```
    },

    on_message: function (message) {
        var full_jid = $(message).attr('from');
        var jid = Strophe.getBareJidFromJid(full_jid);
        var jid_id = Gab.jid_to_id(jid);

        if ($('#chat-' + jid_id).length === 0) {
            $('#chat-area').tabs('add', '#chat-' + jid_id, jid);
            $('#chat-' + jid_id).append(
                "<div class='chat-messages'></div>" +
                "<input type='text' class='chat-input'>");
        }

        $('#chat-' + jid_id).data('jid', full_jid);

        $('#chat-area').tabs('select', '#chat-' + jid_id);
        $('#chat-' + jid_id + ' input').focus();

        var composing = $(message).find('composing');
        if (composing.length > 0) {
            $('#chat-' + jid_id + ' .chat-messages').append(
                "<div class='chat-event'>" +
                Strophe.getNodeFromJid(jid) +
                " is typing..</div>");

            Gab.scroll_chat(jid_id);
        }

        var body = $(message).find("html > body");

        if (body.length === 0) {
            body = $(message).find('body');
            if (body.length > 0) {
                body = body.text()
            } else {
                body = null;
            }
        } else {
            body = body.contents();

            var span = $("<span></span>");
            body.each(function () {
                if (document.importNode) {
                    $(document.importNode(this, true)).appendTo(span);
                } else {
                    // IE workaround
                    span.append(this.xml);
                }
            });

            body = span;
        }

        if (body) {
            // remove notifications since user is now active
```

continues

LISTING 6-3 *(continued)*

```
        $('#chat-' + jid_id + ' .chat-event').remove();

        // add the new message
        $('#chat-' + jid_id + ' .chat-messages').append(
            "<div class='chat-message'>" +
            "&lt;<span class='chat-name'>" +
            Strophe.getNodeFromJid(jid) +
            "</span>&gt;<span class='chat-text'>" +
            "</span></div>");

        $('#chat-' + jid_id + ' .chat-message:last .chat-text')
            .append(body);

        Gab.scroll_chat(jid_id);
    }

    return true;
},

scroll_chat: function (jid_id) {
    var div = $('#chat-' + jid_id + ' .chat-messages').get(0);
    div.scrollTop = div.scrollHeight;
},


presence_value: function (elem) {
    if (elem.hasClass('online')) {
        return 2;
    } else if (elem.hasClass('away')) {
        return 1;
    }

    return 0;
},

insert_contact: function (elem) {
    var jid = elem.find('.roster-jid').text();
    var pres = Gab.presence_value(elem.find('.roster-contact'));

    var contacts = $('#roster-area li');

    if (contacts.length > 0) {
        var inserted = false;
        contacts.each(function () {
            var cmp_pres = Gab.presence_value(
                $(this).find('.roster-contact'));
            var cmp_jid = $(this).find('.roster-jid').text();

            if (pres > cmp_pres) {
                $(this).before(elem);
                inserted = true;
                return false;
```

```
                } else {
                    if (jid < cmp_jid) {
                        $(this).before(elem);
                        inserted = true;
                        return false;
                    }
                }
            });

            if (!inserted) {
                $('#roster-area ul').append(elem);
            }
        } else {
            $('#roster-area ul').append(elem);
        }
    }
};

$(document).ready(function () {
    $('#login_dialog').dialog({
        autoOpen: true,
        draggable: false,
        modal: true,
        title: 'Connect to XMPP',
        buttons: {
            "Connect": function () {
                $(document).trigger('connect', {
                    jid: $('#jid').val(),
                    password: $('#password').val()
                });

                $('#password').val('');
                $(this).dialog('close');
            }
        }
    });

    $('#contact_dialog').dialog({
        autoOpen: false,
        draggable: false,
        modal: true,
        title: 'Add a Contact',
        buttons: {
            "Add": function () {
                $(document).trigger('contact_added', {
                    jid: $('#contact-jid').val(),
                    name: $('#contact-name').val()
                });

                $('#contact-jid').val('');
                $('#contact-name').val('');

                $(this).dialog('close');
            }
```

continues

LISTING 6-3 *(continued)*

```
        }
    });

    $('#new-contact').click(function (ev) {
        $('#contact_dialog').dialog('open');
    });

    $('#approve_dialog').dialog({
        autoOpen: false,
        draggable: false,
        modal: true,
        title: 'Subscription Request',
        buttons: {
            "Deny": function () {
                Gab.connection.send($pres({
                    to: Gab.pending_subscriber,
                    "type": "unsubscribed"}));
                Gab.pending_subscriber = null;

                $(this).dialog('close');
            },

            "Approve": function () {
                Gab.connection.send($pres({
                    to: Gab.pending_subscriber,
                    "type": "subscribed"}));

                Gab.connection.send($pres({
                    to: Gab.pending_subscriber,
                    "type": "subscribe"}));

                Gab.pending_subscriber = null;

                $(this).dialog('close');
            }
        }
    });

    $('#chat-area').tabs().find('.ui-tabs-nav').sortable({axis: 'x'});

    $('.roster-contact').live('click', function () {
        var jid = $(this).find(".roster-jid").text();
        var name = $(this).find(".roster-name").text();
        var jid_id = Gab.jid_to_id(jid);

        if ($('#chat-' + jid_id).length === 0) {
            $('#chat-area').tabs('add', '#chat-' + jid_id, name);
            $('#chat-' + jid_id).append(
                "<div class='chat-messages'></div>" +
                "<input type='text' class='chat-input'>");
            $('#chat-' + jid_id).data('jid', jid);
```

```
        }
        $('#chat-area').tabs('select', '#chat-' + jid_id);

        $('#chat-' + jid_id + ' input').focus();
});

$('.chat-input').live('keypress', function (ev) {
    var jid = $(this).parent().data('jid');

    if (ev.which === 13) {
        ev.preventDefault();

        var body = $(this).val();

        var message = $msg({to: jid,
                            "type": "chat"})
            .c('body').t(body).up()
            .c('active', {xmlns: "http://jabber.org/protocol/chatstates"});
        Gab.connection.send(message);

        $(this).parent().find('.chat-messages').append(
            "<div class='chat-message'>&lt;" +
            "<span class='chat-name me'>" +
            Strophe.getNodeFromJid(Gab.connection.jid) +
            "</span>&gt;<span class='chat-text'>" +
            body +
            "</span></div>");
        Gab.scroll_chat(Gab.jid_to_id(jid));

        $(this).val('');
        $(this).parent().data('composing', false);
    } else {
        var composing = $(this).parent().data('composing');
        if (!composing) {
            var notify = $msg({to: jid, "type": "chat"})
                .c('composing', {xmlns: "http://jabber.org/protocol/chatstates"});
            Gab.connection.send(notify);

            $(this).parent().data('composing', true);
        }
    }
});

$('#disconnect').click(function () {
    Gab.connection.disconnect();
    Gab.connection = null;
});

$('#chat_dialog').dialog({
    autoOpen: false,
    draggable: false,
    modal: true,
    title: 'Start a Chat',
    buttons: {
        "Start": function () {
```

continues

LISTING 6-3 *(continued)*

```
                    var jid = $('#chat-jid').val();
                    var jid_id = Gab.jid_to_id(jid);

                    $('#chat-area').tabs('add', '#chat-' + jid_id, jid);
                    $('#chat-' + jid_id).append(
                        "<div class='chat-messages'></div>" +
                        "<input type='text' class='chat-input'>");

                    $('#chat-' + jid_id).data('jid', jid);

                    $('#chat-area').tabs('select', '#chat-' + jid_id);
                    $('#chat-' + jid_id + ' input').focus();

                    $('#chat-jid').val('');

                    $(this).dialog('close');
                }
            }
        });

        $('#new-chat').click(function () {
            $('#chat_dialog').dialog('open');
        });
    });

    $(document).bind('connect', function (ev, data) {
        var conn = new Strophe.Connection(
            'http://bosh.metajack.im:5280/xmpp-httpbind');

        conn.connect(data.jid, data.password, function (status) {
            if (status === Strophe.Status.CONNECTED) {
                $(document).trigger('connected');
            } else if (status === Strophe.Status.DISCONNECTED) {
                $(document).trigger('disconnected');
            }
        });
        Gab.connection = conn;
    });

    $(document).bind('connected', function () {
        var iq = $iq({type: 'get'}).c('query', {xmlns: 'jabber:iq:roster'});
        Gab.connection.sendIQ(iq, Gab.on_roster);

        Gab.connection.addHandler(Gab.on_roster_changed,
                                  "jabber:iq:roster", "iq", "set");

        Gab.connection.addHandler(Gab.on_message,
                                  null, "message", "chat");
    });

    $(document).bind('disconnected', function () {
```

```
        Gab.connection = null;
        Gab.pending_subscriber = null;

        $('#roster-area ul').empty();
        $('#chat-area ul').empty();
        $('#chat-area div').remove();

        $('#login_dialog').dialog('open');
    });

    $(document).bind('contact_added', function (ev, data) {
        var iq = $iq({type: "set"}).c("query", {xmlns: "jabber:iq:roster"})
            .c("item", data);
        Gab.connection.sendIQ(iq);

        var subscribe = $pres({to: data.jid, "type": "subscribe"});
        Gab.connection.send(subscribe);
    });
```

GABBING MORE

Most chat clients you are probably familiar with have many more features than Gab. You could add some of these to Gab to make it more competitive.

Try adding some of these simple features:

➤ Add support for the other chat notification states like paused and gone.

➤ Allow the user to use text based markup like Markdown or Textile to send rich XHTML-IM messages.

➤ Using the Personal Eventing Protocol (XEP-0163), show the music that a user's contacts are listening to in the chat area; several other chat clients send such notifications.

SUMMARY

Instant messaging is the original XMPP application domain. By creating Gab, you've made a capable IM client that can manage a roster and multiple chat sessions. Gab was quite a bit more complex than the previous chapters' applications, but by sticking with it you learned:

➤ How to get and process a roster

➤ How to deal with roster changes

➤ How to add and edit contacts

➤ How to send and respond to presence subscription requests

➤   How XMPP servers route messages

➤   About jQuery UI's tab control

➤   How to send and interpret activity notifications for chats

The next chapter teaches you how to explore services and their features with XMPP service discovery.

Exploring Services: Service Discovery and Browsing

WHAT'S IN THIS CHAPTER?

➤ The basics of service discovery

➤ Interpreting service discovery results

➤ Service discovery trees

➤ How other XMPP extensions use service discovery

The federated world of XMPP servers and services is a big place, and it's growing every day. Early on, XMPP developers realized that they needed some way to find information about these servers and which services they supported. The XMPP service discovery system was created to fill this need.

Service discovery requests can be sent to nearly every XMPP-addressable entity on the network. Applications can find out which entities are servers, publish-subscribe systems, and multi-user chat services. Service information often includes the list of supported features so that application code never has to guess what functionality is supported.

Most of the extension protocols to XMPP make use of service discovery, usually to communicate feature support. Some also rely on it for service browsing. Multi-user chat services, for example, can be queried for what rooms exist, what settings are applied to a given room, and even which users are present.

Service discovery is a simple but important piece of many XMPP protocols, and your own applications will often need to use it in a variety of tasks. In the course of this chapter, you build a service browser called Dig, which allows users to explore various XMPP services.

APPLICATION PREVIEW

The Dig application is similar to other directory browsing interfaces you may be familiar with, such as Windows Explorer or Mac OS X's Finder. Figure 7-1 shows what the final application will look like.

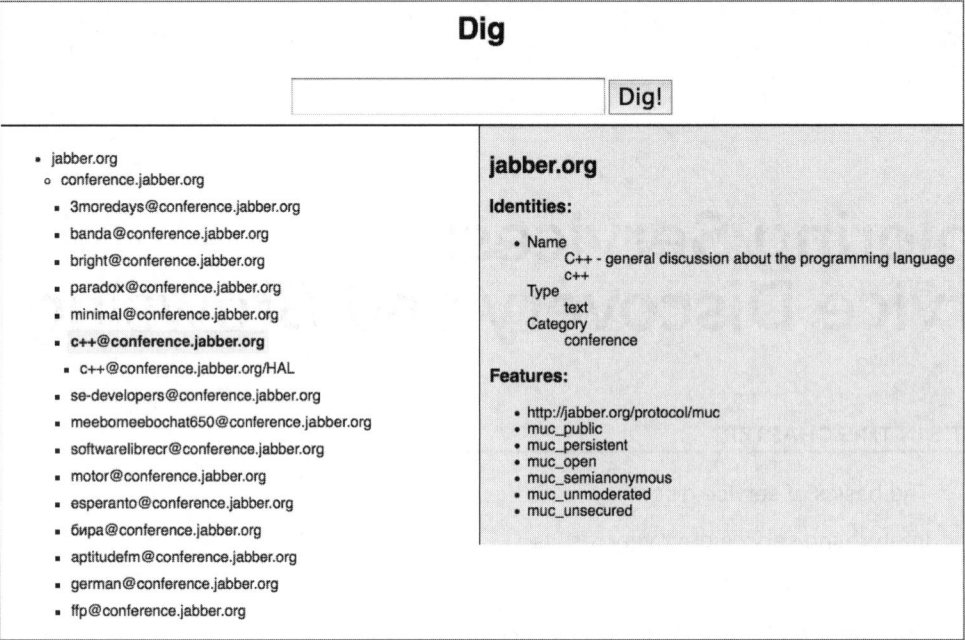

FIGURE 7-1

On the left is the service tree for a given entity. The panel on the right displays information about the selected item in the tree. The user can input the entity for which to query services at the top of the application.

The tree shown in Figure 7-1 is just part of the service tree for jabber.org's multi-user chat server at conference.jabber.org.

DIG DESIGN

Dig must make two kinds of service discovery queries to an entity — disco#info and disco#items. The hash character in their names is taken from their underlying namespace. A disco#info query returns basic identity information and supported features for an entity. Disco#items queries enumerate an entity's children.

Once users input an entity they want to view, both types of queries are run, and the results begin to form a tree in the left pane. Clicking leaves of the tree results in further service discovery queries and further expands the tree. Results from `disco#info` queries appear in the right information pane, and `disco#items` query results are used to expand the tree.

The application's UI is quite simple, but the amount of information the user can learn about XMPP servers and services is immense.

FINDING INFORMATION

Service discovery, defined in XEP-0030 and often called *disco*, consists of a hierarchy of information relating to an entity or service and a pair of queries, `disco#info` and `disco#items`, to request information and traverse the tree, respectively.

Disco#info Queries

Most XMPP entities you will interact with will respond to `disco#info` queries. Generally, these queries are concerned with two kinds of information: identity and features. Identity information contains the entity's name and purpose, and some services may have multiple identities. Feature information is useful to discover which particular features a service supports. For example, a publish-subscribe service may report that it supports all the required and some of the optional features defined in the Publish-Subscribe specification (XEP-0060) and that it also supports several other extensions.

`Disco#info` queries are extremely simple. They consist of an IQ-get stanza using the `http://jabber.org/protocols/disco#info` namespace:

```
<iq to='pemberley.lit'
    from='elizabeth@longbourn.lit/lambton'
    type='get'
    id='info1'>
  <query xmlns='http://jabber.org/protocol/disco#info'/>
</iq>
```

In this example query, Elizabeth is probing the pemberley.lit server for information. This server will respond with a list of identities and features:

```
<iq to='elizabeth@longbourn.lit/lambton'
    from='pemberley.lit'
    type='result'
    id='info1'>
  <query xmlns='http://jabber.org/protocol/disco#info'>
    <identity name='Pemberley XMPP Server'
              category='server'
              type='im'/>
    <feature var='http://jabber.org/protocol/disco#info'/>
    <feature var='jabber:client'/>
    <feature var='jabber:iq:roster'/>
```

```
        <feature var='jabber:iq:version'/>
        <feature var='msgoffline'/>
    </query>
</iq>
```

The pemberley.lit server reports its name and that it is an instant messaging service. It also enumerates the features that the server supports, including `disco#info` support, standard XMPP client support, support for roster commands, support for version queries, and support for the storage of messages for offline users.

XMPP servers vary in their responses to `disco#info` queries, but the responses appear in the same form. Typically, XMPP servers will support a wide range of features, and the list of identities and features will both be much longer than those of the fictional pemberley.lit. `Disco#info` responses are required to contain at least one identity and at least the `disco#info` feature.

Each `<identity>` element contains an optional `name` attribute as well as the required `category` and `type` attributes. A list of standard category and type values is maintained by the XMPP registrar and you can find it at `http://xmpp.org/registrar/disco-categories.html`. Entities that provide multiple services at a single address return multiple `<identity>` elements, usually one per service.

The `<feature>` elements list the basic features the entity provides. The required `var` attribute contains the feature's identifier. These often correspond to namespaces used in various XMPP protocol extensions, and the XMPP registrar maintains the list of registered features at `http://xmpp.org/registrar/disco-features.html`. In the previous example, all but the `msgoffline` feature used the relevant namespaces as identifiers.

Applications can use this information to test what kind of services particular entities provide, or to determine whether a particular service supports some specific feature. For example, not all conference servers support server-side logging of group chats. Those that do can advertise such support in a `<feature>` element.

Disco#items Queries

Service discovery information is organized in the form of a tree. The `disco#items` query requests the list of children for an entity. Some of these children will be other entities and some will be internal nodes. By continuing to do `disco#items` queries on each child, the entire service tree can be expanded.

Requesting `disco#items` on an XMPP server returns the various server-side components that make up the server, each as a separately addressable entity. For example, a publish-subscribe service would return the list of top-level nodes, each of which may also have child nodes. Multi-user chat servers answer `disco#items` queries by returning the list of chat rooms.

`Disco#items` queries are almost exactly the same as `disco#info` queries:

```
<iq to='pemberley.lit'
    from='elizabeth@longbourn.lit/lambton'
    type='get'
    id='items1'>
  <query xmlns='http://jabber.org/protocol/disco#items'/>
</iq>
```

As you can see, only the last portion of the namespace has changed. The response from pemberley.lit appears here:

```
<iq to='elizabeth@longbourn.lit/lambton'
    from='pemberley.lit'
    type='result'
    id='items1'>
  <query xmlns='http://jabber.org/protocol/disco#items'>
    <item jid='pubsub.pemberley.lit'
          name='The Pemberley Pubsub System'/>
    <item jid='chat.pemberley.lit'
          name='The Pemberley Multi-User Chat System'/>
    <item jid='pemberley.lit'
          node='statistics'
          name='Pemberley Server Statistics'/>
  </query>
</iq>
```

Each child item of the entity is represented by an `<item>` element in the response. The preceding example shows three children, two of which are server components, and one of which is an internal node. All of these items will respond to `disco#info` and `disco#items` queries as well.

Disco Nodes

Internal parts of the service tree are exposed as nodes. The `disco#items` query you saw in the last section contained a `statistics` node as one of the pemberley.lit children. Disco nodes are addressable by including a `node` attribute in the `<query>` element of the request:

```
<iq to='pemberley.lit'
    from='elizabeth@longbourn.lit/lambton'
    type='get'
    id='info2'>
  <query xmlns='http://jabber.org/protocol/disco#info'
         node='statistics'/>
</iq>
```

The `statistics` node will respond with one or more `<identity>` elements and one or more `<feature>` elements, just like any other entity. A `disco#items` query to the `statistics` node may also reveal more child nodes.

Aside from the various error cases and other small details, these simple pieces are all there is to service discovery. You have all the knowledge you need to start building Dig.

CREATING DIG

As with previous applications, you start building Dig by first creating its user interface. The screenshot in Figure 7-1 shows the three main pieces: the service input control, the tree pane, and the information pane. The HTML for Dig appears in Listing 7-1, and the CSS styles appear in Listing 7-2.

LISTING 7-1: dig.html

```html
<!DOCTYPE HTML PUBLIC "-//W3C//DTD HTML 4.01//EN"
         "http://www.w3.org/TR/html4/strict.dtd">
<html>
  <head>
    <meta http-equiv="Content-type" content="text/html;charset=UTF-8">
    <title>Dig - Chapter 7</title>

    <link rel='stylesheet' href='http://ajax.googleapis.com/ajax/libs/jqueryu
i/1.7.2/themes/cupertino/jquery-ui.css'>
    <script src='http://ajax.googleapis.com/ajax/libs/jquery/1.3.2/jquery.js'>
    </script>
    <script src='http://ajax.googleapis.com/ajax/libs/jqueryui/1.7.2/jquery-u
i.js'></script>
    <script src='scripts/strophe.js'></script>
    <script src='scripts/flXHR.js'></script>
    <script src='scripts/strophe.flxhr.js'></script>

    <link rel='stylesheet' type='text/css' href='dig.css'>
    <script type='text/javascript' src='dig.js'></script>
  </head>
  <body>
    <h1>Dig</h1>

    <div id='input-bar'>
      <input id='service' type='text'>
      <input id='dig' type='button' value='Dig!' disabled='disabled'>
    </div>

    <div class='clear'></div>

    <div class='left'>
      <ul id='tree'>
      </ul>
    </div>

    <div class='right'>
      <h2 id='selected-name'></h2>
      <div id='disco-info'>
        <h3>Identities:</h3>
        <ul id='identity-list'>
        </ul>

        <h3>Features:</h3>
        <ul id='feature-list'>
        </ul>
      </div>
    </div>

    <!-- login dialog -->
    <div id='login_dialog' class='hidden'>
```

```
          <label>JID:</label><input type='text' id='jid'>
          <label>Password:</label><input type='password' id='password'>
        </div>
      </body>
    </html>
```

LISTING 7-2: dig.css

```css
body {
    font-family: Helvetica;
}

h1 {
    text-align: center;
}

.hidden {
    display: none
}

.left {
    padding: 10px;
    width: 400px;
    float: left;
}

.right {
    padding: 10px;
    border-left: solid 1px black;
    width: 500px;
    float: right;
    background-color: #eee;
}

.clear {
    clear: both;
}

.item {
    padding: 4px;
}

.selected {
    background-color: #ff6;
    font-weight: bold;
}

#input-bar {
    padding: 10px;
    text-align: center;
```

continues

```
        border-bottom: solid 2px black;
    }

    input {
        font-size: 150%;
    }

    #tree ul {
        line-height: 175%;
        margin-left: 0;
        padding-left: 10px;
    }
```

The input control contains a text entry box and a button; the tree pane contains an empty unordered list; and the information pane contains a section for the identities and one for the features. The styles just make the default rendering of these various elements a little more visually pleasing. Selected entities in the tree are highlighted in yellow and bold, and various UI elements have a little extra whitespace or larger fonts.

Listing 7-3 contains the skeleton of the JavaScript code for Dig. You've seen all these elements before in previous chapters, so they won't be explained here.

LISTING 7-3: dig.js (initial skeleton)

```
var Dig = {
    connection: null,
};

$(document).ready(function () {
    $('#login_dialog').dialog({
        autoOpen: true,
        draggable: false,
        modal: true,
        title: 'Connect to XMPP',
        buttons: {
            "Connect": function () {
                $(document).trigger('connect', {
                    jid: $('#jid').val(),
                    password: $('#password').val()
                });

                $('#password').val('');
                $(this).dialog('close');
            }
        }
    });
});

$(document).bind('connect', function (ev, data) {
```

```
        var conn = new Strophe.Connection(
            'http://bosh.metajack.im:5280/xmpp-httpbind');
        conn.connect(data.jid, data.password, function (status) {
            if (status === Strophe.Status.CONNECTED) {
                $(document).trigger('connected');
            } else if (status === Strophe.Status.DISCONNECTED) {
                $(document).trigger('disconnected');
            }
        });
        Dig.connection = conn;
    });

    $(document).bind('connected', function () {
        // nothing here yet
    });
```

With these basics in place, you can start on the real meat of the application.

Initial Disco Queries

Once the user has input a JID into the text entry box and clicked Dig!, the code must send the initial
disco#info and disco#items queries to the designated service.

First, bind the click event for the Dig! button and send the two disco queries. The following code
should be placed in the document ready handler:

```
$('#dig').click(function () {
    var service = $('#service').val();
    $('#service').val('');

    // set up disco info pane
    $('#selected-name').text(service);
    $('#identity-list').empty();
    $('#feature-list').empty();

    // clear tree pane
    $('#tree').empty();

    $('#tree').append("<li><span class='item selected'>" +
                      service +
                      "</span></li>");

    Dig.connection.sendIQ(
        $iq({to: service, type: "get"})
            .c("query", {xmlns:
                          "http://jabber.org/protocol/disco#info"}),
        function (iq) {
            Dig.on_info(iq, $('.selected')[0]);
        });

    Dig.connection.sendIQ(
        $iq({to: service, type: "get"})
```

```
        .c("query", {xmlns:
                    "http://jabber.org/protocol/disco#items"}),
    function (iq) {
        Dig.on_items(iq, $('.selected')[0]);
    });
});
```

This code first gets the name of the service and clears the text entry box. Then the code clears the information pane and creates the initial disco tree. Finally, it sends disco#info and disco#items queries to the service.

Notice that the currently selected element is also passed to both on_info() and on_items(). This extra information is passed so that the handlers know which branch of the tree the result is for. Without this information, a user might see the results for one branch appear under another if the user clicks on a different branch before a response to a query is received.

The on_info() and on_items() functions must now be implemented. The following code adds the first of these functions to the Dig object:

```
on_info: function (iq, elem) {
    // do nothing if the response is not for the selected branch
    if ($('.selected').length > 0 &&
        elem !== $('.selected')[0]) {
        return;
    }

    $('#feature-list').empty();
    $(iq).find("feature").each(function () {
        $('#feature-list').append("<li>" +
                                  $(this).attr('var') +
                                  "</li>");
    });

    $('#identity-list').empty();
    $(iq).find("identity").each(function () {
        $('#identity-list').append("<li><dl><dt>Name</dt><dd>" +
                                   ($(this).attr('name') || "none") +
                                   "</dd><dt>Type</dt><dd>" +
                                   ($(this).attr('type') || "none") +
                                   "</dd><dt>Category</dt><dd>" +
                                   ($(this).attr('category') || "none") +
                                   "</dd></dl></li>");
    });
}
```

The `on_info()` function simply takes each feature and each identity and formats them into list elements. The little-used definition list (`<dl>` element) aids the formatting of each identity's properties.

The `on_items()` function is also quite simple:

```
on_items: function (iq, elem) {
    var items = $(iq).find("item");
    if (items.length > 0) {
        $(elem).parent().append("<ul></ul>");

        var list = $(elem).parent().find("ul");

        $(iq).find("item").each(function () {
            var node = $(this).attr('node');
            list.append("<li><span class='item'>" +
                    $(this).attr("jid") +
                    (node ? ":" + node : "") +
                    "</span></li>");
        });
    }
}
```

code snippet dig.js

If any `<item>` elements are returned, new items are added to the selected branch of the tree in the tree pane. Notice that if the items point to disco nodes as opposed to JIDs, they are written as `jid:node`. This isn't the best way to display the information perhaps, but it will assist you later when you must handle click events for items in the tree.

Finally, you need to enable the Dig! button in the `connected` event handler. Make the highlighted changes to this event handler:

```
$(document).bind('connected', function () {
    $('#dig').removeAttr('disabled');
});
```

code snippet dig.js

Running Dig in this state should allow you to see the top-level children and the basic information about an entity. Next you need to add the ability to browse and expand the tree.

Browsing the Disco Tree

So far, Dig is not much use beyond obtaining a high-level view of a service. You need to extend it to allow users to click various branches of the tree to change what information is displayed in the information pane and expand the tree under the current branch.

Because the `on_items()` and `on_info()` functions are so general, the only thing you must add is a handler for click events in the tree pane. Add the code handler to the document ready handler:

```
$('#tree .item').live('click', function () {
    if ($(this).hasClass("selected")) {
        return;
    }

    $(".selected").removeClass("selected");
    $(this).addClass("selected");

    var serv_node = $(this).text();
    var service, node;
    var idx = serv_node.indexOf(":");
    if (idx < 0) {
        service = serv_node;
        node = null;
    } else {
        service = serv_node.slice(0, idx);
        node = serv_node.slice(idx + 1);
    }

    var query_attrs;
    if (node) {
        query_attrs = { node: node };
    } else {
        query_attrs = {};
    }

    var elem = this;
    query_attrs["xmlns"] = "http://jabber.org/protocol/disco#info";
    Dig.connection.sendIQ(
        $iq({to: service, type: "get"})
            .c("query", query_attrs),
        function (iq) {
            Dig.on_info(iq, elem);
        });

    if ($(".selected").parent().find("ul").length === 0) {
        query_attrs["xmlns"] = "http://jabber.org/protocol/disco#items";
        Dig.connection.sendIQ(
            $iq({to: service, type: "get"})
                .c("query", query_attrs),
            function (iq) {
                Dig.on_items(iq, elem);
            });
    }
});
```

code snippet dig.js

jQuery's `live()` function is used to bind an event handler to matching elements. Unlike using `click()` or `bind()` to do this, `live()` enables the binding even on elements that are added dynamically after the binding is created. You have used `live()` before in Chapter 6.

The code first checks to see if the selected branch was clicked, and if so, returns. There is no need to redo the queries in this case. If the branch that received the click is not selected, the old selection is removed, and the clicked branch becomes selected.

The next block of code parses the text in the selected `<span>` element to determine the service and node for this branch's tree item. Both of these pieces of information are needed to address the disco queries.

Finally, a `disco#info` query is sent to the correct service and node, and if no `disco#items` query was previously done for this part of the tree, a `disco#items` query is also sent. Because `on_items()` creates a sublist for the relevant tree branch, it is sufficient to check for a child `<ul>` element to determine if `on_items()` has already been executed. Both of the disco queries use the same `on_items()` and `on_info()` handlers you created previously.

Dig is complete and can now be used to explore the vast number of public XMPP services. The final source code is shown in Listing 7-4. In the next section, you use Dig to browse a few well-known services.

Available for download on Wrox.com

LISTING 7-4: dig.js (final)

```javascript
var Dig = {
    connection: null,

    on_items: function (iq, elem) {
        var items = $(iq).find("item");
        if (items.length > 0) {
            $(elem).parent().append("<ul></ul>");

            var list = $(elem).parent().find("ul");

            $(iq).find("item").each(function () {
                var node = $(this).attr('node');
                list.append("<li><span class='item'>" +
                        $(this).attr("jid") +
                        (node ? ":" + node : "") +
                        "</span></li>");
            });
        }
    },

    on_info: function (iq, elem) {
        // do nothing if the response is not for the selected branch
        if ($('.selected').length > 0 &&
            elem !== $('.selected')[0]) {
            return;
        }

        $('#feature-list').empty();
```

continues

LISTING 7-4 *(continued)*

```javascript
        $(iq).find("feature").each(function () {
            $('#feature-list').append("<li>" +
                                      $(this).attr('var') +
                                      "</li>");
        });

        $('#identity-list').empty();
        $(iq).find("identity").each(function () {
            $('#identity-list').append("<li><dl><dt>Name</dt><dd>" +
                                      ($(this).attr('name') || "none") +
                                      "</dd><dt>Type</dt><dd>" +
                                      ($(this).attr('type') || "none") +
                                      "</dd><dt>Category</dt><dd>" +
                                      ($(this).attr('category') || "none") +
                                      "</dd></dl></li>");
        });
    }
};

$(document).ready(function () {
    $('#login_dialog').dialog({
        autoOpen: true,
        draggable: false,
        modal: true,
        title: 'Connect to XMPP',
        buttons: {
            "Connect": function () {
                $(document).trigger('connect', {
                    jid: $('#jid').val(),
                    password: $('#password').val()
                });

                $('#password').val('');
                $(this).dialog('close');
            }
        }
    });

    $('#dig').click(function () {
        var service = $('#service').val();
        $('#service').val('');


        // set up disco info pane
        $('#selected-name').text(service);
        $('#identity-list').empty();
        $('#feature-list').empty();

        // clear tree pane
        $('#tree').empty();

        $('#tree').append("<li><span class='item selected'>" +
```

```
                          service +
                          "</span></li>");

    Dig.connection.sendIQ(
        $iq({to: service, type: "get"})
            .c("query", {xmlns:
                        "http://jabber.org/protocol/disco#info"}),
        function (iq) {
            Dig.on_info(iq, $('.selected')[0]);
        });

    Dig.connection.sendIQ(
        $iq({to: service, type: "get"})
            .c("query", {xmlns:
                        "http://jabber.org/protocol/disco#items"}),
        function (iq) {
            Dig.on_items(iq, $('.selected')[0]);
        });
});

$('#tree .item').live('click', function () {
    if ($(this).hasClass("selected")) {
        return;
    }

    $(".selected").removeClass("selected");
    $(this).addClass("selected");

    var serv_node = $(this).text();
    var service, node;
    var idx = serv_node.indexOf(":");
    if (idx < 0) {
        service = serv_node;
        node = null;
    } else {
        service = serv_node.slice(0, idx);
        node = serv_node.slice(idx + 1);
    }

    var query_attrs;
    if (node) {
        query_attrs = { node: node };
    } else {
        query_attrs = {};
    }

    var elem = this;
    query_attrs["xmlns"] = "http://jabber.org/protocol/disco#info";
    Dig.connection.sendIQ(
        $iq({to: service, type: "get"})
            .c("query", query_attrs),
        function (iq) {
```

continues

LISTING 7-4 *(continued)*

```
                    Dig.on_info(iq, elem);
            });

        if ($(".selected").parent().find("ul").length === 0) {
            query_attrs["xmlns"] = "http://jabber.org/protocol/disco#items";
            Dig.connection.sendIQ(
                $iq({to: service, type: "get"})
                    .c("query", query_attrs),
                function (iq) {
                    Dig.on_items(iq, elem);
                });
        }
    });
});

$(document).bind('connect', function (ev, data) {
    var conn = new Strophe.Connection(
        'http://bosh.metajack.im:5280/xmpp-httpbind');

    conn.connect(data.jid, data.password, function (status) {
        if (status === Strophe.Status.CONNECTED) {
            $(document).trigger('connected');
        } else if (status === Strophe.Status.DISCONNECTED) {
            $(document).trigger('disconnected');
        }
    });
    Dig.connection = conn;
});

$(document).bind('connected', function () {
    $('#dig').removeAttr('disabled');
});
```

DIGGING INTO SERVICES

Service discovery can provide a variety of useful functionality. Your applications might use or implement service discovery to:

➤ Determine support for a specific software feature.

➤ Use disco#items results to generate lists of resources such as public multi-user chat rooms.

➤ Crawl the disco tree to look for specific services like proprietary IM network gateways or proxy services.

➤ Communicate metadata about your application to other entities making service discovery requests.

Over the next sections, you will use Dig to accomplish similar tasks. You will try to find whether the jabber.org server offers a proxy service, if the server supports registration, and what public chat rooms you can join at its multi-user chat service.

Finding a Proxy Server

XMPP clients often support peer-to-peer file transfers between contacts. Due to network restrictions, however, many peers are behind NATs (network address translators) or corporate firewalls. In these cases, it is necessary for both sides to use a third-party proxy service to complete the transfer.

It may happen that neither party knows of a proxy service to use, but with service discovery browsing, their client software can determine whether the users' servers provide one. Normally, this check would be done transparently to the end user, but here you use Dig to find an answer manually.

Open the Dig application in your web browser, type `jabber.org` into the text entry box, and click Dig! You should see a result similar to the screenshot in Figure 7-2, although your result may be different if the jabber.org service has changed or upgraded any of its services.

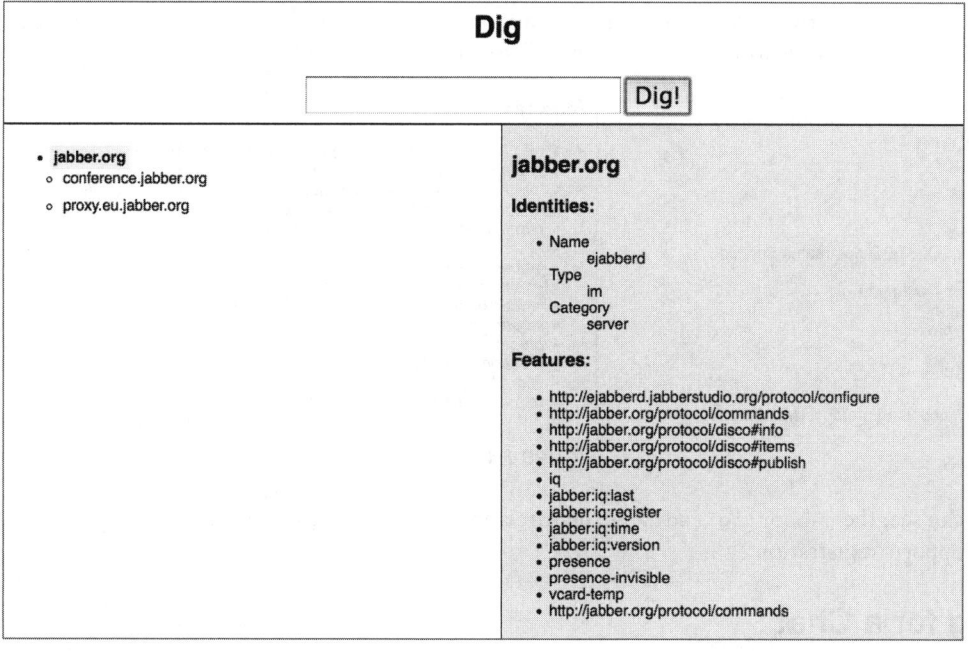

FIGURE 7-2

You should see the promising proxy.eu.jabber.org item. Click it to obtain more information, and you should see something similar to Figure 7-3 in the information pane.

An XMPP Bytestreams (see XEP-0065 for more information) proxy is exactly what is needed to complete a peer-to-peer file transfer.

Normally, your application will search for a particular item by its type, category, or features, not by its name. In this instance, human intuition short-circuited the search by inferring possible features from the name of the service.

Note that the proxy.eu.jabber.org item does not have any children, so the tree is not expanded underneath it.

Discovering Features

Some servers support account creation over XMPP. If your application depends on this feature, it is wise to check whether the feature is supported by the XMPP server using service discovery.

If you have the Dig application open from the previous example, simply click the root item of the tree, jabber.org. Otherwise, open the Dig application and browse to the disco tree for jabber.org. You should see a list of features similar to those listed in Figure 7-4.

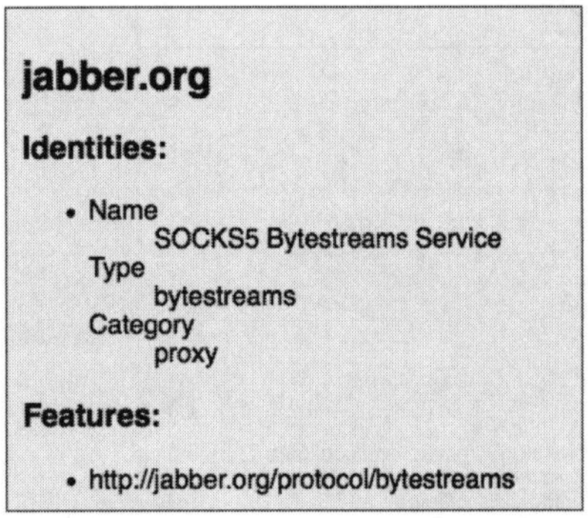

jabber.org

Identities:

- Name
    SOCKS5 Bytestreams Service
  Type
    bytestreams
  Category
    proxy

Features:

- http://jabber.org/protocol/bytestreams

FIGURE 7-3

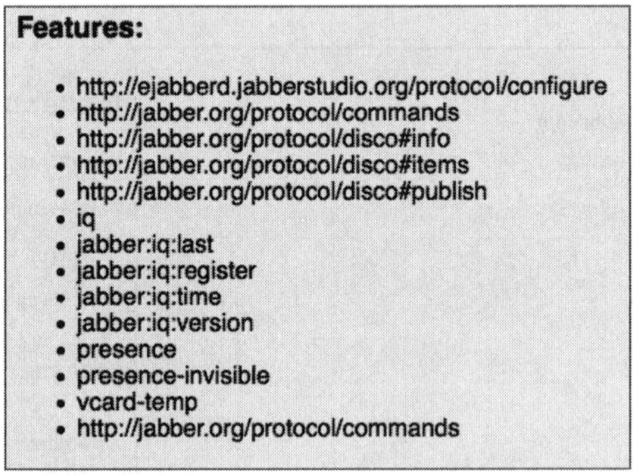

Features:

- http://ejabberd.jabberstudio.org/protocol/configure
- http://jabber.org/protocol/commands
- http://jabber.org/protocol/disco#info
- http://jabber.org/protocol/disco#items
- http://jabber.org/protocol/disco#publish
- iq
- jabber:iq:last
- jabber:iq:register
- jabber:iq:time
- jabber:iq:version
- presence
- presence-invisible
- vcard-temp
- http://jabber.org/protocol/commands

FIGURE 7-4

As you can see, the `jabber:iq:register` feature appears in the list, so you can be assured that the server supports registration.

Looking for a Chat

Service discovery is also used to enumerate lists of publicly available resources, be they publish-subscribe nodes, multi-user chat rooms, or a list of shared files. You've seen from the previous two examples that the jabber.org server hosts a conference.jabber.org service. You can browse this service to get a list of the public rooms.

Use Dig to browse to the disco tree of jabber.org and click the conference.jabber.org item. You should see a long list of chat rooms like those in Figure 7-5.

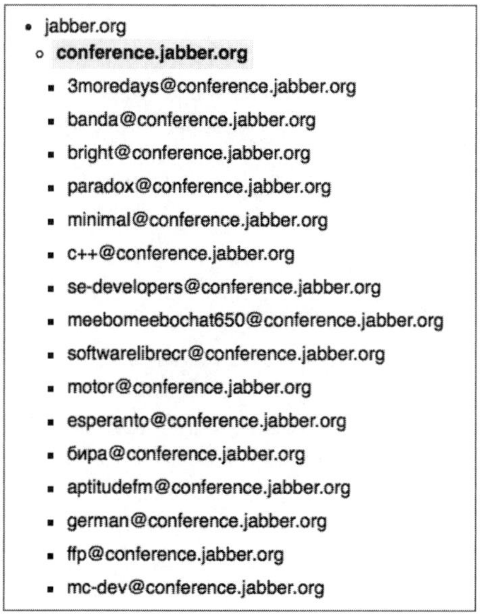

- jabber.org
  - **conference.jabber.org**
    - 3moredays@conference.jabber.org
    - banda@conference.jabber.org
    - bright@conference.jabber.org
    - paradox@conference.jabber.org
    - minimal@conference.jabber.org
    - c++@conference.jabber.org
    - se-developers@conference.jabber.org
    - meebomeebochat650@conference.jabber.org
    - softwarelibrecr@conference.jabber.org
    - motor@conference.jabber.org
    - esperanto@conference.jabber.org
    - бира@conference.jabber.org
    - aptitudefm@conference.jabber.org
    - german@conference.jabber.org
    - ffp@conference.jabber.org
    - mc-dev@conference.jabber.org

FIGURE 7-5

If you click any of the rooms, you will see more information about it in the right pane. You may notice that after you click a specific room, the tree expands beneath it. These subitems are the participants of the chat; the resource part of each JID is the participant's nickname.

Now that you've built Dig and seen service discovery in action, you'll be ready to make use of it in your own applications.

DISCOVERING MORE

Dig is already quite useful for browsing disco trees, but you might try adding a few new features to make it even better:

➤ Add the ability to group the items by category or type instead of only by their names.

➤ Allow the user to filter the tree for specific features they are interested in.

SUMMARY

This chapter covered a simple, but important, XMPP extension called service discovery, often referred to as *disco*. Using service discovery, your application can browse available resources, determine support for specific features, and find metadata about various services. Your application can also implement service discovery to enable other entities to gather information on your application's resources.

You created a simple service discovery browser called Dig, which allowed you to explore several areas of jabber.org's services tree. Along the way you learned:

➤ How to make `disco#info` and `disco#items` queries

➤ How to interpret results and use the items to build a disco tree

➤ How to use disco to determine feature support

➤ How to enumerate public chat rooms and other public resources

➤ How to find specific services needed by your application

The next chapter is all about one of the services you explored here, multi-user chat.

8

Group Chatting:
A Multi-User Chat Client

WHAT'S IN THIS CHAPTER?

➤ Joining group chat rooms

➤ Creating and configuring rooms

➤ Exchanging presence and messages in group chat

➤ Multi-user chat roles and permissions

➤ Moderating rooms

XMPP's multi-user chat extension was originally inspired by the Internet Relay Chat (IRC) protocol. Some clever XMPP protocol designers wanted to improve upon IRC in several ways, while at the same time bringing group chat natively to XMPP.

XMPP's multi-user chat (MUC) has one enormous advantage over its predecessors — structured payloads. IRC and other chat protocols typically transmit plain text back and forth with very little structure. Because of XMPP's extensibility, MUC messages can carry arbitrarily complex payloads even within regular chat messages.

MUC is also a form of message broadcast. A single message sent to a room gets rebroadcast out to all the participants automatically. This makes it similar to Publish-Subscribe, which you see in the next chapter. Unlike Publish-Subscribe, MUC provides a lot of advanced management features typical of group chat services, such as room moderation, and each participant is often allowed to broadcast messages to the room as well.

The combination of structured messaging, automatic broadcast, and group publishing opens the doors to many alternative uses of MUC. It has been used as the basis for rich, collaborative spaces (for example, Drop.io, which was shown in Chapter 2), and in Chapter 11, you build a multi-user Tic-Tac-Toe game on top of MUC.

Multi-user chat is a big protocol, and a full-featured client can become quite sophisticated. In this chapter, you build a simple group chat client called Groupie, which uses the most important pieces of the MUC protocol.

APPLICATION PREVIEW

Figure 8-1 shows a screenshot from the finished Groupie application. Just as in previous chapters, the application's interface is as simple as possible.

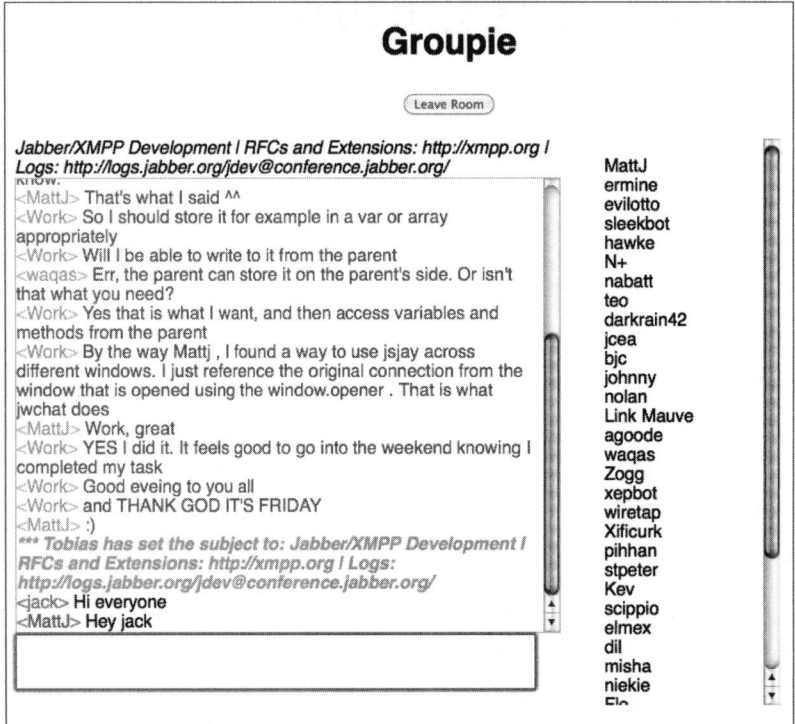

FIGURE 8-1

At the top of the screen are the chat and participant areas. The chat area contains all the messages people send to the room as well as private messages sent to and from the user. The participant area contains the list of current room occupants with whom the user is conversing. Beneath the chat area is a text box for the user to type and send messages.

GROUPIE DESIGN

Although Groupie's UI design appears simplistic, there is some sophistication necessary to make a usable group chat client. Groupie will need to support features like room creation and configuration, topic changes, private messaging between participants, and basic moderation.

When the application starts, the user is presented with an expanded version of the login dialog box you have seen in earlier chapters. This new login dialog box contains new fields for the multi-user chat room the user wants to join as well as the nickname the user wants to use within the room. If the room already exists, the user will join the other participants in the room, and if the room doesn't already exist, the room will be created.

Once in the room, messages from other participants appear in the chat area, and the user can type their own messages in the text entry box. The list of participants to the right of the chat area changes as people join and leave the room. Private messages can be sent to other participants using special commands in the text box, and private messages that get sent to the user show up in the normal chat area but rendered differently.

Two other special commands will be implemented — user actions and topic changes. User actions allow users to describe their own actions, similar to someone talking about himself or herself in the third person. Topic changes allow the user to modify the room's topic if they have adequate permissions within the room.

Group chat rooms have roles and affiliations, which control permissions and access to the room on a short- or long-term basis. Manipulating roles is necessary for silencing or removing users in a room when they get out of hand and changing a participant's affiliation can make them a fellow administrator or ban them permanently. Groupie supports these operations via special text commands. You see more on these topics later in Understanding Roles and Affiliations.

It may seem like a lot to implement, but these features just scratch the surface of possible functionality for multi-user chat rooms. Before you start coding, you should become familiar with the stanzas that make up the multi-user chat protocol.

PUBLIC SPEAKING

Group chat allows multiple people to gather in the same place to discuss a topic. These virtual meeting places are called rooms, and unlike in the real world, users can be in more than one group chat room at the same time. Rooms can have access controls, moderators, administrators, and even automatic logging and archival of the group's communications. Before you can start work on your application, you must first learn how group chat operations are accomplished at the protocol level.

Group Chat Services

Group chat is provided as a service, usually alongside a regular XMPP server. The group chat service has its own domain; for example, the jabber.org server runs a group chat service at conference.jabber.org.

Each room on the group chat service gets its own address, which looks just like a user's JID. The XMPP developer's chat room on the conference.jabber.org service is at jdev@conference.jabber.org, and general XMPP-related chat takes place in jabber@conference.jabber.org.

Many XMPP servers run group chat services, and thousands of chat rooms are spread across these services. As you saw in Chapter 7, service discovery can be used to find and locate group chat services as well as the public rooms hosted on them.

Entering and Leaving a Room

Before you can do much with a group chat room, you must first enter the room. This is also often referred to as *joining* the room. When you are done participating, you leave the room. Because this mirrors the concept of a user coming and going on and offline, the multi-user chat designers decided to model this part of the protocol with <presence> stanzas.

Users can join a group chat room simply by sending available presence to the room, along with a note that they understand the multi-user chat protocol. Sending presence directly to a JID instead of to the user's server is called *directed presence*. Similarly, to leave, unavailable presence is sent to the room.

DIRECTED PRESENCE

Sending presence stanzas directly to a JID instead of to the user's server is called sending directed presence. Directed presence is quite useful in XMPP protocols and extensions because it has some special properties.

Directed presence can be sent to users or services without requiring that presence subscriptions be set up. This is useful for giving another user or an external service temporary access to presence information.

Another property of directed presence is that the server keeps track of who has received direct presence notifications. The server uses this information to ensure that the recipients are notified when the sender goes offline, even if the sender forgets to send unavailable presence before logging off.

There is one limitation to be aware of when using directed presence — only unavailable presence is sent automatically. Presence changes from available to away or away to available are not automatically broadcast on the sender's behalf.

Because group chat services need to keep track of participants' presence, direct presence fulfills a crucial role. The server rarely loses track of a participant's presence, even if that person forgets to send unavailable presence.

Every participant in a group chat room gets their own address as well. Each participant picks a nickname for the room, and their JID within the room is the room's JID with a resource added containing their nickname. For example, Darcy's nickname in the Meryton ball chat room is darcy, so his group chat JID is ball@chat.meryton.lit/darcy.

If Bingley and Jane want to join the group chat room for the Meryton ball, they will both need to send directed presence to their desired identity in the room `ball@chat.meryton.lit`. Their stanzas are shown here:

```
<presence to='ball@chat.meryton.lit/bingley'
          from='bingley@netherfield.lit/meryton'>
  <x xmlns='http://jabber.org/protocol/muc'/>
</presence>

<presence to='ball@chat.meryton.lit/jane'
          from='jane@longbourn.lit/meryton'>
  <x xmlns='http://jabber.org/protocol/muc'/>
</presence>
```

Once they have joined the room, the group chat service will broadcast all the other participants' presence statuses to them. After all the other participants' presence stanzas are sent, the server concludes the presence broadcast by sending the arriving participant's presence to everyone, including the new arrival. Thus, when a new participant sees their own presence broadcast back to them, they know they have fully joined the room.

This is what Jane's client will receive upon joining the room:

```
<presence to='jane@longbourn.lit/meryton'
          from='ball@chat.meryton.lit/elizabeth'>
  <x xmlns='http://jabber.org/protocol/muc'>
    <item affiliation='member' role='participant'/>
  </x>
</presence>

..

<presence to='jane@longbourn.lit/meryton'
          from='ball@chat.meryton.lit/bingley'>
  <x xmlns='http://jabber.org/protocol/muc'>
    <item affiliation='member' role='participant'/>
  </x>
</presence>

<presence to='jane@longbourn.lit/meryton'
          from='ball@chat.meryton.lit/jane'>
  <x xmlns='http://jabber.org/protocol/muc'>
    <item affiliation='member' role='participant'/>
    <status code='110'/>
  </x>
</presence>
```

The room sends the affiliations and roles of each participant along with their presence. Jane's own presence broadcast also includes a status code of 110, which signals that this presence refers to the user herself. Just as with presence updates from Jane's roster, Jane will also receive presence updates from the room as people leave and new people join.

It can happen that someone already in the room has a user's desired nickname. When this happens, the group chat service will respond to the directed presence with a presence error signaling a nickname conflict.

Lydia tries to join the room with her sisters, but someone else has already used her desired nickname:

```
<presence to='ball@chat.meryton.lit/lydia'
          from='lydia@longbourn.lit/meryton'>
  <x xmlns='http://jabber.org/protocol/muc'/>
</presence>
```

The server responds with a nickname conflict error:

```
<presence to='lydia@longbourn.lit/meryton'
          from='ball@chat.meryton.lit'
          type='error'>
  <x xmlns='http://jabber.org/protocol/muc'/>
  <error type='cancel'>
    <conflict xmlns='urn:ietf:params:xml:ns:xmpp-stanzas'/>
  </error>
</presence>
```

Lydia will have to choose a new nickname and attempt to join the room again.

Leaving a room is accomplished by sending unavailable presence to your room JID. Darcy has tired of the conversation in the room and has decided to leave. He sends the following stanza:

```
<presence to='ball@chat.meryton.lit/darcy'
          from='darcy@pemberley.lit/meryton'
          type='unavailable'/>
```

The server will broadcast this out to the other occupants. For example, Jane's client will receive the following stanza marking Darcy's exit:

```
<presence to='jane@longbourn.lit/meryton'
          from='ball@chat.meryton.lit/darcy'
          type='unavailable'>
  <x xmlns='http://jabber.org/protocol/muc'>
    <item affiliation='member' role='none'/>
  </x>
</presence>
```

Darcy will also receive the broadcast from the room. Note that it also contains the status code 110 because it refers to his own presence.

```
<presence to='darcy@pemberley.lit/meryton'
          from='ball@chat.meryton.lit/darcy'
          type='unavailable'>
  <x xmlns='http://jabber.org/protocol/muc'>
    <item affiliation='member' role='none'/>
    <status code='110'/>
  </x>
</presence>
```

Aside from more error cases defined in the specification, that is all there is to joining and leaving group chat rooms.

Sending and Receiving Messages

Once in a room, users can communicate with each other by sending and receiving messages. This works very similarly to private chat messages, which you've seen in previous chapters.

Messages are sent to the room with a special type — groupchat. Messages directed to the bare room JID, ball@chat.meryton.lit, for example, are broadcast out to all occupants. Messages sent to the full JID of an occupant in the room are private and relayed by the room to the real JID of the user.

In the following example, Mr. Bingley addresses Mr. Darcy in the room. First Bingley sends his message to the room:

```
<message to='ball@chat.meryton.lit'
         from='bingley@netherfield.lit/meryton'
         type='groupchat'>
  <body>Come, Darcy, I must have you dance.  I hate to see you standing
    about by yourself in this stupid manner.  You had much better
    dance.</body>
</message>
```

His message will be broadcast out to all occupants, including Mr. Darcy. Darcy's client will receive:

```
<message to='darcy@pemberley.lit/meryton'
         from='ball@chat.meryton.lit/bingley'
         type='groupchat'>
  <body> Come, Darcy, I must have you dance.  I hate to see you standing
    about by yourself in this stupid manner.  You had much better
    dance.</body>
</message>
```

In most group chat rooms, messages will appear just like these, perhaps with XHTML-IM payloads for nicer formatting. Group chat messages can be extended just like anything else in XMPP, and by using extensions, the messages can carry arbitrary structured information. You see this in action in Chapter 11 when you build a game service using group chat.

Anonymity

XMPP multi-user chat rooms have configurable levels of anonymity, unlike many other group chat systems. Three levels are currently defined in the specification: non-anonymous, semi-anonymous, and fully anonymous.

In non-anonymous rooms, each occupant can see the real JID of the other occupants; the room will broadcast an extra jid attribute in the occupant's presence updates.

In semi-anonymous rooms, only owners and admins can see the real JIDs of occupants. Semi-anonymous and non-anonymous rooms are the most common types, and most group chat services will be configured to use one of these as the default for newly created rooms.

Fully anonymous rooms are quite rare, and only server administrators have access to the real JIDs of participants of these rooms. Not even the room's owner can access the real JIDs.

Normal private messages cannot be sent to participants in semi-anonymous or anonymous rooms, as the sender does not have access to the participant's actual JID. This is why private messages in group chat are sent to the participant's room JID.

Creating Rooms

Thousands of rooms in the federated XMPP network are already available for you to participate in, but sometimes you will find that the room you are looking for does not yet exist. Creating rooms is easy, and it is accomplished in much the same manner as joining a room.

Actually, rooms can be created just by joining a non-existent room. Assuming the service allows the user to create new rooms, sending directed presence to the desired room JID of the new room will cause the room to be created and the user to be set as the room's owner. Here, Bingley creates a new room for the Netherfield party:

```
<presence to='chatter@chat.netherfield.lit/bingley'
          from='bingley@netherfield.lit/drawing_room'>
  <x xmlns='http://jabber.org/protocol/muc'/>
</presence>
```

The chat.netherfield.lit service responds with the presence broadcast for the room's new and only occupant:

```
<presence to='bingley@netherfield.lit/drawing_room'
          from='chatter@chat.netherfield.lit/bingley'>
  <x xmlns='http://jabber.org/protocol/muc'>
    <item affiliation='owner' role='moderator'/>
    <status code='110'/>
    <status code='201'/>
  </x>
</presence>
```

Notice that Bingley has the owner affiliation and the moderator role. These attributes give Bingley special powers within the room, and you see more about these later. The 110 status code is sent, just as it was before, and a new status code of 201 is sent. This new status code signals that a new room has been created.

Once the room is created, the owner will usually configure it to behave as desired. Group chat rooms support a wide range of configuration options, including:

➤ Room persistence, or whether the room will continue to exist after all participants have left

➤ Room description

➤ Whether the room's messages should be logged

➤ Whether participants are allowed to change the room's topic

➤ The maximum number of occupants

➤ Access controls like membership lists

Room configuration is done with Data Forms (XEP-0004), which you learn about in the next chapter. Groupie's needs are modest so the default room configuration will be sufficient.

Understanding Roles and Affiliations

You've already seen that every user in a group chat room has a role and an affiliation assigned. Occupants will usually have a role of `participant` and an affiliation of `member`, but as you saw with room creation, the room's creator has a role of `moderator` and an affiliation of `owner`. It's time to learn a little more about roles and affiliations because they are important for one of the most essential pieces of chat rooms, community management.

Roles and affiliations enable or restrict functionality, but they apply on different time scales. An affiliation is a long-term property that persists across visits to the room, but roles apply only to the current visit. For example, when the room's owner joins the room, their role is `moderator`, and when they leave, their role becomes `none`, but even after leaving, their affiliation remains as `owner`.

Roles and affiliations are mostly hierarchical, and each level has all the properties of the previous one as well a few new ones. Table 8-1 lists the defined roles and their normal meanings, and Table 8-2 lists the possible affiliations.

TABLE 8-1: Group Chat Roles

ROLE	PRIVILEGES
None	No permissions — not in the room
Visitor	Can observe conversation, but can't talk
Participant	Can fully participate in public conversation
Moderator	Can remove users from the room, or promote participants to visitors

TABLE 8-2: Group Chat Affiliations

AFFILIATION	PRIVILEGES
Outcast	Banned from the room
None	Can join the room
Member	Can join even if room is members-only, and can retrieve the member list
Admin	Can ban members or unaffiliated users; can add and remove the member affiliation or the moderator role
Owner	Can add and remove admins and owners; can configure or destroy the room

Using the information in Table 8-1 and Table 8-2, you can begin to see how community management is accomplished. Kicking out a rowdy participant is done by setting their role within the room to `none`. If they return and continue to cause problems, you can set their affiliation with the room to `outcast`, and they will no longer be allowed to join. The room's owner can recruit new room administrators by setting their affiliations to `admin`, which will change their role to `moderator` whenever they join the room.

Manipulating roles and affiliations is done via IQ-set and IQ-get stanzas. Modifying the role or affiliation of a participant usually causes new presence information to be broadcast to the room for the affected user.

Wickham has eloped with Lydia, abandoning his post in the militia. Colonel Forster is forced to ban Wickham from the militia's chat room. The colonel sends an IQ-set to change Wickham's affiliation:

```
<iq to='militia@chat.emdashshire.lit'
    from='forster@militia.lit/headquarters'
    type='set'
    id='ban1'>
  <query xmlns='http://jabber.org/protocol/muc#admin'>
    <item jid='wickham@emdashshire.lit'
          affiliation='outcast'/>
    <reason>AWOL</reason>
  </query>
</iq>
```

The chat.emdashshire.lit service will respond with an IQ-result indicating success because Colonel Forster is the owner of the room. If Wickham is not currently in the room, the room does not need to broadcast anything to the rest of the occupants; however, if Wickham is in the room when he is banned, he will be forcibly removed, and all the room occupants will be notified of his presence change.

Wickham will receive the following stanza when he is removed from the room after his banishment:

```
<presence to='wickham@emdashshire.lit/london'
          from='militia@chat.emdashshire.lit'
          type='unavailable'>
  <x xmlns='http://jabber.org/protocol/muc#user'>
    <item affiliation='outcast' role='none'>
      <actor jid='forster@militia.lit'/>
      <reason>AWOL</reason>
    </item>
    <status code='301'/>
  </x>
</presence>
```

The `<actor>` element lets Wickham know who made the affiliation change, and the status code of 301 signals that he has been banned.

The other militia members receive a similar presence stanza.

Role changes are done in the same manner as affiliations. If Lady Catherine wants to grant speaking privileges to Elizabeth within her room, she will send an IQ-set with the desired role change:

```
<iq to='chatter@chat.rosings.lit'
    from='lady_catherine@rosings.lit/parlor'
    type='set'
    id='voice1'>
```

```
      <x xmlns='http://jabber.org/protocol/muc#admin'>
        <item nick='elizabeth' role='participant'/>
      </x>
    </iq>
```

Elizabeth's role changes from `visitor` to `participant`, and the room will send the presence change to all occupants. Note that the `nick` attribute is used to specify Elizabeth by her nickname; because roles apply to a single room visit, changing roles is done by nicknames instead of JIDs.

As you have seen, the multi-user chat protocol has quite a bit of depth. Many more use cases, configuration options, and error flows are enumerated in the extension's specification, but the topics covered in this section are enough for you to build Groupie.

BUILDING THE INTERFACE

Groupie's interface is simple, as you saw in Figure 8-1. It consists of a slightly extended login dialog box, a chat area, a participant area, and the chat input box. The HTML required to build this interface is shown in Listing 8-1, and the CSS for styling it is shown in Listing 8-2.

Available for download on Wrox.com

LISTING 8-1: groupie.html

```html
<!DOCTYPE HTML PUBLIC "-//W3C//DTD HTML 4.01//EN"
        "http://www.w3.org/TR/html4/strict.dtd">
<html>
  <head>
    <meta http-equiv="Content-type" content="text/html;charset=UTF-8">
    <title>Groupie - Chapter 8</title>

    <link rel='stylesheet' href='http://ajax.googleapis.com/ajax/libs/jqueryui
/1.7.2/themes/cupertino/jquery-ui.css'>
    <script src='http://ajax.googleapis.com/ajax/libs/jquery/1.3.2/jquery.js'>
    </script>
    <script src='http://ajax.googleapis.com/ajax/libs/jqueryui/1.7.2/jquery-ui
.js'></script>
    <script src='scripts/strophe.js'></script>
    <script src='scripts/flXHR.js'></script>
    <script src='scripts/strophe.flxhr.js'></script>

    <link rel='stylesheet' type='text/css' href='groupie.css'>
    <script type='text/javascript' src='groupie.js'></script>
  </head>
  <body>
    <h1>Groupie</h1>

    <div id='toolbar'>
      <input id='leave' type='button' value='Leave Room'
             disabled='disabled'>
    </div>

    <div>
      <div>
```

continues

LISTING 8-1 *(continued)*

```
        <span id='room-name'></span>
        <span id='room-topic'></span>
      </div>
      <div id='chat'>
      </div>

      <textarea id='input'></textarea>
    </div>

    <div id='participants'>
      <ul id='participant-list'>
      </ul>
    </div>

    <!-- login dialog -->
    <div id='login_dialog' class='hidden'>
      <label>JID:</label><input type='text' id='jid'>
      <label>Password:</label><input type='password' id='password'>
      <label>Chat Room:</label><input type='text' id='room'>
      <label>Nickname:</label><input type='text' id='nickname'>
    </div>
  </body>
</html>
```

LISTING 8-2: groupie.css

```
body {
    font-family: Helvetica;
}

h1 {
    text-align: center;
}

.hidden {
    display: none
}

#toolbar {
    text-align: center;
    padding: 5px;
    margin-bottom: 15px;
}

#room-name {
    font-size: 150%;
    font-weight: bold;
```

```
}

#room-topic {
    font-style: italic;
}

#chat-area {
    float: left;
    width: 500px;
}

#chat {
    overflow: auto;
    height: 400px;
    border: solid 1px #ccc;
}

#participants {
    float: left;
    width: 200px;
    height: 500px;
    overflow: auto;
}

#input {
    width: 95%;
    font-size: 120%;
}

.notice {
    font-style: italic;
    font-weight: bold;
    color: #3d3;
}

.error {
    color: #d33;
}

.message {
    color: #aaa;
}

.nick {
    color: #66f;
}

.self {
    color: #f66;
}

.body {
    color: #000;
```

continues

LISTING 8-2 *(continued)*

```
}

.delayed {
    opacity: 0.5;
}

.private {
    background-color: #fdd;
}

.action {
    color: #333;
}
```

You'll want the login dialog box to be presented as soon as the application is opened, just as in previous chapters. The JavaScript skeleton in Listing 8-3 has been slightly modified to work with the new fields in the login dialog box, but is otherwise the same as you've seen previously.

LISTING 8-3: groupie.js (skeleton)

```
var Groupie = {
    connection: null,
    room: null,
    nickname: null
};

$(document).ready(function () {
    $('#login_dialog').dialog({
        autoOpen: true,
        draggable: false,
        modal: true,
        title: 'Join a Room',
        buttons: {
            "Join": function () {
                Groupie.room = $('#room').val();
                Groupie.nickname = $('#nickname').val();

                $(document).trigger('connect', {
                    jid: $('#jid').val(),
                    password: $('#password').val()
                });

                $('#password').val('');
                $(this).dialog('close');
            }
        }
    });
```

```
    });

    $(document).bind('connect', function (ev, data) {
        Groupie.connection = new Strophe.Connection(
            'http://bosh.metajack.im:5280/xmpp-httpbind');
        Groupie.connection.connect(
            data.jid, data.password,
            function (status) {
                if (status === Strophe.Status.CONNECTED) {
                    $(document).trigger('connected');
                } else if (status === Strophe.Status.DISCONNECTED) {
                    $(document).trigger('disconnected');
                }
            });
    });

    $(document).bind('connected', function () {
        // nothing here yet
    });

    $(document).bind('disconnected', function () {
        // nothing here yet
    });
```

Now that the boilerplate is done, you can start adding support for joining the group chat room.

JOINING THE ROOM

As you saw in the section Public Speaking, joining group chat rooms is a simple matter of sending directed presence to your desired room JID. However, the room will immediately send you a presence broadcast for all of the other participants when you join, so you will have to handle those too. You'll also need to add support for leaving the room, in case your users care to join a different room.

First, you should add a namespace constant to the `Groupie` object, so that you don't have to keep typing the multi-user chat namespace, `http://jabber.org/protocol/muc`, over and over. Also, a flag is needed for whether the user has joined a room or not. Finally, a dictionary for the room's occupants is needed as well. Add the following attributes to the `Groupie` object:

```
NS_MUC: "http://jabber.org/protocol/muc",
joined: null,
participants: null
```

code snippet groupie.js

Next, modify the `connected` event handler to send initial presence to the server to go online and directed presence to the user's desired room JID to join the room:

```
$(document).bind('connected', function () {
    Groupie.connection.send($pres().c('priority').t('-1'));
    Groupie.connection.send(
        $pres({
```

```
            to: Groupie.room + "/" + Groupie.nickname
        }).c('x', {xmlns: Groupie.NS_MUC}));
    });
```

code snippet groupie.js

The directed presence stanza looks just like the ones you saw as examples before, but the initial presence has something new, a `priority` child.

Presence priorities give information to the user's server about which connected resources are more important for message delivery. Messages will be routed to the resources with the highest positive presence priority, and in the case of a tie, the message will be delivered to one or all of the resources with tied priorities.

The presence priority in Groupie is *negative*, which has a special meaning. Any resource with negative priority will never receive messages addressed to the bare JID. This is very useful for XMPP applications that do not intend to use private messages, because the negative priority will ensure that the application is not delivered messages it won't process. It also ensures that the user does not lose private messages that are sent to resources that are not capable of private chat.

Because Groupie doesn't handle private messages, aside from the special group chat private messages you see later, it sets the presence priority to –1 to avoid accidentally stealing private messages from users.

Now that Groupie starts the process to join a group chat room, you should add support for handling the broadcast of the other participants' presence as well as the broadcast of your own presence, which indicates the room join is complete.

Add the following highlighted lines to the `connected` event handler to set up the incoming presence handler:

```
$(document).bind('connected', function () {
    Groupie.joined = false;
    Groupie.participants = {};

    Groupie.connection.send($pres().c('priority').t('-1'));

    Groupie.connection.addHandler(Groupie.on_presence,
                                  null, "presence");
    Gropuie.connection.send(
        $pres({
            to: Groupie.room + "/" + Groupie.nickname
        }).c('x', {xmlns: Groupie.NS_MUC}));
    });
```

code snippet groupie.js

Now you must implement `on_presence()`. This handler needs to do two things at this stage. First, it must populate the participant area with the current occupants of the room. Second, it will trigger the `room_joined` event when the user's own presence shows up. The modified `Groupie` object is shown here:

```javascript
var Groupie = {
    connection: null,
    room: null,
    nickname: null,

    NS_MUC: "http://jabber.org/protocol/muc",
    joined: null,
    participants: null,

    on_presence: function (presence) {
        var from = $(presence).attr('from');
        var room = Strophe.getBareJidFromJid(from);

        // make sure this presence is for the right room
        if (room === Groupie.room) {
            var nick = Strophe.getResourceFromJid(from);

            if ($(presence).attr('type') === 'error' &&
                !Groupie.joined) {
                // error joining room; reset app
                Groupie.connection.disconnect();
            } else if (!Groupie.participants[nick] &&
                $(presence).attr('type') !== 'unavailable') {
                // add to participant list
                Groupie.participants[nick] = true;
                $('#participant-list').append('<li>' + nick + '</li>');
            }

            if ($(presence).attr('type') !== 'error' &&
                !Groupie.joined) {
                // check for status 110 to see if it's our own presence
                if ($(presence).find("status[code='110']").length > 0) {
                    // check if server changed our nick
                    if ($(presence).find("status[code='210']").length > 0) {
                        Groupie.nickname = Strophe.getResourceFromJid(from);
                    }

                    // room join complete
                    $(document).trigger("room_joined");
                }
            }
        }

        return true;
    }
};
```

The code keeps track of whether or not the room is joined in order to know when to fire the `room_joined` event. It should only fire `room_joined` the first time it receives the user's own presence as indicated by a status code of 110. If a presence error occurs, this usually signals a nickname conflict. Groupie simply resets the application in this case. Note that the group chat service may change the user's requested nickname; this change is signaled by the 210 status code, so in that case, the `nickname` property is updated to reflect the change.

You can add a handler for the `room_joined` event to let the user know their action was successful and enable the Leave Room button. Add the following handler to the end of `groupie.js`:

```
$(document).bind('room_joined', function () {
    Groupie.joined = true;

    $('#leave').removeAttr('disabled');
    $('#room-name').text(Groupie.room);

    $('#chat').append("<div class='notice'>*** Room joined.</div>")
});
```

code snippet groupie.js

All that's left is to enable the user to leave the room by wiring up the Leave Room button. Add the following code to the document ready handler:

```
$('#leave').click(function () {
    Groupie.connection.send(
        $pres({to: Groupie.room + "/" + Groupie.nickname,
               type: "unavailable"}));
    Groupie.connection.disconnect();
});
```

code snippet groupie.js

The preceding code sends directed presence of type `unavailable` to the room to exit nicely and then terminates the XMPP connection. You should make sure that the login dialog box reappears by modifying the `disconnected` event handler:

```
$(document).bind('disconnected', function () {
    Groupie.connection = null;
    $('#participant-list').empty();
    $('#room-name').empty();
    $('#room-topic').empty();
    $('#chat').empty();
    $('#login_dialog').dialog('open');
});
```

code snippet groupie.js

If you run Groupie now, you should see it join the requested room and add the list of all occupants to the participant area. Once your own presence is received, you should see "*** Room joined" printed in the chat area.

DEALING WITH PRESENCE AND MESSAGES

Once in a group chat room, the user needs to be able to send and receive messages, and their participant list should remain updated as people join and leave the room. Private messages sent to the user should be displayed specially, and the user should also be able to send private messages to other participants. You can add all these features to Groupie very easily.

Handling Room Messages

To display messages from people in the room, you must first add a handler for incoming `<message>` stanzas and then display them. You can add the appropriate handler in the `connected` event handler, right after the `addHandler()` for `<presence>` stanzas:

Available for download on Wrox.com

```
Groupie.connection.addHandler(Groupie.on_public_message,
                              null, "message", "groupchat");
```

code snippet groupie.js

Note that each message to the room will have the `type` attribute set to `groupchat`. This differentiates public messages from private ones. Later you add a handler for private messages, which have a `type` attribute equal to `chat` or `normal`.

Now you must implement `on_public_message()`, which should display incoming messages addressed to the room. Add this code to the `Groupie` object:

Available for download on Wrox.com

```
on_public_message: function (message) {
    var from = $(message).attr('from');
    var room = Strophe.getBareJidFromJid(from);
    var nick = Strophe.getResourceFromJid(from);

    // make sure message is from the right place
    if (room === Groupie.room) {
        // is message from a user or the room itself?
        var notice = !nick;

        // messages from ourself will be styled differently
        var nick_class = "nick";
        if (nick === Groupie.nickname) {
            nick_class += " self";
        }

        var body = $(message).children('body').text();

        if (!notice) {
            Groupie.add_message("<div class='message'>" +
                        "&lt;<span class='" + nick_class + "'>" +
                        nick + "</span>&gt; <span class='body'>" +
                        body + "</span></div>");
        } else {
            Groupie.add_message("<div class='notice'>*** " + body +
                        "</div>");
        }
    }
```

```
    }

    return true;
}
```

This function is less complicated than it may appear. First, the function distinguishes messages sent by the room's occupants from messages sent by the room itself and prints the message appropriately. It also uses CSS styles to differentiate messages the user sends from the messages of the other occupants. Finally, just as in previous applications, the function ensures that the content window is scrolled to the bottom when adding new lines by using the add_message() function. The add_message() helper is shown here, and should be added to the Groupie object:

Available for download on Wrox.com

```
add_message: function (msg) {
    // detect if we are scrolled all the way down
    var chat = $('#chat').get(0);
    var at_bottom = chat.scrollTop >= chat.scrollHeight -
        chat.clientHeight;

    $('#chat').append(msg);

    // if we were at the bottom, keep us at the bottom
    if (at_bottom) {
        chat.scrollTop = chat.scrollHeight;
    }
}
```

Next on the list is wiring up the input text box so that the user can send messages to the room. You do this by adding a keypress event handler and watching for the key code that corresponds to the Enter key. Add the following code to the document ready handler:

Available for download on Wrox.com

```
$('#input').keypress(function (ev) {
    if (ev.which === 13) {
        ev.preventDefault();

        var body = $(this).val();

        Groupie.connection.send(
            $msg({
                to: Groupie.room,
                type: "groupchat"}).c('body').t(body));

        $(this).val('');
    }
});
```

With this latest feature, Groupie is moderately useful. Users can join group chat rooms and partici-pate in the conversation. Unfortunately, the participant list does not track the actual state of the room yet, but you will fix that next.

Tracking Presence Changes

The `on_presence()` handler you wrote earlier does a great job of updating the participant list when-ever a new person joins the room, but it isn't kept up-to-date as people leave. You'll need to add logic to `on_presence()` to remove people when they leave the room.

The modified `on_presence()` appears in the following code with the new and modified lines high-lighted. Note that events have been added for people joining and leaving the room. You will make use of these shortly.

```
on_presence: function (presence) {
    var from = $(presence).attr('from');
    var room = Strophe.getBareJidFromJid(from);

    // make sure this presence is for the right room
    if (room === Groupie.room) {
        var nick = Strophe.getResourceFromJid(from);

        if ($(presence).attr('type') === 'error' &&
            !Groupie.joined) {
            // error joining room; reset app
            Groupie.connection.disconnect();
        } else if (!Groupie.participants[nick] &&
            $(presence).attr('type') !== 'unavailable') {
            // add to participant list
            Groupie.participants[nick] = true;
            $('#participant-list').append('<li>' + nick + '</li>');

            if (Groupie.joined) {
                $(document).trigger('user_joined', nick);
            }
        } else if (Groupie.participants[nick] &&
                $(presence).attr('type') === 'unavailable') {
            // remove from participants list
            $('#participant-list li').each(function () {
                if (nick === $(this).text()) {
                    $(this).remove();
                    return false;
                }
            });

            $(document).trigger('user_left', nick);
        }

        if ($(presence).attr('type') !== 'error' &&
            !Groupie.joined) {
            // check for status 110 to see if it's our own presence
            if ($(presence).find("status[code='110']").length > 0) {
```

```
                        // check if server changed our nick
                        if ($(presence).find("status[code='210']").length > 0) {
                            Groupie.nickname = Strophe.getResourceFromJid(from);
                        }

                        // room join complete
                        $(document).trigger("room_joined");
                    }
                }
            }

        return true;
    }
```

code snippet groupie.js

You can print helpful messages to the user whenever people join and leave by writing handlers for these two new events. The following event handlers add notice messages to the chat area on these events; add them to the end of `groupie.js`:

```
$(document).bind('user_joined', function (ev, nick) {
    Groupie.add_message("<div class='notice'>*** " + nick +
                        " joined.</div>");
});

$(document).bind('user_left', function (ev, nick) {
    Groupie.add_message("<div class='notice'>*** " + nick +
                        " left.</div>");
});
```

code snippet groupie.js

Now Groupie keeps track of who is in the room as well as when people join and leave.

Chat History

You might have noticed that often, as soon as you join a group chat room, a lot of messages appear immediately. These represent the recent chat history, and XMPP multi-user chat rooms send a configurable amount of this history to new occupants so that they have some context for the ensuing discussions. If you've ever used IRC, you may be familiar with how confusing it is to join a room in the middle of an active conversation.

It would be nice if Groupie presented this chat history differently. You can modify the `on_public_message()` handler to add a special CSS class to these messages. The room tags historical chat messages with `<delay>` elements just like the stored private messages you saw in Chapter 5. It may be that group chat servers you encounter use the legacy version of delay indication defined in XEP-0091 instead of the current version in XEP-0203. To detect the old-style delay indicators, just check for an `<x>`

element under the `jabber:x:delay` namespace. The following modified version of `on_public_ message()` adds the delayed class to messages that contain delay indicators of either type:

```
on_public_message: function (message) {
    var from = $(message).attr('from');
    var room = Strophe.getBareJidFromJid(from);
    var nick = Strophe.getResourceFromJid(from);

    // make sure message is from the right place
    if (room === Groupie.room) {
        // is message from a user or the room itself?
        var notice = !nick;

        // messages from ourself will be styled differently
        var nick_class = "nick";
        if (nick === Groupie.nickname) {
            nick_class += " self";
        }

        var body = $(message).children('body').text();

        var delayed = $(message).children("delay").length > 0  ||
            $(message).children("x[xmlns='jabber:x:delay']").length > 0;

        if (!notice) {
            var delay_css = delayed ? " delayed": "";
            Groupie.add_message("<div class='message" + delay_css + "'>" +
                                "&lt;<span class='" + nick_class + "'>" +
                                nick + "</span>&gt; <span class='body'>" +
                                body + "</span></div>");
        } else {
            Groupie.add_message("<div class='notice'>*** " + body +
                                "</div>");
        }
    }

    return true;
}
```

code snippet groupie.js

With chat history taken care of, you can now move on to the last messaging-related feature — private room messages.

Keeping It Private

When sending messages for all to see, Groupie addressed the message to the room itself, and the room rebroadcast it to all occupants. You can also address messages to specific occupants, and these messages are sent privately and not shared with the rest of the room. To complete Groupie, you'll want to add support for sending and receiving private messages within the room.

To send a private room message, you need only address the message directly to the occupant's room JID, making sure to set the `type` attribute to `chat` instead of `groupchat`. As discussed in the Anonymity section, the participant's room JID is used since the room may be configured as anonymous or semi-anonymous.

Without a different `type` attribute, the recipient would have no way to distinguish a public message from a private one. To receive private messages, you must watch for incoming messages from room occupants with a `type` attribute of `chat`.

First, add a new `<message>` stanza handler for private messages next to the others in the `connected` event handler:

```
Groupie.connection.addHandler(Groupie.on_private_message,
                              null, "message", "chat");
```

code snippet groupie.js

Next, add the `on_private_message()` function to the `Groupie` object:

```
on_private_message: function (message) {
    var from = $(message).attr('from');
    var room = Strophe.getBareJidFromJid(from);
    var nick = Strophe.getResourceFromJid(from);

    // make sure this message is from the correct room
    if (room === Groupie.room) {
        var body = $(message).children('body').text();
        Groupie.add_message("<div class='message private'>" +
                            "@@ &lt;<span class='nick'>" +
                            nick + "</span>&gt; <span class='body'>" +
                            body + "</span> @@</div>");

    }

    return true;
}
```

code snippet groupie.js

Groupie ensures the message is from a participant of the room before displaying it to the user.

Finally, you need to modify the input text box's `keypress` event handler to detect private messages and send them. Private messages are sent with the `/msg` command, which the user types into the text box. If you've used IRC clients before, this should look pretty familiar. The new handler code must parse out this special command, check it for errors or bad arguments, and then execute the intended action.

The modified `keypress` handler follows, with the changed lines highlighted:

```
$('#input').keypress(function (ev) {
    if (ev.which === 13) {
        ev.preventDefault();

        var body = $(this).val();

        var match = body.match(/^\/(.*?)(?: (.*))?$/);
        var args = null;
        if (match) {
            if (match[1] === "msg") {
                args = match[2].match(/^(.*?) (.*)$/);
                if (Groupie.participants[args[1]]) {
                    Groupie.connection.send(
                        $msg({
                            to: Groupie.room + "/" + args[1],
                            type: "chat"}).c('body').t(body));
                    Groupie.add_message(
                        "<div class='message private'>" +
                            "@@ &lt;<span class='nick self'>" +
                            Groupie.nickname +
                            "</span>&gt; <span class='body'>" +
                            args[2] + "</span> @@</div>");
                } else {
                    Groupie.add_message(
                        "<div class='notice error'>" +
                            "Error: User not in room." +
                            "</div>");
                }
            } else {
                Groupie.add_message(
                    "<div class='notice error'>" +
                        "Error: Command not recognized." +
                        "</div>");
            }
        } else {
            Groupie.connection.send(
                $msg({
                    to: Groupie.room,
                    type: "groupchat"}).c('body').t(body));
        }

        $(this).val('');
    }
});
```

code snippet groupie.js

The preceding code abstracts the command parsing logic because you add more special commands in the next section. For the `/msg` command, Groupie sends the private message to the occupant specified by the user. If the addressed occupant is not in the room or an invalid command was given, an error is shown.

Private messages are now shown in between "@@" markers and with a light red background. Adding support for one command wasn't too hard, but additional commands can be implemented extremely easily. As the final feature in this section, you should add an action command.

Describing Actions

Many chat systems support action descriptions where users describe themselves or what they are doing. Because talking about yourself in the third person is often strange, commands were added to these chat systems to make this more natural. Typically these commands were written /action or /me, and users would type something like this:

```
/me writes another XMPP application
```

You can easily add support for these to Groupie. All you need to do is to add a new clause to the command logic inside the keypress event handler and display messages starting with /me in a special way.

The following code shows the modifications needed to the command interpretation clauses:

```
if (match[1] === "msg") {
    args = match[2].match(/^(.*?) (.*)$/);
    if (Groupie.participants[args[1]]) {
        Groupie.connection.send(
            $msg({
                to: Groupie.room + "/" + args[1],
                type: "chat"}).c('body').t(body));
        Groupie.add_message(
            "<div class='message private'>" +
                "@@ &lt;<span class='nick self'>" +
                Groupie.nickname +
                "</span>&gt; <span class='body'>" +
                args[2] + "</span> @@</div>");
    } else {
        Groupie.add_message(
            "<div class='notice error'>" +
                "Error: User not in room." +
                "</div>");
    }
} else if (match[1] === "me" || match[1] === "action") {
    Groupie.connection.send(
        $msg({
            to: Groupie.room,
            type: "groupchat"}).c('body')
            .t('/me ' + match[2]));
} else {
    Groupie.add_message(
        "<div class='notice error'>" +
            "Error: Command not recognized." +
            "</div>");
}
```

code snippet groupie.js

Lastly, modify the relevant parts of `on_public_message()` to match the parts in the modified version here:

```
if (!notice) {
    var delay_css = delayed ? " delayed": "";

    var action = body.match(/\/me (.*)$/);
    if (!action) {
        Groupie.add_message(
            "<div class='message" + delay_css + "'>" +
                "&lt;<span class='" + nick_class + "'>" +
                nick + "</span>&gt; <span class='body'>" +
                body + "</span></div>");
    } else {
        Groupie.add_message(
            "<div class='message action " + delay_css + "'>" +
                "* " + nick + " " + action[1] + "</div>");
    }
} else {
    Groupie.add_message("<div class='notice'>*** " + body +
                        "</div>");
}
```

code snippet groupie.js

Groupie is nearly done, and it's already quite a usable group chat client. However, if you are a room moderator, you will need some extra functionality for managing the occupants.

MANAGING THE ROOM

The last features you will add to Groupie are all about room management. These are the tools users need to run their own successful group chat rooms, including manipulating the room's topic, kicking and banning users, and managing the room's administrators.

Changing Topics

Every room has a topic, which is typically shown at the top of the room. Depending on the room's configuration, users may be able to change the topic message, or this action may be restricted to administrators. Groupie will need to display the current topic and allow authorized users to change it.

Topic changes are sent out as bodiless messages that contain a `<subject>` element, and the content of the `<subject>` element becomes the new room topic. You can watch for these messages in the `on_public_message()` handler. The following code should be inserted right before the line containing "`if (!notice) {`":

```
// look for room topic change
var subject = $(message).children('subject').text();
if (subject) {
    $('#room-topic').text(subject);
}
```

code snippet groupie.js

You can allow users to change the topic by adding a `/topic` command to the `keypress` event handler. The modified command logic appears here with the new lines highlighted:

```
} else if (match[1] === "me" || match[1] === "action") {
    Groupie.connection.send(
        $msg({
            to: Groupie.room,
            type: "groupchat"}).c('body')
            .t('/me ' + match[2]));
} else if (match[1] === "topic") {
    Groupie.connection.send(
        $msg({to: Groupie.room,
            type: "groupchat"}).c('subject')
            .text(match[2]));
} else {
    Groupie.add_message(
        "<div class='notice error'>" +
            "Error: Command not recognized." +
            "</div>");
}
```

code snippet groupie.js

Groupie's users can now see and change room topics, assuming that the room's configuration allows them to do so.

Dealing with Troublemakers

It is a sad fact that nearly every gathering place on the Internet is prey to those who would disturb peaceful conversations. Luckily, the multi-user chat protocol has quite a few tools for dealing with these troublemakers, and you add two of these to Groupie: kicking out and banning.

Kicking out users from the room simply removes them from the room temporarily and functions as a stern warning. As you saw in the section Public Speaking, kicking out users is accomplished by sending an IQ-set for an occupant that changes the occupant's role to `none`. In order for a user to kick out an occupant, the user must have the role of `moderator`.

Add the `/kick` command by adding the following clause to the command logic:

```
} else if (match[1] === "topic") {
    Groupie.connection.send(
        $msg({to: Groupie.room,
            type: "groupchat"}).c('subject')
            .text(match[2]));
} else if (match[1] === "kick") {
    Groupie.connection.sendIQ(
        $iq({to: Groupie.room,
            type: "set"})
            .c('query', {xmlns: Groupie.NS_MUC + "#admin"})
            .c('item', {nick: match[2],
                        role: "none"}));
} else {
    Groupie.add_message(
```

```
            "<div class='notice error'>" +
                "Error: Command not recognized." +
                "</div>");
    }
```

You can test this feature by creating a new room so that you are the room's owner and then joining the room with another XMPP account. Once the second account is joined, you can type /kick nickname on the first account to remove the second one from the room.

Banning a user is nearly the same, except that you must modify the user's affiliation instead of their role. A banned user has an affiliation of outcast, and won't be able to join the room again until the ban is lifted.

Add the following clause to the command logic to add support for /ban:

```
    } else if (match[1] === "kick") {
        Groupie.connection.sendIQ(
            $iq({to: Groupie.room,
                 type: "set"})
                .c('query', {xmlns: Groupie.NS_MUC + "#admin"})
                .c('item', {nick: match[2],
                            role: "none"}));
    } else if (match[1] === "ban") {
        Groupie.connection.sendIQ(
            $iq({to: Groupie.room,
                 type: "set"})
                .c('query', {xmlns: Groupie.NS_MUC + "#admin"})
                .c('item', {jid: Groupie.participants[match[2]],
                            affiliation: "outcast"}));
    } else {
        Groupie.add_message(
            "<div class='notice error'>" +
                "Error: Command not recognized." +
                "</div>");
    }
```

Users must be banned using their bare JIDs, not their room nicknames. It is also possible to ban an entire domain, but usually moderators try to restrict the ban to avoid inadvertently punishing the innocent. The preceding code uses the participants dictionary to get the JID for an occupant's nickname. Previously, Groupie only stored the value true in this dictionary; you will have to add the following highlighted lines to the on_presence() handler to store the JID if that information is available:

```
    } else if (!Groupie.participants[nick] &&
               $(presence).attr('type') !== 'unavailable') {
        // add to participant list
        var user_jid = $(presence).find('item').attr('jid');
        Groupie.participants[nick] = user_jid || true;
```

```
            $('#participant-list').append('<li>' + nick + '</li>');

            if (Groupie.joined) {
                $(document).trigger('user_joined', nick);
            }
        } else if (Groupie.participants[nick] &&
```

code snippet groupie.js

Groupie can now help room administrators and owners keep the peace as long as one of them is around. Because administrators have to sleep sometime, it is often helpful to recruit new administrators to help out.

Recruiting Help

The final feature you will add to Groupie is granting and revoking administrator privileges. This is done via the /op and /deop commands, named after their IRC counterparts.

Adding or removing administrators is done very similarly to banning users; you need only change someone's affiliation with the room. Add the following highlighted clauses to implement the new commands:

```
        } else if (match[1] === "ban") {
            Groupie.connection.sendIQ(
                $iq({to: Groupie.room,
                     type: "set"})
                    .c('query', {xmlns: Groupie.NS_MUC + "#admin"})
                    .c('item', {jid: Groupie.participants[match[2]],
                                affiliation: "outcast"}));
        } else if (match[1] === "op") {
            Groupie.connection.sendIQ(
                $iq({to: Groupie.room,
                     type: "set"})
                    .c('query', {xmlns: Groupie.NS_MUC + "#admin"})
                    .c('item', {jid: Groupie.participants[match[2]],
                                affiliation: "admin"}));
        } else if (match[1] === "deop") {
            Groupie.connection.sendIQ(
                $iq({to: Groupie.room,
                     type: "set"})
                    .c('query', {xmlns: Groupie.NS_MUC + "#admin"})
                    .c('item', {jid: Groupie.participants[match[2]],
                                affiliation: "none"}));
        } else {
            Groupie.add_message(
                "<div class='notice error'>" +
                    "Error: Command not recognized." +
                    "</div>");
        }
```

code snippet groupie.js

Groupie is finally complete, and can be used by normal participants and moderators alike. The final JavaScript code appears in Listing 8-4.

LISTING 8-4: groupie.js (final)

```javascript
var Groupie = {
    connection: null,
    room: null,
    nickname: null,

    NS_MUC: "http://jabber.org/protocol/muc",
    joined: null,
    participants: null,

    on_presence: function (presence) {
        var from = $(presence).attr('from');
        var room = Strophe.getBareJidFromJid(from);

        // make sure this presence is for the right room
        if (room === Groupie.room) {
            var nick = Strophe.getResourceFromJid(from);

            if ($(presence).attr('type') === 'error' &&
                !Groupie.joined) {
                // error joining room; reset app
                Groupie.connection.disconnect();
            } else if (!Groupie.participants[nick] &&
                $(presence).attr('type') !== 'unavailable') {
                // add to participant list
                var user_jid = $(presence).find('item').attr('jid');
                Groupie.participants[nick] = user_jid || true;
                $('#participant-list').append('<li>' + nick + '</li>');

                if (Groupie.joined) {
                    $(document).trigger('user_joined', nick);
                }
            } else if (Groupie.participants[nick] &&
                    $(presence).attr('type') === 'unavailable') {
                // remove from participants list
                $('#participant-list li').each(function () {
                    if (nick === $(this).text()) {
                        $(this).remove();
                        return false;
                    }
                });

                $(document).trigger('user_left', nick);
            }

            if ($(presence).attr('type') !== 'error' &&
                !Groupie.joined) {
                // check for status 110 to see if it's our own presence
```

continues

LISTING 8-4 *(continued)*

```
            if ($(presence).find("status[code='110']").length > 0) {
                // check if server changed our nick
                if ($(presence).find("status[code='210']").length > 0) {
                    Groupie.nickname = Strophe.getResourceFromJid(from);
                }

                // room join complete
                $(document).trigger("room_joined");
            }
        }
    }

    return true;
},

on_public_message: function (message) {
    var from = $(message).attr('from');
    var room = Strophe.getBareJidFromJid(from);
    var nick = Strophe.getResourceFromJid(from);

    // make sure message is from the right place
    if (room === Groupie.room) {
        // is message from a user or the room itself?
        var notice = !nick;

        // messages from ourself will be styled differently
        var nick_class = "nick";
        if (nick === Groupie.nickname) {
            nick_class += " self";
        }

        var body = $(message).children('body').text();

        var delayed = $(message).children("delay").length > 0  ||
            $(message).children("x[xmlns='jabber:x:delay']").length > 0;

        // look for room topic change
        var subject = $(message).children('subject').text();
        if (subject) {
            $('#room-topic').text(subject);
        }

        if (!notice) {
            var delay_css = delayed ? " delayed": "";

            var action = body.match(/\/me (.*)$/);
            if (!action) {
                Groupie.add_message(
                    "<div class='message" + delay_css + "'>" +
                        "&lt;<span class='" + nick_class + "'>" +
```

```
                                    nick + "</span>&gt; <span class='body'>" +
                                    body + "</span></div>");
                     } else {
                         Groupie.add_message(
                             "<div class='message action " + delay_css + "'>" +
                                 "* " + nick + " " + action[1] + "</div>");
                     }
                 } else {
                     Groupie.add_message("<div class='notice'>*** " + body +
                                         "</div>");
                 }
             }

        return true;
    },

    add_message: function (msg) {
        // detect if we are scrolled all the way down
        var chat = $('#chat').get(0);
        var at_bottom = chat.scrollTop >= chat.scrollHeight -
            chat.clientHeight;

        $('#chat').append(msg);

        // if we were at the bottom, keep us at the bottom
        if (at_bottom) {
            chat.scrollTop = chat.scrollHeight;
        }
    },

    on_private_message: function (message) {
        var from = $(message).attr('from');
        var room = Strophe.getBareJidFromJid(from);
        var nick = Strophe.getResourceFromJid(from);

        // make sure this message is from the correct room
        if (room === Groupie.room) {
            var body = $(message).children('body').text();
            Groupie.add_message("<div class='message private'>" +
                                "@@ &lt;<span class='nick'>" +
                                nick + "</span>&gt; <span class='body'>" +
                                body + "</span> @@</div>");

        }

        return true;
    }
};

$(document).ready(function () {
    $('#login_dialog').dialog({
        autoOpen: true,
        draggable: false,
```

continues

LISTING 8-4 *(continued)*

```
        modal: true,
        title: 'Join a Room',
        buttons: {
            "Join": function () {
                Groupie.room = $('#room').val();
                Groupie.nickname = $('#nickname').val();

                $(document).trigger('connect', {
                    jid: $('#jid').val(),
                    password: $('#password').val()
                });

                $('#password').val('');
                $(this).dialog('close');
            }
        }
});

$('#leave').click(function () {
    $('#leave').attr('disabled', 'disabled');
    Groupie.connection.send(
        $pres({to: Groupie.room + "/" + Groupie.nickname,
                type: "unavailable"}));
    Groupie.connection.disconnect();
});

$('#input').keypress(function (ev) {
    if (ev.which === 13) {
        ev.preventDefault();

        var body = $(this).val();

        var match = body.match(/^\/(.*?)(?: (.*))?$/);
        var args = null;
        if (match) {
            if (match[1] === "msg") {
                args = match[2].match(/^(.*?) (.*)$/);
                if (Groupie.participants[args[1]]) {
                    Groupie.connection.send(
                        $msg({
                            to: Groupie.room + "/" + args[1],
                            type: "chat"}).c('body').t(body));
                    Groupie.add_message(
                        "<div class='message private'>" +
                            "@@ &lt;<span class='nick self'>" +
                            Groupie.nickname +
                            "</span>&gt; <span class='body'>" +
                            args[2] + "</span> @@</div>");
                } else {
                    Groupie.add_message(
                        "<div class='notice error'>" +
```

```
                            "Error: User not in room." +
                            "</div>");
        }
    } else if (match[1] === "me" || match[1] === "action") {
        Groupie.connection.send(
            $msg({
                to: Groupie.room,
                type: "groupchat"}).c('body')
                .t('/me ' + match[2]));
    } else if (match[1] === "topic") {
        Groupie.connection.send(
            $msg({to: Groupie.room,
                type: "groupchat"}).c('subject')
                .text(match[2]));
    } else if (match[1] === "kick") {
        Groupie.connection.sendIQ(
            $iq({to: Groupie.room,
                type: "set"})
                .c('query', {xmlns: Groupie.NS_MUC + "#admin"})
                .c('item', {nick: match[2],
                            role: "none"}));
    } else if (match[1] === "ban") {
        Groupie.connection.sendIQ(
            $iq({to: Groupie.room,
                type: "set"})
                .c('query', {xmlns: Groupie.NS_MUC + "#admin"})
                .c('item', {jid: Groupie.participants[match[2]],
                            affiliation: "outcast"}));
    } else if (match[1] === "op") {
        Groupie.connection.sendIQ(
            $iq({to: Groupie.room,
                type: "set"})
                .c('query', {xmlns: Groupie.NS_MUC + "#admin"})
                .c('item', {jid: Groupie.participants[match[2]],
                            affiliation: "admin"}));
    } else if (match[1] === "deop") {
        Groupie.connection.sendIQ(
            $iq({to: Groupie.room,
                type: "set"})
                .c('query', {xmlns: Groupie.NS_MUC + "#admin"})
                .c('item', {jid: Groupie.participants[match[2]],
                            affiliation: "none"}));
    } else {
        Groupie.add_message(
            "<div class='notice error'>" +
                "Error: Command not recognized." +
                "</div>");
    }
} else {
    Groupie.connection.send(
        $msg({
            to: Groupie.room,
            type: "groupchat"}).c('body').t(body));
```

continues

LISTING 8-4 *(continued)*

```
            }

            $(this).val('');
        }
    });
});

$(document).bind('connect', function (ev, data) {
    Groupie.connection = new Strophe.Connection(
        'http://bosh.metajack.im:5280/xmpp-httpbind');
    Groupie.connection.connect(
        data.jid, data.password,
        function (status) {
            if (status === Strophe.Status.CONNECTED) {
                $(document).trigger('connected');
            } else if (status === Strophe.Status.DISCONNECTED) {
                $(document).trigger('disconnected');
            }
        });
});

$(document).bind('connected', function () {
    Groupie.joined = false;
    Groupie.participants = {};

    Groupie.connection.send($pres().c('priority').t('-1'));

    Groupie.connection.addHandler(Groupie.on_presence,
                                  null, "presence");
    Groupie.connection.addHandler(Groupie.on_public_message,
                                  null, "message", "groupchat");
    Groupie.connection.addHandler(Groupie.on_private_message,
                                  null, "message", "chat");

    Groupie.connection.send(
        $pres({
            to: Groupie.room + "/" + Groupie.nickname
        }).c('x', {xmlns: Groupie.NS_MUC}));
});

$(document).bind('disconnected', function () {
    Groupie.connection = null;
    $('#room-name').empty();
    $('#room-topic').empty();
    $('#participant-list').empty();
    $('#chat').empty();
```

```
        $('#login_dialog').dialog('open');
    });

    $(document).bind('room_joined', function () {
        Groupie.joined = true;

        $('#leave').removeAttr('disabled');
        $('#room-name').text(Groupie.room);

        Groupie.add_message("<div class='notice'>*** Room joined.</div>")
    });

    $(document).bind('user_joined', function (ev, nick) {
        Groupie.add_message("<div class='notice'>*** " + nick +
                            " joined.</div>");
    });

    $(document).bind('user_left', function (ev, nick) {
        Groupie.add_message("<div class='notice'>*** " + nick +
                            " left.</div>");
    });
```

IMPROVING GROUPIE

Groupie is a simple group chat client, but it is full of potential. Try adding some more features to make your users even happier:

➤ Add support for chatting in multiple rooms at the same time.

➤ Let room owners configure some basic settings for newly created rooms.

➤ Combine a version of Chapter 7's browser with Groupie to allow users to find new chat rooms and join them easily.

SUMMARY

XMPP's multi-user chat protocol allows a group of people to create a shared space for communication. Typically, it is used for text communication between human users, but it can also be used for many other purposes. Some people have used group chat to enable bots to exchange data. Others have used it to create rich collaborative environments or to provide the basis for game systems, which you do in Chapter 11.

In this chapter, you created a simple group chat client that implemented an important cross-section of MUC's feature set. By the end you learned:

➤   How to join, leave, and create group chat rooms

➤   How to participate in conversations

➤   How to send and receive private messages within a room

➤   How to manage the room's topic

➤   How roles and affiliations work and the different privileges they enable

➤   How to deal with and ban troublemakers

➤   How to create new room administrators

➤   How to deal with chat history

In the next chapter, you discover a similar protocol called Publish-Subscribe, which is used primarily for notification and one-to-many broadcast systems.

Publishing and Subscribing:
A Shared Sketch Pad Introduction

WHAT'S IN THIS CHAPTER?

> ➤   How publish-subscribe systems work

> ➤   Using Data Forms

> ➤   Creating and configuring pubsub nodes

> ➤   Subscribing and unsubscribing from pubsub nodes

> ➤   Publishing and receiving events

> ➤   Using HTML5's <canvas> element

Chatting online is a great way for teams to communicate, but it is often ineffective at communicating visual ideas. In a face-to-face setting, the speaker can step up to a whiteboard and begin sketching out their ideas. In this chapter, you develop an application called SketchCast, which allows a presenter to broadcast a whiteboard session to a virtually unlimited number of participants. You develop SketchCast using one of XMPP's most powerful extensions, publish-subscribe, or *pubsub* as it is commonly called.

SketchCast is an example of a very simple vector drawing program. Similar programs can be found in almost every introductory book on graphics or GUI programming. SketchCast stretches this functionality to a shared environment, giving the entire audience a view of what the presenter is drawing.

A lot of functionality is required to bring this application to life beyond just the simple graphics. To enable others to see what someone is drawing, you must capture the drawing actions, transform them into a format suitable for transmission, send these actions across a network, and re-create them on the audience's computers. In addition, presenters will need some mechanism for setting up this whole system, keeping track of participants, and ensuring everyone is getting the same data.

XMPP and pubsub make this complex set of actions easy to achieve. It handles the heavy lifting, leaving you free to concentrate on only a few key pieces.

This chapter presents many of the core ideas of the XMPP pubsub system as well as an introduction to working with XMPP's Data Forms, which is used in many XMPP extensions.

SKETCHCAST PREVIEW

Before you get started, Figure 9-1 shows a peek at what the final application will look like.

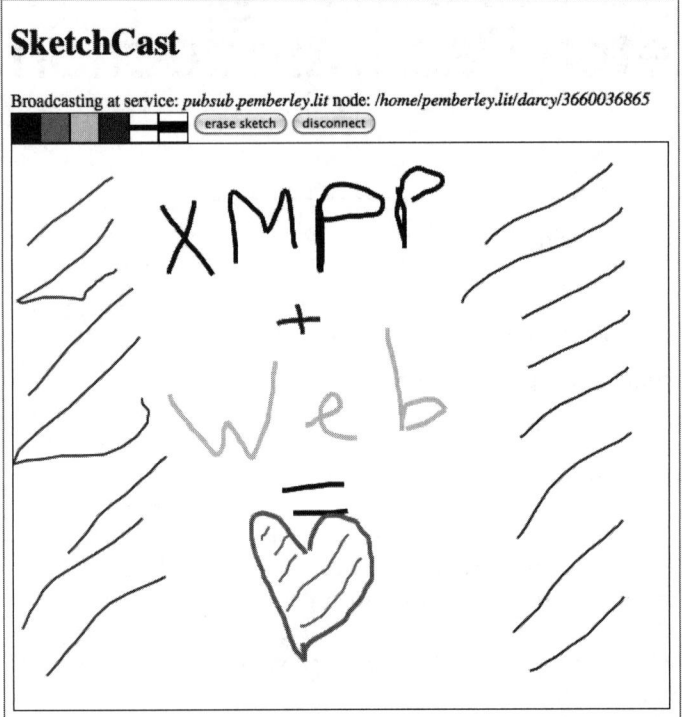

FIGURE 9-1

SketchCast has a simple user interface consisting of a toolbar of various drawing tools and a large sketching area. The presenter can pick from a number of colors or line widths and can also erase the board. These controls will be disabled for the audience.

SKETCHCAST DESIGN

SketchCast has a lot of functionality, but as you will see, it is actually one of the simplest XMPP pubsub applications possible. This is a testament to the immense power and flexibility of the pubsub system. It's time to dive in and see what pubsub has to offer.

Everything Is Pubsub

Publish-subscribe systems are everywhere — newspapers, blogs, television, and even e-mail lists. Almost everything you need to know about how pubsub works is right there in its name. There is a channel of communication, subscribers who are interested in data sent on that channel, and publishers who can send data across the channel.

Imagine that you start a new magazine, *XMPP Aficionado*. The magazine becomes quite popular, and it attracts thousands of subscribers who give you their money and their addresses. Whenever a new issue is ready, you publish it and mail it out to every subscriber's address.

Publishing a magazine is hard work; think about all the time you must spend collecting money and addresses, printing each issue, and driving the truck full of magazines to the post office. Wouldn't it be great if you could just worry about writing the next issue and sending that out to a company that would handle the rest of the work? Oh, look! There is Pubsub, Inc. right there in the yellow pages.

XMPP pubsub takes all the manual labor out of building publish-subscribe systems, just as Pubsub, Inc. promises to make publishing your magazine easier. Computing machines made calculation so easy that sophisticated applications, like spreadsheets and web browsers, were built on top of them. In the same way, XMPP pubsub enables new types of applications to be built on top of its foundations.

Now that you know what pubsub systems are, you can learn to use them to power the SketchCast application.

Presenter's Flow

The first thing the SketchCast application must do for a would-be presenter is to create a channel for them to publish sketches. In XMPP pubsub these channels are called *nodes*.

Pubsub applications vary in their needs, so the system offers a configuration facility to allow for maximum flexibility. SketchCast will need to make some tweaks to the default configuration of its pubsub nodes. Many different XMPP extensions have similar configuration systems so it makes sense to have a standardized way to manipulate these systems. XMPP's Data Forms provides this mechanism, and SketchCast will need to use this to request and submit a configuration form.

Once a node is created and configured, the application needs to publish the user's drawing actions to the node. Once these events are published, pubsub takes over and makes sure that they get delivered to the interested audience members.

While the presenter is sketching, they'll want to know how many people are watching. SketchCast will need to retrieve the subscriber list from the pubsub node so that it can present this data to them.

Once the sketching session is done, it's good to clean up after it by deleting the pubsub node.

Audience's Flow

Once a presenter has created a node and is ready to begin, they'll communicate the existence of the node to potential audience members. You don't need to worry about how this happens; perhaps it is sent inside a company-wide e-mail to all employees.

Each audience member will type in the node to SketchCast, and the application will subscribe to the pubsub node for the sketch. From then on the pubsub system will make sure that any new data that is published will be sent to them.

Some audience members will probably be busy playing Minesweeper and will not notice the presenter's e-mail until after they have already begun drawing. These users will need to catch up to the rest of the group, so SketchCast will need to use pubsub to fetch the drawing actions they have missed.

Each drawing action will need to be rendered in the sketching area, just like it appeared on the presenter's screen. SketchCast will translate the drawing events into graphics on the screen to re-create the sketch.

Finally, once the sketch is over or the audience members' attentions are spent, they will want to stop watching the presentation. The application will have to unsubscribe from the pubsub node to ensure that it doesn't keep getting events that the user isn't interested in.

Keep this design for SketchCast in mind as you learn about the Data Forms and Publish-Subscribe extensions. Once you learn these new XMPP protocols, you start to build SketchCast.

FILLING OUT FORMS

Every application's data is different. A spreadsheet organizes data in one format, whereas a recipe tracker organizes it completely differently. Even different versions of the *same* application may have different needs. Instead of creating new formats for each application, it's often better to create a flexible format that can be used by a wide range of applications. Data Forms is the most widely used such format in the XMPP toolbox.

You'll need to use forms to configure your pubsub nodes for SketchCast.

What Is The Data Forms Extension?

Data Forms takes a bit of inspiration from forms in HTML. It allows applications to define a form with fields of various types — text fields, list fields, and address fields to name a few. It also provides a lightweight workflow on top of these forms enabling applications to request, provide, submit, and cancel forms.

Forms are used in several places in the Pubsub protocol, including configuring pubsub nodes and dealing with subscription options. Many XMPP protocols depend on forms for similar functionality. Multi-User Chat (XEP-0045) uses forms for room configuration among other things; Ad-Hoc Commands (XEP-0050) uses forms for command input and output; and Service Discovery Extensions (XEP-0128) relies on forms as a way to easily add extensibility to a another protocol.

An example form is shown here. This form has a `type` attribute whose value is `form`, which means that the system expects it to be filled it out. You might receive such a form as a result of requesting one from some XMPP service. Don't worry if you don't understand the purpose of some of the attributes yet; you will see these in more detail in the next section.

```
<x xmlns='jabber:x:data' type='form'>
  <title>A Simple Form</title>
  <instructions>Fill out this simple form!</instructions>
  <field type='text-single'
         label="What's your favorite color?"
         var='favorite_color'>
    <required/>
  </field>
</x>
```

Forms of this type often come with labels, and for certain fields, a list of options will also be included. When forms are filled out and returned, usually only the response data is sent, and the metadata for the fields is omitted.

A completed version of the preceding form might look like this:

```
<x xmlns='jabber:x:data' type='submit'>
  <field type='text-single'
         var='favorite_color'>
    <value>orange</value>
  </field>
</x>
```

Forms are easily extensible. If someone later decides that this form should ask about your favorite food, the question can be added to the form without changing the protocol at all. A well-designed user interface could just add the new field to a dialog box and send the user's response back to the server.

Form Elements, Fields, and Types

You saw that forms consist of some metadata and some fields in the examples in the previous section. These elements are all contained inside of a form element, which looks like `<x xmlns='jabber:x:data' type='form'/>`. The `<x>` element is an historical artifact; if protocol designers were building Data Forms today, this would probably have been the more descriptive `<form>`.

Inside the `<x>` element are a few bits of metadata, like the `<instructions>` element you saw in the preceding section, and the form's fields.

The <x> Element's type Attribute

The `type` attribute in a form has four possible values: `form`, `submit`, `cancel`, and `result`. These relate to the form's place in a particular workflow.

A value of `form` means that the form is blank and needs filling out. If you were attempting to open a new bank account, and the bank clerk handed you a clipboard with a form on it, that form would have a `type` attribute with the value of `form`.

The `submit` value is used when you return a completed form. Once you've filled out that new account form at the bank, you hand it back to the teller, and that form now has a `type` of `submit`.

If you change your mind about completing a form, you can send back an empty form with the `cancel` type. As you're sitting in the bank filling out the new account form, you might notice that the bank across the street has a big sign advertising its lower fees. You would stop filling out the form, hand it back to the clerk, and walk across the street to the other bank. The poor clerk is now holding a form with a `type` of `cancel`.

Finally, there is the `result` type. This type is used when the form represents a generic data set, or the result of submitting a form generated some response data. After completing a new account form at the cheaper bank, the clerk creates the account and hands you a document containing your account details. This document is a form with a `type` of `result`.

Form Metadata

In addition to fields, forms may have a title and a set of instructions. These are intended for human consumption in the case that the form is presented directly in the user interface. You saw these elements used in the previous section with the example favorite color form.

Form Fields

The heart of every form is the collection of fields waiting to be filled out or communicating result data. Unlike HTML forms, XMPP's Data Forms has a fairly rich set of data types that can be specified. Form fields can even be flagged as required or optional and contain other metadata to assist with display to users.

Every field can have some metadata associated with it. You've already seen the `label` attribute in the first example. Fields may also contain the `<required>` element, which means that any submission of the form must include a value for that field. And just like the `<instructions>` element in the form itself, each field can have a `<desc>` element containing a human-readable description of the field's purpose.

Every field must have a `var` attribute, which uniquely identifies the field. This can be any identifier you like, but most XMPP extensions use standardized form fields as defined in Field Standardization for Data Forms (XEP-0068). There is more about this in the next section.

Each field has a `type` attribute that describes the type of data for the field. The following types are defined:

➤ `text-single`: A single line of text, similar to `<input type='text'>` in HTML

➤ `text-private`: A single line of text that is obscured during entry, similar to `<input type='password'>` in HTML

➤ `text-multi`: Multiple lines of text, similar to `<textarea>` in HTML

➤ `list-single`: A single value from a predefined list of options, similar to `<select>` in HTML

➤ `list-multi`: Multiple values from a predefined list of options, similar to `<select multiple='multiple'>` in HTML

➤ `jid-single`: A single JID

➤ `jid-multi`: Multiple JIDs

➤ `boolean`: Either true or false

➤ `hidden`: A field hidden from the user and whose value is normally returned unmodified

➤ `fixed`: A human-readable description, used for section headers in the form

The options for `list-single` and `list-multi` fields are specified by including `<option>` elements as children of the field. Each `<option>` element can have a `label` attribute, and the value of the option is specified in a `<value>` child. Take a look at an example `list-single` field with three options:

```
<field type='list-single' var='animals'
       label='Pick an animal'>
  <option label='Fox'>
    <value>fox</value>
  </option>
  <option label='Hare'>
    <value>hare</value>
  </option>
  <option label='Tortoise'>
    <value>tortoise</value>
  </option>
</field>
```

Fields may also specify a default value by including a `<value>` element as an immediate child. If the field can have multiple values, as with `list-multi`, `jid-multi`, and `text-multi` fields, multiple `<value>` children can be present. The same `<value>` elements store the filled out fields' values when forms are returned. The following is an example of a submitted form field that was used to inquire about XMPP server administrators:

```
<field type='jid-multi' var='admins'>
  <value>alice@example.com</value>
  <value>bob@example.com</value>
</field>
```

Forms allow a rich, structured set of data to be manipulated or returned. In Figure 9-2 you can see a screenshot of an XMPP client rendering a form related to multi-user chat room configuration. This form allows a user to make configuration changes easily. Even if the server supports some new feature that wasn't defined in the multi-user chat specification, the user can still customize it due to the flexible nature of forms.

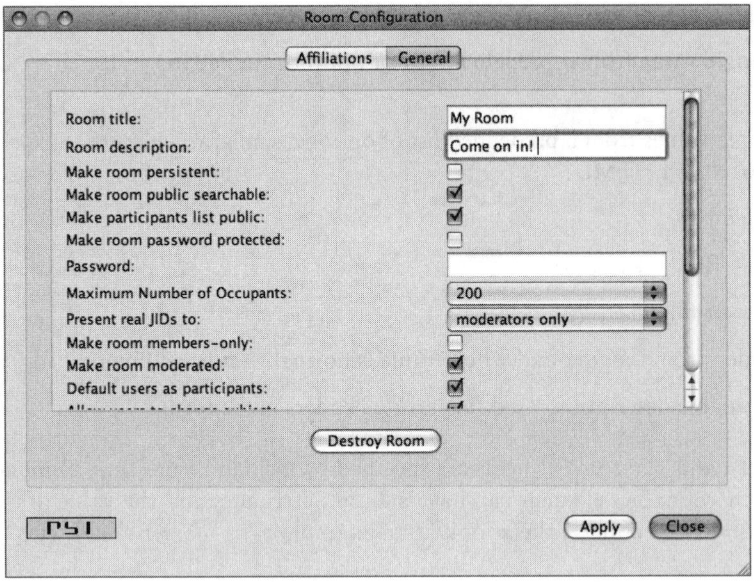

FIGURE 9-2

Standardized Form Fields

Flexibility is a wonderful attribute to have, but having forms be so malleable does have a downside. How do you get everyone to agree what the fields should be for common forms? It didn't take long for the XMPP community to address this problem with Field Standardization for Data Forms (XEP-0068).

Each standardized form has a form type, which is encoded in a special field. The XMPP registrar manages a list of standard types used in XMPP extensions, but custom protocol developers are not required to register their form types. Because you'll be using standardized pubsub-related forms in the SketchCast application, you should see an example of such a form. The following is a node configuration form that has been submitted to change the title of a pubsub node:

```
<x xmlns='jabber:x:data' type='submit'>
  <field var='FORM_TYPE' type='hidden'>
    <value>http://jabber.org/protocol/pubsub#node_config</value>
  </field>
  <field var='pubsub#title'>
    <value>Best Node Ever</value>
  </field>
</x>
```

The standardized form type is included as a special hidden field with a `var` attribute equal to `FORM_TYPE`. The value of this field is the form type's identifier. The pubsub extension defines several different types of forms, and consulting the pubsub specification in XEP-0060, you can see that `http://jabber.org/protocol/pubsub#node_config` is the identifier for the node configuration form.

Fields within a standardized form will have `var` attributes that are defined in the specification for the form. The node configuration form for pubsub is specified in section 16.4.2 of XEP-0060, and an excerpt that includes the `pubsub#title` field is shown here:

```
<form_type>
  <name>http://jabber.org/protocol/pubsub#node_config</name>
  <!-- parts omitted -->
  <field var='pubsub#title'
         type='text-single'
         label='A friendly name for the node'/>
  <!-- parts omitted -->
</form_type>
```

The content of the `<name>` element is what will appear in the `FORM_TYPE` field, and the `<field>` element specifies what kind of field it will be.

The SketchCast application will use standardized forms to configure the pubsub node, and custom forms to transmit drawing information from the publisher to the subscribers. If the SketchCast protocol was published in a XEP of its own, it might define and register a standard form type for the drawing information.

WORKING WITH PUBSUB NODES

Pubsub nodes are the communication hubs of the publish-subscribe system. Users and applications can subscribe to a node that they are interested in, and when data is published there, the node will immediately broadcast that data to all subscribers.

These nodes are provided by pubsub services. Nearly every XMPP server has a built-in pubsub service for its users. For example, the well-known jabber.org XMPP server has a public pubsub service located at pubsub.jabber.org. All you need to know to start using pubsub is the location of a pubsub service. You can create an interesting pubsub node, and to subscribe, a user needs to know the service's address and the node's name.

Pubsub nodes support a wide range of actions and configurations. The SketchCast application will make use of many of the basic actions: creating nodes, configuring nodes, publishing to nodes, deleting nodes, subscribing to nodes, and receiving events from nodes. It may seem like a lot of work, but you see shortly that pubsub nodes are pretty simple.

Creating Nodes

SketchCast's users can't accomplish much unless there is a pubsub node to publish and subscribe to. The presenting user will need to create a node so that all the viewers can subscribe to it.

A pubsub node is created by sending an IQ-set stanza to the pubsub service:

```
<iq to='pubsub.pemberley.lit'
    from='darcy@pemberley.lit/library'
    type='set'
    id='create1'>
```

```
    <pubsub xmlns='http://jabber.org/protocol/pubsub'>
      <create node='latest_books'/>
    </pubsub>
  </iq>
```

Most actions on pubsub nodes will look very similar to this one. You've seen several stanzas like this one in other chapters already; the difference here is the `<pubsub>` element.

Other than Service Discovery queries (see Chapter 7), pubsub-related actions all contain a `<pubsub>` element qualified by one of the pubsub namespaces. Here, `http://jabber.org/protocol/pubsub` is used, which is the main pubsub namespace, but some actions, such as node configuration, require related namespaces like `http://jabber.org/protocol/pubsub#owner`. It's easy when reading these examples to skip over the namespace used and to assume that they are all the same. If you encounter errors with pubsub stanzas, please double-check that you are using the correct namespace for your actions.

Inside the `<pubsub>` element is the action requested, `<create>`. The node to create is specified in the `node` attribute. If there isn't already a node with this name, and if you are allowed to create nodes on this service, the server will acknowledge that your request was successful:

```
<iq from='pubsub.pemberley.lit'
    to='darcy@pemberley.lit/library'
    type='result'
    id='create1'/>
```

If the node already existed, or if you didn't have authorization to create it, the server would have returned an IQ-error with a `<conflict>` or `<forbidden>` condition.

Now your pubsub node is created and ready to receive events.

It's possible to let the server choose the name when you create a node. Sometimes it doesn't matter what the node is called, and if the user doesn't have to pick a name, the application becomes easier to use. You'll be using these *instant nodes* in SketchCast, and the following example shows how to create one:

```
<iq from='darcy@pemberley.lit/library'
    to='pubsub.pemberley.lit'
    type='set'
    id='instant1'>
  <pubsub xmlns='http://jabber.org/protocol/pubsub'>
    <create/>
  </pubsub>
</iq>
```

Creating instant nodes is even easier than named ones. One question remains, though; what node did the server create? Thankfully, when you create an instant node, the server includes the node's name with its response.

```
<iq from='pubsub.pemberley.lit'
    to='darcy@pemberley.lit/library'
    type='result'
    id='instant1'>
  <pubsub xmlns='http://jabber.org/protocol/pubsub'>
    <create node='1390361429'/>
  </pubsub>
</iq>
```

The server's response looks just like your original creation request for a named node. It has generated a random number for the node name because it was instructed that you didn't care what the node was called. Pubsub services may name instant nodes differently; one might name each node with a random string of characters, and another might use a numeric counter.

Configuring Nodes

Newly created pubsub nodes have a default configuration that is useful for many purposes. Normally the default configuration is for a publicly accessible node that persists a few of the most recently published items and allows only the node's creator (also called the owner) to publish to it. The exact configuration that is used depends on the service and its configuration.

Applications with special requirements may need to configure pubsub nodes appropriately to ensure that those requirements are met. SketchCast, for example, should persist quite a few recent drawing actions or new subscribers may be confused by a partial sketch. The pubsub node's configuration also includes things like the title of the node, the access controls, and whether event notifications should include the original data.

Pubsub node configuration is done by submitting a form inside a `<configure>` action. Node configuration must be done by the owner of the node, so the `<pubsub>` element's namespace is slightly different than the previous example. First, request a configuration form to see what options are available:

```
<iq from='darcy@pemberley.lit/library'
    to='pubsub.pemberley.lit'
    type='get'
    id='configure1'>
  <pubsub xmlns='http://jabber.org/protocol/pubsub#owner'>
    <configure node='latest_books'/>
  </pubsub>
</iq>
```

The server returns a blank configuration form. Many of the form fields are omitted in the following form so you can concentrate on the structure of the protocol instead of its fine details. Also, XMPP servers vary in their support of the pubsub feature set, so don't be surprised if a server doesn't return some of these fields.

```
<iq from='pubsub.pemberley.lit'
    to='darcy@pemberley.lit/library'
    type='result'
    id='configure1'>
  <pubsub xmlns='http://jabber.org/protocol/pubsub#owner'>
    <configure node='latest_books'>
      <x xmlns='jabber:x:data' type='form'>
        <field var='FORM_TYPE' type='hidden'>
          <value>http://jabber.org/protocol/pubsub#node_config</value>
        </field>
        <field var='pubsub#title' type='text-single'
               label='A friendly name for the node'/>
        <field var='pubsub#persist_items' type='boolean'
               label='Persist items to storage'>
          <value>true</value>
```

```
          </field>
          <field var='pubsub#max_items' type='text-single'
                label='Max # of items to persist'>
            <value>10</value>
          </field>
          <!-- more fields -->
        </x>
      </configure>
    </pubsub>
  </iq>
```

This configuration form is just like the ones you saw in the section Filling Out Forms. The first field in the form is the form type identifier and after that are the normal fields. The three fields shown in the form are settings that control the title of the node, whether it persists previously published items, and if so, how many items it will persist.

Because you want to change the node's settings, you must submit a completed form back to the server containing your desired configuration. The form submission stanza appears almost identical to the preceding example, but the field labels and types have been removed, the field values filled in, and the form's type attribute changed to submit. Only the three settings from the example have changed here, but you could also change a single setting or all possible settings at the same time:

```
<iq from='darcy@pemberley.lit/library'
    to='pubsub.pemberley.lit'
    type='set'
    id='configure2'>
  <pubsub xmlns='http://jabber.org/protocol/pubsub#owner'>
    <configure node='latest_books'>
      <x xmlns='jabber:x:data' type='submit'>
        <field var='FORM_TYPE'>
          <value>http://jabber.org/protocol/pubsub#node_config</value>
        </field>
        <field var='pubsub#title'>
          <value>Books I've Read Lately</value>
        </field>
        <field var='pubsub#persist_items'>
          <value>true</value>
        </field>
        <field var='pubsub#max_items'>
          <value>100</value>
        </field>
      </x>
    </configure>
  </pubsub>
</iq>
```

The server should respond to your submission with a successful reply:

```
<iq from='pubsub.pemberley.lit'
    to='darcy@pemberley.lit/library'
    type='result'
    id='configure2'/>
```

Now Mr. Darcy has a pubsub node with a nice title to entice subscribers and the ability to persist the data about the most recent 100 books he has read.

Pubsub Events

Pubsub nodes and their configuration are necessary and useful, but they don't do much by themselves. The real value of pubsub nodes is in the events that are published to them and broadcast to subscribers.

Anything can be included in a pubsub event. The pubsub service doesn't know or care what is inside the event; it simply broadcasts this data to a node's subscribers. The content of a pubsub event is called its payload. Generally, subscribers will know what payloads are published at a given node and how to interpret them. Some common event payloads include blog posts in the Atom syndication format or information about songs currently playing in User Tune format (XEP-0118).

When publishing, the event is wrapped in a `<publish>` action within the `<pubsub>` element, and when receiving events, the same event is carried in a `<message>` stanza. In both cases the event payload is the same. Following is an example of an event with a User Tune payload:

```
<tune xmlns='http://jabber.org/protocol/tune'>
  <artist>Elizabeth Bennet</artist>
  <title>A Piano Song for Lady Catherine</title>
</tune>
```

Forms are flexible enough to represent many kinds of payloads, and Mr. Darcy has chosen to use a form to encode the latest books that he has read. Whenever he finishes reading a book, he publishes an event to his pubsub node using the following form-based payload:

```
<x xmlns='jabber:x:data' type='result'>
  <field var='title'>
    <value>A History of Pemberley</value>
  </field>
  <field var='author'>
    <value>Sir Lewis de Bourgh</value>
  </field>
</x>
```

The previous examples both included event payloads, but nodes can also be configured to send only event notifications. In this case, the payload can be retrieved by querying the pubsub node. You see how to publish and receive events as well as how to retrieve payloads in the next sections.

Publishing to a Node

Mr. Darcy, having just finished his latest book, must now publish a new event to his pubsub node. You saw Mr. Darcy's event payloads in the previous section; here is how they are published:

```
<iq from='darcy@pemberley.lit/library'
    to='pubsub.pemberley.lit'
    type='set'
    id='publish1'>
  <pubsub xmlns='http://jabber.org/protocol/pubsub'>
```

```
            <publish node='latest_books'>
              <item>
                <x xmlns='jabber:x:data' type='result'>
                  <field var='title'>
                    <value>A History of Pemberley</value>
                  </field>
                  <field var='author'>
                    <value>Sir Lewis de Bourgh</value>
                  </field>
                </x>
              </item>
            </publish>
          </pubsub>
        </iq>
```

In this example, the event payload is wrapped in an `<item>` element and then placed inside the `<publish>` action. If Mr. Darcy had just finished two books, he would just append the second one in its own `<item>` element.

The server will accept the publish request and return a successful response:

```
<iq from='pubsub.pemberly.lit'
    to='darcy@pemberley.lit/library'
    type='result'
    id='publish1'>
  <pubsub pubsub xmlns='http://jabber.org/protocol/pubsub'>
    <publish node='latest_books'>
      <item id='821b576dfabfc6b358b6ec4139b87f5c'/>
    </publish>
  </pubsub>
</iq>
```

Notice that the server's response also includes an `<item>` element. Because Mr. Darcy's `<item>` element did not contain an `id` attribute, the server created one for him since every item must have an identifier. These identifiers are used for notifications, item retrieval, and retraction.

Mr. Darcy could also have specified an `id` attribute in his original publish stanza, and the server would have used that `id` instead. This is very similar to the earlier examples of normal and instant node creation.

Subscribing and Unsubscribing

Elizabeth and Georgiana are both avid readers and quite curious about what books Mr. Darcy has had his nose in lately. Each of the ladies can subscribe to Mr. Darcy's pubsub node by sending an IQ-set with the `<subscribe>` action:

```
<iq from='elizabeth@longbourn.lit/outside'
    to='pubsub.pemberley.lit'
    type='set'
    id='subscribe1'>
  <pubsub pubsub xmlns='http://jabber.org/protocol/pubsub'>
```

```
        <subscribe node='latest_books'
                   jid='elizabeth@longbourn.lit/outside'/>
    </pubsub>
</iq>
```

Elizabeth has specified both the node she wants to subscribe to as well as the address to which events should be delivered. As long as she stays a subscriber, she'll be immediately notified whenever Mr. Darcy finishes a book and publishes a corresponding event.

The server sends a successful response to Elizabeth's request:

```
<iq from='pubsub.pemberley.lit'
    to='elizabeth@longbourn.lit/outside'
    type='result'
    id='subscribe1'>
    <pubsub pubsub xmlns='http://jabber.org/protocol/pubsub'>
        <subscribe node='latest_books'
                   jid='elizabeth@longbourn.lit/outside'
                   subscription='subscribed'/>
    </pubsub>
</iq>
```

The `subscription` attribute informs Elizabeth about the status of her subscription, and in this example, it informs her she is fully subscribed. Pubsub nodes can be configured with a variety of access models, some of which require the node's owner to approve subscription requests manually. If Mr. Darcy's node were configured this way, the `subscription` attribute would have a value of `pending`.

If for some reason Mr. Darcy had configured his node to allow only a specific set of people to subscribe (called a whitelist access model), Elizabeth's request might have been returned with a `not-allowed` error:

```
<iq from='pubsub.pemberley.lit'
    to='elizabeth@longbourn.lit/outside'
    type='error'
    id='subscribe1'>
    <pubsub pubsub xmlns='http://jabber.org/protocol/pubsub'>
        <subscribe node='latest_books'
                   jid='elizabeth@longbourn.lit/outside'/>
    </pubsub>
    <error type='cancel'>
        <not-allowed xmlns='urn:ietf:params:xml:ns:xmpp-stanzas'/>
        <closed-node xmlns='http://jabber.org/protocol/pubsub#errors'/>
    </error>
</iq>
```

Now that Elizabeth has subscribed, she'll receive event broadcasts when Mr. Darcy finishes a book. Event broadcasts are sent in `<message>` stanzas containing an `<event>` child with the `http://jabber.org/protocol/pubsub#event` namespace. The `<event>` element will contain one or more `<item>` elements wrapped in an `<items>` element; the payloads are contained within the `<item>` elements, if included. In this example, a lone item appears, and the item's `id` attribute matches the one the server returned earlier to Mr. Darcy. The payload is also identical to the one Mr. Darcy published.

```
<message from='pubsub.pemberley.lit'
         to='elizabeth@longbourn.lit/outside'>
  <event xmlns='http://jabber.org/protocol/pubsub#event'>
    <items node='latest_books'>
      <item id='821b576dfabfc6b358b6ec4139b87f5c'>
        <x xmlns='jabber:x:data' type='result'>
          <field var='title'>
            <value>A History of Pemberley</value>
          </field>
          <field var='author'>
            <value>Sir Lewis de Bourgh</value>
          </field>
        </x>
      </item>
    </items>
  </event>
</message>
```

Unlike Elizabeth, Georgiana sees Darcy all the time, and this frequent contact has the benefit of keeping her informed about Darcy's reading habits without having a pubsub subscription. After a few days of being subscribed to Darcy's pubsub node, she's decided the information published there is not useful to her. She can unsubscribe by sending an IQ-set with the <unsubscribe> action:

```
<iq from='georgiana@pemberley.lit/piano'
    to='pubsub.pemberley.lit'
    type='set'
    id='unsubscribe1'>
  <pubsub pubsub xmlns='http://jabber.org/protocol/pubsub'>
    <unsubscribe node='latest_books'
                 jid='georgiana@pemberley.lit/piano'/>
  </pubsub>
</iq>
```

The server responds with a successful result:

```
<iq from='pubsub.pemberley.lit'
    to='georgiana@pemberley.lit/piano'
    type='result'
    id='unsubscribe1'/>
```

Any future book updates from Mr. Darcy will no longer be sent to Georgiana.

Retrieving Subscriptions

Mr. Darcy is of an inquisitive mind, and though he loathes admitting it, he often wants to see how popular his book updates have become. When he publishes a new update, he gets no indication of how many people have received his event. Luckily, Mr. Darcy can easily query the list of subscribers to his pubsub node:

```
<iq from='darcy@pemberley.lit/library'
    to='pubsub.pemberley.lit'
```

```
      type='get'
      id='subscribers1'>
   <pubsub xmlns='http://jabber.org/protocol/pubsub#owner'>
      <subscriptions node='latest_books'/>
   </pubsub>
</iq>
```

You can see that Mr. Darcy has used the `http://jabber.org/protocol/pubsub#owner` namespace because retrieving the subscriber list is an action restricted to the node's owner. Inside the normal `<pubsub>` element he's placed a `<subscriptions>` action referencing his pubsub node. The server returns an unfortunately short subscriber list:

```
<iq from='pubsub.pemberley.lit'
    to='darcy@pemberley.lit/library'
    type='result'
    id='subscribers1'>
   <pubsub xmlns='http://jabber.org/protocol/pubsub#owner'>
      <subscriptions node='latest_books'>
         <subscription jid='elizabeth@longbourn.lit/outside'
                       subscription='subscribed'/>
         <subscription jid='bingley@netherfield.lit/house'
                       subscription='subscribed'/>
      </subscriptions>
   </pubsub>
</iq>
```

Only his dear friend Charles and that willful girl Elizabeth care to know what books he's been reading.

Retrieving Items

Elizabeth just subscribed to Mr. Darcy's `latest_books` node, and she has missed his event broadcasts from earlier in the week. She must investigate his past reading material if she wishes to learn more about him.

Remember that Mr. Darcy configured his node to persist items. Anyone can query his node for the most recently published items. Here, Elizabeth requests the last five items by sending an IQ-get stanza to the node with the `<items>` action:

```
<iq from='elizabeth@longbourn.lit/outside'
    to='pubsub.pemberley.lit'
    type='get'
    id='items1'>
   <pubsub xmlns='http://jabber.org/protocol/pubsub'>
      <items node='latest_books' max_items='3'/>
   </pubsub>
</iq>
```

The `<items>` element contains a `node` attribute just like the other actions you've seen previously. Elizabeth has also set the `max_items` attribute to 3 because she is only interested in the recent history. If she had omitted `max_items`, the server would interpret it as a request to send all the historical data it has been configured to keep. If she had set `max_items` to 500, which is much larger than the configured maximum for the node, the server would have sent as many as were available.

The server responds with the requested items along with their payloads:

```
<iq from='pubsub.pemberley.lit'
    to='elizabeth@longbourn.lit/outside'
    type='result'
    id='items1'>
  <pubsub xmlns='http://jabber.org/protocol/pubsub'>
    <items node='latest_books'>
      <item id='4f900045977f0ccd372c4a670bcba27f'>
        <x xmlns='jabber:x:data' type='result'>
          <field var='title'>
            <value>Of Acquaintances and Persuasion</value>
          </field>
          <field var='author'>
            <value>Daleforth Carnham</value>
          </field>
        </x>
      </item>
      <item id='16ddab0d5b3572388446c552d1bdf793'>
        <x xmlns='jabber:x:data' type='result'>
          <field var='title'>
            <value>Managing Temperment</value>
          </field>
          <field var='author'>
            <value>Sarah Pratt</value>
          </field>
        </x>
      </item>
      <item id='e4139c9d583558c172a28f68ec036c6c'>
        <x xmlns='jabber:x:data' type='result'>
          <field var='title'>
            <value>The Haunting at Hertfordshire</value>
          </field>
          <field var='author'>
            <value>Sir William Lucas</value>
          </field>
        </x>
      </item>
    </items>
  </pubsub>
</iq>
```

The node could have been configured to send only notifications, in which case the payloads would be missing. Had Mr. Darcy's node been configured this way, the server's response would have appeared like this:

```
<iq from='pubsub.pemberley.lit'
    to='elizabeth@longbourn.lit/outside'
    type='result'
    id='items1'>
  <pubsub xmlns='http://jabber.org/protocol/pubsub'>
    <items node='latest_books'>
      <item id='4f900045977f0ccd372c4a670bcba27f'/>
      <item id='16ddab0d5b3572388446c552d1bdf793'/>
```

```
            <item id='e4139c9d583558c172a28f68ec036c6c'/>
        </items>
      </pubsub>
  </iq>
```

A separate request must be sent to the server to retrieve the items with their payloads. Elizabeth would send an IQ-get with an `<items>` action as before, but the `<items>` element would contain the list of items she is interested in. An example is shown here:

```
<iq from='elizabeth@longbourn.lit/outside'
    to='pubsub.pemberley.lit'
    type='get'
    id='items2'>
  <pubsub xmlns='http://jabber.org/protocol/pubsub'>
    <items node='latest_books'>
      <item id='4f900045977f0ccd372c4a670bcba27f'/>
      <item id='16ddab0d5b3572388446c552d1bdf793'/>
      <item id='e4139c9d583558c172a28f68ec036c6c'/>
    </items>
  </pubsub>
</iq>
```

The server will then respond with the payloads just as in the original example.

If a node is configured to send only notifications, subscribers will receive `<message>` containing a list of items that are new. A similar retrieval process is necessary to get the event payloads for these items.

Subscription Management

You saw that when subscribing to a pubsub node, you must include the JID at which you want to receive event notifications. This JID can be either the bare JID (as with elizabeth@longbourn.lit) or a full JID (as with darcy@pemberley.lit/library). Because delivery of events is done with `<message>` stanzas, the delivery semantics are different depending on whether a subscription is for the bare or full JID. Whether an application should use the bare or full JID depends on the situation.

Normally, each subscription will last as long as the pubsub node exists or until the user unsubscribes. A pubsub node can also have a different subscription life cycle; the specification contains several examples of expiring subscriptions (see section 12.18 of XEP-0060 for an example). For instance, anonymously connected users' subscriptions will be removed when their session terminates, even if they never unsubscribe explicitly. Some clever developers are even working on presence-based subscriptions that can be canceled as soon as the subscriber goes offline.

Considering the number of available pubsub services and nodes, Elizabeth might forget just what she is subscribed to and where events are supposed to be sent. If Elizabeth remembers the pubsub services that she might have subscriptions on, she can ask them for a list of her subscriptions:

```
<iq from='elizabeth@longbourn.lit/outside'
    to='pubsub.pemberley.lit'
    type='get'
```

```
        id='mysubs1'>
    <pubsub xmlns='http://jabber.org/protocol/pubsub'>
      <subscriptions/>
    </pubsub>
  </iq>
```

Elizabeth asks the service at pubsub.pemberley.lit to list her subscriptions across all nodes on the service. She could also specify a `node` attribute on the `<subscriptions>` action to limit her query to a specific node. Here, the server informs her that in addition to her subscription to Mr. Darcy's latest books, she also has a forgotten subscription to Georgiana's public diary:

```
<iq from='pubsub.pemberley.lit'
    to='elizabeth@longbourn.lit/outside'
    type='result'
    id='mysubs1'>
  <pubsub xmlns='http://jabber.org/protocol/pubsub'>
    <subscriptions>
      <subscription node='latest_books'
                    jid='elizabeth@longbourn.lit/outside'
                    subscription='subscribed'/>
      <subscription node='public_diary'
                    jid='elizabeth@longbourn.lit'
                    subscription='subscribed'/>
    </subscriptions>
  </pubsub>
</iq>
```

You've now seen many of the major use cases in pubsub, and this is enough knowledge about the protocol to create this chapter's application.

BROADCASTING SKETCHES USING PUBSUB

It's time to put theory into practice. You've spent the bulk of this chapter getting familiar with Data Forms and Publish-Subscribe, and this new knowledge will make it easy to build the SketchCast application.

The presenting user must create a pubsub node, turn drawing events into form-based payloads, publish the events to the node, and delete the node once finished. Users in the audience need to subscribe to the presenter's pubsub node, retrieve the past drawing events, translate events into drawing commands, handle new event notifications, and eventually unsubscribe from the node. All the while the application should be user friendly, handle common errors, and enable users to communicate visually.

Building the Interface

The SketchCast user interface needs only a few major pieces. First you need someplace to draw. You'll also need some buttons to change the color being used, to change the thickness of the lines, to erase the drawing, and to disconnect. You also need a small status bar to report what's going on to the user. Finally, you need a login dialog box and an error dialog box.

The HTML for the application, shown in Listing 9-1, contains all of these interface elements.

LISTING 9-1: sketchcast.html

```html
<!DOCTYPE HTML PUBLIC "-//W3C//DTD HTML 4.01//EN"
         "http://www.w3.org/TR/html4/strict.dtd">
<html>
  <head>
    <meta http-equiv="Content-type" content="text/html;charset=UTF-8" />
    <title>SketchCast - Chapter 9</title>

<link rel='stylesheet' href='http://ajax.googleapis.com/ajax/libs/jqueryui/1.
7.2/themes/cupertino/jquery-ui.css'>
    <script src='http://ajax.googleapis.com/ajax/libs/jquery/1.3.2/jquery.js'>
    </script>
    <script src='http://ajax.googleapis.com/ajax/libs/jqueryui/1.7.2/jquery-u
i.js'></script>
    <script src='scripts/strophe.js'></script>
    <script src='scripts/flXHR.js'></script>
    <script src='scripts/strophe.flxhr.js'></script>

    <link rel='stylesheet' type='text/css' href='sketchcast.css'>
    <script type='text/javascript' src='sketchcast.js'></script>
  </head>
  <body>
    <h1>SketchCast</h1>

    <!-- status bar -->
    <div id='status'></div>

    <!-- drawing tool buttons.  The ids are the button values -->
    <div class='button disabled color' id='color-000'></div>
    <div class='button disabled color' id='color-f00'></div>
    <div class='button disabled color' id='color-0f0'></div>
    <div class='button disabled color' id='color-00f'></div>
    <div class='button disabled linew' id='color-2'><div></div></div>
    <div class='button disabled linew' id='color-4'><div></div></div>
    <input id='erase' type='button' value='erase sketch'
           disabled>
    <input id='disconnect' type='button' value='disconnect'
           disabled>
    <div class='clear'></div>

    <!-- drawing area -->
    <canvas id='sketch' class='disabled' width='600'
           height='500'></canvas>

    <!-- login dialog -->
    <div id='login_dialog' class='hidden'>
```

continues

LISTING 9-1 *(continued)*

```
    <label>JID:</label><input type='text' id='jid'>
    <label>Password:</label><input type='password' id='password'>
    <label>Pubsub service:</label><input type='text' id='service'>
    <label>Pubsub node:</label><input type='text' id='node'>
  </div>

  <!-- empty error dialog -->
  <div id='error_dialog' class='hidden'>
    <p></p>
  </div>
</body>
</html>
```

The CSS for this application is shown in Listing 9-2.

LISTING 9-2: sketchcast.css

```css
.clear {
    clear: both;
}

.button {
    border: solid 1px black;
    width: 25px;
    height: 25px;
    float: left;
}

div.disabled {
    -moz-opacity: 0.25;
    opacity: 0.25;
}

.hidden {
    display: none;
}

#sketch {
    border: solid 1px black;
}

#color-000 {
    background-color: #000;
}

#color-f00 {
    background-color: #f00;
}

#color-0f0 {
    background-color: #0f0;
```

```
    }

    #color-00f {
        background-color: #00f;
    }

    #width-2 div {
        background-color: #000;
        height: 5px;
        margin-top: 10px;
    }

    #width-4 div {
        background-color: #000;
        height: 10px;
        margin-top: 7px;
    }

    #erase {
        margin-left: 5px;
    }
```

The two dialog boxes start off hidden and the status bar starts empty. All other controls are shown but disabled. When the presenter starts publishing a sketch, the toolbar and drawing area will be enabled. Viewers' toolbars will remain disabled, but the drawing area will be become enabled once they are subscribed to a sketch.

Sketching with Canvas

Before you worry about the XMPP parts of the application, you should wire up the drawing area and the drawing tools so that you can make some test sketches.

Sketching is done with a virtual pen, similar to the ones found in many consumer graphics applications. The end of the pen is the mouse pointer, and it will leave ink on the drawing area while the mouse button is pressed. The toolbar buttons are used to change the color of the ink, the thickness of the lines produced, and to erase the entire sketch.

First, you must keep track of whether the pen is up or down and connect these to the `mouseup` and `mousedown` events. Next, whenever the mouse moves, you should check if the pen is down and, if so, draw a line from its old position to the current position. Create a file called `sketchcast.js` and add the following code to it:

Available for download on Wrox.com

```
var SketchCast = {
    pen_down: false,
    old_pos: null
};

$(document).ready(function () {
    $('#sketch').mousedown(function () {
        SketchCast.pen_down = true;
    });

    $('#sketch').mouseup(function () {
```

```javascript
            SketchCast.pen_down = false;
    });

    $('#sketch').mousemove(function (ev) {
        // get the position of the drawing area, our offset
        var offset = $(this).offset();
        // calculate our position within the drawing area
        var pos = {x: ev.pageX - offset.left,
                   y: ev.pageY - offset.top};

        if (SketchCast.pen_down) {
            if (!SketchCast.old_pos) {
                SketchCast.old_pos = pos;
                return;
            }

            // render the line segment
            var ctx = $('#sketch').get(0).getContext('2d');
            ctx.beginPath();
            ctx.moveTo(SketchCast.old_pos.x, SketchCast.old_pos.y);
            ctx.lineTo(pos.x, pos.y);
            ctx.stroke();

            SketchCast.old_pos = pos;
        } else {
            SketchCast.old_pos = null;
        }
    });
});
```

code snippet sketchcast.js

Once your application has loaded, it binds the mousedown, mouseup, and mousemove events. The mousedown and mouseup events simply change the pen state; all the real work is in mousemove.

In order to draw anything, you'll need to know exactly where you are inside the drawing area. This is slightly tricky because the coordinate system for the <canvas> element begins at its upper-left corner but the mouse coordinates from the mousemove event are relative to the top left of the browser's viewport. jQuery helps resolve this difference with its offset() function, which will give you the coordinates of an element relative to the viewport. If you subtract these from the mousemove event coordinates, the result is a set of coordinates relative to the top left of the drawing area.

The HTML5 <canvas> element is capable of some amazing things, but this application's needs are quite modest. All the drawing logic needed for SketchCast is explained shortly, but if you are interested in what else canvas elements can do, there is a great tutorial on the Opera developer's site at http://dev.opera.com/articles/view/html-5-canvas-the-basics/.

All canvas operations require a drawing context, which contains drawing information like the current color and line width. If you've ever done graphics programming before, it's very likely you've seen drawing contexts like these. Because SketchCast is only capable of two-dimensional drawing, you create a 2d context using the getContext() function from the canvas API as shown here:

```javascript
var ctx = $('#sketch').get(0).getContext('2d');
```

Call `beginPath()` on the context to start defining a path. Paths can be quite complex, but you'll only be using simple line segments in SketchCast. `moveTo()` is used to go to the last known position of the mouse without marking the canvas and `lineTo()` is used to add a line segment from the previous position to the current location. The path is now completed, so you can make it appear on the canvas by calling `stroke()`. That's all there is to it!

Load SketchCast into a web browser and try a few sketches.

It's pretty fun to play around with, but before long it gets boring drawing thin, black lines. You can make sketches more interesting by enabling the buttons on the toolbar so that the pen's color and width are changeable. Bind the `click` event on each of the toolbar buttons and implement them as shown here. Make the highlighted modifications to `sketchcast.js`:

```
var SketchCast = {
    pen_down: false,
    old_pos: null,
    color: '000',
    line_width: 4
};

$(document).ready(function () {
    $('#sketch').mousedown(function () {
        SketchCast.pen_down = true;
    });

    $('#sketch').mouseup(function () {
        SketchCast.pen_down = false;
    });

    $('#sketch').mousemove(function (ev) {
        // get the position of the drawing area, our offset
        var offset = $(this).offset();
        // calculate our position within the drawing area
        var pos = {x: ev.pageX - offset.left,
                   y: ev.pageY - offset.top};

        if (SketchCast.pen_down) {
            if (!SketchCast.old_pos) {
                SketchCast.old_pos = pos;
                return;
            }

            // render the line segment
            var ctx = $('#sketch').get(0).getContext('2d');
            ctx.strokeStyle = '#' + SketchCast.color;
            ctx.lineWidth = SketchCast.line_width;
            ctx.beginPath();
            ctx.moveTo(SketchCast.old_pos.x, SketchCast.old_pos.y);
            ctx.lineTo(pos.x, pos.y);
            ctx.stroke();

            SketchCast.old_pos = pos;
        } else {
```

```
            SketchCast.old_pos = null;
        }
    });

    $('.color').click(function (ev) {
        SketchCast.color = $(this).attr('id').split('-')[1];
    });

    $('.linew').click(function (ev) {
        SketchCast.line_width = $(this).attr('id').split('-')[1];
    });

    $('#erase').click(function () {
        var ctx = $('#sketch').get(0).getContext('2d');
        ctx.fillStyle = '#fff';
        ctx.strokeStyle = '#fff';
        ctx.fillRect(0, 0, 600, 500);
    });
});
```

code snippet sketchcast.js

Two new state variables have been added — `color` and `line_width` — and the code has been modified to use these values while drawing. The erase button implementation is straightforward; it draws a white rectangle over the whole canvas. The toolbar buttons, however, warrant a little more explanation.

All the color buttons work almost identically except for the actual color value they set. Instead of writing several different handlers, one for each button, you can use the button's `id` attribute to store the color the button will set. All the color buttons have the CSS class `color`, and whenever one of them is pressed, you can grab the color value out of its `id` attribute to set the drawing color. The same trick also works for the line width buttons. This saves a lot of typing!

Reload the SketchCast page in your web browser and exercise your new creative options!

Logging In and Making Nodes

The next step in bringing SketchCast to life is to start building in pubsub support so that users can share drawings with others. First, you'll want to enable the login dialog box and ensure that it pops up when the application starts. Then you'll connect to the XMPP server and either create and configure a pubsub node if the user is presenting or subscribe to an existing one if he is just watching.

The login dialog box has the normal fields for the username and password, but it also contains two fields for the pubsub service and the pubsub node. If a presenter wants to create a new sketch, they will leave the pubsub node blank, and if a viewer wants to watch a sketch, they simply enter the sketch's node. Put the following code at the top of your document ready handler:

```
$('#login_dialog').dialog({
    autoOpen: true,
    draggable: false,
    modal: true,
    title: 'Connect to a SketchCast',
```

```
        buttons: {
            "Connect": function () {
                $(document).trigger('connect', {
                    jid: $('#jid').val(),
                    password: $('#password').val(),
                    service: $('#service').val(),
                    node: $('#node').val()
                });

                $('#password').val('');
                $(this).dialog('close');
            }
        }
    });
```

As with the other applications, SketchCast will need to keep track of the connection; it must also store the pubsub service and node. SketchCast also needs some namespace constants for pubsub and forms. Add the following attributes to the `SketchCast` object:

```
connection: null,
service: null,
node: null,

NS_DATA_FORMS: "jabber:x:data",
NS_PUBSUB: "http://jabber.org/protocol/pubsub",
NS_PUBSUB_OWNER: "http://jabber.org/protocol/pubsub#owner",
NS_PUBSUB_ERRORS: "http://jabber.org/protocol/pubsub#errors",
NS_PUBSUB_NODE_CONFIG: "http://jabber.org/protocol/pubsub#node_config"
```

You also need to hook up the error dialog box. For simplicity, all errors are treated as fatal and terminate the connection when they occur. You don't want to confuse users, so when they close the error dialog box, you must re-open the login dialog box so that they can start over. Later, you'll add a function to report errors that opens this dialog box. Add this code to the document ready handler:

```
$('#error_dialog').dialog({
    autoOpen: false,
    draggable: false,
    modal: true,
    title: 'Whoops!  Something Bad Happened!',
    buttons: {
        "Ok": function () {
            $(this).dialog('close');
            $('#login_dialog').dialog('open');
        }
    }
});
```

Now add the familiar connection logic event handlers at the end of `sketchcast.js`:

```
$(document).bind('connect', function (ev, data) {
    $('#status').html('Connecting..');

    var conn = new Strophe.Connection(
        'http://bosh.metajack.im:5280/xmpp-httpbind');

    conn.connect(data.jid, data.password, function (status) {
        if (status === Strophe.Status.CONNECTED) {
            $(document).trigger('connected');
        } else if (status === Strophe.Status.DISCONNECTED) {
            $(document).trigger('disconnected');
        }
    });

    SketchCast.connection = conn;
    SketchCast.service = data.service;
    SketchCast.node = data.node;
});

$(document).bind('connected', function () {
    // nothing here yet
});
```

code snippet sketchcast.js

Once SketchCast is connected, it must send initial presence and set up or subscribe to a pubsub node. Modify the `connected` event handler to accomplish this:

```
$(document).bind('connected', function () {
    $('#status').html("Connected.");

    // send negative presence since we're not a chat client
    SketchCast.connection.send($pres().c('priority').t('-1'));

    if (SketchCast.node.length > 0) {
        // a node was specified, so we attempt to subscribe to it

        // first, set up a callback for the events
        SketchCast.connection.addHandler(
            SketchCast.on_event,
            null, "message", null, null, SketchCast.service);

        // now subscribe
        var subiq = $iq({to: SketchCast.service,
                         type: "set"})
            .c('pubsub', {xmlns: SketchCast.NS_PUBSUB})
            .c('subscribe', {node: SketchCast.node,
                             jid: SketchCast.connection.jid});
        SketchCast.connection.sendIQ(subiq,
                                     SketchCast.subscribed,
```

```
                                    SketchCast.subscribe_error);
    } else {
        // a node was not specified, so we start a new sketchcast
        var createiq = $iq({to: SketchCast.service,
                            type: "set"})
            .c('pubsub', {xmlns: SketchCast.NS_PUBSUB})
            .c('create');
        SketchCast.connection.sendIQ(createiq,
                                    SketchCast.created,
                                    SketchCast.create_error);
    }
});
```

A negative presence priority is used because SketchCast is not capable of dealing with normal chat messages. You used this before in Chapter 8 to avoid accidentally stealing private messages from the user's other connected resources.

If the user has supplied a node, the application prepares a pubsub event handler, builds a subscription stanza — just like the ones from the "Working with Pubsub Nodes" section — and sends the request to the server. If they receive a successful reply, the `subscribed()` function is called; otherwise, an error has occurred and `subscribe_error()` is invoked. A `<message>` handler is added so that when a pubsub event is received, `on_event()` can process it.

If a node is not supplied, SketchCast builds and sends a similar IQ-set stanza to create a node. Once the node is created, the code calls `created()`, or, on any IQ-error response, `create_error()` is called.

The initial implementation of `SketchCast.on_event()` does nothing. You'll be adding more to it later. Add this placeholder to the `SketchCast` object:

```
on_event: function (msg) {
    // blank for now
}
```

Now add the subscription handlers to the `SketchCast` object:

```
subscribed: function (iq) {
    $(document).trigger("reception_started");
},

subscribe_error: function (iq) {
    SketchCast.show_error("Subscription failed with " +
                        SketchCast.make_error_from_iq(iq));
}
```

Once successfully subscribed, the code fires a custom `reception_started` event. If the subscription fails, an error is shown. You'll need to implement the two error helper functions, `show_error()` and `make_error_from_iq()`, by adding the following to the `SketchCast` object:

```
make_error_from_iq: function (iq) {
    var error = $(iq)
        .find('*[xmlns="' + Strophe.NS.STANZAS + '"]')
        .get(0).tagName;
    var pubsub_error = $(iq)
        .find('*[xmlns="' + SketchCast.NS_PUBSUB_ERRORS + '"]');
    if (pubsub_error.length > 0) {
        error = error + "/" + pubsub_error.get(0).tagName;
    }

    return error;
},

show_error: function (msg) {
    SketchCast.connection.disconnect();
    SketchCast.connection = null;
    SketchCast.service = null;
    SketchCast.node = null;

    $('#error_dialog p').text(msg);
    $('#error_dialog').dialog('open');
}
```

code snippet sketchcast.js

The `make_error_from_iq()` function looks at the `<error>` element of the IQ-error stanza and pulls out the generic error type and, if present, the application-specific error type. It combines these into a simple string for presentation to the user. `show_error()` disconnects, resets the XMPP state, and pops up the error dialog box with the supplied message. These error messages aren't the most user-friendly, but they are simple to generate and get the job done. In a real-world application, more care should be taken to present more helpful errors.

Subscriptions are taken care of, so you can move on to node creation for the presenter. Following are the node creation callback implementations, which should be added to the `SketchCast` object:

```
created: function (iq) {
    // find pubsub node
    var node = $(iq).find("create").attr('node');
    SketchCast.node = node;

    // configure the node
    var configiq = $iq({to: SketchCast.service,
                        type: "set"})
        .c('pubsub', {xmlns: SketchCast.NS_PUBSUB_OWNER})
        .c('configure', {node: node})
        .c('x', {xmlns: SketchCast.NS_DATA_FORMS,
                 type: "submit"})
        .c('field', {"var": "FORM_TYPE"})
        .c('value').t(SketchCast.NS_PUBSUB_NODE_CONFIG)
```

```
                       .up().up()
                       .c('field', {"var": "pubsub#deliver_payloads"})
                       .c('value').t("1")
                       .up().up()
                       .c('field', {"var": "pubsub#send_last_published_item"})
                       .c('value').t("never")
                       .up().up()
                       .c('field', {"var": "pubsub#persist_items"})
                       .c('value').t("true")
                       .up().up()
                       .c('field', {"var": "pubsub#max_items"})
                       .c('value'),t("20");
              SketchCast.connection.sendIQ(configiq,
                                            SketchCast.configured,
                                            SketchCast.configure_error);
          },

          create_error: function (iq) {
              SketchCast.show_error("SketchCast creation failed with " +
                          SketchCast.make_error_from_iq(iq));
          }
```

code snippet sketchcast.js

The pubsub node creation stanza requests an instant node; the first thing the `created()` callback must do is store the name of the node created.

After the presenter begins sketching, any viewers that arrive will see new drawing events, but they won't get any of the events from before they subscribed. To remedy this situation, the viewers must retrieve the most recent items from the pubsub node to give the drawing events some context. Because you usually have no idea what the configuration defaults might be on any given pubsub service, the code must configure the pubsub node to store a reasonable amount of past events.

The `created()` callback that follows builds a configuration form for the pubsub node and submits it. Notice that you do not need to ask for a form from the server; you already know what values need changing. The callback sends the configuration form and assigns `configured()` and `configure_error()` to handle the success and error cases, respectively.

`create_error()` just displays an error message to the user.

Both callbacks are shown here:

```
          configured: function (iq) {
              $(document).trigger("broadcast_started");
          },

          configure_error: function (iq) {
              SketchCast.show_error("SketchCast configuration failed with " +
                          SketchCast.make_error_from_iq(iq));
          }
```

code snippet sketchcast.js

When the server acknowledges that your node is successfully configured, SketchCast triggers the custom event `broadcast_started`. If something bad happens during configuration, the error dialog box is opened.

A placeholder handler for the `broadcast_started` event is shown here and should be added at the end of `sketchcast.js`; it updates the status area and enables the drawing controls:

```
$(document).bind('broadcast_started', function () {
    $('#status').html('Broadcasting at service: <i>' +
                    SketchCast.service + '</i> node: <i>' +
                    SketchCast.node + "</i>");

    $('.button').removeClass('disabled');
    $('#sketch').removeClass('disabled');
    $('#erase').removeAttr('disabled');
});
```

code snippet sketchcast.js

Publishing and Receiving Sketch Events

The next tasks to implement are generating the sketch events from the presenter's drawing actions, publishing those events to the node, receiving the events on the subscriber side, and translating event payloads back into drawing actions. Once you've written these pieces, the rest of the application is just polish.

Sketch Events

A form is a convenient way to store sketch events, but first you must decide what data needs to be encoded to re-create a drawing action. Look again at the lines that control drawing inside the `mousemove` handler you wrote earlier:

```
// render the line segment
var ctx = $('#sketch').get(0).getContext('2d');
ctx.strokeStyle = '#' + SketchCast.color;
ctx.lineWidth = SketchCast.line_width;
ctx.beginPath();
ctx.moveTo(SketchCast.old_pos.x, SketchCast.old_pos.y);
ctx.lineTo(pos.x, pos.y);
ctx.stroke();
```

code snippet sketchcast.js

Only a few pieces of data are needed to draw the line segment — the color, line width, and the old and new coordinates of the mouse pointer.

To build a pubsub event payload, you can encode these four pieces of data into a form like this:

```
<x xmlns='jabber:x:data' type='result'>
  <field var='color'>
    <value>f00</value>
  </field>
  <field var='line_width'>
```

```
        <value>6</value>
      </field>
      <field var='from_pos'>
        <value>50,123</value>
      </field>
      <field var='to_pos'>
        <value>72,89</value>
      </field>
    </x>
```

Publishing Sketch Events

The drawing code must be modified to publish events to the node in the format outlined previously. Also, only the presenter should be able to draw and only when the sketching area is enabled. Modify the `mousemove` event handler to match the one shown here:

Available for download on Wrox.com

```
$('#sketch').mousemove(function (ev) {
    // get the position of the drawing area, our offset
    var offset = $(this).offset();
    // calculate our position within the drawing area
    var pos = {x: ev.pageX - offset.left,
               y: ev.pageY - offset.top};

    if (SketchCast.pen_down) {
        if (!SketchCast.old_pos) {
            SketchCast.old_pos = pos;
            return;
        }

        if (!$('#sketch').hasClass('disabled') &&
            (Math.abs(pos.x - SketchCast.old_pos.x) > 2 ||
             Math.abs(pos.y - SketchCast.old_pos.y) > 2)) {
            // render the line segment
            var ctx = $('#sketch').get(0).getContext('2d');
            ctx.strokeStyle = '#' + SketchCast.color;
            ctx.lineWidth = SketchCast.line_width;
            ctx.beginPath();
            ctx.moveTo(SketchCast.old_pos.x, SketchCast.old_pos.y);
            ctx.lineTo(pos.x, pos.y);
            ctx.stroke();

            SketchCast.publish_action({
                color: SketchCast.color,
                line_width: SketchCast.line_width,
                from: SketchCast.old_pos,
                to: pos
            });

            SketchCast.old_pos = pos;
        }
    } else {
        SketchCast.old_pos = null;
    }
});
```

code snippet sketchcast.js

Note that any line segment must be at least two pixels high or two pixels wide before it will be drawn in this new version of the code. This is needed to prevent excessive amounts of drawing events from being published. In some browsers, the `mousemove` event will be sent many times within the same pixel.

Next, implement `publish_action()` by adding the following code to the `SketchCast` object:

```
publish_action: function (action) {
    SketchCast.connection.sendIQ(
        $iq({to: SketchCast.service,
            type: "set"})
        .c('pubsub', {xmlns: SketchCast.NS_PUBSUB})
        .c('publish', {node: SketchCast.node})
        .c('item')
        .c('x', {xmlns: SketchCast.NS_DATA_FORMS,
                type: "result"})
        .c('field', {"var": "color"})
        .c('value').t(action.color)
        .up().up()
        .c('field', {"var": "line_width"})
        .c('value').t('' + action.line_width)
        .up().up()
        .c('field', {"var": "from_pos"})
        .c('value').t('' + action.from.x + ',' + action.from.y)
        .up().up()
        .c('field', {"var": "to_pos"})
        .c('value').t('' + action.to.x + ',' + action.to.y));
}
```

code snippet sketchcast.js

This function may look complex, but it's just building the form you saw previously and sending it to the server wrapped in a pubsub IQ-set stanza containing a `<publish>` action. Once this data is published to the node, the pubsub service will broadcast it out to all subscribers.

Receiving Sketch Events

You already created a blank `on_event()` handler that is executed whenever new events come in. You must now fill in the missing pieces to extract the data from the event and turn it into a line segment on the canvas.

You will build an action object like the one you used for `publish_action()` in the previous section, and then send that to the `render_action()` function. The new `on_event()` code is shown here:

```
on_event: function (msg) {
    if ($(msg).find('x').length === 0) {
        // this message wasn't for us!
        return true;
    }

    var color = $(msg).find('field[var="color"] value').text();
    var line_width = $(msg).find('field[var="line_width"] value').text();
```

```js
var from_pos = $(msg).find('field[var="from_pos"] value').text()
    .split(',');
var to_pos =1 $(msg).find('field[var="to_pos"] value').text()
    .split(',');

var action = {
    color: color,
    line_width: line_width,
    from: {x: parseFloat(from_pos[0]),
           y: parseFloat(from_pos[1])},
    to: {x: parseFloat(to_pos[0]),
         y: parseFloat(to_pos[1])}
};

SketchCast.render_action(action);

return true;
}
```

code snippet sketchcast.js

Now implement `render_action()` and add it to the `SketchCast` object:

Available for download on Wrox.com

```js
render_action: function (action) {
    // render the line segment
    var ctx = $('#sketch').get(0).getContext('2d');
    ctx.strokeStyle = '#' + action.color;
    ctx.lineWidth = action.line_width;
    ctx.beginPath();
    ctx.moveTo(action.from.x, action.from.y);
    ctx.lineTo(action.to.x, action.to.y);
    ctx.stroke();
}
```

code snippet sketchcast.js

Don't be surprised if this code looks familiar; it's just a slightly modified version of the drawing code from the `mousemove` event handler. It's bad practice to be copying slightly modified code around, so replace the old drawing code with another call to `render_action()`. This puts all the drawing logic in one place where it is easier to find and modify and won't get out of sync. You can replace the old drawing code by modifying the `mousemove` event handler:

Available for download on Wrox.com

```js
$('#sketch').mousemove(function (ev) {
    // get the position of the drawing area, our offset
    var offset = $(this).offset();
    // calculate our position within the drawing area
    var pos = {x: ev.pageX - offset.left,
               y: ev.pageY - offset.top};

    if (SketchCast.pen_down) {
        if (!SketchCast.old_pos) {
```

```
            SketchCast.old_pos = pos;
            return;
        }

    if (!$('#sketch').hasClass('disabled') &&
        (Math.abs(pos.x - SketchCast.old_pos.x) > 2 ||
         Math.abs(pos.y - SketchCast.old_pos.y) > 2)) {
        SketchCast.render_action({
            color: SketchCast.color,
            line_width: SketchCast.line_width,
            from: {x: SketchCast.old_pos.x,
                   y: SketchCast.old_pos.y},
            to: {x: pos.x,
                 y: pos.y}});

        SketchCast.publish_action({
            color: SketchCast.color,
            line_width: SketchCast.line_width,
            from: SketchCast.old_pos,
            to: pos
        });

        SketchCast.old_pos = pos;
        }
    } else {
        SketchCast.old_pos = null;
    }
});
```

code snippet sketchcast.js

You now have a working version of SketchCast!

Joining Late and Catching Up

When late joining users arrive, they need to request the drawing events that they have missed from the pubsub service. As shown previously, this is easily done with an IQ-get stanza containing an `<items>` command. Add the following highlighted code to the `reception_started` event handler:

```
$(document).bind('reception_started', function () {
    $('#status').html('Receiving SketchCast.');

    // get missed events
    SketchCast.connection.sendIQ(
        $iq({to: SketchCast.service, type: "get"})
            .c('pubsub', {xmlns: SketchCast.NS_PUBSUB})
            .c('items', {node: SketchCast.node}),
        SketchCast.on_old_items);
});
```

code snippet sketchcast.js

Now, add the implementation of `on_old_items()` to the SketchCast object:

```
on_old_items: function (iq) {
    $(iq).find('item').each(function () {
        SketchCast.on_event(this);
    });
}
```

code snippet sketchcast.js

Because the `on_event()` handler only looks for a form containing drawing actions, you can just send each `<item>` child to it. As far as `on_event()` knows, the action was received just like any other event.

When a straggler joins an in-progress sketching session, they will receive past drawing actions, and they will have some context for the new parts of the sketch they will see. In this case, they will receive up to twenty previous actions because the node configuration was set to persist up to twenty items. Note that some XMPP servers place limits on how many items can be persisted, so if you need a lot of persistence, you may have to specially configure the server to support your application.

Gracefully Ending the Session

To finish off SketchCast, you should make sure the presenter and the viewers can gracefully quit. In order to clean up after itself, the application must delete the pubsub node if the user is a presenter and unsubscribe if they are a viewer. In both cases, you should also disconnect and reset the application to its starting state.

Start with the publisher case by implementing the Disconnect button in the toolbar. The best place to add the handler for the button is when you get the `broadcast_started` event; when this event is received you know the user is a publisher and that they have just created a pubsub node. The modified event handler is shown here:

```
$(document).bind('broadcast_started', function (ev, data) {
    $('#status').html('Broadcasting at service: <i>' +
                    SketchCast.service + '</i> node: <i>' +
                    data.node + "</i>");

    $('.button').removeClass('disabled');
    $('#sketch').removeClass('disabled');
    $('#erase').removeAttr('disabled');
    $('#disconnect').removeAttr('disabled');

    $('#disconnect').click(function () {
        $('.button').addClass('disabled');
        $('#sketch').addClass('disabled');
        $('#erase').attr('disabled', 'disabled');
        $('#disconnect').attr('disabled', 'disabled');

        SketchCast.connection.sendIQ(
            $iq({to: SketchCast.service,
                type: "set"})
            .c('pubsub', {xmlns: SketchCast.NS_PUBSUB_OWNER})
```

```
                .c('delete', {node: SketchCast.node}));

        SketchCast.disconnect();
    });
});
```

The code binds the `click` event for the Disconnect button in order to delete the pubsub node using the `<delete>` pubsub action and then disconnect. You must now write the `disconnect()` function and add it to the `SketchCast` object:

```
disconnect: function () {
    $('#erase').click();
    SketchCast.connection.disconnect();
    SketchCast.connection = null;
    SketchCast.service = null;
    SketchCast.node = null;
    $('#login_dialog').dialog('open');
}
```

After disconnecting the XMPP stream, the code resets the application state, clears the drawing area, and opens the login dialog box. SketchCast is then ready for another round.

The viewer's disconnection sequence is slightly more complicated. You must unsubscribe from the pubsub node and disconnect, which is very similar to the publisher's actions, but there is a possibility that the publisher of the sketch has disconnected before all the subscribers. In this case, the pubsub service will notify the user of the node's deletion, and you must extend `on_event()` to deal with this new kind of event.

First, enable the disconnect button once you receive the `reception_started` event, just like you did for the publisher's side. The modified event handler is shown here:

```
$(document).bind('reception_started', function (ev, data) {
    $('#status').html('Receiving SketchCast.');

    $('#disconnect').removeAttr('disabled');
    $('#disconnect').click(function () {
        $('#disconnect').attr('disabled', 'disabled');
        SketchCast.connection.sendIQ(
            $iq({to: SketchCast.service,
                type: "set"})
            .c('pubsub', {xmlns: SketchCast.NS_PUBSUB_OWNER})
            .c('unsubscribe', {node: SketchCast.node
                               jid: SketchCast.connection.jid}));

        SketchCast.disconnect();
```

```
        });

        // get missed events
        SketchCast.connection.sendIQ(
            $iq({to: SketchCast.service, type: "get"})
                .c('pubsub', {xmlns: SketchCast.NS_PUBSUB})
                .c('items', {node: SketchCast.node}),
            SketchCast.on_old_items);
    });
```

Next, you must modify the pubsub event handler, on_event(). Simply show an error if the pubsub node gets deleted while the user is still subscribed. Replace the old handler with the following:

```
on_event: function (msg) {
    if ($(msg).find('x').length > 0) {
        var color = $(msg).find('field[var="color"] value').text();
        var line_width = $(msg).find('field[var="line_width"] value').text();
        var from_pos = $(msg).find('field[var="from_pos"] value').text()
            .split(',');
        var to_pos =1 $(msg).find('field[var="to_pos"] value').text()
            .split(',');

        var action = {
            color: color,
            line_width: line_width,
            from: {x: parseFloat(from_pos[0]),
                    y: parseFloat(from_pos[1])},
            to: {x: parseFloat(to_pos[0]),
                  y: parseFloat(to_pos[1])}
        };

        SketchCast.render_action(action);
    } else if ($(msg).find('delete[node="' + SketchCast.node + '"]')
            .length > 0) {
        SketchCast.show_error("SketchCast ended by presenter.");
    }

    return true;
}
```

This new version first looks for a sketch drawing event, and if it doesn't find one, it looks for a node delete notification.

Your job is done, and it's time to alert the marketing department! The complete JavaScript file is shown in Listing 9-3.

LISTING 9-3: sketchcast.js

```javascript
var SketchCast = {
    // drawing state
    pen_down: false,
    old_pos: null,
    color: '000',
    line_width: 4,

    // xmpp state
    connection: null,
    service: null,
    node: null,

    // namespace constants
    NS_DATA_FORMS: "jabber:x:data",
    NS_PUBSUB: "http://jabber.org/protocol/pubsub",
    NS_PUBSUB_OWNER: "http://jabber.org/protocol/pubsub#owner",
    NS_PUBSUB_ERRORS: "http://jabber.org/protocol/pubsub#errors",
    NS_PUBSUB_NODE_CONFIG: "http://jabber.org/protocol/pubsub#node_config",

    on_event: function (msg) {
        if ($(msg).find('x').length > 0) {
            var color = $(msg).find('field[var="color"] value').text();
            var line_width = $(msg)
                .find('field[var="line_width"] value').text();
            var from_pos = $(msg).find('field[var="from_pos"] value').text()
                .split(',');
            var to_pos = $(msg).find('field[var="to_pos"] value').text()
                .split(',');

            var action = {
                color: color,
                line_width: line_width,
                from: {x: parseFloat(from_pos[0]),
                       y: parseFloat(from_pos[1])},
                to: {x: parseFloat(to_pos[0]),
                     y: parseFloat(to_pos[1])}
            };

            SketchCast.render_action(action);
        } else if ($(msg).find('delete[node="' + SketchCast.node + '"]')
                .length > 0) {
            SketchCast.show_error("SketchCast ended by presenter.");
        }

        return true;
    },

    on_old_items: function (iq) {
        $(iq).find('item').each(function () {
            SketchCast.on_event(this);
        });
```

```
    },

    // subscription callbacks
    subscribed: function (iq) {
        $(document).trigger("reception_started");
    },

    subscribe_error: function (iq) {
        SketchCast.show_error("Subscription failed with " +
                              SketchCast.make_error_from_iq(iq));
    },

    // error handling helpers
    make_error_from_iq: function (iq) {
        var error = $(iq)
            .find('*[xmlns="' + Strophe.NS.STANZAS + '"]')
            .get(0).tagName;
        var pubsub_error = $(iq)
            .find('*[xmlns="' + SketchCast.NS_PUBSUB_ERRORS + '"]');
        if (pubsub_error.length > 0) {
            error = error + "/" + pubsub_error.get(0).tagName;
        }

        return error;
    },

    show_error: function (msg) {
        SketchCast.connection.disconnect();
        SketchCast.connection = null;
        SketchCast.service = null;
        SketchCast.node = null;

        $('#error_dialog p').text(msg);
        $('#error_dialog').dialog('open');
    },

    // node creation callbacks
    created: function (iq) {
        // find pubsub node
        var node = $(iq).find("create").attr('node');
        SketchCast.node = node;

        // configure the node
        var configiq = $iq({to: SketchCast.service,
                            type: "set"})
            .c('pubsub', {xmlns: SketchCast.NS_PUBSUB_OWNER})
            .c('configure', {node: node})
            .c('x', {xmlns: SketchCast.NS_DATA_FORMS,
                     type: "submit"})
            .c('field', {"var": "FORM_TYPE"})
            .c('value').t(SketchCast.NS_PUBSUB_NODE_CONFIG)
            .up().up()
            .c('field', {"var": "pubsub#deliver_payloads"})
            .c('value').t("1")
```

continues

LISTING 9-3 *(continued)*

```
            .up().up()
            .c('field', {"var": "pubsub#send_last_published_item"})
            .c('value').t("never")
            .up().up()
            .c('field', {"var": "pubsub#persist_items"})
            .c('value').t("true")
            .up().up()
            .c('field', {"var": "pubsub#max_items"})
            .c('value').t("20");
        SketchCast.connection.sendIQ(configiq,
                                    SketchCast.configured,
                                    SketchCast.configure_error);
    },

    create_error: function (iq) {
        SketchCast.show_error("SketchCast creation failed with " +
                            SketchCast.make_error_from_iq(iq));
    },

    configured: function (iq) {
        $(document).trigger("broadcast_started");
    },

    configure_error: function (iq) {
        SketchCast.show_error("SketchCast configuration failed with " +
                            SketchCast.make_error_from_iq(iq));
    },

    publish_action: function (action) {
        SketchCast.connection.sendIQ(
            $iq({to: SketchCast.service, type: "set"})
                .c('pubsub', {xmlns: SketchCast.NS_PUBSUB})
                .c('publish', {node: SketchCast.node})
                .c('item')
                .c('x', {xmlns: SketchCast.NS_DATA_FORMS,
                        type: "result"})
                .c('field', {"var": "color"})
                .c('value').t(action.color)
                .up().up()
                .c('field', {"var": "line_width"})
                .c('value').t('' + action.line_width)
                .up().up()
                .c('field', {"var": "from_pos"})
                .c('value').t('' + action.from.x + ',' + action.from.y)
                .up().up()
                .c('field', {"var": "to_pos"})
                .c('value').t('' + action.to.x + ',' + action.to.y));
    },

    render_action: function (action) {
        // render the line segment
```

```javascript
        var ctx = $('#sketch').get(0).getContext('2d');
        ctx.strokeStyle = '#' + action.color;
        ctx.lineWidth = action.line_width;
        ctx.beginPath();
        ctx.moveTo(action.from.x, action.from.y);
        ctx.lineTo(action.to.x, action.to.y);
        ctx.stroke();
    },

    disconnect: function () {
        $('#erase').click();
        SketchCast.connection.disconnect();
        SketchCast.connection = null;
        SketchCast.service = null;
        SketchCast.node = null;
        $('#login_dialog').dialog('open');
    }
};

$(document).ready(function () {
    $('#login_dialog').dialog({
        autoOpen: true,
        draggable: false,
        modal: true,
        title: 'Connect to a SketchCast',
        buttons: {
            "Connect": function () {
                $(document).trigger('connect', {
                    jid: $('#jid').val(),
                    password: $('#password').val(),
                    service: $('#service').val(),
                    node: $('#node').val()
                });

                $('#password').val('');
                $(this).dialog('close');
            }
        }
    });

    $('#error_dialog').dialog({
        autoOpen: false,
        draggable: false,
        modal: true,
        title: 'Whoops!  Something Bad Happened!',
        buttons: {
            "Ok": function () {
                $(this).dialog('close');
                $('#login_dialog').dialog('open');
            }
        }
    });

    $('#sketch').mousedown(function () {
```

continues

LISTING 9-3 *(continued)*

```
        SketchCast.pen_down = true;
});

$('#sketch').mouseup(function () {
    SketchCast.pen_down = false;
});

$('#sketch').mousemove(function (ev) {
    // get the position of the drawing area, our offset
    var offset = $(this).offset();
    // calculate our position within the drawing area
    var pos = {x: ev.pageX - offset.left,
               y: ev.pageY - offset.top};

    if (SketchCast.pen_down) {
        if (!SketchCast.old_pos) {
            SketchCast.old_pos = pos;
            return;
        }

        if (!$('#sketch').hasClass('disabled') &&
            (Math.abs(pos.x - SketchCast.old_pos.x) > 2 ||
             Math.abs(pos.y - SketchCast.old_pos.y) > 2)) {
            SketchCast.render_action({
                color: SketchCast.color,
                line_width: SketchCast.line_width,
                from: {x: SketchCast.old_pos.x,
                       y: SketchCast.old_pos.y},
                to: {x: pos.x,
                     y: pos.y}});

            SketchCast.publish_action({
                color: SketchCast.color,
                line_width: SketchCast.line_width,
                from: SketchCast.old_pos,
                to: pos
            });

            SketchCast.old_pos = pos;
        }
    } else {
        SketchCast.old_pos = null;
    }
});

$('.color').click(function (ev) {
    SketchCast.color = $(this).attr('id').split('-')[1];
});

$('.linew').click(function (ev) {
```

```
            SketchCast.line_width = $(this).attr('id').split('-')[1];
        });

        $('#erase').click(function () {
            var ctx = $('#sketch').get(0).getContext('2d');
            ctx.fillStyle = '#fff';
            ctx.strokeStyle = '#fff';
            ctx.fillRect(0, 0, 600, 500);
        });
    });

    $(document).bind('connect', function (ev, data) {
        $('#status').html('Connecting..');

        var conn = new Strophe.Connection(
            'http://bosh.metajack.im:5280/xmpp-httpbind');
        conn.connect(data.jid, data.password, function (status) {
            if (status === Strophe.Status.CONNECTED) {
                $(document).trigger('connected');
            } else if (status === Strophe.Status.DISCONNECTED) {
                $(document).trigger('disconnected');
            }
        });

        SketchCast.connection = conn;
        SketchCast.service = data.service;
        SketchCast.node = data.node;
    });

    $(document).bind('connected', function () {
        $('#status').html("Connected.");

        // send negative presence send we're not a chat client
        SketchCast.connection.send($pres().c('priority').t('-1'));

        if (SketchCast.node.length > 0) {
            // a node was specified, so we attempt to subscribe to it

            // first, set up a callback for the events
            SketchCast.connection.addHandler(
                SketchCast.on_event,
                null, "message", null, null, SketchCast.service);

            // now subscribe
            var subiq = $iq({to: SketchCast.service,
                             type: "set"})
                .c('pubsub', {xmlns: SketchCast.NS_PUBSUB})
                .c('subscribe', {node: SketchCast.node,
                                 jid: SketchCast.connection.jid});
            SketchCast.connection.sendIQ(subiq,
                                         SketchCast.subscribed,
                                         SketchCast.subscribe_error);
        } else {
            // a node was not specified, so we start a new sketchcast
```

continues

LISTING 9-3 *(continued)*

```
            var createiq = $iq({to: SketchCast.service,
                                type: "set"})
                .c('pubsub', {xmlns: SketchCast.NS_PUBSUB})
                .c('create');
            SketchCast.connection.sendIQ(createiq,
                                    SketchCast.created,
                                    SketchCast.create_error);
    }
});

$(document).bind('broadcast_started', function () {
    $('#status').html('Broadcasting at service: <i>' +
                    SketchCast.service + '</i> node: <i>' +
                    SketchCast.node + "</i>");

    $('.button').removeClass('disabled');
    $('#sketch').removeClass('disabled');
    $('#erase').removeAttr('disabled');
    $('#disconnect').removeAttr('disabled');

    $('#disconnect').click(function () {
        $('.button').addClass('disabled');
        $('#sketch').addClass('disabled');
        $('#erase').attr('disabled', 'disabled');
        $('#disconnect').attr('disabled', 'disabled');

        SketchCast.connection.sendIQ(
            $iq({to: SketchCast.service,
                type: "set"})
                .c('pubsub', {xmlns: SketchCast.NS_PUBSUB_OWNER})
                .c('delete', {node: SketchCast.node}));

        SketchCast.disconnect();
    });
});

$(document).bind('reception_started', function () {
    $('#status').html('Receiving SketchCast.');

    $('#disconnect').removeAttr('disabled');
    $('#disconnect').click(function () {
        $('#disconnect').attr('disabled', 'disabled');
        SketchCast.connection.sendIQ(
            $iq({to: SketchCast.service,
                type: "set"})
                .c('pubsub', {xmlns: SketchCast.NS_PUBSUB_OWNER})
                .c('unsubscribe', {node: SketchCast.node,
                                jid: SketchCast.connection.jid}));

        SketchCast.disconnect();
```

```
    });

    // get missed events
    SketchCast.connection.sendIQ(
        $iq({to: SketchCast.service, type: "get"})
            .c('pubsub', {xmlns: SketchCast.NS_PUBSUB})
            .c('items', {node: SketchCast.node}),
        SketchCast.on_old_items);
});
```

A Better SketchPad

Software can always be improved. Perhaps you'd like to try adding some new features to SketchCast?
The marketing department says that the top three user requests are:

➤   Show drawing events that happened before viewers subscribed.

➤   Enable writing on the board using fonts.

➤   Browse for available SketchCasts instead of typing in their names.

SUMMARY

XMPP pubsub is an extremely powerful tool. Even in its simplest forms, it makes creating applications
like SketchCast quite easy. In this chapter, you used XMPP pubsub to develop a sketch presentation
application and learned about:

➤   The basics of pubsub

➤   Creating and using forms

➤   Subscribing, unsubscribing, and retrieving items from pubsub nodes

➤   Creating, configuring, and deleting pubsub nodes

➤   Publishing and dealing with pubsub events

➤   HTML5's `<canvas>` element

In the next chapter, you see a truly collaborative application, which allows two users to edit a
shared document, and you learn how to extend XMPP stanzas with your own elements.

10

Writing with Friends: A Collaborative Text Editor

WHAT'S IN THIS CHAPTER?

➤ Learning the Operational Transformation algorithm

➤ Using service discovery to probe features

➤ Extending XMPP stanzas

People used to mail manuscripts back and forth to collaborate. Over the years, as technology improved, this turned into file sharing via disks and then sharing over e-mail. Technology has now reached a point where multiple people, even in large groups, can simultaneously edit the same document over the network, and the familiarity of the Web has made it both easy and common. Given your previous experience with XMPP applications, it should be no surprise to you that XMPP provides an ideal medium for collaborative document editing.

One of the latest examples of such applications is Google Wave, a rich, media-filled, collaborative space for groups of people to work on shared documents. When Google needed a protocol to facilitate such a platform, it turned to XMPP. On top of XMPP, Google has built a fantastic platform for collaborative editing based on the principles of *operational transformation*. It has also chosen to do its protocol design work on the Wave protocol in the open at `http://www.waveprotocol.org`.

In this chapter, you will build a collaborative text editor based on the same principles as Google Wave — operational transformation. Although the application is designed for collaboration between a pair of users, the underlying algorithms can be scaled to arbitrary numbers of collaborators. You see through this and other applications how simple it is to build sophisticated software on top of XMPP's core technology.

APPLICATION PREVIEW

The final version of the NetPad application is shown in Figure 10-1. It has a simple UI, but is nevertheless quite powerful.

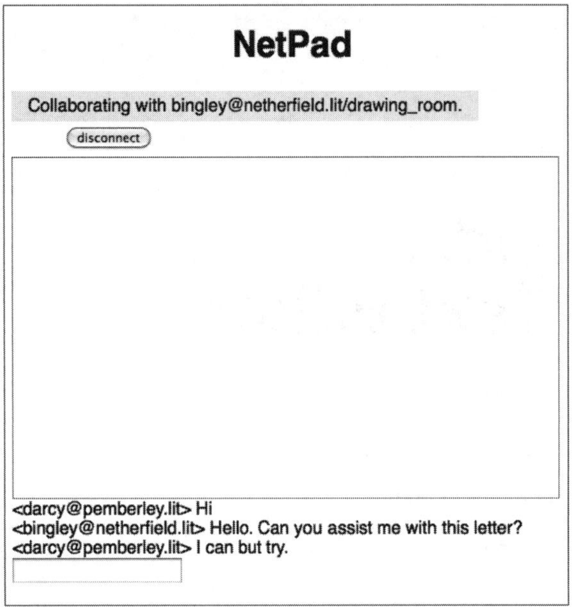

FIGURE 10-1

A large editing area takes up most of the screen. A status area and a disconnect button appear at the top, and the chat area appears at the bottom. Not only can the two collaborators work on the same text, but they can also chat with each other about their ideas.

NETPAD DESIGN

Like any text editor, NetPad's primary focus is to edit text. It is easy to accept local edits to the text, but NetPad must also support editing operations coming from a remote user. Most of the work of building NetPad is supporting these remote operations. The chat area is a slimmed-down version of the functionality from Chapter 6's Gab application, and by now you should be comfortable with the private messaging pieces that are needed.

To allow users to collaborate on the same text, NetPad uses the theory of operational transformation. Local editing actions are expressed as operations on the text and sent to the remote party. Remote operations are received and transformed into slightly modified versions; after these modified versions are applied, both parties end up with a consistent view of the text.

NetPad must establish an editing session between a pair of users, send local operations to the other party, and process incoming remote operations. These operations will be encoded into XML as an extension to the XMPP protocol. The application uses `<presence>` stanzas for establishing sessions and `<message>` stanzas for communicating editing operations.

Of course, not every user will be capable of collaborating on a NetPad document, so NetPad must first determine whether the potential collaborator's client has support for this editing functionality. This can be done with Service Discovery, which you saw in Chapter 7.

NetPad's design is rather simple, but operational transformation and XMPP protocol extensions are both worthy of a thorough investigation. Once these concepts are explained, you will be ready to design the NetPad protocol and build NetPad.

OPERATIONAL TRANSFORMATION

Ellis and Gibbs first presented the concept behind operational transformation in their paper "Concurrency Control in Groupware Systems." This paper is an excellent example of an academic article that is extremely readable, turning a complex topic into a simple description. The algorithm that NetPad uses is based directly on the work of these fine researchers.

Collaborative editing is a form of real-time *groupware*. These types of applications have many interesting and important properties. First, they are highly interactive, real-time, distributed network applications. These properties are true of most of the applications in this book. Groupware applications are ad-hoc and volatile in nature; there is no telling what actions users will take or what order they take them in, and the users may come and go freely. Finally, these types of applications are quite focused; each user of the system is interacting with the same data and often making conflicting changes.

The main challenge of groupware applications is consistency. The view that one user has of a document should be as close as possible to the other users' views of the same information. When editing operations have stopped, the resulting documents should all be identical. It does users no good to work collaboratively if at the end of their session each has a different result.

Concurrency problems are not unique to groupware applications, but the real-time and distributed properties of these systems make most common solutions to the concurrency impractical. For example, database management systems have often supported various forms of concurrency control, but they accomplish this by disallowing conflicting operations altogether. Other systems allow only one editor at a time, and this ability passes from user to user. The low latency and interactivity required by groupware necessitates a different approach.

Basic Principles

The operational transformation algorithm is concerned with a group of users, the operations these users can perform, and the order in which each user executes these operations.

The set of operations that NetPad needs is quite simple — inserting a character and deleting a character. The insertion operation takes two arguments — the character to insert and the position at which to place it. This operation is written as `insert(pos, char)`. The deletion operation needs only the position at which to delete a character and is written as `delete(pos)`.

Each user's editing actions will generate a sequence of these two operations. It is important that the sequence of operations be executed in the proper order. For example, consider the four operations `insert(0, 'c')`, `insert(0, 'b')`, `insert(0, 'a')`, and `delete(0)`. Permuting the order of these operations would result in a different string. In the order listed, these operations result in the string `bc`. If the middle two operations are switched, the resulting string becomes `ac`.

Each user's operations are ordered, and other users must execute them in the same order. In addition, the total set of operations has an order as well, although unlike local operations, this ordering is not always complete. It is possible for two users to generate different operations simultaneously on the same string. These operations are overlapping and cannot be ordered in relation to each other.

Figure 10-2 and Figure 10-3 illustrate these two cases. In both figures each user, u_1 and u_2, generates an operation, o_1 and o_2, respectively. In Figure 10-2, o_1 is executed by u_2 before they generate o_2. However, in Figure 10-3, u_1 and u_2 perform simultaneous operations that overlap.

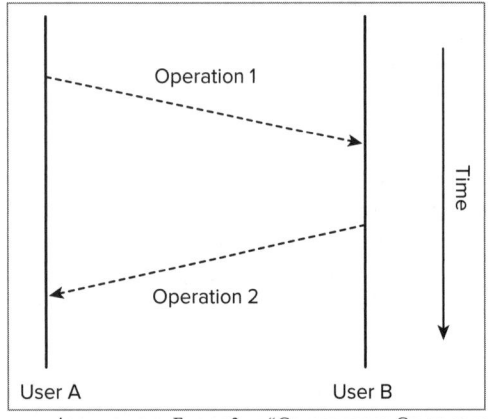

ADAPTED FROM FIGURE 2 OF "CONCURRENCY CONTROL IN GROUPWARE SYSTEMS" BY ELLIS AND GIBBS, ACM SIGMOD RECORD, ACM 18(2), 1989.

FIGURE 10-2

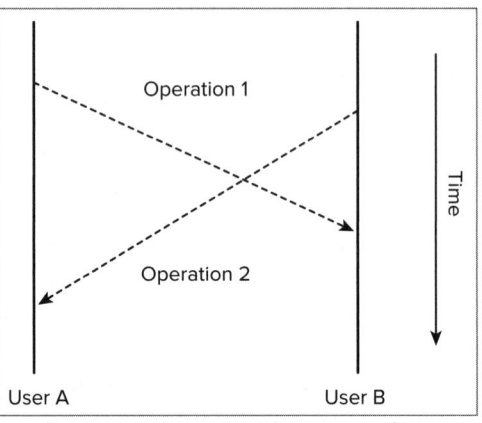

ADAPTED FROM FIGURE 2 OF "CONCURRENCY CONTROL IN GROUPWARE SYSTEMS" BY ELLIS AND GIBBS, ACM SIGMOD RECORD, ACM 18(2), 1989.

FIGURE 10-3

The case where operations overlap is the real crux of the collaborative editing problem. The non-overlapping cases can easily be handled by keeping track of the order of operations, and enforcing execution in the correct order. Overlapping operations, however, have no ordering. How are these to be executed?

Overlapping operations must be transformed into new operations that can be ordered, and this is where the name "operational transformation" comes from. Because u_1 knows the state on which o_2 operated, they can transform o_2 into an operation that accounts for the local operation o_1. Similarly, u_2 can transform o_1 to account for the changes made by o_2.

Imagine that both u_1 and u_2 have the string `ace` in their editors. Each user simultaneously does an insert operation; o_1, performed by u_1, is `insert(1, 'b')`, and o_2, performed by u_2, is `insert(2, 'd')`.

First, watch what happens when these operations are not transformed. The first user executes o_1 and then receives and executes o_2; the resulting string is `abdce`. The second user executes o_2 and then o_1 and ends up with the string `abcde`. Each user now has an inconsistent view of the data, and only one of them has the correct version.

Now, observe the result when each user transforms the operations they receive. The first user executes o_1 and then receives o_2. Because the user has added a character to the string, he or she applies a transformation turning o_2 into o_2' adding one to the position of the insert operation; `insert(2, 'd')` becomes `insert(3, 'd')`. The o_1 operation that u_2 receives needs no transformation because the position it references has not been changed by o_2; o_1' is the same as o_1. Applying o_1, o_2' or o_2, o_1' results in the same result — the string `abcde`.

Similar transformations are possible between any pair of operations.

Details of the Algorithm

As you've learned, operational transformation solves a complex problem in a relatively simple and straightforward manner. However, you have a few important details to consider before the algorithm can be implemented in NetPad. The structure of operation requests must be defined. Executing groups of operations will need some care, and the algorithm has the concept of priorities to address this. Also, it is necessary for each user to maintain a queue of outstanding operations, to know the state for which a given operation applies, and to track the history of operations that have already been performed.

State

Each user must keep a state vector with one element for each user participating in the session. There will be two participants in every NetPad session, and the state vectors for both users will have two elements. The elements of the state vector are simple counters that start at zero. For every operation executed, the operation initiator's element of the state vector is incremented by one. For example, if the first position in the state vector represents the local user and the second position represents the remote user, a state vector of <10, 23> means that 10 locally generated operations and 23 remotely generated operations were executed on the local document.

Each user's place in the state vector must be the same for all state vectors. This can be achieved easily by lexicographically ordering the users by their JIDs.

Operation Requests

When any user executes a local operation, they will broadcast a corresponding operation request to the other users. Operation requests can be represented as a four-element vector in the form <j, s, o, p>. The first element, j, is the initiator's position in the state vector. The next element, s, is the state vector of the jth user at the time the operation was generated. The element o is the operation requested, and p is the operation's priority.

Each request carries not only the operation and its parameters but also the state vector at the time the operation was first executed and its priority. This extra information will allow the other participants to determine when they can execute the request. For example, one user may generate an operation that comes after a second user's; a third user, who has received the second user's operation first, must wait for the first user's operation before they can execute either. Without knowledge of the operation's corresponding state, it would not be possible to order execution properly.

Request Queue and Execution Log

Each user must keep a queue for incoming requests. All requests, both local and remote, will be appended to the queue, and a user must traverse the queue to execute operations that are ready. An operation is ready for execution if the current state vector for the user is less than or equal to the queued request's state vector.

State vectors are compared in a special way, described in the Implementation section. If the state vectors are equal, the operation was performed on the same state, and can be executed without any transformation. If the request's state vector is less than the current local state vector, some overlapping operations have already been executed and the request's operation must be transformed before execution.

After any request's operation is executed, the request is appended to the user's execution log. This log is used to transform overlapping operations — operations executed simultaneously by different users — by taking into account operations that have already been executed. The execution log will be traversed in reverse chronological order to look for operations that affect a given request.

Priorities

Every request has a priority, which is calculated at the operation's origin at the time of its execution. These priorities must take into account previous operations' priorities at the same location, so they are composed of two parts. The first part is the priority of the most recent request in the execution log whose operation had an original position equal to the current operation's position. The second part is the user's position in the state vector. If no request in the execution log applies, the priority consists of just the user's position in the state vector.

This may sound complex, but it is necessary for the algorithm to function perfectly. Using a simpler scheme for priorities doesn't work in all cases, so this scheme is needed. The outline of a proof for the correctness of this approach is provided in the paper; the paper also shows why a simpler scheme cannot work.

Implementation

The implementation of operational transformation is taken directly from the aforementioned paper. The details are explained here along with the source code, but if you need more details or are just curious, please read the original paper.

Initial Code

You start by setting up the `OpTrans` object and its basic properties and initialization function. Place the following code into a new file called `optrans.js`:

```
var OpTrans = {
    log: null, // the request log
    queue: null, // the request queue
    state: null, // our state vector
    jid: null, // our jid
    jid_map: null, // maps jids to positions in state vectors
    buffer: null, // the text buffer being affected by operations
```

```
            update_func: null, // callback function

        init: function (jids, buffer, update_func) {
            this.log = [];
            this.queue = [];
            this.state = [];
            this.jid_map = {};
            this.buffer = buffer.split('');
            this.jid = jids[0];
            this.update_func = update_func;

            $.each(jids.sort(), function (i) {
                OpTrans.jid_map[this] = i;
                OpTrans.state.push(0);
            });
        }
    };
```

code snippet optrans.js

The init() function's parameters are a list of JIDs of the participants, the initial buffer contents, and a callback function. The first item in the list of JIDs must be the JID of the local user. The initial buffer will normally be an empty string, but it may be a partial document if the hosting user has done some editing before the other user has connected. The callback function will be invoked every time an operation is executed, and it will be passed the new buffer as well as a flag indicating whether the update came from the local user or a remote one.

The init() function sets the various properties to their default values. The execution log and request queue start empty. The list of JIDs passed into the function is used to create the jid_map property, which maps each JID to a corresponding index in a state vector. Each state vector is the same length as the list of JIDs, and the initial state vector starts with each value set to zero. The jid property stores the local user's JID.

Each user in the session will initialize their own OpTrans object when the session begins. Except for the jid property, which will be different for each user, all participants start with the same initial state.

Comparison Functions

A state vector will need to be compared against other state vectors in order to determine operation precedence. Similarly, priority values will also need to be compared to each other. Because both of these objects are not simple numbers or strings, you will write special comparison functions for them.

Add the following code for the compare_state() and compare_priority() functions to the ObTrans object:

```
compare_state: function (s1, s2) {
    var i, smaller = false;
    for (i = 0; i < s1.length; i++) {
        if (s1[i] > s2[i]) {
            return 1;
        } else if (s1[i] < s2[i]) {
            smaller = true;
```

```
                }
            }

        if (smaller) {
            return -1;
        }

        return 0;
    },


    compare_priority: function (p1, p2) {
        if (p1.length > p2.length) {
            return -1;
        } else if (p1.length < p2.length) {
            return 1;
        } else {
            var i;
            for (i = 0; i < p1.length; i++) {
                if (p1[i] > p2[i]) {
                    return -1;
                } else if (p1[i] < p2[i]) {
                    return 1;
                }
            }
        }

        return 0;
    }
```

code snippet optrans.js

State vectors are compared element by element. A state vector s_i is equal to another state vector s_j if all its elements are equal. If all elements of s_i are less than or equal to s_j but at least one element in s_i is less than its corresponding element in s_j, s_i is less than s_j. Otherwise, s_i is considered greater than s_j.

Priorities are also compared element-wise. Whereas state vectors are always of equal length, priorities can be arbitrarily long. Two priorities are equal if they have the same length and each element is the same. Otherwise, either one priority is a sub list of the other, or they differ at some specific element. In the former case, the longer priority is the greater one. In the latter case, the result of the first differing elements' comparison is the result of the priorities' comparison.

Handling Requests

The first step in operational transformation is to handle the request. A request may be a result of a local user operation, or it may be received over the network from a remote user. For local operations, a priority must be calculated and a request constructed; remote operations are wrapped in a request before they are sent. In both cases, the request must be added to the requests queue, and then the execution stage is begun.

Add the following `do_local()` and `do_remote()` functions to the `ObTrans` object:

```
do_local: function (op, pos, chr) {
    // calculate p
    var l, maxp = [];
    for (l = 0; l < this.log.length; l++) {
        if (this.log[l][4] === pos) {
            if (this.compare_priority(maxp, this.log[l][3]) == 1) {
                maxp = this.log[l][3];
            }
        }
    }

    var p = maxp.concat(this.jid_map[this.jid]);

    // append request to queue
    var req = [this.jid_map[this.jid],
                this.state.concat(),
                [op, pos, chr],
                p];
    this.queue.push(req);

    this.execute();

    return req;
},

do_remote: function (jid, state, op, pos, chr, pri) {
    // append request
    var req = [this.jid_map[jid], state, [op, pos, chr], pri];
    this.queue.push(req);

    this.execute();
}
```

code snippet optrans.js

For `do_local()` only the operation's details are passed in, but for `do_remote()` you must pass in all the necessary components of the request, which are used to create a request object.

The `do_local()` function is more involved than `do_remote()` due to the priority calculation. The `do_local()` function must also return the constructed request back to the caller in order for the request to be broadcast to the remote users. The priority calculation was described previously in the "Priorities" section.

NetPad calls `init()` once the editing session has started, and from then on it calls `do_local()` when the local user performs editing operations and `do_remote()` when requests are received from the remote user. After each request is executed, the callback function will be invoked to notify NetPad about the new text changes. All the other functions of the `OpTrans` object are for use internally.

Execution

The `execute()` function contains most of the core logic of the operational transformation algorithm. It finds requests that are ready to be executed on the request queue, potentially transforms these based on past operations in the execution log, and then applies the operation to the buffer. The following `execute()` function should be added to the `OpTrans` object:

```
execute: function () {
    var r, cmp, new_queue = [];
    for (r = 0; r < this.queue.length; r++) {
        var remstate = this.queue[r][1];
        var cmp = this.compare_state(remstate, this.state);
        if (cmp < 1) {
            var op = this.queue[r][2];
            var orig_pos = op[1];
            if (cmp < 0) {
                var l = -1;
                while (l = this.find_prev(remstate, l) >= 0) {
                    var k = this.log[l][0];
                    if (remstate[k] <= this.log[l][1][k]) {
                        op = this.transform_op(op,
                                               this.log[l][2],
                                               this.queue[r][3],
                                               this.log[l][3]);
                    }
                }
            }

            var remote = this.queue[r][0] !== this.jid_map[this.jid];

            this.perform_op.apply(this, [remote].concat(op, orig_pos));
            this.log.push(this.queue[r].concat(orig_pos));
            this.state[this.queue[r][0]] += 1;
        } else {
            new_queue.push(this.queue[r]);
        }
    }

    this.queue = new_queue;
}
```

code snippet optrans.js

The `execute()` function traverses the request queue in the order the requests were added, looking for requests that are ready for execution. Each request whose state vector is less than or equal to the local user's current state vector can be executed. If the request's state vector is strictly less than the local user's state vector, the request must be transformed before it can be executed; the local buffer has been modified by operations that weren't executed at the request's origin. If the two state vectors are equal, the request can be executed immediately.

To transform a request, the execution log is searched for requests whose state vectors are less than or equal to the current request. The `find_next()` function returns the index of the next such request from the execution log or -1 if no such request is found. Additionally, only some of these requests from the log will affect the transformation; the logged request's and the current request's state vectors are compared at the element corresponding to the logged request's origin, and if the element in the logged request's state vector is greater than or equal to the element of the current request's state vector, that request must be transformed against. Each such request found in the execution log will trigger a transformation done by `transform_op()`; it is possible that several transformations will take place.

Add the following `find_prev()` function to the `OpTrans` object:

```
find_prev: function (state, last_idx) {
    if (last_idx < 0) {
        last_idx = this.log.length;
    }

    var k;
    for (k = last_idx; k >= 0; k--) {
        if (this.compare_state(this.log[k][1], state) < 1) {
            break;
        }
    }

    return k;
}
```

code snippet optrans.js

Once the potentially transformed operation is ready for execution, `perform_op()` does the buffer manipulation, and then the request is added to the execution log. Note that the original position of the operation is also stored in the execution log because this is needed for the priority calculation shown previously in `do_local()`.

The following `perform_op()` function should be added to the `OpTrans` object:

```
perform_op: function (remote, op, pos, chr) {
    if (op === 'insert') {
        this.buffer.splice(pos, 0, [chr]);
    } else if (op === 'delete') {
        this.buffer.splice(pos, 1);
    }

    this.update_func(this.buffer.join(''), remote);
}
```

code snippet optrans.js

The final operations are very easy to perform. The `splice()` method of JavaScript's `Array` class makes it easy to insert or delete a character at any position. Once the operation is done, the callback function is notified with the new buffer. Note that inside the `OpTrans` object the buffer is stored as an array, but `perform_op()` passes it as a string to the callback function.

Transformation

The only piece of the algorithm left is to perform the transformation of operations. The `transform_op()` function takes both an operation to transform and also an operation to transform against. The first operation will always be the current operation, and the operation to transform against will come from the execution log. Once it has finished the transformation, it returns the new, transformed operation.

The `transform_op()` function that follows should be added to the `OpTrans` object:

```
transform_op: function (op1, op2, pri1, pri2) {
    var idx1 = op1[1];
    var idx2 = op2[1];

    if (op1[0] === 'insert' && op2[0] === 'insert') {
        if (idx1 < idx2) {
            return op1;
        } else if (idx1 > idx2) {
            return [op1[0], idx1 + 1, op1[2]];
        } else {
            if (op1[2] === op2[2]) {
                return null;
            } else {
                var cmp = this.compare_priority(pri1, pri2);
                if (cmp === -1) {
                    return [op1[0], idx1 + 1, op1[2]];
                } else {
                    return op1;
                }
            }
        }
    } else if (op1[0] === 'delete' && op2[0] === 'delete') {
        if (idx1 < idx2) {
            return op1;
        } else if (idx1 > idx2) {
            return [op1[0], idx1 - 1, op1[2]];
        } else {
            return null;
        }
    } else if (op1[0] === 'insert' && op2[0] === 'delete') {
        if (idx1 < idx2) {
            return op1;
        } else {
            return [op1[0], idx1 - 1, op1[2]];
        }
    } else if (op2[0] === 'delete' && op2[0] === 'insert') {
        if (idx1 < idx2) {
            return op1;
        } else {
            return [op1[0], idx1 + 1, op1[2]];
        }
    }
}
```

code snippet is part of optrans.js

There are four possible combinations of operations — `insert()` transformed against an `insert()` or a `delete()` and `delete()` transformed against an `insert()` or `delete()`. In each case the transformed operation may shift position forward or backward, be discarded, or remain unchanged.

Consider the case where a `delete()` is transformed by a previous `delete()` operation. If the index where the current `delete()` will occur is less than the old `delete()`, no change is necessary. If the index is the same, then the delete has already happened and the operation is superfluous. Otherwise, the index must be decremented by one so account for the missing character. The other operation transformations are similar.

The one slightly tricky case is when both operations are `insert()`s. In this case, if two `insert()` operations occur at the same index, the algorithm must use the priorities of the operations to determine the final transformation. If this priority comparison were not done, it would be possible for users to perform the operations in different orders, resulting in different buffers.

The final `optrans.js` file appears in Listing 10-1. Although NetPad uses this to enable collaborative editing between two users, the operational transformation algorithm — and this particular implementation of it — is not limited to two users; arbitrary numbers of participants can work simultaneously on the same buffer just as easily.

LISTING 10-1: optrans.js

```
var OpTrans = {
    log: null, // the request log
    queue: null, // the request queue
    state: null, // our state vector
    jid: null, // our jid
    jid_map: null, // maps jids to positions in state vectors
    buffer: null, // the text buffer being affected by operations
    update_func: null, // callback function

    init: function (jids, buffer, update_func) {
        this.log = [];
        this.queue = [];
        this.state = [];
        this.jid_map = {};
        this.buffer = buffer.split('');
        this.jid = jids[0];
        this.update_func = update_func;

        $.each(jids.sort(), function (i) {
            OpTrans.jid_map[this] = i;
            OpTrans.state.push(0);
        });
    },

    getState: function (jid) {
    },

    do_local: function (op, pos, chr) {
        // calculate p
```

continues

LISTING 10-1 *(continued)*

```
            var l, maxp = [];
            for (l = 0; l < this.log.length; l++) {
                if (this.log[l][4] === pos) {
                    if (this.compare_priority(maxp, this.log[l][3]) == 1) {
                        maxp = this.log[l][3];
                    }
                }
            }

            var p = maxp.concat(this.jid_map[this.jid]);

            // append request to queue
            var req = [this.jid_map[this.jid],
                        this.state.concat(),
                        [op, pos, chr],
                        p];
            this.queue.push(req);

            this.execute();

            return req;
        },

        do_remote: function (jid, state, op, pos, chr, pri) {
            // append request
            var req = [this.jid_map[jid], state, [op, pos, chr], pri];
            this.queue.push(req);

            this.execute();
        },

        compare_state: function (s1, s2) {
            var i, smaller = false;
            for (i = 0; i < s1.length; i++) {
                if (s1[i] > s2[i]) {
                    return 1;
                } else if (s1[i] < s2[i]) {
                    smaller = true;
                }
            }

            if (smaller) {
                return -1;
            }

            return 0;
        },

        compare_priority: function (p1, p2) {
            if (p1.length > p2.length) {
                return -1;
            } else if (p1.length < p2.length) {
```

```
            return 1;
        } else {
            var i;
            for (i = 0; i < p1.length; i++) {
                if (p1[i] > p2[i]) {
                    return -1;
                } else if (p1[i] < p2[i]) {
                    return 1;
                }
            }
        }

        return 0;
    },

    execute: function () {
        var r, cmp, new_queue = [];
        for (r = 0; r < this.queue.length; r++) {
            var remstate = this.queue[r][1];
            var cmp = this.compare_state(remstate, this.state);
            if (cmp < 1) {
                var op = this.queue[r][2];
                var orig_pos = op[1];
                if (cmp < 0) {
                    var l = -1;
                    while (l = this.find_prev(remstate, l) >= 0) {
                        var k = this.log[l][0];
                        if (remstate[k] <= this.log[l][1][k]) {
                            op = this.transform_op(op,
                                                   this.log[l][2],
                                                   this.queue[r][3],
                                                   this.log[l][3]);
                        }
                    }
                }

                var remote = this.queue[r][0] !== this.jid_map[this.jid];

                this.perform_op.apply(this, [remote].concat(op, orig_pos));
                this.log.push(this.queue[r].concat(orig_pos));
                this.state[this.queue[r][0]] += 1;
            } else {
                new_queue.push(this.queue[r]);
            }
        }

        this.queue = new_queue;
    },

    perform_op: function (remote, op, pos, chr) {
        if (op === 'insert') {
            this.buffer.splice(pos, 0, [chr]);
        } else if (op === 'delete') {
            this.buffer.splice(pos, 1);
```

continues

LISTING 10-1 *(continued)*

```
        }

        this.update_func(this.buffer.join(''), remote);
    },

    find_prev: function (state, last_idx) {
        if (last_idx < 0) {
            last_idx = this.log.length;
        }

        var k;
        for (k = last_idx; k >= 0; k--) {
            if (this.compare_state(this.log[k][1], state) < 1) {
                break;
            }
        }

        return k;
    },

    transform_op: function (op1, op2, pri1, pri2) {
        var idx1 = op1[1];
        var idx2 = op2[1];

        if (op1[0] === 'insert' && op2[0] === 'insert') {
            if (idx1 < idx2) {
                return op1;
            } else if (idx1 > idx2) {
                return [op1[0], idx1 + 1, op1[2]];
            } else {
                if (op1[2] === op2[2]) {
                    return null;
                } else {
                    var cmp = this.compare_priority(pri1, pri2);
                    if (cmp === -1) {
                        return [op1[0], idx1 + 1, op1[2]];
                    } else {
                        return op1;
                    }
                }
            }
        } else if (op1[0] === 'delete' && op2[0] === 'delete') {
            if (idx1 < idx2) {
                return op1;
            } else if (idx1 > idx2) {
                return [op1[0], idx1 - 1, op1[2]];
            } else {
                return null;
            }
```

```
        } else if (op1[0] === 'insert' && op2[0] === 'delete') {
            if (idx1 < idx2) {
                return op1;
            } else {
                return [op1[0], idx1 - 1, op1[2]];
            }
        } else if (op2[0] === 'delete' && op2[0] === 'insert') {
            if (idx1 < idx2) {
                return op1;
            } else {
                return [op1[0], idx1 + 1, op1[2]];
            }
        }
    }
};
```

EXTENDING THE XMPP PROTOCOL

In previous applications you have seen much of the core XMPP protocol and several important extensions, but you've not yet created your own extensions. Creating protocol extensions is an important part of XMPP development, and sometimes you'll even need to create extensions of another extension.

XML documents are easily extensible through the use of namespaces. Every attribute or element is attached to some namespace, and new elements and attributes can be added under different namespaces. XMPP systems are designed to ignore XML under namespaces they don't recognize, but they will forward these payloads along to their final destinations. This combination of features makes XMPP easy to extend, and the community around developing extensions has used these features to create nearly 300 protocol extensions.

Ignoring the Unknown

XMPP extensions work because XMPP systems do not require knowledge of every bit of XML passing through. New things can be added without breaking existing XMPP software, and anything unknown will not only be ignored, but it will also be preserved until it is finally delivered to its destination.

This principle of ignoring the unknown is adhered to by every piece of the XMPP stack. For example, servers do not know anything about typing notifications, but these can still be sent from one client to another. Clients, likewise, may not understand some features of other clients; this does not cause them to break, and the strange features are simply ignored.

It is hard to know how developers or even end users will use a protocol. Therefore, it is best to remain as flexible as possible, leaving room for future growth and change. If XMPP did not ignore unknown protocol elements, it is likely that it would still be limited to the few uses for which it was originally designed.

XML Namespaces

Many people are familiar with XML, but few seem to have much experience with XML namespaces. Namespaces are important for defining XMPP extensions because they allow the addition of elements and attributes that will be interpreted in a new context.

An XML namespace is simply a URI, or uniform resource identifier. It is important to note that although a URI may sometimes look like a URL, it does not necessarily reference an actual location on the Web.

In XMPP, the URIs take several forms. Originally URIs of the form `jabber:foo` or `jabber:x:foo` were used. Eventually the community adopted more URL-like URIs such as `http://jabber.org/protocol/muc`. Today, XMPP URIs look like `urn:xmpp:jingle:1`. These differences are due to the community's increasing knowledge of and sophistication with URIs.

Official XMPP extensions register their URIs with the XMPP registrar as part of the standardization process. Application-specific namespaces that are not intended for standardization typically use URL-style URIs such as `http://metajack.im/ns/netpad`. If you intend to submit your protocol extension to the XSF, you can contact the XMPP registrar to obtain a temporary namespace to use until your extension reaches draft status and is assigned a permanent namespace.

XML elements can have a default namespace, and this namespace is inherited by child elements that have no namespace declaration of their own. For instance, XMPP client streams use a default namespace of `jabber:client`; a `<message>` element in the stream does not need to declare itself part of the `jabber:client` namespace because it will inherit this property from the default namespace. This inheritance is quite handy because it saves having to declare the namespace of every element; most of the time, elements will all be in a common, inherited namespace.

Extended Elements

Extended elements are just new child elements that live under a different namespace. You've seen several examples of these including XHTML-IM's `<html>` child and inside every IQ-get and IQ-set stanza in the book.

There's no restriction on where you can place extended elements, except that you cannot normally place an extended element at the XMPP stanza level. XMPP extensions routinely add extended elements even to other XMPP extensions' elements.

Extended elements for a particular protocol extension can generally appear only in a few specific places. It makes little sense, for example, to place a `jabber:iq:roster` element anywhere but as the first child of an `<iq>` stanza. Some extensions do have more generic properties; Data Forms in particular can go nearly anywhere.

Extended elements can appear two ways. Either they can declare a new default namespace by including the `xmlns` attribute in the element, or they can use namespace prefixes.

Changing the Default Namespace

Changing the default namespace is the most common method used with extended elements, and all the examples in this book have used this method. Any element can declare the default namespace by setting the value of the `xmlns` attribute to the namespace desired. The following example shows a `<message>` stanza with an extended `<event>` child under a new default namespace. Some children under the `<event>` element are also under the new namespace because they have no namespace specifically declared, and the `<x>` element declares another default namespace for the form and its children.

```
<message to='elizabeth@longbourn.lit/bedroom'
         from='pubsub.pemberley.lit'>
  <event xmlns='http://jabber.org/protocol/pubsub#event'>
    <items node='latest_books'>
      <item id='821b576dfabfc6b358b6ec4139b87f5c'>
        <x xmlns='jabber:x:data' type='result'>
          <field var='title'>
            <value>A History of Pemberley</value>
          </field>
          <field var='author'>
            <value>Sir Lewis de Bourgh</value>
          </field>
        </x>
      </item>
    </items>
  </event>
</message>
```

Namespace Prefixes

Instead of changing the default namespace, XML elements may define namespace prefixes. You've seen these briefly in Chapter 1; the `<stream:stream>` element that opens an XMPP stream is a prefixed element.

Prefixes must be defined before or at the time of their use, and descendants of an element that defines a prefix will also inherit the prefix's definition. The prefix is defined by including an `xmlns:foo` attribute, where `foo` is the prefix you want you use. The value of this attribute is the namespace to which the prefix is bound. Prefixes appear before element names and are separated from the name by a colon.

The following example shows the same `<message>` stanza as before, but uses prefixes instead of changing the default namespace:

```
<message to='elizabeth@longbourn.lit/bedroom'
         from='pubsub.pemberley.lit'>
  <pubsub:event xmlns:pubsub='http://jabber.org/protocol/pubsub#event'>
    <pybsub:items node='latest_books'>
      <pubsub:item id='821b576dfabfc6b358b6ec4139b87f5c'>
        <form:x xmlns:form='jabber:x:data' type='result'>
          <form:field var='title'>
            <form:value>A History of Pemberley</form:value>
          </form:field>
          <form:field var='author'>
            <form:value>Sir Lewis de Bourgh</form:value>
          </form:field>
        </form:x>
      </pubsub:item>
    </pubsub:items>
  </pubsub:event>
</message>
```

In this case, prefixes are more verbose than changing the default namespace. However, if the children of the `<pubsub:event>` element were replaced with elements under the `jabber:client` namespace, the use of prefixes would be an improvement. This is why the `<stream:stream>` element of an XMPP stream is prefixed; most of the elements it contains belong to a different namespace.

Note that changing the default namespace and using prefixes can be done in the same element; in fact, this is exactly what the `<stream:stream>` element does:

```
<stream:stream xmlns='jabber:client'
               xmlns:stream='http://etherx.jabber.org/streams'
               version='1.0'
               from='pemberley.lit'
               id='893ca401f5ff2ec29499984e9b7e8afc'
               xml:lang='en'>
```

Extended Attributes

Extended attributes can also be created, but these are rarely used in protocol extensions. Attributes are treated somewhat differently in XML than elements; an attribute with no prefix does not belong to the default namespace, but to the element in which it appears. What interpretation an element gives to such an attribute is application defined. For this reason, it is suggested that only prefixed attributes be used for extending XMPP.

Prefixed attributes work very similarly to prefixed elements, and the prefix must be defined in the same manner as with prefixed elements. The following example uses a prefixed attribute on a message's `<body>` element to add an explicit emotion to the text:

```
<message to='darcy@pemberley.lit'
         from='elizabaeth@longbourn.lit/ballroom'
         type='chat'>
  <body emote:emotion='annoyed' xmlns:emote='http://metajack.im/ns/emote-0'>
    I cannot talk of books in a ball-room; my head is always full of
    something else.
  </body>
</message>
```

You could easily have made the emotion attribute an element instead, perhaps so the emoticon could pertain to the entire stanza, not just the `<body>` element. Indeed, elements are the preferred way to extend XMPP. Few protocol extensions use attributes, but the capability exists if you ever need it. For an example of them in real-world use, see SOAP over XMPP in XEP-0072.

One prefix is always defined — `xml` — and this prefix is often used to add attributes to various XMPP elements. In addition, any prefix beginning with "xml" (or "XML", "xMl", and so on) is reserved. Most often you will see the `xml:lang` attribute used to designate which language is used for a piece of text. It can also be used to provide alternate translations. For example, you could send a message with two `<body>` elements, each with a different `xml:lang` value. Unlike other prefixes, the `xml` prefix does not need to be defined; it is always implicitly defined in XML, as is the `xmlns` attribute.

Contributing Extensions

If you develop an interesting extension that you think might be useful to the community at large, you should consider submitting it to the XSF and participating in the standardization process. The XSF welcomes new and interesting ideas from both within and outside the XMPP community.

Submitting a proposal is very easy. A document template for XEPs is provided at `http://xmpp.org/extensions/submit.shtml`, which you can modify to describe your extension. The entire process of standardization is described in XEP-0001, XMPP Extension Protocols, and a set of guidelines to help you is provided by Guidelines for Authors of XMPP Extension Proposals in XEP-0143.

Once submitted, you send your proposal to the XMPP extensions editor, and the proposal will be placed in the XEP inbox. The XSF elects a group of members every year to form the XMPP Council, and this council votes on whether to accept new proposals or modify existing ones.

The XMPP Council and the XMPP extensions editor are very friendly, and they will be more than happy to help you with your proposal by providing feedback and answering any questions you may have.

Another way to participate is to join one of the many discussion lists run by the XSF. You can find these lists at `http://xmpp.org/about/discuss.shtml`. The standards@xmpp.org list is where most protocol discussions happen. List members propose new ideas, point out errors or missing functionality in existing protocols, and ask and answer protocol-related questions. Lists also exist for a variety of specialized topics, and there is even a list for real-time web services, ws-xmpp@xmpp.org.

You can also apply for XSF membership. The XSF holds membership elections every quarter, and the XSF membership elects the XSF Council, the board of directors, and new members; they also vote on changes to the organization's structure and rules.

For the past several years, the XSF has had two summits every year — one in the U.S. and one in Europe. These summits are open to everyone, and many of the most prolific community members often attend as well as developers from a variety of companies. You can find more information at `http://xmpp.org/summit/`.

DESIGNING THE PROTOCOL

The NetPad protocol is a combination of other XMPP protocols plus a new set of elements specific to the application. These new elements will belong to a special namespace, `http://metajack.im/ns/netpad`. First, support for the NetPad protocol is discoverable using standard Service Discovery queries. Then, users establish sessions by include new elements within directed presence stanzas. Finally, commands to start and stop the session along with the editing operations themselves travel inside normal <message> stanzas.

The actual application specific bits are sparing, and they are layered within fairly standard pieces of existing XMPP protocols. This type of protocol construction is typical and demonstrates why so many developers are able to build amazing things with such little effort.

Testing for Support

A client can signal support for the NetPad protocol by responding appropriately to service discovery requests. The client must watch for disco#info queries and return a `<feature>` element containing a `var` attribute of `http://metajack.im/ns/netpad`.

Here is an example response from a client claiming to support the NetPad protocol:

```
<iq to='darcy@pemberley.lit/library'
    from='bingley@netherfield.lit/drawing_room'
    type='result'
    id='netpad1'>
  <query xmlns='http://jabber.org/protocol/disco#info'>
    <identity category='client'
              type='pc'
              name='NetPad'/>
    <feature var='http://jabber.org/protocol/disco#info'/>
    <feature var='http://metajack.im/ns/netpad'/>
  </query>
</iq>
```

Once the application knows that the remote party supports the NetPad protocol, it can start to interact with them using the protocol.

Requesting and Controlling Sessions

Once an editing session is established, the hosting user will want to be notified if the other party leaves. Directed presence is well suited to provide a base protocol for this situation. The remote user can send directed presence along with a new NetPad protocol element requesting an editing session.

This new element is called `<collaborate>`, and here is an example of a request for an editing session:

```
<presence to='bingley@netherfield.lit/drawing_room'
          from='darcy@pemberley.lit/library'>
  <collaborate xmlns='http://metajack.im/ns/netpad'/>
</presence>
```

Bingley receives not only the request for collaboration, but he will also receive notification if Darcy goes offline, implicitly ending any session.

It's possible that Bingley is already in a session with another user, so an appropriate error must be returned in this case. XMPP stanza errors may contain application specific error conditions, so you can create the `<already-collaborating>` condition for this situation. Here's an example error response from Bingley:

```
<presence to='darcy@pemberley.lit/library'
          from='bingley@netherfield.lit/drawing_room'
          type='error'>
  <collaborate xmlns='http://metajack.im/ns/netpad'/>
  <error type='wait'>
    <recipient-unavailable xmlns='urn:ietf:params:xml:ns:xmpp-stanzas'/>
```

```
      <already-collaborating xmlns='http://metajack.im/ns/netpad'/>
    </error>
</presence>
```

This error's general condition is `<recipient-unavailable>`, which is the most appropriate choice for the situation. The type of the error is `wait`, signaling that retrying in the future may prove successful. The original contents of the failed request are also included.

Alternatively, if the session request is successful, Bingley should send an acknowledgement to Darcy. Also, Bingley may have already started working on his document; Darcy must be sent the current text so that Bingley's future editing commands will make sense.

You can use a `<message>` stanza to respond to the session request and include the contents of the document along with it. A new element is needed to signal that this `<message>` stanza is part of the NetPad protocol and to hold the document's contents. Since this is the official start of the editing session, it seems reasonable to call this element `<start>`. The following example shows Bingley's response to Darcy's session request:

```
<message to='darcy@pemberley.lit/library'
         from='bingley@netherfield.lit/drawing_room'
         type='chat'>
   <start xmlns='http://metajack.im/ns/netpad'>
     Dearest Jane
   </start>
</message>
```

Darcy receives the `<start>` acknowledgement along with what appears to be the beginnings of a letter to Jane. If Bingley had not yet written anything, the `<start>` element would be empty.

Darcy can terminate the editing session at anytime by sending unavailable presence or going offline, but Bingley also needs the ability to stop the session. You can add a `<stop>` element to a `<message>` stanza to accomplish this, and this is shown in the following example:

```
<message to='darcy@pemberley.lit/library'
         from='bingley@netherfield.lit/drawing_room'
         type='chat'>
   <stop xmlns='http://metajack.im/ns/netpad'/>
</message>
```

Now both parties can terminate a session.

Editing Operations

Once a session is underway, the parties need to send editing operations to each other. These can easily be carried by new elements inside `<message>` stanzas. The new element is called `<op>`, and it must carry the name of the operation and its parameters. Also, operation requests must include the state vector and the operation's priorty.

Because the name, position, and character attributes of an operation are single values, they are placed in the attributes of an `<op>` element. The state vector and priority value are lists of numbers, so each of these is encoded as a container of child elements holding the individual cell values. State vectors are encoded in `<state>` elements, priorities in `<priority>` elements. Each cell value appears in a `<cell>` element. This is very similar to the encoding process that Chapter 9's SketchPad application used, except that instead of using a form, a custom protocol is employed.

The following stanzas show operations in action:

```
<message to='bingley@netherfield.lit/drawing_room'
         from='darcy@pemberley.lit/library'
         type='chat'>
  <op name='insert' pos='12' char=',' xmlns='http://metajack.im/ns/netpad'>
    <state>
      <cell>0</cell>
      <cell>0</cell>
    </state>
    <priority>
      <cell>1</cell>
    </priority>
  </op>
</message>

<message to='darcy@pemberley.lit/library'
         from='bingley@netherfield.lit/drawing_room'
         type='chat'>
  <op name='delete' pos='4' xmlns='http://metajack.im/ns/netpad'>
    <state>
      <cell>0</cell>
      <cell>1</cell>
    </state>
    <priority>
      <cell>0</cell>
    </priority>
  </op>
</message>
```

Darcy has added a comma, and Bingley has started to delete the "est" from "Dearest".

These are all the pieces necessary for the NetPad protocol. By layering the protocol on top of existing primitives, the new elements remain simple but accomplish much. You see shortly that this protocol is not just easy to understand; it is also easy to implement.

BUILDING THE EDITOR

With the fundamentals of operational transformation and XMPP protocol extensions in hand, you can start building the NetPad collaborative editor. You build the editor in three stages. First, you must determine feature support and set up the editing session between the users. Next, you add chat capabilities between the two users. Finally, you enable both users to collaborate on a single document in the editing window.

The Initial Skeleton

Before you start writing code, NetPad needs a user interface, some styling, and the initial skeleton of the code. These are all similar to the other applications you've seen in previous chapters.

The basic layout of the application appears in Listing 10-2. Aside from the familiar header and login dialog box, the application consists of a status area, a Disconnect button, an editing area, and a chat area.

LISTING 10-2: netpad.html

```html
<!DOCTYPE HTML PUBLIC "-//W3C//DTD HTML 4.01//EN"
          "http://www.w3.org/TR/html4/strict.dtd">
<html>
  <head>
    <title>NetPad - Chapter 10</title>

    <link rel='stylesheet' href='http://ajax.googleapis.com/ajax/libs/jqueryu
i/1.7.2/themes/cupertino/jquery-ui.css'>
    <script src='http://ajax.googleapis.com/ajax/libs/jquery/1.3.2/jquery.js'>
    </script>
    <script src='http://ajax.googleapis.com/ajax/libs/jqueryui/1.7.2/jquery-u
i.js'></script>
    <script src='scripts/strophe.js'></script>
    <script src='flxhr/flXHR.js'></script>
    <script src='scripts/strophe.flxhr.js'></script>

    <link rel='stylesheet' href='netpad.css'>
    <script src='optrans.js'></script>
    <script src='netpad.js'></script>
  </head>
  <body>
    <h1>NetPad</h1>

    <div id='status' class='no-collab'>
      Not collaborating.
    </div>
    <input id='disconnect' type='button' value='disconnect'
           disabled='disabled'>
    <div class='clear'></div>

    <textarea id='pad' disabled='disabled'></textarea>

    <div id='chat-area'>
      <div id='chat'></div>
      <input id='input' type='text' disabled='disabled'>
    </div>

    <!-- login dialog -->
    <div id='login_dialog' class='hidden'>
      <label>JID:</label><input type='text' id='jid'>
      <label>Password:</label><input type='password' id='password'>
      <label>Collaborator:</label><input type='collaborator' id='collaborator'>
    </div>
  </body>
</html>
```

The login dialog box contains a field called Collaborator. If this field is left blank, NetPad will start a session with no collaborator, and it will allow another user to join the editing session. If a collaborator is given, it will attempt to join an editing session with the given user.

The `optrans.js` file is included, because it will be needed later when the operational transformation library you created is used to power the editing features.

Listing 10-3 contains the CSS for the NetPad application and does nothing out of the ordinary.

LISTING 10-3: netpad.css

```css
body {
    font-family: Helvetica;
}

h1 {
    text-align: center;
}

.hidden {
    display: none;
}

.clear {
    clear: both;
}

#pad {
    width: 500px;
    height: 300px;
}

#disconnect {
    margin: 5px 5px 5px 50px;
}

#status {
    padding: 5px 15px 5px 15px;
    float: left;
}

.no-collab {
    background-color: #fcc;
}

.try-collab {
    background-color: #ccf;
}

.collab {
    background-color: #cfc;
}
```

The initial JavaScript skeleton appears in Listing 10-4. By now this initial connection code should be quite familiar. The only difference from previous chapters' applications is the extra collaborator field.

LISTING 10-4: netpad.js (skeleton)

```javascript
var NetPad = {
    connection: null,
    collaborator: null
};

$(document).ready(function () {
    $('#login_dialog').dialog({
        autoOpen: true,
        draggable: false,
        modal: true,
        title: 'Connect to XMPP',
        buttons: {
            "Connect": function () {
                $(document).trigger('connect', {
                    jid: $('#jid').val(),
                    password: $('#password').val(),
                    collaborator: $('#collaborator').val()
                });

                $('#password').val('');
                $(this).dialog('close');
            }
        }
    });
});

$(document).bind('connect', function (ev, data) {
    var conn = new Strophe.Connection(
        "http://bosh.metajack.im:5280/xmpp-httpbind");

    conn.connect(data.jid, data.password, function (status) {
        if (status === Strophe.Status.CONNECTED) {
            $(document).trigger('connected');
        } else if (status === Strophe.Status.DISCONNECTED) {
            $(document).trigger('disconnected');
        }
    });

    NetPad.connection = conn;
    NetPad.collaborator = data.collaborator || null;
});

$(document).bind('connected', function () {
    // nothing here yet
});

$(document).bind('disconnected', function () {
    // nothing here yet
});
```

Starting Editing Sessions

Once a user clicks the Connect button, either they will wait for someone to start an editing session with them, or they will attempt to start an editing session with a remote user. Because not every user will be running NetPad, or a NetPad-compatible editor, you must first test for support for collaborative editing. If support is available, you then initiate an editing session.

The NetPad protocol you developed earlier in this chapter includes some basic session establishment support. It's important to know when a collaborator comes and goes, and so the session establishment is done with directed presence, just like joining and leaving multi-user chat rooms.

Determining Feature Support

Feature support is signaled by responding with the NetPad namespace when replying to a disco#info query. You'll need to add a namespace constant to the NetPad application to keep track of this namespace.

In addition to this, you also need to know whether the application is running as the master editor. Though the master editor has no special power among the collaborators, the master editor serves as the contact point for the session. If the user starts NetPad with no collaborator given, the application becomes a master editor and waits for collaborators.

Add the following attributes to your `NetPad` object:

```
NS_NETPAD: 'http://metajack.im/ns/netpad',
master: null
```

code snippet netpad.js

When a collaborator is specified, NetPad must send a service discovery request to the collaborator to determine if their client supports the NetPad protocol. When running as the master editor, NetPad must listen for these requests and respond with the correct feature to confirm it supports the protocol. You can modify the `connected` event handler to add this functionality:

```
$(document).bind('connected', function () {
    if (NetPad.collaborator) {
        NetPad.master = false;

        $('#status')
            .text('Checking feature support for ' + NetPad.collaborator + '.')
            .attr('class', 'try-collab');

        // check for feature support
        NetPad.connection.sendIQ(
            $iq({to: NetPad.collaborator, type: 'get'})
                .c('query', {xmlns: Strophe.NS.DISCO_INFO}),
            function (iq) {
                var f = $(iq).find(
                    'feature[var="' + NetPad.NS_NETPAD + '"]');

                if (f.length > 0) {
                    $('#status')
```

```
                            .text('Establishing session with ' +
                                    NetPad.collaborator + '.')
                            .attr('class', 'try-collab');

                        // request editing session
                    } else {
                        $('#status')
                            .text('Collaboration not supported with ' +
                                    NetPad.collaborator + '.')
                            .attr('class', 'no-collab');

                        NetPad.connection.disconnect();
                    }
                });
        } else {
            NetPad.master = true;

            // handle incoming discovery requests
            NetPad.connection.addHandler(NetPad.on_disco_info,
                                    Strophe.NS.DISCO_INFO, "iq", "get");
        }
    });
```

The `connected` event handler checks if the collaborator has been specified, and if not, it sets the `master` attribute to false. It updates the status area to inform the user of what is happening, and then it sends the service discovery request to the collaborator.

Once the collaborator has answered the service discovery request, NetPad checks whether the response contains the desired feature. If the feature is supported, the status area is updated, and an editing session is requested. If the feature is unsupported, the status area displays an appropriate message and the connection is terminated.

If the collaborator is specified, `master` is set to true, and a handler for service discovery requests is added. You need to implement this handler, `on_disco_info()`. The following code should be added to the `NetPad` object:

```
on_disco_info: function (iq) {
    NetPad.connection.sendIQ(
        $iq({to: $(iq).attr('from'),
             id: $(iq).attr('id'),
             type: "result"})
            .c('query', {xmlns: Strophe.NS.DISCO_INFO})
            .c('identity', {category: 'client',
                            type: 'pc'}).up()
            .c('feature', {'var': NetPad.NS_NETPAD}));

    return true;
}
```

The handler sends an IQ-result with the appropriate `<identity>` and `<feature>` elements. NetPad identifies itself as a chat client with NetPad protocol support. Note that the response's `id` attribute must match the original request's `id` attribute.

If you run NetPad now, you should be able to see the feature negotiation in action. Try collaborating both with another NetPad user and also a regular XMPP user, and watch the different behavior.

Unfortunately, there is no way to disconnect yet, so you should wire up the Disconnect button.

First, modify the `disconnected` event handler to reset the application:

```
$(document).bind('disconnected', function () {
    NetPad.connection = null;
    NetPad.collaborator = null;

    $('#login_dialog').dialog('open');
});
```

code snippet netpad.js

Next, enable the Disconnect button once the connection has been established. Add the following line as the first line of the `connected` event handler:

```
$('#disconnect').removeAttr('disabled');
```

code snippet netpad.js

Finally, add the `click` event handler for the button. The following code should be added to the document ready handler:

```
$('#disconnect').click(function () {
    $('#disconnect').attr('disabled', 'disabled');

    NetPad.connection.disconnect();
});
```

code snippet netpad.js

Now the application will behave as the user expects.

Establishing NetPad Sessions

Once NetPad has determined a collaborator supports the protocol, it can request an editing session. In the NetPad protocol you designed, this is done with directed presence containing a special `<collaborate>` element.

After the directed presence is sent to request an editing session, the master editor responds with a special message containing the `<start>` element to begin the session or with an `<already-collaborating>` error. The master editor can also send a session stop message using the `<stop>` element when it terminates the session. If the other user terminates their connection, the master editor needs to stop the collaboration; it handles this by watching for the unavailable presence.

First, you'll modify the `connected` event handler to add a handler for the session request. At the same time, the master editor can start manipulating text, so the edit area will need to be enabled. The highlighted code that follows are the new additions to the `connected` event handler:

```
    } else {
        NetPad.master = true;

        $('#pad').removeAttr('disabled');

        // handle incoming discovery and collaboration requests
        NetPad.connection.addHandler(NetPad.on_disco_info,
                                Strophe.NS.DISCO_INFO, "iq", "get");
        NetPad.connection.addHandler(NetPad.on_collaborate,
                                NetPad.NS_NETPAD, "presence");
    }
```

code snippet netpad.js

Now add the following `on_collaborate()` function to the `NetPad` object:

```
on_collaborate: function (presence) {
    var from = $(presence).attr('from');

    if (NetPad.collaborator) {
        // we already have a collaborator
        NetPad.connection.send(
            $pres({to: from, type: 'error'})
                .c('error', {type: 'wait'})
                .c('recipient-unavailable', {xmlns: Strophe.NS.STANZAS})
                .up()
                .c('already-collaborating', {xmlns: NetPad.NS_NETPAD}));
    } else {
        NetPad.collaborator = from;

        NetPad.start_collaboration(true);
    }

    return true;
}
```

code snippet netpad.js

The `on_collaborate()` handler checks that there is not already a session in progress. If an existing session is found, it returns an appropriate error `<presence>` stanza, like the one shown in the protocol design examples. Otherwise, the collaborator is set and `start_collaboration()` is called to begin the session.

The `start_collaboration()` function follows, and, as discussed earlier, it sends the session start message to the collaborator to inform them the request was successful:

```
start_collaboration: function () {
    $('#status')
        .text('Collaborating with ' + NetPad.collaborator + '.')
```

```
                    .attr('class', 'collab');

        if (NetPad.master) {
            // set up and send initial collaboration state
            NetPad.connection.send(
                $msg({to: NetPad.collaborator, type: 'chat'})
                    .c('start', {xmlns: NetPad.NS_NETPAD}));
        } else {
            $('#pad').removeAttr('disabled');
        }
    }
```

code snippet netpad.js

The status text is updated to reflect the new editing session. The master editor sends a `<message>` stanza with a `<start>` child under the NetPad namespace to acknowledge that a session has begun. Because both parties will call this function, it is necessary to send the message only for the master editor. When the other participant calls this function, it will just enable their editing area.

The collaborating user will need to handle this message in order to begin the session as well. Modify the connected event handler by adding the following highlighted line:

```
$(document).bind('connected', function () {
    $('#disconnect').removeAttr('disabled');

    NetPad.connection.addHandler(NetPad.on_message, null, "message");

    if (NetPad.collaborator) {
        NetPad.master = false;
```

code snippet netpad.js

You'll also need to add the following `on_message()` function to the `NetPad` object:

```
on_message: function (message) {
    var from = $(message).attr('from');

    if (NetPad.collaborator === from) {
        var collab = $(message)
            .find('*[xmlns="' + NetPad.NS_NETPAD + '"]');
        if (collab.length > 0) {
            if (NetPad.master) {
                // handle state changes
            } else {
                var command = collab[0].tagName;
                if (command === "start") {
                    NetPad.start_collaboration();
                } else if (command === "stop") {
                    NetPad.stop_collaboration();
                } else {
                    // handle state changes
                }
            }
        }
```

```
        }
    }

    return true;
}
```

The `on_message()` handler watches for elements under the NetPad namespace. Three possible elements may arrive — the `<start>` element, signaling the beginning of the session, the `<stop>` element, signaling the termination of the session by the master editor, and the actual editing operations, which you implement later.

When the master editor's client disconnects, it first notifies the other participant that the session is ended by sending the stop message. Make the highlighted modifications to the Disconnect button's `click` handler:

```
$('#disconnect').click(function () {
    if (NetPad.collaborator) {
        NetPad.stop_collaboration(true);
    }

    $('#disconnect').attr('disabled', 'disabled');

    NetPad.connection.disconnect();
});
```

The argument to `stop_collaboration()` controls whether a stop message is sent to the collaborator. The master editor must send this when the end of the session is initiated, but the rest of the time no notification is needed.

Add the following `stop_collaboration()` function to the NetPad object:

```
stop_collaboration: function (notify) {
    $('#status')
        .text('Not collaborating.')
        .attr('class', 'no-collab');

    if (notify) {
        NetPad.connection.send(
            $msg({to: NetPad.collaborator, type: 'chat'})
                .c('stop', {xmlns: NetPad.NS_NETPAD}));
    }
}
```

This function simply updates the status area, and if `notify` is set, sends the stop message to the collaborator.

The master editor can now end a session, but it doesn't yet detect when the other participant disconnects. Because the other participant sent directed presence, the master editor can watch for unavailable <presence> stanzas. You can add a handler for these stanzas by making the following modifications to the connected event handler:

```
    } else {
        NetPad.master = true;

        $('#pad').removeAttr('disabled');

        // handle incoming discovery and collaboration requests
        NetPad.connection.addHandler(NetPad.on_disco_info,
                                Strophe.NS.DISCO_INFO, "iq", "get");
        NetPad.connection.addHandler(NetPad.on_collaborate,
                                NetPad.NS_NETPAD, "presence");
        NetPad.connection.addHandler(NetPad.on_unavailable,
                                null, "presence", "unavailable");
    }
```

code snippet netpad.js

Now add the following on_unavailable() handler to the NetPad object:

```
on_unavailable: function (presence) {
    var from = $(presence).attr('from');

    if (from === NetPad.collaborator) {
        NetPad.stop_collaboration();
    }

    return true;
}
```

code snippet netpad.js

This handler just calls stop_collaboration() when the other participant leaves. Because the other participant is disconnected, there is no reason to send a notification that the session is over.

If you test NetPad at this point, you should see the collaborative editing session start and end as one or the other party joins and disconnects. Now that sessions can be started and stopped, you just need to send and process editing commands to have a functional editor. Before that though, there is another handy feature you should add.

Chatting About Work

An important part of every collaborative process is communication. Two people working together on a document will have much to discuss, and it is up to you to give NetPad's users the ability to chat with each other.

You've already built several types of chat functionality, and NetPad's chat is actually simpler than your previous private chat client, Gab, from Chapter 6. You see shortly how easy it is to add an important feature by leveraging the stock tools of XMPP.

The input box starts disabled, so you need to enable it when the session is started and disable it once the session is over. The following highlighted modifications must be made to `start_collaboration()` and `stop_collaboration()`:

```javascript
start_collaboration: function () {
    $('#status')
        .text('Collaborating with ' + NetPad.collaborator + '.')
        .attr('class', 'collab');

    $('#input').removeAttr('disabled');

    if (NetPad.master) {
        // set up and send initial collaboration state
        NetPad.connection.send(
            $msg({to: NetPad.collaborator, type: 'chat'})
                .c('start', {xmlns: NetPad.NS_NETPAD}));
    } else {
        $('#pad').removeAttr('disabled');
    }
},

stop_collaboration: function (notify) {
    $('#status')
        .text('Not collaborating.')
        .attr('class', 'no-collab');

    $('#input').attr('disabled', 'disabled');

    if (notify) {
        NetPad.connection.send(
            $msg({to: NetPad.collaborator, type: 'chat'})
                .c('stop', {xmlns: NetPad.NS_NETPAD}));
    }
}
```

code snippet netpad.js

Next, you wire up the input box to send messages when the user presses the Enter key. Add the following `keypress` event handler to the document ready handler:

```javascript
$('#input').keypress(function (ev) {
    if (ev.which === 13) {
        ev.preventDefault();

        var body = $(this).val();
        $('#chat').append("<div class='message'>" +
                        "&lt;<span class='nick self'>" +
                        Strophe.getBareJidFromJid(
                            NetPad.connection.jid) +
```

```
                                  "</span>&gt; " +
                                  "<span class='message'>" +
                                  body +
                                  "</span>" +
                                  "</div>");

            NetPad.scroll_chat();

            NetPad.connection.send(
                $msg({to: NetPad.collaborator, type: 'chat'})
                    .c('body').t(body));

            $(this).val('');
        }
    });
```

The function formats the chat text and adds it to the chat area, and then it sends a `<message>` stanza to the collaborator. Once the message is sent, the function clears the input box, preparing it for the next message.

The chat area must be scrolled once content is added so that the new messages appear correctly. Add the following `scroll_chat()` function to the NetPad object to do this:

```
scroll_chat: function () {
    var chat = $('#chat').get(0);
    chat.scrollTop = chat.scrollHeight;
}
```

Finally, NetPad must watch for incoming messages and display them. Modify the `on_message()` function to match the one shown here:

```
on_message: function (message) {
    var from = $(message).attr('from');

    if (NetPad.collaborator === from) {
        var collab = $(message)
            .find('*[xmlns="' + NetPad.NS_NETPAD + '"]');
        if (collab.length > 0) {
            if (NetPad.master) {
                // handle state changes
            } else {
                var command = collab[0].tagName;
                if (command === "start") {
                    NetPad.start_collaboration();
                } else if (command === "stop") {
                    NetPad.stop_collaboration();
                } else {
                    // handle state changes
                }
```

```
            }
        } else {
            // add regular message to the chat
            var body = $(message).find('body').text();
            $('#chat').append("<div class='message'>" +
                                "&lt;<span class='nick'>" +
                                Strophe.getBareJidFromJid(from) +
                                "</span>&gt; " +
                                "<span class='message'>" +
                                body +
                                "</span>" +
                                "</div>");
            NetPad.scroll_chat();
        }
    }

    return true;
}
```

With just those few changes, NetPad now supports chat between the collaborators.

Making Edits

You have only one task left — to add the primary feature of collaborative editing. Much of the work has already been done by creating the OpTrans object, but there is still a little bit of glue needed to stick everything together.

To finish everything off, you'll need to initialize the OpTrans object, generate and broadcast local operations, receive and process remote operations, and keep the editing area updated with the latest changes.

Initializing OpTrans

OpTrans's init() method needs to be invoked by all participants at the start of a session. You can do this easily by modifying the start_collaboration() function:

```
start_collaboration: function () {
    $('#status')
        .text('Collaborating with ' + NetPad.collaborator + '.')
        .attr('class', 'collab');

    $('#input').removeAttr('disabled');

    var buffer = $('#pad').val();
    OpTrans.init([NetPad.connection.jid, NetPad.collaborator],
                buffer,
                NetPad.update_pad);

    if (NetPad.master) {
        // set up and send initial collaboration state
```

```
        var msg = $msg({to: NetPad.collaborator, type: 'chat'})
            .c('start', {xmlns: NetPad.NS_NETPAD});
        if (buffer) {
            msg.t(buffer);
        }

        NetPad.connection.send(msg);
    } else {
        $('#pad').removeAttr('disabled');
    }
}
```

code snippet netpad.js

The initial contents of the editing area and the relevant JIDs are passed into `init()`. The start message is also modified to include any text that the master editor created before the session began.

The `on_message()` handler, which processes the start message, must also be modified to deal with this initial data. Make the highlighted modifications to `on_message()`:

```
if (command === "start") {
    $('#pad').val(collab.text());
    NetPad.start_collaboration();
} else if (command === "stop") {
    NetPad.stop_collaboration();
} else {
```

code snippet netpad.js

The `start_collaboration()` function also passes the `update_pad()` function to `OpTrans.init()`, which will be called whenever buffer modifications occur due to editing operations. Add the following implementation of `update_pad()` to the `NetPad` object:

```
update_pad: function (buffer, remote) {
    var old_pos = $('#pad')[0].selectionStart;
    var old_buffer = $('#pad').val();
    $('#pad').val(buffer);

    if (buffer.length > old_buffer.length && !remote) {
        old_pos += 1;
    }

    $('#pad')[0].selectionStart = old_pos;
    $('#pad')[0].selectionEnd = old_pos;
}
```

code snippet netpad.js

Most of the code in `update_pad()` handles saving and restoring the cursor position so that it stays in the same place during an update. Otherwise, the cursor would jump to the end of the buffer after every edit. Unfortunately, IE 6 does not support the `selectionStart` and `selectionEnd` properties, so this code will not work there. It should work fine in later versions of IE and in other browsers.

Local and Remote Operations

The next step is to generate and broadcast local editing events. While the user is in the editing area, certain key presses will cause the contents of the buffer to change. These keys include normal alphanumeric keys, the Delete and Backspace keys, as well as the shortcuts for copy and paste. It is a lot of work to handle the full range of possibilities, so for the sake of simplicity, NetPad will be limited to the most basic operations and will disallow the others.

The following `keypress` event handler processes local editing events. After it determines which event is intended, it calls the `send_op()` function to update the `OpTrans` object and broadcast the operation to the other user. Add this code to the document ready handler:

Available for download on Wrox.com

```javascript
$('#pad').keypress(function (ev) {
    if (NetPad.collaborator) {
        var idx = this.selectionStart;
        var handled = true;
        if (ev.which === 8) {
            this.selectionStart = idx - 1;
            this.selectionEnd = idx - 1;
            NetPad.send_op('delete', idx - 1);
        } else if (ev.which === 46) {
            NetPad.send_op('delete', idx);
        } else if ((ev.which >= 32 && ev.which <= 127) ||
                    ev.which >= 256) {
            NetPad.send_op('insert', idx, String.fromCharCode(ev.which));
        }

        ev.preventDefault();
    }
});
```

code snippet netpad.js

The key codes 8 and 46 are for the Backspace and Delete keys, respectively. The range of key codes in the last case handle the normal printable ASCII character set as well as the printable non-ASCII characters. The handler passes the `send_op()` function the operation, the index at which the operation occurred, and, for an insert operation, the character that was inserted. Any characters not explicitly handled here will be ignored because the default behaviors are switched off with the call to `preventDefault()`.

The `send_op()` function takes a local operation, encodes it into the NetPad protocol XML format you designed previously, and sends it to the collaborator. Its counterpart, `process_op()`, handles decoding the NetPad protocol stanza and passing the operation request to `OpTrans`'s `do_remote()` function. Add the following two functions to the `NetPad` object:

Available for download on Wrox.com

```javascript
send_op: function (op, pos, chr) {
    var req = OpTrans.do_local(op, pos, chr);

    var op_attrs = {xmlns: NetPad.NS_NETPAD,
                    name: op,
```

```
                      pos: pos};
        if (chr) {
            op_attrs['char'] = chr;
        }

        var msg = $msg({to: NetPad.collaborator, type: 'chat'})
            .c('op', op_attrs)
            .c('state');

        var i;
        for (i = 0; i < req[1].length; i++) {
            msg.c('cell').t('' + req[1][i]).up();
        }

        msg.up().c('priority');
        for (i = 0; i < req[3].length; i++) {
            msg.c('cell').t('' + req[3][i]).up();
        }

        NetPad.connection.send(msg);
    },

    process_op: function (op) {
        var name = op.attr('name');
        var pos = parseInt(op.attr('pos'), 10);
        var chr = op.attr('char');
        var pri = [];
        var state = [];

        op.find('state > cell').each(function () {
            state.push(parseInt($(this).text(), 10));
        });

        op.find('priority > cell').each(function () {
            priority.push(parseInt($(this).text(), 10));
        });

        OpTrans.do_remote(NetPad.collaborator,
                          state,
                          name, pos, chr,
                          pri);
    }
```

code snippet netpad.js

The last step is to call `process_op()` whenever remote operations are received. Because they arrive in `<message>` stanzas, you can modify the `on_message()` handler by adding the following high-lighted lines:

```
if (collab.length > 0) {
    if (NetPad.master) {
        NetPad.process_op(collab);
    } else {
```

```
            var command = collab[0].tagName;
            if (command === "start") {
                $('#pad').val(collab.text());
                NetPad.start_collaboration();
            } else if (command === "stop") {
                NetPad.stop_collaboration();
            } else {
                console.log("got remote op");
                NetPad.process_op(collab);
            }
        }
    }
} else {
```

code snippet netpad.js

NetPad can now send and receive editing operations, process them with the OpTrans object, and update the buffer contents to reflect both local and remote changes. Give it a try with a friend or by running multiple copies of the application yourself. At the end of every editing session, you will notice that both users have the same resulting text.

The final version of netpad.js appears in Listing 10-5.

Available for download on Wrox.com

LISTING 10-5: netpad.js (final)

```
var NetPad = {
    connection: null,
    collaborator: null,
    NS_NETPAD: 'http://metajack.im/ns/netpad',
    master: null,

    on_disco_info: function (iq) {
        NetPad.connection.sendIQ(
            $iq({to: $(iq).attr('from'),
                id: $(iq).attr('id'),
                type: "result"})
                .c('query', {xmlns: Strophe.NS.DISCO_INFO})
                .c('identity', {category: 'client',
                                type: 'pc'}).up()
                .c('feature', {'var': NetPad.NS_NETPAD}));

        return true;
    },

    on_collaborate: function (presence) {
        var from = $(presence).attr('from');

        if (NetPad.collaborator) {
            // we already have a collaborator
            NetPad.connection.send(
                $pres({to: from, type: 'error'})
                    .c('error', {type: 'wait'})
                    .c('recipient-unavailable', {xmlns: Strophe.NS.STANZAS})
```

continues

LISTING 10-5 *(continued)*

```
                    .up()
                    .c('already-collaborating', {xmlns: NetPad.NS_NETPAD}));
        } else {
            NetPad.collaborator = from;

            NetPad.start_collaboration(true);
        }

        return true;
    },

    start_collaboration: function () {
        $('#status')
            .text('Collaborating with ' + NetPad.collaborator + '.')
            .attr('class', 'collab');

        $('#input').removeAttr('disabled');

        var buffer = $('#pad').val();
        OpTrans.init([NetPad.connection.jid, NetPad.collaborator],
                    buffer,
                    NetPad.update_pad);

        if (NetPad.master) {
            // set up and send initial collaboration state
            var msg = $msg({to: NetPad.collaborator, type: 'chat'})
                .c('start', {xmlns: NetPad.NS_NETPAD});
            if (buffer) {
                msg.t(buffer);
            }

            NetPad.connection.send(msg);
        } else {
            $('#pad').removeAttr('disabled');
        }
    },

    on_message: function (message) {
        var from = $(message).attr('from');

        if (NetPad.collaborator === from) {
            var collab = $(message)
                .find('*[xmlns="' + NetPad.NS_NETPAD + '"]');
            if (collab.length > 0) {
                if (NetPad.master) {
                    NetPad.process_op(collab);
                } else {
                    var command = collab[0].tagName;
                    if (command === "start") {
                        $('#pad').val(collab.text());
                        NetPad.start_collaboration();
                    } else if (command === "stop") {
```

```
                    NetPad.stop_collaboration();
                } else {
                    NetPad.process_op(collab);
                }
            }
        } else {
            // add regular message to the chat
            var body = $(message).find('body').text();
            $('#chat').append("<div class='message'>" +
                            "&lt;<span class='nick'>" +
                            Strophe.getBareJidFromJid(from) +
                            "</span>&gt; " +
                            "<span class='message'>" +
                            body +
                            "</span>" +
                            "</div>");
            NetPad.scroll_chat();
        }
    }

    return true;
},

stop_collaboration: function (notify) {
    $('#status')
        .text('Not collaborating.')
        .attr('class', 'no-collab');

    $('#input').attr('disabled', 'disabled');

    if (notify) {
        NetPad.connection.send(
            $msg({to: NetPad.collaborator, type: 'chat'})
                .c('stop', {xmlns: NetPad.NS_NETPAD}));
    }
},

on_unavailable: function (presence) {
    var from = $(presence).attr('from');

    if (from === NetPad.collaborator) {
        NetPad.stop_collaboration();
    }

    return true;
},

scroll_chat: function () {
    var chat = $('#chat').get(0);
    chat.scrollTop = chat.scrollHeight;
},

update_pad: function (buffer, remote) {
    var old_pos = $('#pad')[0].selectionStart;
```

continues

LISTING 10-5 *(continued)*

```
        var old_buffer = $('#pad').val();
        $('#pad').val(buffer);

        if (buffer.length > old_buffer.length && !remote) {
            old_pos += 1;
        }

        $('#pad')[0].selectionStart = old_pos;
        $('#pad')[0].selectionEnd = old_pos;
    },

    send_op: function (op, pos, chr) {
        var req = OpTrans.do_local(op, pos, chr);

        var op_attrs = {xmlns: NetPad.NS_NETPAD,
                        name: op,
                        pos: posK};
        if (chr) {
            op_attrs['char'] = chr;
        }

        var msg = $msg({to: NetPad.collaborator, type: 'chat'})
            .c('op', op_attrs)
            .c('state');

        var i;
        for (i = 0; i < req[1].length; i++) {
            msg.c('cell').t('' + req[1][i]).up();
        }

        msg.up().c('priority');
        for (i = 0; i < req[3].length; i++) {
            msg.c('cell').t('' + req[3][i]).up();
        }

        NetPad.connection.send(msg);
    },

    process_op: function (op) {
        var name = op.attr('name');
        var pos = parseInt(op.attr('pos'), 10);
        var chr = op.attr('char');
        var pri = [];
        var state = [];

        op.find('state > cell').each(function () {
            state.push(parseInt($(this).text(), 10));
        });

        op.find('priority > cell').each(function () {
            priority.push(parseInt($(this).text(), 10));
```

```
            });

        OpTrans.do_remote(NetPad.collaborator,
                          state,
                          name, pos, chr,
                          pri);
    }
};

$(document).ready(function () {
    $('#login_dialog').dialog({
        autoOpen: true,
        draggable: false,
        modal: true,
        title: 'Connect to XMPP',
        buttons: {
            "Connect": function () {
                $(document).trigger('connect', {
                    jid: $('#jid').val(),
                    password: $('#password').val(),
                    collaborator: $('#collaborator').val()
                });

                $('#password').val('');
                $(this).dialog('close');
            }
        }
    });

    $('#disconnect').click(function () {
        if (NetPad.collaborator) {
            NetPad.stop_collaboration(true);
        }

        $('#disconnect').attr('disabled', 'disabled');

        NetPad.connection.disconnect();
    });

    $('#input').keypress(function (ev) {
        if (ev.which === 13) {
            ev.preventDefault();

            var body = $(this).val();
            $('#chat').append("<div class='message'>" +
                              "&lt;<span class='nick self'>" +
                              Strophe.getBareJidFromJid(
                                  NetPad.connection.jid) +
                              "</span>&gt; " +
                              "<span class='message'>" +
                              body +
                              "</span>" +
```

continues

LISTING 10-5 *(continued)*

```
                            "</div>");

          NetPad.connection.send(
              $msg({to: NetPad.collaborator, type: 'chat'})
                  .c('body').t(body));

          $(this).val('');
      }
  });

  $('#pad').keypress(function (ev) {
      if (NetPad.collaborator) {
          var idx = this.selectionStart;
          var handled = true;
          if (ev.which === 8) {
              this.selectionStart = idx - 1;
              this.selectionEnd = idx - 1;
              NetPad.send_op('delete', idx - 1);
          } else if (ev.which === 46) {
              NetPad.send_op('delete', idx);
          } else if ((ev.which >= 32 && ev.which <= 127) ||
                     ev.which >= 256) {
              NetPad.send_op('insert', idx, String.fromCharCode(ev.which));
          }

          ev.preventDefault();
      }
  });
});

$(document).bind('connect', function (ev, data) {
    var conn = new Strophe.Connection(
        "http://bosh.metajack.im:5280/xmpp-httpbind");

    conn.connect(data.jid, data.password, function (status) {
        if (status === Strophe.Status.CONNECTED) {
            $(document).trigger('connected');
        } else if (status === Strophe.Status.DISCONNECTED) {
            $(document).trigger('disconnected');
        }
    });

    NetPad.connection = conn;
    NetPad.collaborator = data.collaborator || null;
});

$(document).bind('connected', function () {
    $('#disconnect').removeAttr('disabled');

    NetPad.connection.addHandler(NetPad.on_message, null, "message");

    if (NetPad.collaborator) {
```

```javascript
            NetPad.master = false;

            $('#status')
                .text('Checking feature support for ' + NetPad.collaborator + '.')
                .attr('class', 'try-collab');

            // check for feature support
            NetPad.connection.sendIQ(
                $iq({to: NetPad.collaborator, type: 'get'})
                    .c('query', {xmlns: Strophe.NS.DISCO_INFO}),
                function (iq) {
                    var f = $(iq).find(
                        'feature[var="' + NetPad.NS_NETPAD + '"]');

                    if (f.length > 0) {
                        $('#status')
                            .text('Establishing session with ' +
                                NetPad.collaborator + '.')
                            .attr('class', 'try-collab');

                        NetPad.connection.send(
                            $pres({to: NetPad.collaborator})
                                .c('collaborate', {xmlns: NetPad.NS_NETPAD}));
                    } else {
                        $('#status')
                            .text('Collaboration not supported with ' +
                                NetPad.collaborator + '.')
                            .attr('class', 'no-collab');

                        NetPad.connection.disconnect();
                    }
                });
        } else {
            NetPad.master = true;

            $('#pad').removeAttr('disabled');

            // handle incoming discovery and collaboration requests
            NetPad.connection.addHandler(NetPad.on_disco_info,
                                         Strophe.NS.DISCO_INFO, "iq", "get");
            NetPad.connection.addHandler(NetPad.on_collaborate,
                                         NetPad.NS_NETPAD, "presence");
            NetPad.connection.addHandler(NetPad.on_unavailable,
                                         null, "presence");
        }
    });

    $(document).bind('disconnected', function () {
        NetPad.connection = null;

        $('#login_dialog').dialog('open');
    });
```

EXPANDING NETPAD

NetPad is quite functional, but it is lacking a lot of nice features. You should try making NetPad a more competitive product by adding some of these features:

➤ The collaborating user does not receive notifications when the master editor disconnects without sending the session stop message. Modify the protocol to include this case, and implement it.

➤ Allow more than two collaborators. You could even use a multi-user chat room to broadcast the editing operations.

➤ Fix the edit area so that it handles more advanced functions like arrow key movement and copy and paste.

➤ Add a shared whiteboard, perhaps based on Chapter 9's SketchPad, to the application so that collaborators can draw pictures. Each user could draw with a different color.

SUMMARY

In this chapter you built a sophisticated application that allowed two users to collaboratively edit the same document in real time. Applications such as NetPad are becoming more common, and the XMPP protocol makes them fun and easy to build.

Hopefully you learned a lot in this chapter, including:

➤ The principles behind operational transformation

➤ The various ways XMPP stanzas can be extended to make custom protocols

➤ Using directed presence to do your own session management

➤ The ease of adding chat and other social features to existing applications

In the next chapter, you build the biggest application yet — a multi-user, real-time gaming system for Tic-Tac-Toe players.

11

Playing Games: Head to Head Tic-Tac-Toe

WHAT'S IN THIS CHAPTER?

➤ Writing an XMPP bot

➤ Creating sophisticated protocols

➤ Collaborative spaces on top of multi-user chat

Almost everyone enjoys playing games, and if the successes of the massively multi-player online role-playing games (MMORPGs) like World of Warcraft are any indication, people enjoy playing games with others. Many games depend on low-latency interaction between players, and others need features for players to find each other and communicate. XMPP offers a lot of built-in functionality perfect for games, and more complex features are just a few extended stanzas away.

XMPP excels at sending small bits of structured information back and forth, which games can use to pass around changes to the game's world or state. This is really not such a different problem from other forms of collaboration; the only real difference is in the purpose of the data. Just replace the buffer full of text in Chapter 10's NetPad with a dungeon full of monsters. To XMPP, it's all just bits of XML.

As long as players are not playing alone, communication is an important part of game play. As you've discovered throughout this book, XMPP has a wide variety of tools for communication of all kinds, and most of these tools are built-in and ready for use without much work required. Remember just how easy it was to add chat to the NetPad application? The same can be done in games. Add some game-related information alongside players' presence, and what was once a chat roster is now a guild of fellow adventurers.

You will put XMPP to this pleasurable use in this chapter, developing a Tic-Tac-Toe game that users all over the world can play.

APPLICATION PREVIEW

Toetem has a lot of different pieces for the UI. Figure 11-1 shows the initial screen, which displays the current list of games and the list of waiting players.

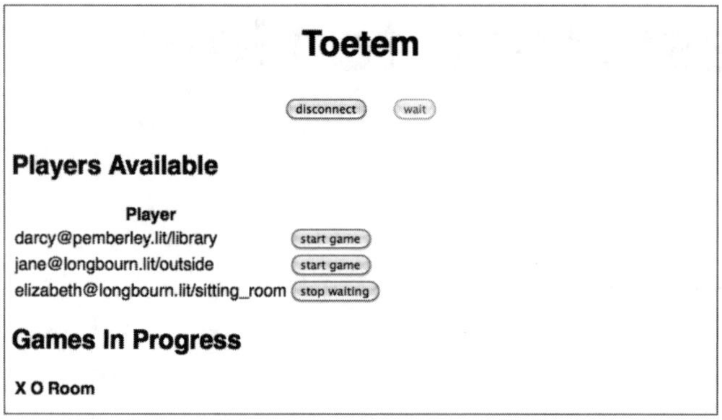

FIGURE 11-1

Several buttons line the top of the interface. You've seen the Disconnect button before, but the other one is new. The Wait button adds the user to the list of players waiting to play a game.

Underneath the button bar is the list of waiting players. These are players who are ready to play a Tic-Tac-Toe game. Next to each player is a Play button the user can click to start a game with that player, or if that player is also the user, a Stop Waiting button appears.

At the bottom is the list of active games. Anytime a new game starts, it shows up in this list, and when the game finishes, the game is removed. Next to each game is a Watch button, allowing the user to join the game as an observer to watch the action.

The game board and chat are shown in Figure 11-2. Players interact with the board by clicking on it during their turn. The button at the top allows them to resign. The chat area allows all the players and observers to talk to each other.

This is the biggest application you build in this book, but you see soon that it is composed of parts you have already worked with.

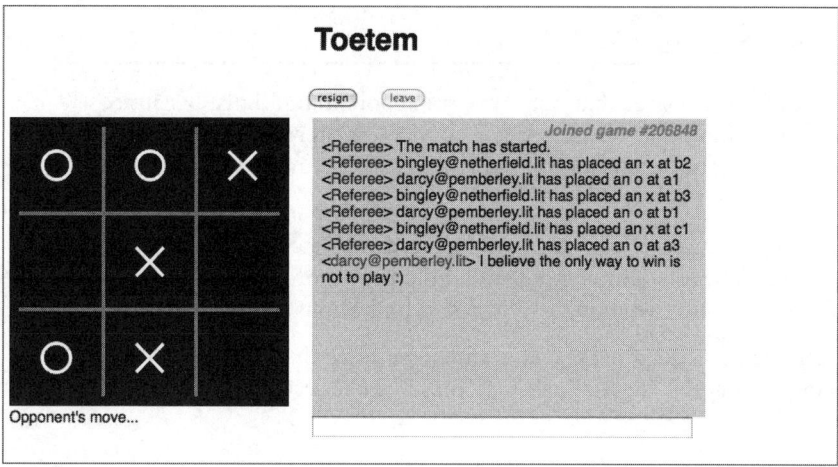

FIGURE 11-2

TOETEM DESIGN

Toetem consists of two major pieces: the referee and the game client.

The referee is an XMPP bot that enforces game rules and keeps track of the active games and waiting players. Users interact with the referee only indirectly through the actions they take in the game client. Only one referee is needed for all the players in the system, but without a referee, there would be no way to prevent cheating and abuse by malicious players.

The game client is the application that each player uses to access the system and play games. Actions that the user takes are sent to the referee and then broadcast out to the other players and observers.

Because the referee is a bot, it does not need a user interface. It simply maintains a connection and listens for commands from users, checks their legality, and then broadcasts them out to other users or updates its internal state.

The referee understands a number of commands, and these are covered in detail in the following "Designing the Game Protocol" section. The protocol you create is a healthy mix of all three stanza types — `<iq>`, `<presence>`, and `<message>` — and makes use of existing extensions like multi-user chat.

Games are organized around multi-user chat rooms. Each game has an associated room, and all players and observers join this room to play or watch the game. This chat room provides the communication area for all the game's participants, and it also is used to broadcast the players' moves to everyone. Multi-user chat rooms already provide most of the functionality needed, so they make a great building block for the Toetem protocol.

BOTS AND COMPONENTS

Toetem uses a bot for the referee, but bots have some potential pitfalls. Because bots are normal users on the server, they come complete with rosters and all the normal message routing that clients have. Usually this extra functionality is not necessary and can get in the way as your bot scales in size.

In a more robust system, the referee would be replaced with a component that performed the same function. The component would have more control over its resources and routing, and it wouldn't run into size limitations as quickly.

For more information on components and scaling please see the "Components" section in Chapter 1 and the "Spreading Out Components" section in Chapter 13.

Users wishing to play games will need to know the JID of the referee when they connect. Once connected, they will be able to view the list of current games and the list of waiting players. They can choose to start a game with one of the waiting players, to wait for someone to play, or to watch one of the active games being played by others.

If they start a game or join a game as an observer they will be switched to the game view. In the game view, the user will see the Tic-Tac-Toe board as well as the game's chat. Whenever a player moves, the board will update in real time for all the players and observers. An observer can leave the game at any time, but players must wait until the game has concluded before they can leave.

Most of the work will be defining and implementing the Toetem protocol and creating the game board control. The protocol you design in this chapter is not limited to Tic-Tac-Toe games; in fact, it is a simplification of the same protocol that Chesspark uses for its chess games. Changing the game board and the particular kinds of moves and state is all that you need to turn it into any other kind of game. Tic-Tac-Toe was chosen because it has extremely simple rules, allowing you to concentrate on the protocol and interactions between users instead of complex game logic.

DESIGNING THE GAME PROTOCOL

You designed a simple protocol in the previous chapter, and in this chapter, you design a much more complex protocol for managing and running a game system. Each piece of the protocol is built out of the protocol blocks that you've seen in previous chapters, but the combination of these simple pieces results in a sophisticated system.

The Toetem protocol comprises four main areas. First, you need some way to keep track of players in the system, and just as in the previous chapter, you use directed presence for this task. Next, you need to manage the list of players who are waiting for a game. You also need to manage the active games and their corresponding chat rooms. Finally, you must deal with the player interactions within each game.

Keeping Track of Users

Keeping track of users is quite important. For starters, the other players will want to know who is available to play and who is already playing. Even more importantly, the referee must gracefully handle the situation where players leave unexpectedly.

If a player leaves who is not playing or in the waiting list, it is not a concern. However, if a player in a game or a player in the waiting list leaves, the consequences will be felt by other users. It will be frustrating for users if they click a waiting player's Play button and that player is no longer there. Even worse is the exit of a player during a game.

The first case is easily handled by removing the player from the list of waiting players. In the second case, a decision must be made on how to handle the situation. In Toetem, the simplest solution is used, which is to forfeit the player who leaves the game. This solution is not optimal, but it prevents the most common form of abuse — cheating by leaving the game in a losing position.

The Toetem protocol uses directed presence to keep track of players. To interact with the referee, the user must first send it directed presence. From then on, the referee will know when the user becomes unavailable, and the referee can take the appropriate action. This is the same technique used by NetPad in Chapter 10 and by multi-user chat rooms.

The following example `<presence>` stanza shows Darcy registering himself with the referee. Note that the namespace used for the Toetem protocol is `http://metajack.im/ns/toetem`.

```
<presence to='referee@pemberley.lit/toetem'
          from='darcy@pemberley.lit/library'>
  <register xmlns='http://metajack.im/ns/toetem'/>
</presence>
```

When a player leaves, the referee will receive a stanza similar to the following:

```
<presence to='referee@pemberley.lit/toetem'
          from='darcy@pemberley.lit/library'
          type='unavailable'/>
```

Once a player registers with the referee, the current list of waiting players and active games will be sent in a pair of `<message>` stanzas. Darcy receives the following `<message>` stanzas after registering:

```
<message to='darcy@pemberley.lit/library'
         from='referee@pemberley.lit/toetem'>
  <waiting xmlns='http://metajack.im/ns/toetem'>
    <player jid='elizabeth@longbourn.lit/sitting_room'/>
  </waiting>
</message>

<message to='darcy@pemberley.lit/library'
         from='referee@pemberley.lit/toetem'>
  <games xmlns='http://metajack.im/ns/toetem'>
```

```
        <game x-player='jane@longbourn.lit/outside'
              o-player='bingley@netherfield.lit/drawing_room'
              room='toetem-1045@games.pemberley.lit'/>
     </games>
  </message>
```

The `<waiting>` element contains a `<player>` element for each waiting player along with the player's JID. Similarly, the `<games>` element contains a `<game>` for each active game along with its players and its room.

Managing Players

Players need to signal that they are waiting to start a game and also when they stop waiting. These tasks are easily done with the help of `<iq>` stanzas. The players also need to handle changes to the list of currently waiting players, which the referee sends in `<message>` stanzas.

If users want to add themselves to the waiting list, they send the `<waiting>` command in an IQ-set stanza. To remove themselves from the list, they send a `<stop-waiting>` command in an IQ-set stanza. Elizabeth adds and removes herself from the list in the following stanzas:

```
<iq to='referee@pemberley.lit/toetem'
    from='elizabeth@longbourn.lit/sitting_room'
    type='set'
    id='waiting2'>
  <waiting xmlns='http://metajack.im/ns/toetem'/>
</iq>

<iq to='elizabeth@longbourn.lit/sitting_room'
    from='referee@pemberley.lit/toetem'
    type='result'
    id='waiting2'/>

<iq to='referee@pemberley.lit/toetem'
    from='elizabeth@longbourn.lit/sitting_room'
    type='set'
    id='waiting3'>
  <stop-waiting xmlns='http://metajack.im/ns/toetem'/>
</iq>

<iq to='elizabeth@longbourn.lit/sitting_room'
    from='referee@pemberley.lit/toetem'
    type='result'
    id='waiting3'/>
```

These stanzas are all fairly simple commands with empty responses, but it is enough to fulfill Toetem's requirements.

It's possible that someone could send a `<waiting>` command while they are already waiting, or a `<stop-waiting>` command when they are not yet waiting. The Toetem protocol needs to handle these cases as well. In the first case, there is no reason to throw an error; the referee can simply pretend it has added the user to the list and return a successful response. In the other case, the referee must return an appropriate error. The following example shows the `bad-request` condition sent in response to a strange `<stop-waiting>` command from Jane:

```
<iq to='jane@longbourn.lit/outside'
    from='referee@pemberley.lit/toetem'
    type='error'
    id='stop1'>
  <stop-waiting xmlns='http://metajack.im/ns/toetem'/>
  <error type='cancel'>
    <bad-request xmlns='urn:ietf:params:xml:ns:xmpp-stanzas'/>
  </error>
</iq>
```

Every time the waiting list changes, the referee will broadcast out the update to every registered player. Each player will receive `<message>` stanzas like the following:

```
<message to='darcy@pemberley.lit/library'
         from='referee@pemberley.lit/toetem'>
  <waiting xmlns='http://metajack.im/ns/toetem'>
    <player jid='jane@longbourn.lit/outside'/>
  </waiting>
</message>

<message to='darcy@pemberley.lit/library'
         from='referee@pemberley.lit/toetem'>
  <not-waiting xmlns='http://metajack.im/ns/toetem'>
    <player jid='jane@longbourn.lit/outside'/>
  </not-waiting>
</message>
```

The first stanza is exactly like the one players receive when first registering, except that updates contain only a single `<player>` element. Updates about players leaving the waiting list are nearly the same, except with a `<not-waiting>` element instead of `<waiting>`.

Users will always see an accurate waiting list of players because they start with the current list and receive updates as it changes. There is no need for each user to poll the waiting list; updates are delivered and processed in real time.

These simple interactions, in addition to the unavailable presence notifications described previously, are all that is needed for the referee to manage the waiting list of players.

Managing Games

Managing games is a little more complex. From the user's perspective, the same three kinds of actions are needed as for the waiting player's list — handle updates to the list of active games, start a game, and resign a game. However, the referee must create or destroy a multi-user chat room as the result of a game beginning or ending, and this makes its job a little more involved.

Once a game starts, the game's players receive a message from the referee with the name of the game's room. These players must then join the room for the game to begin. After a game is concluded, the players can leave at their leisure; they may want to continue chatting with each other after the match.

Handling updates to the list of active games is done exactly like updates to the waiting list. A message is broadcast to all registered players when games begin or end. Here are the stanzas Darcy sees as Jane and Elizabeth start and finish their game:

```
<message to='darcy@pemberley.lit/library'
         from='referee@pemberley.lit/toetem'>
  <games xmlns='http://metajack.im/ns/toetem'>
    <game x-player='jane@longbourn.lit/outside'
          o-player='elizabeth@longbourn.lit/sitting_room'
          room='toetem-123@games.pemberley.lit'/>
  </games>
</message>

<message to='darcy@pemberley.lit/library'
         from='referee@pemberley.lit/toetem'>
  <game-over xmlns='http://metajack.im/ns/toetem'>
    <game x-player='jane@longbourn.lit/outside'
          o-player='elizabeth@longbourn.lit/sitting_room'
          room='toetem-123@games.pemberley.lit'/>
  </game-over>
</message>
```

Like the waiting list, game notifications are delivered immediately so that each player always has the most current information without having to continuously ask for it.

If Elizabeth wants to watch a game, she can simply join the game's room. The referee will then start broadcasting game moves to her as described in the next section.

To start her own game, Elizabeth must send the `<start>` command to the referee along with the player she wishes to start a game with. A successful request and its response are shown in the following example:

```
<iq to='referee@pemberley.lit/toetem'
    from='elizabeth@longbourn.lit/sitting_room'
    type='set'
    id='start1'>
  <start xmlns='http://metajack.im/ns/toetem'
         with='jane@longbourn.lit/outside'/>
</iq>

<iq to='elizabeth@longbourn.lit/sitting_room'
    from='referee@pemberley.lit/toetem'
    type='result'
    id='start1'/>
```

The referee then creates the game room and invites the players. These invitations are sent by the room on behalf of the referee and can be seen in the following example. The format of these invitations is defined in section 7.5.2 of XEP-0045, Mediated Invitation.

```
<message to='elizabeth@longbourn.lit/sitting_room'
         from='toetem-456@games.pemberley.lit'>
  <x xmlns='http://jabber.org/protocol/muc#user'>
```

```
      <invite from='referee@pemberley.lit/toetem'/>
    </x>
  </message>

  <message to='jane@longbourn.lit/outside'
           from='toetem-456@games.pemberley.lit'>
    <x xmlns='http://jabber.org/protocol/muc#user'>
      <invite from='referee@pemberley.lit/toetem'/>
    </x>
  </message>
```

Once the invitations are received, both players must join the room. The protocol interactions from there are covered in the next section.

A few possible error cases exist for game starts. If a player tries to start a game with a user who is not currently on the waiting list, the server returns an item not found error stanza like the following:

```
<iq to='jane@longbourn.lit/outside'
    from='referee@pemberley.lit/toetem'
    type='error'
    id='start2'>
  <start xmlns='http://metajack.im/ns/toetem'
         with='elizabeth@longbourn.lit/library'/>
  <error type='modify'>
    <item-not-found xmlns='urn:ietf:params:xml:ns:xmpp-stanzas'/>
  </error>
</iq>
```

Also, it is possible that the requested player has already started a game with someone else and is currently busy playing. In this case, the referee returns a not allowed error such as the following:

```
<iq to='jane@longbourn.lit/outside'
    from='referee@pemberley.lit/toetem'
    type='error'
    id='start3'>
  <start xmlns='http://metajack.im/ns/toetem'
         with='darcy@pemberley.lit/library'/>
  <error type='cancel'>
    <not-allowed xmlns='urn:ietf:params:xml:ns:xmpp-stanzas'/>
  </error>
</iq>
```

While in a game, a player may wish to resign instead of await their obvious fate. Resigning is done by sending the <resign> command in an IQ-set to the referee. Beaten by her clever sister, Jane resigns in the following example:

```
<iq to='referee@pemberley.lit/toetem'
    from='jane@longbourn.lit/outside'
    type='set'
    id='resign1'>
  <resign xmlns='http://metajack.im/ns/toetem'/>
```

```
    </iq>

    <iq to='jane@longbourn.lit/outside'
        from='referee@pemberley.lit/toetem'
        type='result'
        id='resign1'/>
```

A user who tries to resign while not in a game will receive the same bad request error you saw in a previous example.

All that is left to finish the Toetem protocol is the interaction between players once they are in the game room.

Playing and Watching the Game

When a game start request is received, the referee creates a room for the game, joins the room, and then invites each of the players. Once both players have joined the room, the game is started. The referee manages the game state, receives moves from the players, and broadcasts the game's moves and state as needed.

The first task for the referee is to notify everyone in the room when the game has started and when it has finished. It is easy to do this by sending a message to the room containing some Toetem protocol elements alongside the regular message contents. The following example stanzas show these <game-started> and <game-ended> elements:

```
    <message to='elizabeth@longbourn.lit/sitting_room'
             from='toetem-789@games.pemberley.lit/referee'
             type='groupchat'>
      <body>The match has started.</body>
      <game-started xmlns='http://metajack.im/ns/toetem'
                    x-player='elizabeth@longbourn.lit/sitting_room'
                    o-player='jane@longbourn.lit/outside'/>
    </message>

    <message to='elizabeth@longbourn.lit/sitting_room'
             from='toetem-789@games.pemberley.lit/referee'
             type='groupchat'>
      <body>elizabeth has won the match.</body>
      <game-ended xmlns='http://metajack.im/ns/toetem'
                  winner='elizabeth@longbourn.lit/sitting_room'/>
    </message>
```

Once a game has begun, the player with the X pieces can make the first move. Each player makes a move by sending an IQ-set stanza with a <move> command to the referee. The players send moves to the referee instead of broadcasting them directly to the room so that the referee can check that each move is legal. If the move is accepted, the referee forwards it to everyone in the room. If a move is illegal, the referee returns an IQ-error stanza and will not relay the message to the room.

The following example shows Elizabeth making her first move:

```
    <iq to='referee@pemberley.lit/toetem'
        from='elizabeth@longbourn.lit/sitting_room'
```

```
         type='set'
         id='move1'>
    <move xmlns='http://metajack.im/ns/toetem'
          col='b' row='2'/>
  </iq>
```

The referee determines that this move is legal and responds to Elizabeth with an IQ-result stanza. Then, the referee forwards the move on to the other player and the observers in the room:

```
<iq to='elizabeth@longbourn.lit/sitting_room'
    from='referee@pemberley.lit/toetem'
    type='result'
    id='move1'/>

<message to='toetem-789@games.pemberley.lit'
         from='referee@pemberley.lit/toetem'
         type='groupchat'>
  <body>elizabeth has marked an x at b2.</body>
  <move xmlns='http://metajack.im/ns/toetem'
        col='b' row='2'/>
</message>
```

The rest of the game continues in the same way until its conclusion.

Elizabeth may attempt to move out of turn or send an illegal move. The referee must return a proper error in both of these cases. In the former case, the correct error is unexpected request, and in the latter case, not acceptable. The unexpected request can also be used if a player sends a move before the game has officially started and the not allowed error will suffice for the case where the game has already ended. These errors are nearly identical to the error stanzas you've already seen; only the error condition element is changed.

Note that it is important that all participants in the game room check the sender of the game state messages. Only game state changes broadcast by the referee are legal. A rogue player could impersonate the referee if the participants were not paying attention to the origin of the messages.

These simple bits of protocol handle most of the interaction within a game. One problem remains, however; if a new observer joins in the middle of a game, they won't know the current state of the game. The referee must send the current game state to anyone who joins the room. Once the user has joined and received the state, the user can watch for game state broadcasts just like the other participants.

The game state consists of the phase of the game, the players and their pieces, the current board position, and the result if one is known. The phase of the game may be waiting, playing, or finished. If the state is waiting, only the players and pieces are needed to communicate the rest of the state. During the playing state, the players, pieces, and board position are needed. In the finished state, all the information is necessary.

The referee can send this information in a `<game>` element inside a direct room message to the user who has joined. The `<game>` element can use a `phase` attribute for the game's phase. The `x-player` and `o-player` attributes you saw earlier can be reused to communicate the players and their pieces if needed. Finally, the board position can be stored in the `pos` attribute encoded as a string.

A Tic-Tac-Toe board consists of nine squares, which can be filled with either an X or an O. You can turn this information into a nine-character string in which each character is a Space, an X, or an O. The characters fill the board's squares starting from the top left and moving right and continuing the same way with the other two rows.

For example, the string for the position shown in Figure 11-3 would be `"o  xxox  "`.

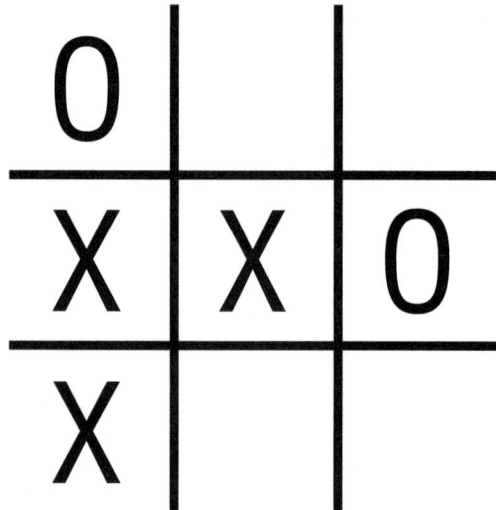

FIGURE 11-3

The following example shows a game state stanza broadcast to Bingley who has joined the game after it has finished. A participant joining during other game phases would see something very similar, just with less information.

```
<message to='toetem-789@games.pemberley.lit/bingley'
         from='referee@pemberley.lit/toetem'
         type='chat'>
  <game-state xmlns='http://metajack.im/ns/toetem'
              phase='finished'
              x-player='elizabeth@longbourn.lit/sitting_room'
              o-player='jane@lonbourn.lit/outside'
              pos='oxoxxooxx'
              winner='elizabeth@longbourn.lit/sitting_room'/>
</message>
```

If the game was aborted or tied, the `winner` attribute will not be present. An observer arriving after the game is over can distinguish between these states by noting whether the `pos` attribute is completely full of moves. If all moves are exhausted, the game was tied; otherwise, it was aborted.

Now any participant who joins will know what the current state is and can follow along with any new moves.

The Toetem protocol is completed. The protocol consists of lots of individual pieces, but each piece is simple. The end result, however, is a flexible gaming platform for connoisseurs of Tic-Tac-Toe.

GETTING STARTED ON TOETEM

Unlike the other applications in this book, Toetem consists of two large pieces of code — the referee and the game client. Each of these pieces requires its own HTML, CSS, and JavaScript files. In order to play a game, three users are needed — two players running the game client and one referee — and a multi-user chat service is needed to host each game's room.

Before you implement the Toetem protocol, you need to get the skeletons of the application set up.

The HTML and CSS for the referee are shown in Listing 11-1 and Listing 11-2, and Listing 11-3 has the initial skeleton JavaScript file. Note that there is very little UI for the referee; it contains just enough UI to enable whoever runs the referee to see what is happening.

LISTING 11-1: referee.html

```html
<!DOCTYPE HTML PUBLIC "-//W3C//DTD HTML 4.01//EN"
          "http://www.w3.org/TR/html4/strict.dtd">
<html>
  <head>
    <title>Toetem Referee - Chapter 3</title>

    <link rel='stylesheet' href='http://ajax.googleapis.com/ajax/libs/jqueryu
i/1.7.2/themes/cupertino/jquery-ui.css'>
    <script src='http://ajax.googleapis.com/ajax/libs/jquery/1.3.2/jquery.js'>
    </script>
    <script src='http://ajax.googleapis.com/ajax/libs/jqueryui/1.7.2/jquery-u
i.js'></script>
    <script src='scripts/strophe.js'></script>
    <script src='flxhr/flXHR.js'></script>
    <script src='scripts/strophe.flxhr.js'></script>

    <link rel='stylesheet' href=referee.css'>
    <script src='referee.js'></script>
    <script src='board.js'></script>
  </head>
  <body>
    <h1>Toetem Referee</h1>

    <div id='log'>
    </div>

    <!-- login dialog -->
    <div id='login_dialog' class='hidden'>
      <label>JID:</label><input type='text' id='jid'>
      <label>Password:</label><input type='password' id='password'>
    </div>
  </body>
</html>
```

LISTING 11-2: referee.css

```css
body {
    font-family: Helvetica;
}

h1 {
    text-align: center;
}

.hidden {
    display: none;
}

#log {
    padding: 10px;
}
```

LISTING 11-3: referee.js (skeleton)

```javascript
var Referee = {
    connection: null
};

$(document).ready(function () {
    $('#login_dialog').dialog({
        autoOpen: true,
        draggable: false,
        modal: true,
        title: 'Connect to XMPP',
        buttons: {
            "Connect": function () {
                $(document).trigger('connect', {
                    jid: $('#jid').val(),
                    password: $('#password').val()
                });

                $('#password').val('');
                $(this).dialog('close');
            }
        }
    });
});

$(document).bind('connect', function (ev, data) {
    var conn = new Strophe.Connection(
        "http://bosh.metajack.im:5280/xmpp-httpbind");

    conn.connect(data.jid, data.password, function (status) {
        if (status === Strophe.Status.CONNECTED) {
            $(document).trigger('connected');
        } else if (status === Strophe.Status.DISCONNECTED) {
            $(document).trigger('disconnected');
```

```
        }
    });

    Referee.connection = conn;
});

$(document).bind('connected', function () {
    // nothing here yet
});
```

The HTML, CSS, and skeleton JavaScript for the game client are in Listing 11-4, Listing 11-5, and
Listing 11-6. The login dialog box takes an extra Referee input to tell the client the location of the
service's referee. The UI has two main sections — one for when users are not playing or observing
a game and one for when they are participating in a game. Both are fairly simple. The participant
UI has a game board and a chat area, and the non-participant UI contains the list of waiting players and the list of active games. These two layouts were shown at the beginning of the chapter in
Figure 11-1 and Figure 11-2.

LISTING 11-4: toetem.html

Available for
download on
Wrox.com

```html
<!DOCTYPE HTML PUBLIC "-//W3C//DTD HTML 4.01//EN"
        "http://www.w3.org/TR/html4/strict.dtd">
<html>
  <head>
    <title>Toetem - Chapter 11</title>

    <link rel='stylesheet' href='http://ajax.googleapis.com/ajax/libs/jqueryu
i/1.7.2/themes/cupertino/jquery-ui.css'>
    <script src='http://ajax.googleapis.com/ajax/libs/jquery/1.3.2/jquery.js'>
    </script>
    <script src='http://ajax.googleapis.com/ajax/libs/jqueryui/1.7.2/jquery-u
i.js'></script>
    <script src='scripts/strophe.js'></script>
    <script src='flxhr/flXHR.js'></script>
    <script src='scripts/strophe.flxhr.js'></script>

    <link rel='stylesheet' href='toetem.css'>
    <script src='toetem.js'></script>
  </head>
  <body>
    <h1>Toetem</h1>

    <div id='browser'>
      <div class='buttons'>
        <input id='disconnect' class='button' type='button' value='disconnect'>
        <input id='wait' class='button' type='button' value='wait'>
      </div>

      <h2>Players Available</h2>
      <table id='waiting'>
        <thead>
          <tr>
```

continues

LISTING 11-4 *(continued)*

```html
            <th>Player</th>
            <th></th>
          </tr>
        </thead>
        <tbody>
        </tbody>
      </table>

      <h2>Games In Progress</h2>
      <table id='games'>
        <thead>
          <tr>
            <th>X</th>
            <th>O</th>
            <th>Room</th>
            <th></th>
          </tr>
        </thead>
        <tbody>
        </tbody>
      </table>
    </div>

    <div id='game' class='hidden'>
      <div class='buttons'>
        <input id='resign' class='button' type='button'
               value='resign' disabled='disabled'>
        <input id='leave' class='button' type='button'
               value='leave' disabled='disabled'>
      </div>

      <div id='board-area'>
        <canvas id='board' width='300' height='300'>
        </canvas>
        <div id='board-status'></div>
      </div>

      <div id='chat'>
        <div id='messages'>
        </div>
        <input type='text' id='input'>
      </div>
    </div>

    <!-- login dialog -->
    <div id='login_dialog' class='hidden'>
      <label>JID:</label><input type='text' id='jid'>
      <label>Password:</label><input type='password' id='password'>
      <label>Toetem Referee</label><input type='text' id='referee'>
    </div>
  </body>
</html>
```

LISTING 11-5: toetem.css

```css
body {
    font-family: Helvetica;
}

h1 {
    text-align: center;
}

.hidden {
    display: none;
}

.buttons {
    text-align: center;
}

input.button {
    margin: 10px;
}

#board {
    width: 300px;
    height: 300px;
    background-color: #000;
}

#board-area {
    float: left;
}

#chat {
    padding-left: 25px;
    float: left;
}

#messages {
    padding: 5px 10px;
    width: 400px;
    height: 300px;
    background-color: #ddd;
}

#messages .system {
    text-align: right;
    font-style: italic;
    font-weight: bold;
    color: #999;
}

#input {
```

continues

```css
    width: 400px;
}

.nick {
    color: #00c;
}

.me {
    color: #c00;
}
```

LISTING 11-6: toetem.js (skeleton)

```javascript
var Toetem = {
    connection: null,
    referee: null
};

$(document).ready(function () {
    $('#login_dialog').dialog({
        autoOpen: true,
        draggable: false,
        modal: true,
        title: 'Connect to XMPP',
        buttons: {
            "Connect": function () {
                $(document).trigger('connect', {
                    jid: $('#jid').val(),
                    password: $('#password').val(),
                    referee: $('#referee').val()
                });

                $('#password').val('');
                $(this).dialog('close');
            }
        }
    });
});

$(document).bind('connect', function (ev, data) {
    var conn = new Strophe.Connection(
        "http://bosh.metajack.im:5280/xmpp-httpbind");

    conn.connect(data.jid, data.password, function (status) {
        if (status === Strophe.Status.CONNECTED) {
            $(document).trigger('connected');
        } else if (status === Strophe.Status.DISCONNECTED) {
            $(document).trigger('disconnected');
        }
```

```
        });

        Toetem.connection = conn;
        Toetem.referee = data.referee;
    });

    $(document).bind('connected', function () {
        // nothing here yet
    });

    $(document).bind('disconnected', function () {
        // nothing here yet
    });
```

With the initial bits of drudgery out of the way, you can start implementing the first bits of the protocol.

IMPLEMENTING SESSIONS AND THE WAITING LIST

The place to start on Toetem is with session tracking and the waiting player's list. Session tracking is needed before players can interact with the referee, and the waiting list is the easiest piece of the protocol in Toetem. Because you build both the service and the client in this chapter, you implement both sides in parallel.

The referee must keep track of players' presence and maintain a list of players who are waiting for games. The referee will add and remove players from the list at their request. This list must be sent to all players whenever they register, and changes to the list must be broadcast to players as they happen.

The user must send directed presence to the referee to establish a gaming session and gain access to the game functionality. Once the referee is tracking the player's presence, the player can query the list or add or remove themselves from the list by clicking various buttons in the UI.

Referee Version One

First, the referee will need structures to track player presence and to store the waiting list. Also, it is handy to create a Toetem protocol namespace constant to save typing. Add the following to the `Referee` object:

```
waiting: [],
presence: {},
NS_TOETEM: "http://metajack.im/ns/toetem"
```

code snippet referee.js

The waiting list will be stored in an array and the players' presence in a dictionary keyed on their JID.

To track presence and answer players' queries, the referee will need handlers for `<presence>` and `<iq>` stanzas. You can make the following modifications to the `connected` event handler to set up these handlers:

```
$(document).bind('connected', function () {
    var conn = Referee.connection;

    $('#log').prepend("<p>Connected as " + conn.jid + "</p>");

    conn.addHandler(Referee.on_presence, null, "presence");
    conn.addHandler(Referee.on_iq, null, "iq");

    conn.send($pres());
});
```

code snippet referee.js

Both of these handlers will need to be implemented.

Add the following `on_presence()` function to the `Referee` object:

```
on_presence: function (pres) {
    var from = $(pres).attr('from');
    var bare_from = Strophe.getBareJidFromJid(from);
    var type = $(pres).attr('type');
    var bare_jid = Strophe.getBareJidFromJid(Referee.connection.jid);

    // only look for direct presence from other users
    if ((!type || type === "unavailable") && from !== bare_jid) {
        if (type === "unavailable") {
            delete Referee.presence[bare_from];

            // remove from lists
            Referee.remove_waiting(from);

            $('#log').prepend("<p>Unregistered " + bare_from + ".</p>");
        } else if ($(pres).find('register').length > 0) {
            Referee.presence[bare_from] = from;

            $('#log').prepend("<p>Registered " + bare_from + ".</p>");

            Referee.send_waiting(from);
        }
    }

    return true;
}
```

code snippet referee.js

The `on_presence()` function ignores any `<presence>` stanza from the referee itself or its other resources. For available `<presence>` stanzas containing `<register>`, it will add the sender to the tracked player list and send the list of waiting players. For unavailable `<presence>` stanzas, the referee will remove the sender from the tracked player list and remove them from the waiting list in case they forget to remove themselves. In each case the referee makes sure to keep the user informed with nice log messages.

Note that the waiting list and the presence tracking use bare JIDs. This limits users to interacting with the Toetem system with a single connected resource. It is possible to extend the referee to support multiple gaming sessions for a single user, but this can make the interactions more complicated. The simple solution has been chosen here.

The `remove_waiting()` function does exactly what its name implies and also broadcasts any waiting list changes to all the registered players. If the requested JID is not in the list, the function does nothing. The implementation that follows should be added to the `Referee` object:

```
remove_waiting: function (jid) {
    var bare_jid = Strophe.getBareJidFromJid(jid);

    var i;
    for (i = 0; i < Referee.waiting.length; i++) {
        var wjid = Strophe.getBareJidFromJid(Referee.waiting[i]);
        if (wjid === bare_jid) {
            break;
        }
    }

    if (i < Referee.waiting.length) {
        Referee.waiting.splice(i, 1);

        Referee.broadcast(function (msg) {
            return msg.c('not-waiting', {xmlns: Referee.NS_TOETEM})
                .c('player', {jid: jid});
        });
    }

    $('#log').prepend("<p>Removed " + bare_jid + " from " +
                                "waiting list</p>");
}
```

code snippet referee.js

The code simply scans through the entire list until it finds a matching JID, and when a match is found, deletes that entry from the array and notifies all the players using `broadcast()`. The `broadcast()` function takes a function that adds on to a `<message>` stanza that will be sent to every registered player; in this way, `broadcast()` makes it easy to send notifications. Add the `broadcast()` function to the `Referee` object:

```
broadcast: function (func) {
    $.each(Referee.presence, function () {
        var msg = func($msg({to: this}));
        Referee.connection.send(msg);
    });
}
```

code snippet referee.js

The referee will also need to send errors to clients that make illegal or unexpected requests. Create the following function, `send_error()`, and add it to the `Referee` object:

```
send_error: function (iq, etype, ename, app_error) {
    var error = $iq({to: $(iq).attr('from'),
                     id: $(iq).attr('id'),
                     type: 'error'})
        .cnode(iq.cloneNode(true)).up()
        .c('error', {type: etype})
        .c(ename, {xmlns: Strophe.NS.STANZAS}).up();

    if (app_error) {
        error.c(app_error, {xmlns: Referee.NS_TOETEM});
    }

    Referee.connection.send(error);
}
```

code snippet referee.js

This function is quite handy because the referee will have to deal with a lot of error cases.

Because the referee will often need to check to see if a player is on the waiting list, the `is_waiting()` function is also helpful to have. Add the following code to the `Referee` object to implement this:

```
is_waiting: function (jid) {
    var bare_jid = Strophe.getBareJidFromJid(jid);

    var i;
    for (i = 0; i < Referee.waiting.length; i++) {
        var wjid = Strophe.getBareJidFromJid(Referee.waiting[i]);
        if (wjid === bare_jid) {
            return true;
        }
    }

    return false;
}
```

code snippet referee.js

Just like the `remove_waiting()` function, `is_waiting()` looks for a player's JID by traversing the list.

Now you can implement the `on_iq()` function, which handles many of the interactions with players. In this version, only the `waiting` and `stop-waiting` commands are implemented. Add the following code to the `Referee` object:

```
on_iq: function (iq) {
    var id = $(iq).attr('id');
    var from = $(iq).attr('from');
```

```
        var type = $(iq).attr('type');

        // make sure we know the user's presence first
        if (!Referee.presence[Strophe.getBareJidFromJid(from)]) {
            Referee.send_error(iq, 'auth', 'forbidden');
        } else {
            var child = $(iq).find('*[xmlns="' + Referee.NS_TOETEM +
                                   '"]:first');
            if (child.length > 0) {
                if (type === 'get') {
                    Referee.send_error(iq, 'cancel', 'bad-request');
                    return true;
                } else if (type !== 'set') {
                    // ignore IQ-error and IQ-result
                    return true;
                }

                switch (child[0].tagName) {
                case 'waiting':
                    Referee.on_waiting(id, from, child);
                    break;

                case 'stop-waiting':
                    Referee.on_stop_waiting(id, from, child);
                    break;

                default:
                    Referee.send_error(iq, 'cancel', 'bad-request');
                }
            } else {
                Referee.send_error(iq, 'cancel', 'feature-not-implemented');
            }
        }

        return true;
    }
```

code snippet referee.js

This function first checks whether the referee is tracking the user making the request; the appropriate error is sent if this is not the case. If the request is from a tracked client, the function looks for a Toetem command in an IQ-set stanza and, if not found, responds with an error. For the `waiting` command, `on_iq()` delegates the behavior to `on_waiting()`; the `stop-waiting` command is delegated to `on_stop_waiting()`.

The last two functions `on_waiting()` and `on_stop_waiting()`, are implemented in the following code:

```
on_waiting: function (id, from, elem) {
    // if they were already waiting, remove them so their resource
    // can be updated
    if (Referee.is_waiting(from)) {
```

```
            Referee.remove_waiting(from);
        }

        Referee.waiting.push(from);

        Referee.connection.send($iq({to: from, id: id, type: 'result'}));

        Referee.broadcast(function (msg) {
            return msg.c('waiting', {xmlns: Referee.NS_TOETEM})
                .c('player', {jid: from});
        });

        $('#log').prepend("<p>Added " +
                        Strophe.getBareJidFromJid(from) + " to " +
                        "waiting list.</p>");
    },

    on_stop_waiting: function (id, from, elem) {
        if (Referee.is_waiting(from)) {
            Referee.remove_waiting(from);
        }

        Referee.connection.send($iq({to: from, id: id, type: 'result'}));
    }
```

code snippet referee.js

The on_waiting() function adds users to the waiting list, taking care to remove them if they are already waiting. It also broadcasts the change to the waiting list to all players. Finally, the on_stop_waiting() function removes the user from the waiting list.

Notice that these functions always return successful responses. There is no need to send an error to the user if the action can simply be ignored. If for some reason the user's client is out of sync, returning success will generally correct the problem. The referee tries to be liberal in what it accepts, but strict in what it sends, just like any good Internet service or client application should.

The first version of the referee is now ready to be put to work, but first you must implement the initial Toetem client.

Toetem Client Version One

Just as with the referee, the Toetem client needs a protocol constant; the protocol's namespace will be used in nearly every stanza sent. Add the following NS_TOETEM attribute to the Toetem object:

```
NS_TOETEM: "http://metajack.im/ns/toetem"
```

code snippet toetem.js

When the client connects, it must send directed presence to the referee to start a gaming session. Once registered with the referee, it must then handle the incoming list of waiting players. After disconnecting, it must clear the list, reset the application state, and re-open the login dialog box. Add the following highlighted code to the `connected` and `disconnected` event handlers:

```
$(document).bind('connected', function () {
    $('#disconnect').removeAttr('disabled');
    $('#wait').removeAttr('disabled');

    Toetem.connection.addHandler(Toetem.on_message, null, "message");

    // tell the referee we're online
    Toetem.connection.send(
        $pres({to: Toetem.referee})
            .c('register', {xmlns: Toetem.NS_TOETEM}));
});

$(document).bind('disconnected', function () {
    Toetem.referee = null;
    Toetem.connection = null;

    $('#waiting tbody').empty();
    $('#games tbody').empty();

    $('#login_dialog').dialog('open');
});
```

code snippet toetem.js

The `on_message()` handler listens for the initial waiting list as well as the change notifications. Its implementation follows and should be added to the `Toetem` object:

```
on_message: function (message) {
    var from = $(message).attr('from');

    if ($(message).find('waiting').length > 0) {
        $(message).find('waiting > player').each(function () {
            $('#waiting tbody').append(
                "<tr><td class='jid'>" +
                    $(this).attr('jid') +
                    "</td><td>" +
                    ($(this).attr('jid') === Toetem.connection.jid ?
                     "<input type='button' class='stop_button' " +
                     "value='stop waiting'>":
                     "<input type='button' class='start_button' " +
                     "value='start game'>") +
                    "</td></tr>");
        });
    } else if ($(message).find('not-waiting').length > 0) {
        $(message).find('not-waiting > player').each(function () {
            var jid = $(this).attr('jid');
            $('#waiting td.jid').each(function () {
                if ($(this).text() === jid) {
                    $(this).parent().remove();
```

```
                        return false;
                    }
                });
            });
        }

        return true;
    }
```

Whenever a `<waiting>` or `<not-waiting>` message comes in, the waiting list will be updated. Note that an action button is displayed next to the JID of the waiting player. If the player in the list is actually the user, this button will remove the user from the waiting list. Otherwise, the button will start a game with the player. You can add the following event handler to the document ready handler in order to implement the Stop Waiting button:

```
$('input.stop_button').live('click', function () {
    Toetem.connection.sendIQ(
        $iq({to: Toetem.referee, type: "set"})
            .c('stop-waiting', {xmlns: Toetem.NS_TOETEM}));
});
```

You should also implement the handlers for the Disconnect and Wait buttons on this screen. Add the following code to the document ready handler:

```
$('#disconnect').click(function () {
    Toetem.connection.disconnect();
});

$('#wait').click(function () {
    Toetem.connection.sendIQ(
        $iq({to: Toetem.referee, type: "set"})
            .c("waiting", {xmlns: Toetem.NS_TOETEM}));
});
```

The Wait button sends the appropriate IQ-set stanza with the `<waiting>` command to the referee. There is no need to update the waiting list on the screen because the referee will broadcast out the change, triggering the `on_message()` handler and causing the new information to appear.

This completes the first version of the referee and the game client. If you launch an instance of the referee and point several game clients at it, you should be able to monitor and manipulate the waiting player list.

IMPLEMENTING GAME MANAGEMENT

The next step on the path to a complete game system is to implement the game management features as well as game chat.

For the referee this includes the ability to create new games between players, make chat rooms for these games, and invite the players to the rooms to interact. The referee must also handle the list of active games as well as keep this new list, the waiting player list, and the players up-to-date as games begin and end.

The game page of the Toetem client will need to be activated and its various widgets enabled. The Start Game button you saw in the previous section must also be implemented. Finally, the client will need to be able to send and receive regular chat messages in the room.

Referee Version Two

The enhanced referee must now keep track of active games and it will interact with a multi-user chat server to create game rooms. Add the following new attributes to the `Referee` object, which add a `games` dictionary and protocol namespace constants for MUC:

```
games: {},

NS_MUC: "http://jabber.org/protocol/muc",
NS_MUC_USER: "http://jabber.org/protocol/muc#user",
NS_MUC_OWNER: "http://jabber.org/protocol/muc#owner",
MUC_SERVICE: 'games.pemberley.lit'
```

code snippet referee.js

Note that you must change the `MUC_SERVICE` value to an appropriate multi-user chat service; the value used here is only a placeholder. Your favorite XMPP server probably runs a service at *conference*.domain.com.

The referee's `on_iq()` handler, created earlier, will need to respond to two new commands — `start` and `resign`. These new commands will start a new game and end a game. Add the following new cases to the `switch` statement in your `on_iq()` handler:

```
case 'start':
    Referee.on_game_start(iq, id, from, child);
    break;

case 'resign':
    Referee.on_resign(iq, id, from);
    break;
```

code snippet referee.js

Next, you implement `on_game_start()` and `on_resign()`.

The following implementation of on_game_start() is simple, but only because it relies on other functions to do its dirty work. The function first checks that the players involved are not already playing, removes them from the waiting list, and creates the game room. Add the following code to the Referee object:

```
on_game_start: function (iq, id, from, elem) {
    var with_jid = $(elem).attr('with');
    var with_bare = Strophe.getBareJidFromJid(with_jid);

    // check that the players are available
    if (!Referee.is_waiting(with_jid)) {
        Referee.send_error(iq, 'modify', 'item-not-found');
        return;
    }

    if (Referee.is_playing(with_jid) ||
        Referee.is_playing(from)) {
        Referee.send_error(iq, 'cancel', 'not-allowed');
        return;
    }

    Referee.connection.send($iq({to: from, id: id, type: 'result'}));

    // remove players from waiting list
    Referee.remove_waiting(from);
    Referee.remove_waiting(with_jid);

    // create game room and invite players
    Referee.create_game(from, with_jid);
}
```

code snippet referee.js

Two new functions are referenced in the preceding code — is_playing() and create_game().

Similar to the is_waiting() function, is_playing() checks if a user is already in a game. Add its implementation to the Referee object:

```
is_playing: function (jid) {
    var bare = Strophe.getBareJidFromJid(jid);

    var found = false;
    $.each(Referee.games, function () {
        if (Strophe.getBareJidFromJid(this.x_player) === jid ||
            Strophe.getBareJidFromJid(this.o_player) === jid) {
            found = true;
            return false;
        }
    });

    return found;
}
```

code snippet referee.js

The `create_game()` function is more involved. Because the referee is not integrated with the multi-user chat service, it's possible that any room the referee attempts to create already exists. To deal with this possibility, the referee chooses a random room name and attempts to create the room. If the room already exists, the referee leaves the room and starts over. Once a new room has been created, the referee initializes the game and invites the players to the room.

Add the following code for `create_game()` to the `Referee` object:

```javascript
create_game: function (player1, player2) {
    // generate a random room name, and make sure it
    // doesn't already exist to our knowledge
    var room;
    do {
        room = "" + Math.floor(Math.random() * 1000000);
    } while (Referee.games[room]);

    var room_jid = room + "@" + Referee.MUC_SERVICE + "/Referee";
    Referee.connection.addHandler(function (presence) {
        var game;

        if ($(presence).find('status[code="201"]').length > 0) {
            // room was freshly created
            game = Referee.new_game();
            game.room = room;

            // create initial game state with randomized sides
            if (Math.random() < 0.5) {
                game.x_player = player1;
                game.o_player = player2;
                Referee.games[room] = game;
            } else {
                game.x_player = player2;
                game.o_player = player1;
                Referee.games[room] = game;
            }

            // invite players to start the game
            Referee.invite_players(game);

            // notify everyone about the game
            Referee.broadcast(function (msg) {
                return msg.c('games', {xmlns: Referee.NS_TOETEM})
                    .c('game', {'x-player': game.x_player,
                                'o-player': game.o_player,
                                'room': Referee.game_room(room)});
            });

            $('#log').prepend("<p>Created game room " + room + ".</p>");
        } else {
            // room was already in use, we need to start over
            Referee.connection.send(
                $pres({to: room_jid, type: 'unavailable'}));
            Referee.create_game(player1, player2);
```

```
            }

        return false;
    }, null, "presence", null, null, room_jid);

    Referee.connection.send(
        $pres({to: room_jid})
            .c("x", {xmlns: Referee.NS_MUC}));
}
```

The initial game state is created by the call to `new_game()`. Once the game object exists, the referee randomly assigns each player to a side — either the Xs or the Os — invites the players to the game, and broadcasts the game's existence to all registered players.

The `<presence>` handler defined in this function checks for the special 201 status from the room. This status, previously discussed in Chapter 8, is sent whenever the room has been freshly created. The handler is only needed to check this first `<presence>` stanza, so it returns false and is deleted after it finishes.

Take a look at the code for `new_game()`. You've already seen the `room`, `x_player`, and `o_player` attributes, but there are several more.

```
new_game: function () {
    return {
        room: null,
        waiting: 2,
        status: 'starting',
        x_player: null,
        o_player: null,
        winner: null
    };
}
```

Most of these attributes are self-explanatory. The `waiting` attribute starts at two because the referee is waiting for two players to join the room before the game starts. Each time a player joins the room, this value is decremented. When `waiting` reaches zero, the game is officially started. The `status` attribute describes what is happening with the game. It may contain the values `starting`, `playing`, `finished`, and `aborted`. These values are explained in detail as you implement more of the referee. Finally, the `winner` attribute stores the JID of the winning player when the game is finished.

With the game's room and object created, both players must be invited to the room. Add the following code to the `Referee` object, which sends the invitations:

```
invite_players: function (game) {
    // send room invites
    $.each([game.x_player, game.o_player], function () {
        Referee.connection.send(
```

```
                    $msg({to: game.room + "@" + Referee.MUC_SERVICE})
                        .c('x', {xmlns: Referee.NS_MUC_USER})
                        .c('invite', {to: this}));
            });
    }
```

The referee will get <presence> stanzas from each player as they join the game's room. You need to modify the referee's on_presence() handler to look for these and start the game once both players have joined. Also, if a player leaves before the game is over, you must forfeit that player and end the game. Therefore, the on_presence() handler must watch for both available and unavailable presence from the players in the room.

Modify your referee's on_presence() handler to match the following implementation. The changed lines are highlighted:

```
on_presence: function (pres) {
    var from = $(pres).attr('from');
    var bare_from = Strophe.getBareJidFromJid(from);
    var type = $(pres).attr('type');
    var bare_jid = Strophe.getBareJidFromJid(Referee.connection.jid);
    var domain = Strophe.getDomainFromJid(from);

    if (domain === Referee.MUC_SERVICE) {
        // handle room presence
        var room = Strophe.getNodeFromJid(from);
        var player = Strophe.getResourceFromJid(from);
        var game = Referee.games[room];

        // make sure it's a game and player we care about
        if (game &&
            (game.status === 'starting' || game.status === 'playing') &&
            (player === game.x_player || player === game.o_player)) {
            if (game.status === 'starting') {
                if (type !== 'unavailable') {
                    // waiting for one less player; if both are
                    // now present, the game is started
                    game.waiting -= 1;

                    $('#log').prepend("<p>Player " + bare_from +
                                    " arrived to game " + game.room +
                                    ".</p>");

                    if (game.waiting === 0) {
                        Referee.start_game(game);
                    }
                } else {
                    // one of the players left before the game even
                    // started, so abort the game
                    Referee.end_game(game, 'aborted');
                }
```

```
            } else {
                // during play, forfeit a player if they leave the room
                if (type === 'unavailable') {
                    if (player === game.x_player) {
                        game.winner = game.o_player;
                    } else {
                        game.winner = game.x_player;
                    }

                    Referee.end_game(game, 'finished');
                }
            }
        }
    } else if ((!type || type === "unavailable") &&
            bare_from !== bare_jid) {
        // handle directed presence from players
        if (type === "unavailable") {
            delete Referee.presence[bare_from];

            // remove from lists
            Referee.remove_waiting(bare_from);

            $('#log').prepend("<p>Unregistered " + bare_from + ".</p>");
        } else {
            Referee.presence[bare_from] = from;

            $('#log').prepend("<p>Registered " + bare_from + ".</p>");

            Referee.send_waiting(from);
            Referee.send_games(from);
        }
    }

    return true;
}
```

code snippet referee.js

The new `if` clause watches for `<presence>` stanzas that originate from the domain of the multi-user chat service. The room and sender are extracted from the JID and the game object is looked up. If the game exists, is active, and this stanza is from one of the players, then the stanza warrants closer inspection.

While in the `starting` state, the referee is waiting for players to join the game. Once both players have joined, it calls `start_game()`, and the state becomes `playing`. If one player joins and then leaves before the other player arrives, the game is aborted with a call to `end_game()`.

In the `playing` state, the referee is watching for the premature exit of one of the players, at which point that player will be forfeited.

Before you implement `start_game()` and `end_game()`, you must implement `send_games()` to send out the initial game list just like the current waiting list is sent when player's register. Add the `send_games()` function and the following helper functions to the `Referee` object. The helpers are for constructing the JID of the game room and sending messages to the room.

```javascript
send_games: function (jid) {
    var msg = $msg({to: jid})
        .c('games', {xmlns: Referee.NS_TOETEM});

    $.each(Referee.games, function (room) {
        msg.c('game', {'x-player': this.x_player,
                       'o-player': this.o_player,
                       'room': Referee.game_room(room)}).up();
    });

    Referee.connection.send(msg);
},

game_room: function (game) {
    return game.room + "@" + Referee.MUC_SERVICE;
},

muc_msg: function (game) {
    return $msg({to: Referee.game_room(game.room), type: "groupchat"});
}
```

code snippet referee.js

`send_game()` builds the list of currently active games and sends that to the player. The `game_room()` function takes the base room name and constructs the appropriate JID for the game's room. This is used by `muc_msg()`, which returns a partially built stanza for communication with the room's occupants. Because the referee will be sending a number of different messages to the game's room, this function is useful in reducing the programming work required.

The `start_game()` function broadcasts the `<game-started>` message to the room and sets the game's `status` to `playing`. Add its implementation to the `Referee` object:

```javascript
start_game: function (game) {
    game.status = 'playing';
    Referee.connection.send(
        Referee.muc_msg(game)
            .c('body').t('The match has started.').up()
            .c('game-started', {xmlns: Referee.NS_TOETEM,
                                'x-player': game.x_player,
                                'o-player': game.o_player}));

    $('#log').prepend("<p>Started game " + game.room + ".</p>");
}
```

code snippet referee.js

The referee includes both the `<game-started>` element and a normal `<body>` element. This provides a human-readable message in the room as well as the machine-friendly trigger for the client code.

The `end_game()` function is a bit longer because it needs to send a similar message to the room, clean up the game, and leave the room. Add the following code for `end_game()` to the `Referee` object:

```
end_game: function (game, status) {
    game.status = status;

    // let room know the result of the game
    var attrs = {xmlns: Referee.NS_TOETEM};
    if (game.winner) {
        attrs.winner = game.winner;
    }

    var msg = "";
    if (game.winner) {
        msg += Strophe.getBareJidFromJid(game.winner) +
            " has won the match.";
    } else if (status === 'finished') {
        msg += "The match was tied.";
    } else {
        msg += "The match was aborted.";
    }

    Referee.connection.send(
        Referee.muc_msg(game)
            .c('body').t(msg).up()
            .c('game-ended', attrs));

    // delete the game
    delete Referee.games[game.room];

    // leave the room
    Referee.connection.send(
        $pres({to: game.room + "@" + Referee.MUC_SERVICE + "/Referee",
            type: "unavailable"}));

    // notify all the players
    Referee.broadcast(function (msg) {
        return msg.c('game-over', {xmlns: Referee.NS_TOETEM})
            .c('game', {'x-player': game.x_player,
                        'o-player': game.o_player,
                        'room': Referee.game_room(game.room)});
    });

    $('#log').prepend("<p>Finished game " + game.room + ".</p>");
}
```

code snippet referee.js

The winner of the game, if there is one, is also included in the <game-ended> element sent to the room.

Note that even though the referee has left and the game is concluded, the players may continue to chat in the room for as long as they want.

The last task for this version of the referee is to implement on_resign() to handle a player resigning the game. Remember that on_resign() was one of the three new functions added in the on_iq() handler earlier in this section.

The referee must first find the game the user wants to resign; this is done by the helper function find_game(). Add the following code for find_game() and on_resign() to the Referee object:

```
find_game: function (player) {
    var game = null;
    $.each(Referee.games, function (r, g) {
        if (g.x_player === player || g.o_player === player) {
            game = g;
            return false;
        }
    });

    return game;
},

on_resign: function (iq, id, from) {
    var game = Referee.find_game(from);
    if (!game || game.status === 'finished' ||
        game.status === 'aborted' ||
        game.status === 'starting' ) {
        Referee.send_error(iq, 'cancel', 'bad-request');
    } else {
        if (from === game.x_player) {
            game.winner = game.o_player;
        } else {
            game.winner = game.x_player;
        }

        Referee.end_game(game, 'finished');

        Referee.connection.send($iq({to: from, id: id, type: 'result'}));

        $('#log').prepend("<p>" + Strophe.getBareJidFromJid(from) +
                          " resigned game " + game.room + ".</p>");
    }
}
```

code snippet referee.js

The on_resign() function makes sure the game exists and is in the playing state; otherwise, it sends an error. The other player is set as the game's winner, and then the previously implemented end_game() function is called to conclude the game. Note that the player's IQ-set stanza to resign requires a corresponding IQ-result reply, and this is sent at the end of the function.

The referee now supports game management. The only thing still lacking is the game logic and in-game events.

Toetem Client Version Two

Because the referee supports creating games, you can implement the Start Game button in the list of waiting players as well as the active games list. Starting the game results in the referee inviting the player to a new game room, and the client will need to listen for these invitations and join the room. The client must then shift into the game mode, and you will make the game page's buttons and chat area do their jobs.

The client will need to keep track of the game it is currently involved in. Add the game attribute to the Toetem object:

```
game: null
```

The main path to starting a game is through the Start Game button. When clicked, the button's handler sends a <start> command to the referee. Add the following handler to the client's document ready function:

```
$('input.start_button').live('click', function () {
    Toetem.connection.sendIQ(
        $iq({to: Toetem.referee, type: "set"})
            .c('start', {xmlns: Toetem.NS_TOETEM,
                        "with": $(this).parent().prev().text()}));
});
```

Notice that the name of the player is gleaned from the previous <td> element of the waiting player's table in the HTML.

Eventually the referee will send an invitation to the game's room to the player. Because this invitation is sent as a <message> stanza, you'll modify the on_message() handler to deal with it. At the same time, you can add support for the active game notifications that the referee broadcasts. Make the highlighted modifications to on_message():

```
on_message: function (message) {
    var from = $(message).attr('from');

    if ($(message).find('waiting').length > 0) {
        $(message).find('waiting > player').each(function () {
            $('#waiting tbody').append(
                "<tr><td class='jid'>" +
```

```
                            $(this).attr('jid') +
                            "</td><td>" +
                            ($(this).attr('jid') === Toetem.connection.jid ?
                             "<input type='button' class='stop_button' " +
                             "value='stop waiting'>":
                             "<input type='button' class='start_button' " +
                             "value='start game'>") +
                            "</td></tr>");
            });
        } else if ($(message).find('not-waiting').length > 0) {
            $(message).find('not-waiting > player').each(function () {
                var jid = $(this).attr('jid');
                $('#waiting td.jid').each(function () {
                    if ($(this).text() === jid) {
                        $(this).parent().remove();
                        return false;
                    }
                });
            });
        } else if ($(message).find('games').length > 0) {
            $(message).find('games > game').each(function () {
                if ($(this).attr('x-player') !== Toetem.connection.jid &&
                    $(this).attr('o-player') !== Toetem.connection.jid) {
                    $('#games tbody').append(
                        "<tr><td>" +
                            $(this).attr('x-player') +
                            "</td><td>" +
                            $(this).attr('o-player') +
                            "</td><td class='jid'>" +
                            $(this).attr('room') +
                            "</td><td>" +
                            "<input type='button' class='watch_button' " +
                            "value='watch game'>" +
                            "</td></tr>");
                }
            });
        } else if ($(message).find('game-over').length > 0) {
            $(message).find('game-over > game').each(function () {
                var jid = $(this).attr('room');
                $('#games td.jid').each(function () {
                    if ($(this).text() === jid) {
                        $(this).parent().remove();
                        return false;
                    }
                });
            });
        } else if ($(message)
                    .find('x > invite').attr('from') === Toetem.referee) {
            Toetem.game = from;

            $('#messages').empty();
            $('#messages').append("<div class='system'>" +
```

```
                                        "Joined game #" +
                                        Strophe.getNodeFromJid(from) +
                                        "</div>");
                    Toetem.scroll_chat();

                    $('#wait').removeAttr('disabled');
                    $('#browser').hide();
                    $('#game').show();

                    var nick = Toetem.connection.jid;

                    Toetem.connection.send(
                        $pres({to: Toetem.game + '/' + nick})
                            .c('x', {xmlns: Toetem.NS_MUC}));
                }

            return true;
        }
```

code snippet toetem.js

When game notifications are received, the on-screen active games list is updated appropriately. When a game invitation is received, on_message() sets the game attribute to the room's JID, switches the client to the game screen, and joins the room. Before switching to the game screen, the message area is cleared and a brief message is added to let the user know what's happening. The browser screen is hidden, the game screen is shown, and because the user is no longer waiting for a game, the Wait button is re-enabled.

Players join the room with their nickname set to their own JID. This is not the most user-friendly, but it makes the code easier and shorter. In a real game system, you might handle nicknames more elegantly.

Eventually, both players should join the room and the referee will send the <game-started> element. The on_message() handler needs to watch for these elements in messages sent to the room. Add this final else clause to the main if statement in on_message():

Available for download on Wrox.com

```
        } else {
            var body = $(message).children('body').text();
            if (body) {
                var who = Strophe.getResourceFromJid(from);
                var nick_style = 'nick';
                if (who === Toetem.connection.jid) {
                    nick_style += ' me';
                }

                $('#messages').append(
                    "<div>&lt;<span class='" + nick_style + "'>" +
                        Strophe.getBareJidFromJid(who) +
                        "</span>&gt; " +
                        body + "</div>");

                Toetem.scroll_chat();
```

```
            }

            if ($(message).find('delay').length > 0) {
                // skip command processing of old messages
                return true;
            }

            var cmdNode = $(message)
                .find('*[xmlns="' + Toetem.NS_TOETEM + '"]');
            var cmd = null;
            if (cmdNode.length > 0) {
                cmd = cmdNode.get(0).tagName;
            }
            if (cmd === 'game-started') {
                $('#resign').removeAttr('disabled');
            } else if (cmd === 'game-ended') {
                $('#resign').attr('disabled', 'disabled');
                $('#leave').removeAttr('disabled');
            }
        }
```

code snippet toetem.js

The new code first adds the contents of any `<body>` element to the chat area. If any commands are received from the referee, it takes the appropriate actions, but it ignores any delayed commands from the chat history. For the `game-started` command, it simply enables the Resign button; for the `game-ended` command, the Resign button is disabled and the Leave button is enabled.

This code also displays any messages sent by the other occupants of the game room. Of course, the user will want to communicate as well and be able to use the new buttons. Add the following event handlers to the client's document ready function:

```
$('#input').keypress(function (ev) {
    if (ev.which === 13) {
        ev.preventDefault();

        var input = $(this).val();
        $(this).val('');

        Toetem.connection.send(
            $msg({to: Toetem.game, type: 'groupchat'})
                .c('body').t(input));
    }
});

$('#resign').click(function () {
    Toetem.connection.sendIQ(
        $iq({to: Toetem.referee, type: 'set'})
            .c('resign', {xmlns: Toetem.NS_TOETEM}));
});

$('#leave').click(function () {
    Toetem.connection.send(
```

```
            $pres({to: Toetem.game + '/' + Toetem.connection.jid,
                    type: 'unavailable'}));
        $('#game').hide();
        $('#browser').show();
    });
```

code snippet toetem.js

The `keypress` handler is nearly identical to similar handlers you've created in previous chapters to allow the user to input and send text. Clicking the Resign button simply sends the `<resign>` command to the referee, which will cause a `<game-ended>` command to be sent to the room. The Leave button exits the room and puts the client back on the browser screen.

The final function needed is the `scroll_chat()` function, which you've also seen before. Add this function to the `Toetem` object:

```
scroll_chat: function () {
    var div = $('#messages').get(0);
    div.scrollTop = div.scrollHeight;
}
```

code snippet toetem.js

The second version of the Toetem client is complete. Try running the new referee along with several clients and create, resign, and leave games. You may even chat with yourself if you are so inclined.

IMPLEMENTING THE GAME LOGIC

The last step on the path to Tic-Tac-Toe madness is to implement the game rules, player moves, display the Tic-Tac-Toe board, and allow observers to watch games.

First, the referee will need to manage the board for each Tic-Tac-Toe game, and you will create a small library that tracks the previous moves on the board and makes sure new moves are legal. This library will also determine when the game is over, either by one player winning or by all possible moves having been made without anyone achieving three Xs or Os in a row.

Once the board's logic is finished, you extend the referee to use it as well as react to the incoming moves from players.

The referee must also send intermediate game state to any observer that joins the room.

Finally, you'll add a graphical display of the Tic-Tac-Toe board to the client and allow players to make their moves by clicking directly on the board. Observers will be able to join games in progress and watch the action.

The Tic-Tac-Toe Library

The Tic-Tac-Toe library abstracts all the game-specific logic into a single place. The referee will create a board for each game and send moves to the board. After a move, it can find out whether the game is over in order to take the appropriate action. In this section, you create a Board class with this functionality.

First, create a file called `board.js` and add the Board constructor function to it:

Available for
download on
Wrox.com

```
Referee.Board = function () {
    this.board = [[' ', ' ', ' '], [' ', ' ', ' '], [' ', ' ', ' ']];
};
```

code snippet board.js

Notice that the Board object is defined under the Referee object. The referee can create new boards with `new Referee.Board()`.

The board's internal state consists of a single attribute, board. This attribute is just a three-by-three matrix of characters, which will have the value `'x'`, `'o'`, or `' '`.

Moves are sent to the referee as a column and a row. The column is a letter, either a, b, or c, and the row is a number from 1 to 3. The Board class will need to convert these values to internal coordinates it can use to index the board matrix. Create the following helper function, `moveToCoords()`. Add this code right after the constructor function:

Available for
download on
Wrox.com

```
Referee.Board.prototype = {
    moveToCoords: function (col, row) {
        var map = {'a': 0, 'b': 1, 'c': 2, '1': 0, '2': 1, '3': 2};
        var coords = {row: null, col: null};
        coords.col = map[col];
        coords.row = map[row];
        return coords;
    }
};
```

code snippet board.js

Methods of JavaScript classes can be defined by setting the class's prototype object to an object containing the desired methods. When a Board object is created, the new object will inherit these methods from the prototype. You augment this prototype with more methods throughout the rest of this section.

The `moveToCoords()` function takes the column and row and creates a simple object with col and row properties set to the converted values. The map variable defines a simple mapping from user-supplied coordinates to numerical indexes; this makes the conversion extremely simple.

Another handy helper function that is needed is `toString()`, which will convert the state of the board into a short string. Add the following code to the prototype:

Available for
download on
Wrox.com

```
toString: function () {
    var r, s = '';

    for (r = 0; r < 3; r++) {
```

```
        s += this.board[r].join('');
    }

    return s;
}
```

To determine if moves are legal or if the game is over, the `Board` class must know whose turn it is. Add the following `currentSide()` function to the prototype. This function counts the Xs and Os to determine which side can make the next move:

```
currentSide: function () {
    var r, c;
    var x = 0, o = 0;

    for (r = 0; r < 3; r++) {
        for (c = 0; c < 3; c++) {
            if (this.board[r][c] === 'x') {
                x += 1;
            } else if (this.board[r][c] === 'o') {
                o += 1;
            }
        }
    }

    if (x === o) {
        return 'x';
    }

    return 'o';
}
```

Given a move consisting of an X or an O and target coordinates, you can easily determine whether the move is legal. An X move can be made only when it is the X side's turn to move, and the same applies for O moves. Also, no move can be made to a square that already contains a move. These rules are codified in the following implementation of `validMove()`, which should be added to the prototype:

```
validMove: function (side, col, row) {
    var curSide = this.currentSide();
    if (side !== curSide) {
        return false;
    }

    var coords = this.moveToCoords(col, row);
    if (this.board[coords.row][coords.col] !== ' ') {
        return false;
```

```
        }

        return true;
    }
```

The move() function calls validMove() to make sure a move is actually allowed. If the move is legal, the board matrix can be updated to reflect the new move. Add move() to the prototype:

```
move: function (side, col, row) {
    if (this.validMove(side, col, row)) {
        var coords = this.moveToCoords(col, row);
        this.board[coords.row][coords.col] = side;
    } else {
        throw {
            name: "BoardError",
            message: "Move invalid"
        };
    }
}
```

If the move is not legal, an exception is raised, which the referee will catch in order to send an error to the offending client.

Once a move is made, the referee must determine whether the game has finished. Create a function called gameOver() to handle this task, and add it to the prototype:

```
gameOver: function () {
    var r, c;

    // check for row wins
    for (r = 0; r < 3; r++) {
        if (this.board[r][0] === 'x' &&
            this.board[r][1] === 'x' &&
            this.board[r][2] === 'x') {
            return 'x';
        } else if (this.board[r][0] === 'o' &&
                   this.board[r][1] === 'o' &&
                   this.board[r][2] === 'o') {
            return 'o';
        }
    }

    // check for column wins
    for (c = 0; c < 3; c++) {
        if (this.board[0][c] === 'x' &&
            this.board[1][c] === 'x' &&
            this.board[2][c] === 'x') {
```

```
            return 'x';
        } else if (this.board[0][c] === 'o' &&
                    this.board[1][c] === 'o' &&
                    this.board[2][c] === 'o') {
            return 'o';
        }
    }

    // check for diagonal wins
    if (this.board[0][0] === 'x' &&
        this.board[1][1] === 'x' &&
        this.board[2][2] === 'x') {
        return 'x';
    } else if (this.board[0][0] === 'o' &&
                this.board[1][1] === 'o' &&
                this.board[2][2] === 'o') {
        return 'o';
    } else if (this.board[0][2] === 'x' &&
                this.board[1][1] === 'x' &&
                this.board[2][0] === 'x') {
        return 'x';
    } else if (this.board[0][2] === 'o' &&
                this.board[1][1] === 'o' &&
                this.board[2][0] === 'o') {
        return 'o';
    }

    // check for a tie
    var tie = true;
    for (r = 0; r < 3; r++) {
        if (this.board[r].indexOf(' ') >= 0) {
            tie = false;
            break;
        }
    }

    if (tie) {
        return "=";
    }

    return false;
}
```

code snippet board.js

This function is long but quite simple. It simply checks for all the winning Tic-Tac-Toe patterns within the board matrix. If no such pattern is detected, it then checks to see if all squares contain a move, in which case the game is a tie. It will return 'x', 'o', or '=' if the game is over and false otherwise.

This is all the logic needed for the simple game of Tic-Tac-Toe. The complete code for board.js appears in Listing 11-8 at the end of the chapter.

Referee Version Three

With the help the new `Board` class, it won't take long to make the referee fully functional. Most of the work is adding the new `<move>` command.

First, modify the `new_game()` function to initialize a `Board` object for the game:

```
new_game: function () {
    return {
        room: null,
        board: new Referee.Board(),
        waiting: 2,
        status: 'starting',
        x_player: null,
        o_player: null,
        winner: null
    };
}
```

code snippet referee.js

Next, add the new `switch` statement clause for the `<move>` command to the referee's `on_iq()` handler:

```
case 'move':
    Referee.on_move(iq, id, from, child);
    break;
```

code snippet referee.js

Just like the other commands, this command delegates its implementation to another function, `on_move()`. Add the following function to the `Referee` object:

```
on_move: function (iq, id, from, elem) {
    var game = Referee.find_game(from);
    var row = elem.attr('row');
    var col = elem.attr('col');

    if (!game) {
        Referee.send_error(iq, 'cancel', 'not-allowed');
    } else if (!row || !col) {
        Referee.send_error(iq, 'modify', 'bad-request');
    } else if (!game || game.status !== 'playing' ||
            (game.board.currentSide() === 'x' &&
             from === game.o_player) ||
            (game.board.currentSide() === 'o' &&
             from === game.x_player)) {
        Referee.send_error(iq, 'wait', 'unexpected-request');
    } else {
        var side = null;
        if (from === game.x_player) {
            side = 'x';
        } else {
```

```
            side = 'o';
        }

    try {
        game.board.move(side, col, row);

        Referee.connection.send(
            $iq({to: from, id: id, type: 'result'}));

        Referee.connection.send(
            Referee.muc_msg(game)
                .c('body').t(
                    Strophe.getBareJidFromJid(from) +
                        ' has placed an ' + side + ' at ' +
                        col + row).up()
                .c('move', {xmlns: Referee.NS_TOETEM,
                        col: col,
                        row: row}));

        $('#log').prepend("<p>" + Strophe.getBareJidFromJid(from) +
                        " moved in game " + game.room + ".</p>");

        // check for end of game
        var winner = game.board.gameOver();
        if (winner) {
            if (winner === 'x') {
                game.winner = game.x_player;
            } else if (winner === 'o') {
                game.winner = game.o_player;
            }

            Referee.end_game(game, 'finished');
        }
    } catch (e) {
        Referee.send_error(iq, 'cancel', 'not-acceptable');
    }
}
}
```

code snippet referee.js

The function does a few checks to ensure that a game exists for the player that sent the move and that the game is in the correct state with the player allowed to move. If these conditions are satisfied, the board's `move()` function is called to make the move and the `gameOver()` function used to determine if the game is over and whether there is a winner. If an error is encountered, the appropriate response is sent back to the player. If all is well, the referee will broadcast out the move to the entire room.

Finally, the referee must send intermediate game state to any observers who join the room. These observers may enter the room after several moves have been made, so they will need the current board moves and other game state. The referee is notified when observers join via their presence to the room, so you must modify the `on_presence()` handler to send game state. Add the following `if else` clause to the end of the `if` statement beginning "`if (game && (game.status === 'starting'`" in `on_presence()`:

```
    } else if (game && type !== 'unavailable') {
        // handle observers joining
        var msg = $msg({to: from, type: 'chat'});
        if (game.status === 'starting') {
            msg.c('body').t('Waiting for players..').up()
                .c('game-state', {xmlns: Referee.NS_TOETEM,
                                  'phase': game.status,
                                  'x-player': game.x_player,
                                  'o-player': game.o_player});
        } else if (game.status === 'playing') {
            msg.c('body').t('Game in progress.').up()
                .c('game-state', {xmlns: Referee.NS_TOETEM,
                                  'phase': game.status,
                                  'x-player': game.x_player,
                                  'o-player': game.o_player,
                                  'pos': game.board.toString()});
        } else {
            msg.c('body').t('Game over.').up()
                .c('game-state', {xmlns: Referee.NS_TOETEM,
                                  'phase': 'finished',
                                  'x-player': game.x_player,
                                  'o-player': game.o_player,
                                  'pos': game.board.toString()});
            if (game.winner) {
                msg.attr({winner: game.winner});
            }
        }

        Referee.connection.send(msg);

        $('#log').prepend("<p>Sent state to observer " + bare_from +
                          " in game " + game.room + ".</p>");
    }
```

code snippet referee.js

That's it! The referee is now ready to officiate Tic-Tac-Toe games.

Toetem Client Version Three

The final Toetem client needs a pretty Tic-Tac-Toe board to show the game in progress as well as allow the player to make moves. Toetem will also need to watch for <move> commands sent to the room by the referee in order to keep the board up to date, and if the user is observing the game, react to game state messages when the user joins.

The graphical board will be drawn with the HTML5 <canvas> API, which was also used for the sketching area in Chapter 9's SketchPad application. Like SketchPad, the final Toetem client will not work in Internet Explorer due to its lack of support for the <canvas> element.

A Tic-Tac-Toe board is comprised of nine squares separated by four straight lines that cross each other. Add the following draw_board() function to the Toetem object to draw the board:

```
draw_board: function () {
    var ctx = $('#board')[0].getContext('2d');

    // clear board
    ctx.fillStyle = '#000';
    ctx.beginPath();
    ctx.fillRect(0, 0, 300, 300);

    // draw grid lines
    ctx.strokeStyle = '#999';
    ctx.lineWidth = 4;

    ctx.beginPath();

    ctx.moveTo(100, 10);
    ctx.lineTo(100, 290);
    ctx.moveTo(200, 10);
    ctx.lineTo(200, 290);
    ctx.moveTo(10, 100);
    ctx.lineTo(290, 100);
    ctx.moveTo(10, 200);
    ctx.lineTo(290, 200);

    ctx.stroke();
}
```

code snippet toetem.js

First, the entire area is filled with black. Four lines are then drawn in gray to create the nine squares. The <canvas> API calls are fairly self-explanatory, and you can find more details about them in Chapter 9.

When a player moves, an X or an O must be placed at the appropriate location. You draw an X with two diagonal lines and an O as a circle. Add the following draw_piece() function to the Toetem object:

```
draw_piece: function (piece, x, y) {
    var ctx = $('#board')[0].getContext('2d');

    ctx.strokeStyle = '#fff';

    var center_x = (x * 100) + 50;
    var center_y = (y * 100) + 50;

    ctx.beginPath();

    if (piece === 'x') {
```

```
        ctx.moveTo(center_x - 15, center_y - 15);
        ctx.lineTo(center_x + 15, center_y + 15);

        ctx.moveTo(center_x + 15, center_y - 15);
        ctx.lineTo(center_x - 15, center_y + 15);
    } else {
        ctx.arc(center_x, center_y, 15, 0, 2 * Math.PI, true);
    }

    ctx.stroke();
}
```

code snippet toetem.js

The position is calculated for the center of the appropriate square, and then the correct shape is drawn relative to that position.

The fancy graphics are now out of the way, but they still need to be integrated into the game client. To draw the initial board and set the `watching` attribute correctly, add the following highlighted line to the `on_message()` handler, just after the game area is shown:

```
Toetem.game = from;
Toetem.watching = false;

$('#messages').empty();
$('#messages').append("<div class='system'>" +
                      "Joined game #" +
                      Strophe.getNodeFromJid(from) +
                      "</div>");
Toetem.scroll_chat();

$('#wait').removeAttr('disabled');
$('#browser').hide();
$('#game').show();
Toetem.draw_board();
$('#board-status').html('Waiting for other player..');
```

code snippet toetem.js

The Watch Game button also needs similar code to switch to the game view and draw the board as well as code to join the game's room. Add the following code to the document event handler:

```
$('input.watch_button').live('click', function () {
    // join the game room
    Toetem.game = $(this).parent().prev().text();
    Toetem.watching = true;

    $('#browser').hide();
    $('#game').show();
```

```
        Toetem.draw_board();
        $('#board-status').html('');

        Toetem.connection.send(
            $pres({to: Toetem.game + '/' + Toetem.connection.jid}));
    });
```

To make new moves, the player clicks an empty square on the board. This action causes the appropriate <move> command to be sent to the referee. There's no point in letting players move out of turn, so moving should only be allowed during a player's own turn.

To keep track of whose turn it is, what pieces the players are using, and whether the user is watching or playing, add the following new attributes to the Toetem object:

Available for download on Wrox.com

```
x_player: null,
o_player: null,
turn: null,
my_side: null,
watching: false
```

code snippet toetem.js

These new attributes will be initialized when the game starts or is joined and maintained as the players make moves.

Add the following handler to the document ready handler to enable the player to make moves:

Available for download on Wrox.com

```
$('#board').click(function (ev) {
    if (Toetem.turn && Toetem.turn === Toetem.my_side) {
        var pos = $(this).position();
        var x = Math.floor((ev.pageX - pos.left) / 100);
        var y = Math.floor((ev.pageY - pos.top) / 100);

        Toetem.connection.sendIQ(
            $iq({to: Toetem.referee, type: 'set'})
                .c('move', {xmlns: Toetem.NS_TOETEM,
                            col: ['a', 'b', 'c'][x],
                            row: y + 1}));
    }
});
```

code snippet toetem.js

If it's the player's turn, the coordinates of the mouse click are used to calculate the square on the board the player clicked. Because the event's pageX and pageY coordinates are provided relative to the page — not the element — they must be transformed by subtracting the position of the board's top-left corner. Because each square is 100 pixels on a side, the code divides the final coordinates by 100 to obtain integers from 0 to 2, indicating one of the three possible squares in each dimension.

Once the square is known, the `<move>` command is sent to the referee. Notice that the on-screen board is not updated yet; it will be updated once the referee broadcasts out the verified move to the game room.

The game start, game state, and move processing logic are all that remain before Toetem is able to play real Tic-Tac-Toe games. The referee broadcasts game starts and moves to the room, but sends game state to oservers directly; all of these notifications arrive to the `on_message()` handler. Make the highlighted modifications to the command processing logic inside `on_message()`:

```javascript
var cmdNode = $(message)
    .find('*[xmlns="' + Toetem.NS_TOETEM + '"]');
var cmd = null;
var row, col;
if (cmdNode.length > 0) {
    cmd = cmdNode.get(0).tagName;
}
if (cmd === 'game-started') {
    var me = Toetem.connection.jid;
    Toetem.x_player = cmdNode.attr('x-player');
    Toetem.o_player = cmdNode.attr('o-player');
    Toetem.turn = 'x';

    if (Toetem.x_player === me) {
        Toetem.my_side = 'x';
        $('#board-status').html('Your move..');
    } else if (Toetem.o_player === me) {
        Toetem.my_side = 'o';
        $('#board-status').html("Opponent's move..");
    }

    if (!Toetem.watching) {
        $('#resign').removeAttr('disabled');
    } else {
        $('#leave').removeAttr('disabled');
    }
} else if (cmd === 'game-ended') {
    $('#resign').attr('disabled', 'disabled');
    $('#leave').removeAttr('disabled');
    var winner = cmdNode.attr('winner');
    if (winner === Toetem.connection.jid) {
        $('#board-status').html('You won!');
    } else if (winner && !Toetem.watching) {
        $('#board-status').html('You lost!');
    } else if (!Toetem.watching) {
        $('#board-status').html('You tied!');
    }
} else if (cmd === 'move') {
    var map = {'a': 0, 'b': 1, 'c': 2, '1': 0, '2': 1, '3': 2};
    col = cmdNode.attr('col');
    row = cmdNode.attr('row');

    Toetem.draw_piece(Toetem.turn, map[col], map[row]);

    if (Toetem.turn === 'x') {
```

```
            Toetem.turn = 'o';
        } else {
            Toetem.turn = 'x';
        }

        if (!Toetem.watching) {
            Toetem.my_turn = Toetem.turn === Toetem.my_side;

            if (Toetem.my_turn) {
                $('#board-status').html("Your move..");
            } else {
                $('#board-status').html("Opponent's move..");
            }
        }
    } else if (cmd === 'game-state') {
        Toetem.x_player = cmdNode.attr('x-player');
        Toetem.o_player = cmdNode.attr('o-player');

        var pos = cmdNode.attr('pos');
        var blanks = 0;
        if (pos) {
            var idx = 0;
            for (row = 0; row < 3; row++) {
                for (col = 0; col < 3; col++) {
                    if (pos[idx] !== ' ') {
                        Toetem.draw_piece(pos[idx], col, row);
                    } else {
                        blanks += 1;
                    }

                    idx += 1;
                }
            }
        }

        if (blanks % 2 === 0) {
            Toetem.turn = 'o';
        } else {
            Toetem.turn = 'x';
        }
    }
}
```

code snippet toetem.js

The game-started command now sets up the x_player, o_player, turn and my_side attributes and updates the board's status area appropriately.

When <move> commands are received, they are transformed to board coordinates and used to draw the piece on the board. Then the turn attribute is flipped, and the board's status area is updated.

The game-ended command updates the states of the Buttons for the player and prints a message about the winner to the board's status area.

Finally, the `game-state` command causes the previous moves to be drawn and the game's attributes to be set up.

The Toetem client is finished. Fire up a referee and invite several of your friends to play Tic-Tac-Toe online with you. Tell the world about your new game service and watch the games of other players.

The final code for the referee, the `Board` class, and the client are shown in Listing 11-7, Listing 11-8, and Listing 11-9, respectively.

LISTING 11-7: referee.js (final)

```
var Referee = {
    connection: null,

    games: {},
    waiting: [],
    presence: {},

    NS_TOETEM: "http://metajack.im/ns/toetem",
    NS_MUC: "http://jabber.org/protocol/muc",
    NS_MUC_USER: "http://jabber.org/protocol/muc#user",
    NS_MUC_OWNER: "http://jabber.org/protocol/muc#owner",

    MUC_SERVICE: 'chat.cactus.local',

    is_waiting: function (jid) {
        var bare_jid = Strophe.getBareJidFromJid(jid);

        var i;
        for (i = 0; i < Referee.waiting.length; i++) {
            var wjid = Strophe.getBareJidFromJid(Referee.waiting[i]);
            if (wjid === bare_jid) {
                return true;
            }
        }

        return false;
    },

    is_playing: function (jid) {
        var bare = Strophe.getBareJidFromJid(jid);

        var found = false;
        $.each(Referee.games, function () {
            if (Strophe.getBareJidFromJid(this.x_player) === jid ||
                Strophe.getBareJidFromJid(this.o_player) === jid) {
                found = true;
                return false;
            }
        });

        return found;
```

continues

LISTING 11-7 *(continued)*

```
        },

        remove_waiting: function (jid) {
            var bare_jid = Strophe.getBareJidFromJid(jid);

            var i;
            for (i = 0; i < Referee.waiting.length; i++) {
                var wjid = Strophe.getBareJidFromJid(Referee.waiting[i]);
                if (wjid === bare_jid) {
                    break;
                }
            }

            if (i < Referee.waiting.length) {
                Referee.waiting.splice(i, 1);

                Referee.broadcast(function (msg) {
                    return msg.c('not-waiting', {xmlns: Referee.NS_TOETEM})
                        .c('player', {jid: jid});
                });

                $('#log').prepend("<p>Removed " + bare_jid + " from " +
                                  "waiting list</p>");
            }
        },

        send_error: function (iq, etype, ename, app_error) {
            var error = $iq({to: $(iq).attr('from'),
                             id: $(iq).attr('id'),
                             type: 'error'})
                .cnode(iq.cloneNode(true)).up()
                .c('error', {type: etype})
                .c(ename, {xmlns: Strophe.NS.STANZAS}).up();

            if (app_error) {
                error.c(app_error, {xmlns: Referee.NS_TOETEM});
            }

            Referee.connection.send(error);
        },

        on_presence: function (pres) {
            var from = $(pres).attr('from');
            var bare_from = Strophe.getBareJidFromJid(from);
            var type = $(pres).attr('type');
            var bare_jid = Strophe.getBareJidFromJid(Referee.connection.jid);
            var domain = Strophe.getDomainFromJid(from);

            if (domain === Referee.MUC_SERVICE) {
                // handle room presence
                var room = Strophe.getNodeFromJid(from);
                var player = Strophe.getResourceFromJid(from);
```

```
var game = Referee.games[room];

// make sure it's a game and player we care about
if (game &&
    (game.status === 'starting' || game.status === 'playing') &&
    (player === game.x_player || player === game.o_player)) {
    if (game.status === 'starting') {
        if (type !== 'unavailable') {
            // waiting for one less player; if both are
            // now present, the game is started
            game.waiting -= 1;

            $('#log').prepend("<p>Player " + bare_from +
                             " arrived to game " + game.room +
                             ".</p>");

            if (game.waiting === 0) {
                Referee.start_game(game);
            }
        } else {
            // one of the players left before the game even
            // started, so abort the game
            Referee.end_game(game, 'aborted');
        }
    } else {
        // during play, forfeit a player if they leave the room
        if (type === 'unavailable') {
            if (player === game.x_player) {
                game.winner = game.o_player;
            } else {
                game.winner = game.x_player;
            }

            Referee.end_game(game, 'finished');
        }
    }
} else if (game && type !== 'unavailable') {
    // handle observers joining
    var msg = $msg({to: from, type: 'chat'});
    if (game.status === 'starting') {
        msg.c('body').t('Waiting for players..').up()
            .c('game-state', {xmlns: Referee.NS_TOETEM,
                             'phase': game.status,
                             'x-player': game.x_player,
                             'o-player': game.o_player});
    } else if (game.status === 'playing') {
        msg.c('body').t('Game in progress.').up()
            .c('game-state', {xmlns: Referee.NS_TOETEM,
                             'phase': game.status,
                             'x-player': game.x_player,
                             'o-player': game.o_player,
                             'pos': game.board.toString()});
    } else {
        msg.c('body').t('Game over.').up()
```

continues

LISTING 11-7 *(continued)*

```
                              .c('game-state', {xmlns: Referee.NS_TOETEM,
                                        'phase': 'finished',
                                        'x-player': game.x_player,
                                        'o-player': game.o_player,
                                        'pos': game.board.toString()}});
                    if (game.winner) {
                        msg.attr({winner: game.winner});
                    }
                }

                Referee.connection.send(msg);

                $('#log').prepend("<p>Sent state to observer " + bare_from +
                                " in game " + game.room + ".</p>");
            }
        } else if ((!type || type === "unavailable") &&
                bare_from !== bare_jid) {
            // handle directed presence from players
            if (type === "unavailable") {
                delete Referee.presence[bare_from];

                // remove from lists
                Referee.remove_waiting(bare_from);

                $('#log').prepend("<p>Unregistered " + bare_from + ".</p>");
            } else {
                Referee.presence[bare_from] = from;

                $('#log').prepend("<p>Registered " + bare_from + ".</p>");

                Referee.send_waiting(from);
                Referee.send_games(from);
            }
        }

        return true;
    },

    broadcast: function (func) {
        $.each(Referee.presence, function () {
            var msg = func($msg({to: this}));
            Referee.connection.send(msg);
        });
    },

    send_waiting: function (jid) {
        var msg = $msg({to: jid})
            .c('waiting', {xmlns: Referee.NS_TOETEM});

        $.each(Referee.waiting, function () {
            msg.c('player', {jid: this}).up();
```

```
            });

        Referee.connection.send(msg);
},

on_iq: function (iq) {
    var id = $(iq).attr('id');
    var from = $(iq).attr('from');
    var type = $(iq).attr('type');

    // make sure we know the user's presence first
    if (!Referee.presence[Strophe.getBareJidFromJid(from)]) {
        Referee.send_error(iq, 'auth', 'forbidden');
    } else {
        var child = $(iq).find('*[xmlns="' + Referee.NS_TOETEM +
                              '"]:first');
        if (child.length > 0) {
            if (type === 'get') {
                Referee.send_error(iq, 'cancel', 'bad-request');
                return true;
            } else if (type !== 'set') {
                // ignore IQ-error and IQ-result
                return true;
            }

            switch (child[0].tagName) {
            case 'waiting':
                Referee.on_waiting(id, from, child);
                break;

            case 'stop-waiting':
                Referee.on_stop_waiting(id, from, child);
                break;

            case 'start':
                Referee.on_game_start(iq, id, from, child);
                break;

            case 'resign':
                Referee.on_resign(iq, id, from);
                break;

            case 'move':
                Referee.on_move(iq, id, from, child);
                break;

            default:
                Referee.send_error(iq, 'cancel', 'bad-request');
            }
        } else {
            Referee.send_error(iq, 'cancel', 'feature-not-implemented');
        }
    }

    return true;
```

continues

LISTING 11-7 *(continued)*

```
    },

    on_waiting: function (id, from, elem) {
        // if they were already waiting, remove them so their resource
        // can be updated
        if (Referee.is_waiting(from)) {
            Referee.remove_waiting(from);
        }

        Referee.waiting.push(from);

        Referee.connection.send($iq({to: from, id: id, type: 'result'}));

        Referee.broadcast(function (msg) {
            return msg.c('waiting', {xmlns: Referee.NS_TOETEM})
                .c('player', {jid: from});
        });

        $('#log').prepend("<p>Added " +
                        Strophe.getBareJidFromJid(from) + " to " +
                        "waiting list.</p>");
    },

    on_stop_waiting: function (id, from, elem) {
        if (Referee.is_waiting(from)) {
            Referee.remove_waiting(from);
        }

        Referee.connection.send($iq({to: from, id: id, type: 'result'}));
    },

    send_games: function (jid) {
        var msg = $msg({to: jid})
            .c('games', {xmlns: Referee.NS_TOETEM});

        $.each(Referee.games, function (room) {
            msg.c('game', {'x-player': this.x_player,
                        'o-player': this.o_player,
                        'room': Referee.game_room(room)}).up();
        });

        Referee.connection.send(msg);
    },

    new_game: function () {
        return {
            room: null,
            board: new Referee.Board(),
            waiting: 2,
            status: 'starting',
            x_player: null,
            o_player: null,
```

```
                winner: null
            };
        },

        on_game_start: function (iq, id, from, elem) {
            var with_jid = elem.attr('with');
            var with_bare = Strophe.getBareJidFromJid(with_jid);

            // check that the players are available
            if (!Referee.is_waiting(with_jid)) {
                Referee.send_error(iq, 'modify', 'item-not-found');
                return;
            }

            if (Referee.is_playing(with_jid) ||
                Referee.is_playing(from)) {
                Referee.send_error(iq, 'cancel', 'not-allowed');
                return;
            }

            Referee.connection.send($iq({to: from, id: id, type: 'result'}));

            // remove players from waiting list
            Referee.remove_waiting(from);
            Referee.remove_waiting(with_jid);

            // create game room and invite players
            Referee.create_game(from, with_jid);
        },

        create_game: function (player1, player2) {
            // generate a random room name, and make sure it
            // doesn't already exist to our knowledge
            var room;
            do {
                room = "" + Math.floor(Math.random() * 1000000);
            } while (Referee.games[room]);

            var room_jid = room + "@" + Referee.MUC_SERVICE + "/Referee";
            Referee.connection.addHandler(function (presence) {
                var game;

                if ($(presence).find('status[code="201"]').length > 0) {
                    // room was freshly created
                    game = Referee.new_game();
                    game.room = room;

                    // create initial game state with randomized sides
                    if (Math.random() < 0.5) {
                        game.x_player = player1;
                        game.o_player = player2;
                        Referee.games[room] = game;
                    } else {
                        game.x_player = player2;
```

continues

LISTING 11-7 *(continued)*

```
                    game.o_player = player1;
                    Referee.games[room] = game;
                }

                // invite players to start the game
                Referee.invite_players(game);

                // notify everyone about the game
                Referee.broadcast(function (msg) {
                    return msg.c('games', {xmlns: Referee.NS_TOETEM})
                        .c('game', {'x-player': game.x_player,
                                    'o-player': game.o_player,
                                    'room': Referee.game_room(room)});
                });

                $('#log').prepend("<p>Created game room " + room + ".</p>");
            } else {
                // room was already in use, we need to start over
                Referee.connection.send(
                    $pres({to: room_jid, type: 'unavailable'}));
                Referee.create_game(player1, player2);
            }

            return false;
        }, null, "presence", null, null, room_jid);

        Referee.connection.send(
            $pres({to: room_jid})
                .c("x", {xmlns: Referee.NS_MUC}));
    },

    invite_players: function (game) {
        // send room invites
        $.each([game.x_player, game.o_player], function () {
            Referee.connection.send(
                $msg({to: game.room + "@" + Referee.MUC_SERVICE})
                    .c('x', {xmlns: Referee.NS_MUC_USER})
                    .c('invite', {to: this}));
        });
    },

    game_room: function (room) {
        return room + "@" + Referee.MUC_SERVICE;
    },

    muc_msg: function (game) {
        return $msg({to: Referee.game_room(game.room), type: "groupchat"});
    },

    start_game: function (game) {
        game.status = 'playing';
        Referee.connection.send(
```

```
            Referee.muc_msg(game)
                .c('body').t('The match has started.').up()
                .c('game-started', {xmlns: Referee.NS_TOETEM,
                                    'x-player': game.x_player,
                                    'o-player': game.o_player}));

        $('#log').prepend("<p>Started game " + game.room + ".</p>");
    },

    end_game: function (game, status) {
        game.status = status;

        // let room know the result of the game
        var attrs = {xmlns: Referee.NS_TOETEM};
        if (game.winner) {
            attrs.winner = game.winner;
        }

        var msg = "";
        if (game.winner) {
            msg += Strophe.getBareJidFromJid(game.winner) +
                " has won the match."
        } else if (status === 'finished') {
            msg += "The match was tied.";
        } else {
            msg += "The match was aborted.";
        }

        Referee.connection.send(
            Referee.muc_msg(game)
                .c('body').t(msg).up()
                .c('game-ended', attrs));

        // delete the game
        delete Referee.games[game.room];

        // leave the room
        Referee.connection.send(
            $pres({to: game.room + "@" + Referee.MUC_SERVICE + "/Referee",
                    type: "unavailable"}));

        // notify all the players
        Referee.broadcast(function (msg) {
            return msg.c('game-over', {xmlns: Referee.NS_TOETEM})
                .c('game', {'x-player': game.x_player,
                            'o-player': game.o_player,
                            'room': Referee.game_room(game.room)});
        });

        $('#log').prepend("<p>Finished game " + game.room + ".</p>");
    },

    find_game: function (player) {
        var game = null;
```

continues

LISTING 11-7 *(continued)*

```
        $.each(Referee.games, function (r, g) {
            if (g.x_player === player || g.o_player === player) {
                game = g;
                return false;
            }
        });

        return game;
    },

    on_resign: function (iq, id, from) {
        var game = Referee.find_game(from);
        if (!game || game.status === 'finished' ||
            game.status === 'aborted' ||
            game.status === 'starting' ) {
            Referee.send_error(iq, 'cancel', 'bad-request');
        } else {
            if (from === game.x_player) {
                game.winner = game.o_player;
            } else {
                game.winner = game.x_player;
            }

            Referee.end_game(game, 'finished');

            Referee.connection.send($iq({to: from, id: id, type: 'result'}));

            $('#log').prepend("<p>" + Strophe.getBareJidFromJid(from) +
                            " resigned game " + game.room + ".</p>");
        }
    },

    on_move: function (iq, id, from, elem) {
        var game = Referee.find_game(from);
        var row = elem.attr('row');
        var col = elem.attr('col');

        if (!game) {
            Referee.send_error(iq, 'cancel', 'not-allowed');
        } else if (!row || !col) {
            Referee.send_error(iq, 'modify', 'bad-request');
        } else if (!game || game.status !== 'playing' ||
                    (game.board.currentSide() === 'x' &&
                     from === game.o_player) ||
                    (game.board.currentSide() === 'o' &&
                     from === game.x_player)) {
            Referee.send_error(iq, 'wait', 'unexpected-request');
        } else {
            var side = null;
            if (from === game.x_player) {
                side = 'x';
            } else {
```

```
                    side = 'o';
                }

            try {
                game.board.move(side, col, row);

                Referee.connection.send(
                    $iq({to: from, id: id, type: 'result'}));

                Referee.connection.send(
                    Referee.muc_msg(game)
                        .c('body').t(
                            Strophe.getBareJidFromJid(from) +
                                ' has placed an ' + side + ' at ' +
                                col + row).up()
                        .c('move', {xmlns: Referee.NS_TOETEM,
                                    col: col,
                                    row: row}));

                $('#log').prepend("<p>" + Strophe.getBareJidFromJid(from) +
                                    " moved in game " + game.room + ".</p>");

                // check for end of game
                var winner = game.board.gameOver();
                if (winner) {
                    if (winner === 'x') {
                        game.winner = game.x_player;
                    } else if (winner === 'o') {
                        game.winner = game.o_player;
                    }

                    Referee.end_game(game, 'finished');
                }
            } catch (e) {
                Referee.send_error(iq, 'cancel', 'not-acceptable');
            }
        }
    }
};

$(document).ready(function () {
    $('#login_dialog').dialog({
        autoOpen: true,
        draggable: false,
        modal: true,
        title: 'Connect to XMPP',
        buttons: {
            "Connect": function () {
                $(document).trigger('connect', {
                    jid: $('#jid').val(),
                    password: $('#password').val()
                });

                $('#password').val('');
```

continues

LISTING 11-7 *(continued)*

```
                    $(this).dialog('close');
                }
            }
        });
    });

    $(document).bind('connect', function (ev, data) {
        var conn = new Strophe.Connection(
            "http://bosh.metajack.im:5280/xmpp-httpbind");

        conn.connect(data.jid, data.password, function (status) {
            if (status === Strophe.Status.CONNECTED) {
                $(document).trigger('connected');
            } else if (status === Strophe.Status.DISCONNECTED) {
                $(document).trigger('disconnected');
            }
        });

        Referee.connection = conn;
    });

    $(document).bind('connected', function () {
        var conn = Referee.connection;

        $('#log').prepend("<p>Connected as " + conn.jid + "</p>");

        conn.addHandler(Referee.on_presence, null, "presence");
        conn.addHandler(Referee.on_iq, null, "iq");

        conn.send($pres());
    });

    $(document).bind('disconnected', function () {
        // nothing here yet
    });
```

Available for download on Wrox.com

LISTING 11-8: board.js

```
Referee.Board = function () {
    this.board = [[' ', ' ', ' '], [' ', ' ', ' '], [' ', ' ', ' ']];
};

Referee.Board.prototype = {
    validMove: function (side, col, row) {
        var curSide = this.currentSide();
        if (side !== curSide) {
            return false;
        }

        var coords = this.moveToCoords(col, row);
        if (this.board[coords.row][coords.col] !== ' ') {
```

```
            return false;
        }

        return true;
    },

    move: function (side, col, row) {
        if (this.validMove(side, col, row)) {
            var coords = this.moveToCoords(col, row);
            this.board[coords.row][coords.col] = side;
        } else {
            throw {
                name: "BoardError",
                message: "Move invalid"
            };
        }
    },

    moveToCoords: function (col, row) {
        var map = {'a': 0, 'b': 1, 'c': 2, '1': 0, '2': 1, '3': 2};
        var coords = {row: null, col: null};
        coords.col = map[col];
        coords.row = map[row];
        return coords;
    },

    currentSide: function () {
        var r, c;
        var x = 0, o = 0;

        for (r = 0; r < 3; r++) {
            for (c = 0; c < 3; c++) {
                if (this.board[r][c] === 'x') {
                    x += 1;
                } else if (this.board[r][c] === 'o') {
                    o += 1;
                }
            }
        }

        if (x === o) {
            return 'x';
        }

        return 'o';
    },

    gameOver: function () {
        var r, c;

        // check for row wins
        for (r = 0; r < 3; r++) {
            if (this.board[r][0] === 'x' &&
                this.board[r][1] === 'x' &&
```

continues

LISTING 11-8 *(continued)*

```
            this.board[r][2] === 'x') {
            return 'x';
        } else if (this.board[r][0] === 'o' &&
                this.board[r][1] === 'o' &&
                this.board[r][2] === 'o') {
            return 'o';
        }
    }

    // check for column wins
    for (c = 0; c < 3; c++) {
        if (this.board[0][c] === 'x' &&
            this.board[1][c] === 'x' &&
            this.board[2][c] === 'x') {
            return 'x';
        } else if (this.board[0][c] === 'o' &&
                this.board[1][c] === 'o' &&
                this.board[2][c] === 'o') {
            return 'o';
        }
    }

    // check for diagonal wins
    if (this.board[0][0] === 'x' &&
        this.board[1][1] === 'x' &&
        this.board[2][2] === 'x') {
        return 'x';
    } else if (this.board[0][0] === 'o' &&
            this.board[1][1] === 'o' &&
            this.board[2][2] === 'o') {
        return 'o';
    } else if (this.board[0][2] === 'x' &&
            this.board[1][1] === 'x' &&
            this.board[2][0] === 'x') {
        return 'x';
    } else if (this.board[0][2] === 'o' &&
            this.board[1][1] === 'o' &&
            this.board[2][0] === 'o') {
        return 'o';
    }

    // check for a tie
    var tie = true;
    for (r = 0; r < 3; r++) {
        if (this.board[r].indexOf(' ') >= 0) {
            tie = false;
            break;
        }
    }

    if (tie) {
        return "=";
```

```
            }

            return false;
        },

        toString: function () {
            var r, s = '';

            for (r = 0; r < 3; r++) {
                s += this.board[r].join('');
            }

            return s;
        }
    };
```

LISTING 11-9: toetem.js (final)

```
var Toetem = {
    connection: null,
    referee: null,
    NS_TOETEM: "http://metajack.im/ns/toetem",
    game: null,
    x_player: null,
    o_player: null,
    turn: null,
    my_side: null,
    watching: false,

    on_message: function (message) {
        var from = $(message).attr('from');

        if ($(message).find('waiting').length > 0) {
            $(message).find('waiting > player').each(function () {
                $('#waiting tbody').append(
                    "<tr><td class='jid'>" +
                        $(this).attr('jid') +
                        "</td><td>" +
                        ($(this).attr('jid') === Toetem.connection.jid ?
                         "<input type='button' class='stop_button' " +
                         "value='stop waiting'>":
                         "<input type='button' class='start_button' " +
                         "value='start game'>") +
                        "</td></tr>");
            });
        } else if ($(message).find('not-waiting').length > 0) {
            $(message).find('not-waiting > player').each(function () {
                var jid = $(this).attr('jid');
                $('#waiting td.jid').each(function () {
                    if ($(this).text() === jid) {
                        $(this).parent().remove();
                        return false;
                    }
```

continues

LISTING 11-9 *(continued)*

```
                });
            });
        } else if ($(message).find('games').length > 0) {
            $(message).find('games > game').each(function () {
                if ($(this).attr('x-player') !== Toetem.connection.jid &&
                    $(this).attr('o-player') !== Toetem.connection.jid) {
                    $('#games tbody').append(
                        "<tr><td>" +
                            $(this).attr('x-player') +
                            "</td><td>" +
                            $(this).attr('o-player') +
                            "</td><td class='jid'>" +
                            $(this).attr('room') +
                            "</td><td>" +
                            "<input type='button' class='watch_button' " +
                            "value='watch game'>" +
                            "</td></tr>");
                }
            });
        } else if ($(message).find('game-over').length > 0) {
            $(message).find('game-over > game').each(function () {
                var jid = $(this).attr('room');
                $('#games td.jid').each(function () {
                    if ($(this).text() === jid) {
                        $(this).parent().remove();
                        return false;
                    }
                });
            });
        } else if ($(message)
                    .find('x > invite').attr('from') === Toetem.referee) {
            Toetem.game = from;
            Toetem.watching = false;

            $('#messages').empty();
            $('#messages').append("<div class='system'>" +
                                "Joined game #" +
                                Strophe.getNodeFromJid(from) +
                                "</div>");
            Toetem.scroll_chat();

            $('#wait').removeAttr('disabled');
            $('#browser').hide();
            $('#game').show();
            Toetem.draw_board();
            $('#board-status').html('Waiting for other player..');

            var nick = Toetem.connection.jid;

            Toetem.connection.send(
                $pres({to: Toetem.game + '/' + nick})
                    .c('x', {xmlns: Toetem.NS_MUC}));
```

```
    } else {
        var body = $(message).children('body').text();
        if (body) {
            var who = Strophe.getResourceFromJid(from);
            var nick_style = 'nick';
            if (who === Toetem.connection.jid) {
                nick_style += ' me';
            }

            $('#messages').append(
                "<div>&lt;<span class='" + nick_style + "'>" +
                    Strophe.getBareJidFromJid(who) +
                    "</span>&gt; " +
                    body + "</div>");

            Toetem.scroll_chat();
        }

        if ($(message).find('delay').length > 0) {
            // skip command processing of old messages
            return true;
        }

        var cmdNode = $(message)
            .find('*[xmlns="' + Toetem.NS_TOETEM + '"]');
        var cmd = null;
        var row, col;
        if (cmdNode.length > 0) {
            cmd = cmdNode.get(0).tagName;
        }
        if (cmd === 'game-started') {
            var me = Toetem.connection.jid;
            Toetem.x_player = cmdNode.attr('x-player');
            Toetem.o_player = cmdNode.attr('o-player');
            Toetem.turn = 'x';

            if (Toetem.x_player === me) {
                Toetem.my_side = 'x';
                $('#board-status').html('Your move..');
            } else if (Toetem.o_player === me) {
                Toetem.my_side = 'o';
                $('#board-status').html("Opponent's move..");
            }

            if (!Toetem.watching) {
                $('#resign').removeAttr('disabled');
            } else {
                $('#leave').removeAttr('disabled');
            }
        } else if (cmd === 'game-ended') {
            $('#resign').attr('disabled', 'disabled');
            $('#leave').removeAttr('disabled');
            var winner = cmdNode.attr('winner');
            if (winner === Toetem.connection.jid) {
```

continues

LISTING 11-9 *(continued)*

```
            $('#board-status').html('You won!');
        } else if (winner && !Toetem.watching) {
            $('#board-status').html('You lost!');
        } else if (!Toetem.watching) {
            $('#board-status').html('You tied!');
        }
    } else if (cmd === 'move') {
        var map = {'a': 0, 'b': 1, 'c': 2, '1': 0, '2': 1, '3': 2};
        var col = cmdNode.attr('col');
        var row = cmdNode.attr('row');

        Toetem.draw_piece(Toetem.turn, map[col], map[row]);

        if (Toetem.turn === 'x') {
            Toetem.turn = 'o';
        } else {
            Toetem.turn = 'x';
        }

        if (!Toetem.watching) {
            Toetem.my_turn = Toetem.turn === Toetem.my_side;

            if (Toetem.my_turn) {
                $('#board-status').html("Your move..");
            } else {
                $('#board-status').html("Opponent's move..");
            }
        }
    } else if (cmd === 'game-state') {
        var pos = cmdNode.attr('pos');
        if (pos) {
            var idx = 0;
            for (row = 0; row < 3; row++) {
                for (col = 0; col < 3; col++) {
                    if (pos[idx] !== ' ') {
                        Toetem.draw_piece(pos[idx], col, row);
                    }

                    idx += 1;
                }
            }
        }
    }
}

return true;
},

scroll_chat: function () {
    var div = $('#messages').get(0);
    div.scrollTop = div.scrollHeight;
```

```
        },

    draw_board: function () {
        var ctx = $('#board')[0].getContext('2d');

        // clear board
        ctx.fillStyle = '#000';
        ctx.beginPath();
        ctx.fillRect(0, 0, 300, 300);

        // draw grid lines
        ctx.strokeStyle = '#999';
        ctx.lineWidth = 4;

        ctx.beginPath();

        ctx.moveTo(100, 10);
        ctx.lineTo(100, 290);
        ctx.moveTo(200, 10);
        ctx.lineTo(200, 290);
        ctx.moveTo(10, 100);
        ctx.lineTo(290, 100);
        ctx.moveTo(10, 200);
        ctx.lineTo(290, 200);

        ctx.stroke();
    },

    draw_piece: function (piece, x, y) {
        var ctx = $('#board')[0].getContext('2d');

        ctx.strokeStyle = '#fff';

        var center_x = (x * 100) + 50;
        var center_y = (y * 100) + 50;

        ctx.beginPath();

        if (piece === 'x') {
            ctx.moveTo(center_x - 15, center_y - 15);
            ctx.lineTo(center_x + 15, center_y + 15);

            ctx.moveTo(center_x + 15, center_y - 15);
            ctx.lineTo(center_x - 15, center_y + 15);
        } else {
            ctx.arc(center_x, center_y, 15, 0, 2 * Math.PI, true);
        }

        ctx.stroke();
    }
};

$(document).ready(function () {
    $('#login_dialog').dialog({
```

continues

LISTING 11-9 *(continued)*

```
            autoOpen: true,
            draggable: false,
            modal: true,
            title: 'Connect to XMPP',
            buttons: {
                "Connect": function () {
                    $(document).trigger('connect', {
                        jid: $('#jid').val(),
                        password: $('#password').val(),
                        referee: $('#referee').val()
                    });

                    $('#password').val('');
                    $(this).dialog('close');
                }
            }
        });

        $('#disconnect').click(function () {
            $(this).attr('disabled', 'disabled');

            Toetem.connection.disconnect();
        });

        $('#wait').click(function () {
            $(this).attr('disabled', 'disabled');

            Toetem.connection.sendIQ(
                $iq({to: Toetem.referee, type: "set"})
                    .c("waiting", {xmlns: Toetem.NS_TOETEM}));
        });

        $('input.stop_button').live('click', function () {
            Toetem.connection.sendIQ(
                $iq({to: Toetem.referee, type: "set"})
                    .c('stop-waiting', {xmlns: Toetem.NS_TOETEM}),
                function () {
                    $('#wait').removeAttr('disabled');
                });
        });

        $('input.start_button').live('click', function () {
            Toetem.connection.sendIQ(
                $iq({to: Toetem.referee, type: "set"})
                    .c('start', {xmlns: Toetem.NS_TOETEM,
                                "with": $(this).parent().prev().text()}));
        });

        $('input.watch_button').live('click', function () {
            // join the game room
            Toetem.game = $(this).parent().prev().text();
            Toetem.watching = true;
```

```
        $('#browser').hide();
        $('#game').show();
        Toetem.draw_board();
        $('#board-status').html('');

        Toetem.connection.send(
            $pres({to: Toetem.game + '/' + Toetem.connection.jid}));
    });

    $('#input').keypress(function (ev) {
        if (ev.which === 13) {
            ev.preventDefault();

            var input = $(this).val();
            $(this).val('');

            Toetem.connection.send(
                $msg({to: Toetem.game, type: 'groupchat'})
                    .c('body').t(input));
        }
    });

    $('#resign').click(function () {
        Toetem.connection.sendIQ(
            $iq({to: Toetem.referee, type: 'set'})
                .c('resign', {xmlns: Toetem.NS_TOETEM}));
    });

    $('#leave').click(function () {
        Toetem.connection.send(
            $pres({to: Toetem.game + '/' + Toetem.connection.jid,
                   type: 'unavailable'}));
        $('#game').hide();
        $('#browser').show();
    });

    $('#board').click(function (ev) {
        if (Toetem.turn && Toetem.turn === Toetem.my_side) {
            var pos = $(this).position();
            var x = Math.floor((ev.pageX - pos.left) / 100);
            var y = Math.floor((ev.pageY - pos.top) / 100);

            Toetem.connection.sendIQ(
                $iq({to: Toetem.referee, type: 'set'})
                    .c('move', {xmlns: Toetem.NS_TOETEM,
                                col: ['a', 'b', 'c'][x],
                                row: y + 1}));
        }
    });
});

$(document).bind('connect', function (ev, data) {
    var conn = new Strophe.Connection(
```

continues

LISTING 11-9 *(continued)*

```
        "http://bosh.metajack.im:5280/xmpp-httpbind");

    conn.connect(data.jid, data.password, function (status) {
        if (status === Strophe.Status.CONNECTED) {
            $(document).trigger('connected');
        } else if (status === Strophe.Status.DISCONNECTED) {
            $(document).trigger('disconnected');
        }
    });

    Toetem.connection = conn;
    Toetem.referee = data.referee;
});

$(document).bind('connected', function () {
    $('#disconnect').removeAttr('disabled');
    $('#wait').removeAttr('disabled');

    Toetem.connection.addHandler(Toetem.on_message, null, "message");

    // tell the referee we're online
    Toetem.connection.send(
        $pres({to: Toetem.referee})
            .c('register', {xmlns: Toetem.NS_TOETEM}));
});

$(document).bind('disconnected', function () {
    Toetem.referee = null;
    Toetem.connection = null;

    $('#waiting tbody').empty();
    $('#games tbody').empty();

    $('#login_dialog').dialog('open');
});
```

MAKING THE GAME MORE FUN

Toetem is a simple example of an XMPP-powered gaming system. Try creating an even better and more fun version. You might:

➤ Add support for another game like Texas Hold'em or chess.

➤ Add the ability for the system to handle more than one type of game.

➤ Allow players to watch multiple games simultaneously.

➤ Allow players to *play* multiple games simultaneously. Chess masters can easily beat dozens of lesser players at the same time!

SUMMARY

In this final application, you created a real-time, multi-user game system for Tic-Tac-Toe. Players from all over the world can use their XMPP accounts to connect to the system, find other players, and have fun playing with each other. Unlike previous applications, Toetem required you to implement both the service logic and the client logic. You also had to design an appropriate protocol leveraging multi-user chat to tie it all together.

Along the way you:

➤ Created an XMPP bot

➤ Managed external resources on behalf of users

➤ Designed a game protocol built on top of multi-user chat and simple interactions

➤ Implemented a complex application using the tools you've learned in previous chapters

A game system like Toetem can be created without the aid of the XMPP protocol, but by now you should be convinced that doing so would be a lot more painful and a lot less fun. Interactive applications like Toetem are easy to design and easy to build when you have the power of XMPP at your fingertips.

The third and final part of this book covers several advanced topics including XMPP session attachment, deploying XMPP applications, and writing Strophe plug-ins.

PART III
Advanced Topics

12

Getting Attached: Bootstrapping BOSH

WHAT'S IN THIS CHAPTER?

➤ How BOSH keeps track of sessions

➤ Using Strophe to attach to sessions

➤ Improving performance with attachment

➤ Using attachment for persistence

➤ Increasing security with attachment

One of the more advanced uses of Strophe is session attachment. Instead of initiating a fresh XMPP connection when the application starts, a connection is provided that is already set up along with a little extra information that Strophe can use to attach to it. The connection may have been set up by server-side logic or by a previous page in the application.

Session attachment can solve a variety of problems relating to security, session persistence, and performance. Most of the time you probably won't need session attachment, but when your application does need it, it really comes in handy.

Although session attachment can provide faster application startup times or enhanced security, it comes with the cost of doing more work to prepare and manage the connection.

Knowing when to use session attachment is as important as knowing how to use it. In this chapter you are introduced to the common use cases and mechanics of attaching to already-established sessions.

Unlike the other chapters in this book, it is impossible to demonstrate session attachment with pure JavaScript code. This chapter contains some additional server-side code to handle session creation that will not be fully covered in the text.

SESSION ATTACHMENT

Session attachment is one of those features whose purpose is limited but indispensable. At its core, it is extremely simple; instead of starting a new connection and authenticating with the server, you simply attach to a connection that has already been set up. However, exactly how this works and what kinds of things it is useful for are not quite as obvious.

The Mechanics of Sessions

XMPP is a TCP-based protocol, just like HTTP, and communication happens over an established, mostly reliable socket between two endpoints. As you may remember from Chapter 2, the BOSH extension to XMPP provides a bridge between this bidirectional, stateful protocol and HTTP, which is unidirectional and stateless. To understand how session attachment works, it's necessary to peek under the covers a little bit to see how BOSH achieves the translation.

Because a web browser cannot directly connect to an XMPP server, a BOSH connection manager responds to requests from a browser using HTTP and uses them to manage an XMPP connection on behalf of the user. Aside from the socket needed for XMPP communication, each managed connection has two other pieces of data associated with it: the SID and the RID.

SID stands for Session Identifier. This uniquely identifies the managed XMPP connection, and it is often a long, opaque alphanumeric string. Even though it is enough to identify the session, it is not very useful on its own.

The Request Identifier (RID) identifies a particular HTTP request associated with a BOSH-managed connection. Before a connection is established, the client sends a random RID to the connection manager along with its first request. Each subsequent request increments the RID by one.

The SID and the RID together provide enough information to interact with the underlying XMPP connection. Because the RID is generated randomly from a very large range of numbers, it is virtually impossible to guess the RID if you do not know one of the previous ones. Also, the connection manager will reject RIDs that fall outside of a narrow window around the current request. In this way, the BOSH-managed connection is tolerant of small errors like out of order delivery but robust to attacks like hijacking the connection.

Because these two identifiers are enough to both address and make use of a managed XMPP session, if an application knows the SID and the RID, it can *take over* or *attach* to the underlying session. All it must do is send a request to the BOSH connection manager using the unchanged SID and the RID incremented by one.

Note that it is very difficult to *share* a session in this manner, because the two applications (or two instances of the same application) will need to know the current RID at all times. If this were an easy problem to solve, you wouldn't need XMPP to shuttle data around in the first place!

Of course, attaching to a session does not give the application access to the previous history of what happened on the connection before attachment. For this reason, it is often used very early during the session's life or at other well defined, known points.

If your code knows the SID and the RID of the session you want to attach to, you can use Strophe's `attach()` function to take over the session. Instead of a username and password, you pass the SID and the RID, but like `connect()`, it still takes a connection status callback function. The `attach()` function also takes the JID used in the session, but this isn't strictly necessary. If you didn't know the JID used for the underlying session, you could discover it once you were attached.

The `attach()` function is demonstrated in the following code, but it should look very familiar after seeing `connect()` in previous chapters:

```
var connection = new Strophe.Connection(BOSH_URL);
connection.attach(jid, sid, rid, callback);
```

Using session attachment with Strophe is pretty easy; the tricky part is getting the SID and RID to Strophe in the first place and establishing the connection outside of the application.

Typically the SID and RID are transmitted as the result of an AJAX call to set up a session or embedded within the HTML served from the backend web application. The underlying connection is usually established by backend code doing the initial HTTP requests that the JavaScript code would normally be doing.

Even with the knowledge of how attachment works, you might still be wondering why you would need such a feature. After all, every application you built in this book was possible without it.

Use Cases

Session attachment is typically employed to solve issues of security, performance, and persistence. New use cases for technology appear every day, so this small list is by no means exhaustive, but these uses have emerged as the main motivations for session attachment in the few years the technique has been around.

Increased or Easier Security

BOSH sessions can be encrypted, and often the underlying XMPP sessions are encrypted as well. Because XMPP makes use of SASL, the authentication mechanisms tend to be quite strong. How then can session attachment improve on this situation?

In web applications, authentication starts with the user typing in a username and password. The server assigns and returns a session identifier, and from then on all the HTTP requests sent and received contain this identifier, which verifies the identity of the client without asking for credentials repeatedly. This use case is still desirable in XMPP-enabled web applications.

This same use case for cached credentials is similar to token-based authentication. Just imagine that the SID and the RID are tokens, and you can see why session attachment is useful here.

If the XMPP-enabled piece of your application is a part of a larger web site, it is much more convenient if the users do not have to both log in to the web site and also to the XMPP application. In this situation, it is best if the web site can serve the pages for the XMPP application with credentials already embedded. To avoid leaking the user's password by placing it in the web page (and therefore also in the browser's cache, and so on), the session and request identifiers can be embedded instead, and used to attach to a running session that has already been pre-authenticated by the server. In a worst-case scenario, only a single session becomes compromised.

Pushing Performance

Another common use case is to increase the performance of application startup. Typically it takes half a dozen requests and responses to initiate and set up an XMPP connection over BOSH. Pre-establishing the connection on the server side eliminates precious round-trip cycles when startup latency is important, and if well done, can mean essentially instant-on connections.

Fewer requests at startup puts a smaller load on the HTTP infrastructure of your web application, especially when large numbers of clients are reconnecting after an outage or failure. Imagine the traffic spike if ten thousand clients suddenly connected and each had to make six or seven requests to get set up!

Session creation performance is also drastically increased if the XMPP session is established to a server local to the backend web infrastructure. Instead of each round trip being across the Internet, they could all be across a local network. Assuming an average ping time on the open Internet of 100ms, the six setup requests would take more than half a second. With a typical local network ping time of 10ms, start up latency is suddenly an order of magnitude faster. Even better, the session creation could happen completely internal to the XMPP server itself, involving no round trips or extra requests at all.

Persisting Connections

Session attachment can also be used to persist a connection across multiple pages. This use case is much trickier though because nothing prevents a user from opening the same web page in a second window or tab, so care must be taken that there is only one page using the underlying session at a time.

One way to achieve session persistence might be to store the SID and RID in a cookie, and reattach to the session once the next page has loaded. In this way, the XMPP session would follow the user from page to page, becoming detached and reattached multiple times.

Now that you are familiar with the main use cases for session attachment as well as the basics of how it works, it is time to see an example of it in action.

AUTOMATIC LOGINS WITH SESSION ATTACHMENT

Most of the work of session attachment is outside the JavaScript application code. This chapter departs from the JavaScript-only examples in the rest of the book by also implementing a backend web application built in Python on top of the Django framework. The same work could be done by a Ruby on Rails application or one written in Java, but Python code is quite readable even for those unfamiliar with it and that makes for a nice example.

First, you must install a few dependencies for the example. You need:

➤ Django version 1.1 or later, http://www.djangoproject.com

➤ Twisted Python version 8.2.0 or later, http://twistedmatrix.com

➤ Punjab version 0.13 or later, http://code.stanziq.com/pubjab

Note that although Punjab is a fully functional BOSH connection manager, it is used in this example only for its ready-made BOSH library routines. It is not necessary to run a Punjab server, only to install the code so that it can be found by the session establishment code inside the Django application.

Please refer to the instructions provided with these packages for installation instructions for your particular platform. You can also find some basic instructions for Punjab in Appendix B. Once you have the software installed, you can create the project.

Creating the Django Project

You create a Django project called `attach` by using Django's included `django-admin.py` command. Find a suitable directory for your project, and run:

```
django-admin.py startproject attach
```

This should create a directory called `attach` filled with a project skeleton. The contents of this directory should include files named `settings.py`, `__init__.py`, `urls.py`, and `manage.py`.

Next, you must create a Django application inside this project called `attacher`. You can do this with the `manage.py` command. From inside the `attach` directory, run:

```
python manage.py startapp attacher
```

Like `startproject`, this creates a directory called `attacher` that contains skeleton files for the application.

Next, you must set up `urls.py` to map URLs in the application to specific views in the code. The `urls.py` file shown in Listing 12-1 creates a mapping from the root URL to the `attacher` application's `index` view.

Available for download on Wrox.com

LISTING 12-1: urls.py

```
from django.conf.urls.defaults import *

urlpatterns = patterns('',
    (r'^$', 'attach.attacher.views.index'),
    (r'^static/(?P<path>.*)$', 'django.views.static.serve',
     {'document_root':
       '/path/to/attach/media/'}),

)
```

Be sure to replace /path/to/attach/media/ with the real, absolute path to the attach directory with /media/ appended. This is where the static resources for the application are stored, and you will create this directory shortly.

The index view is defined in attacher/views.py, which appears in Listing 12-2.

LISTING 12-2: views.py

```python
from django.http import HttpResponse
from django.template import Context, loader

from attach.settings import BOSH_SERVICE, JABBERID, PASSWORD
from attach.boshclient import BOSHClient

def index(request):
    bc = BOSHClient(JABBERID, PASSWORD, BOSH_SERVICE)
    bc.startSessionAndAuth()

    t = loader.get_template("attacher/index.html")
    c = Context({
        'jid': bc.jabberid.full(),
        'sid': bc.sid,
        'rid': bc.rid,
    })

    return HttpResponse(t.render(c))
```

This view creates an XMPP session via the BOSHClient object using credentials and configuration defined in the project settings file. Once created, it renders a response page from the index.html template. The jid, sid, and rid properties provided in the Context object will be substituted inside the template. When the browser receives the rendered page, it will have access to the real JID, SID, and RID for the established connection.

The file boshclient.py handles session establishment, and you will need to download it from the book's web site and copy it into your project directory. It is not shown here because its source code is too long to list in the text.

To create the HTML template, create a directory under the attach project directory called templates. Create the attacher directory under the templates directory, and place the HTML code from Listing 12-3 into an index.html file there.

LISTING 12-3: index.html

```html
<!DOCTYPE HTML PUBLIC "-//W3C//DTD HTML 4.01//EN"
                      "http://www.w3.org/TR/html4/strict.dtd">
<html>
  <head>
    <title>Strophe Attach Example</title>
```

```
<script src='http://ajax.googleapis.com/ajax/libs/jquery/1.3.2/jquery.js'>
</script>
<script src='scripts/strophe.js'></script>
<script src='scripts/flXHR.js'></script>
<script src='scripts/strophe.flxhr.js'></script>

<script type='text/javascript'>
  <!--
      var Attacher = {
          JID: '{{ jid }}',
          SID: '{{ sid }}',
          RID: '{{ rid }}'
      };
      // -->
</script>

<link rel='stylesheet' type='text/css' href='attacher.css'>
<script type='text/javascript' src='attacher.js'></script>
</head>
<body>
  <h1>Strophe Attach Example</h1>

  <p>This example shows how to attach to an existing BOSH session with
  Strophe.</p>

  <h2>Log</h2>

  <div id='log'>
  </div>
</body>
</html>
```

The `Attacher` object's properties will be substituted during template rendering to be the actual JID, SID, and RID values for the established session. The JavaScript code will then be able to access these in order to call Strophe's `attach()` function.

You must edit the `settings.py` file in the project directory to provide the configuration information for your preferred XMPP server and BOSH server. Add the following lines to the end of `settings.py`, but be sure to use real domain names and values:

```
BOSH_SERVICE = 'http://pemberley.lit/xmpp-httpbind'
JABBERID = 'darcy@pemberley.lit/bosh'
PASSWORD = 'lizzy'
```

The CSS and HTML files in Listing 12-4 and Listing 12-5 should be placed in a directory called `media` inside the `attach` project directory. You'll need to set the `MEDIA_ROOT` setting to the absolute path to this directory along with the trailing slash character. For example, on Windows systems, this might be:

```
MEDIA_ROOT = 'c:\\projects\\attach\\media\\'
```

On Mac OS X or GNU/Linux systems, this might be:

```
MEDIA_ROOT = '/projects/attach/media/'
```

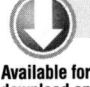

LISTING 12-4: attacher.css

```css
body {
    font-family: Helvetica;
}

h1, h2 {
    text-align: center;
}

#log {
    background-color: #ccc;
}
```

LISTING 12-5: attacher.js

```javascript
$(document).ready(function () {
    Attacher.connection = new Strophe.Connection(
        "http://bosh.metajack.im:5280/xmpp-httpbind");

    Attacher.connection.attach(
        Attacher.JID, Attacher.SID, Attacher.RID, null);

    $('#log').append("<div>Session attached!</div>");

    Attacher.connection.sendIQ(
        $iq({to: Strophe.getDomainFromJid(Attacher.JID),
            type: "get"})
            .c('query', {xmlns:
                    'http://jabber.org/protocol/disco#info'}),
        function () {
            $('#log').append("<div>Response received " +
                            "from server!</div>");
        });
});
```

The application is now complete, and you can use Django's built-in web server to test it out. Start the server with:

```
python manage.py runserver
```

This starts a web server at `http://127.0.0.1:8000/`, which you can connect to with your web browser. If everything is set up correctly, you should see log messages appear on the web page stating that it has connected to the session and communicated with the server.

As you can see, session attachment is a lot more complicated to set up, but from the JavaScript application's point of view, is extremely easy. If you don't have a current need for pre-established sessions and session attachment, just remember that it is available to use when such a need arises.

SUMMARY

Session attachment is an advanced use of Strophe and XMPP to attach to a pre-established session from JavaScript. Attaching to sessions created out of band allows XMPP applications to increase security in the face of convenience demanded by users, improve startup performance, and to persist a session across multiple page loads.

In this chapter, you:

➤   Discovered why session attachment is useful

➤   Learned how attached sessions work

➤   Learned how to make Strophe attach to an existing session

➤   Built a small automatic login example using Django for the backend

In the next chapter, you will discover some considerations, best practices, and guidelines for deploying and scaling XMPP applications.

13

Deploying XMPP Applications

WHAT'S IN THIS CHAPTER?

➤   Load balancing connection managers

➤   Clustering XMPP servers

➤   Distributing components

➤   Reducing latency and serialization

➤   Optimizing client side operations

Developing an application with XMPP is only the beginning. Once you have put the finishing touches on your latest creation, you'll likely want to share it with the world at large. Because the world is a big place, full of lots of potential users, you'll want to ensure that your application is deployed in such a way that it will scale and run as efficiently as possible.

You can scale your application in quite a few ways, both horizontally, spreading it across multiple machines, and vertically, optimizing the application and running it on better hardware. For example, many XMPP servers have a clustered operation mode, enabling more than one server to provide services under a single domain.

If your application has only modest amounts of users or traffic, feel free to skip this chapter. After all, you can always come back when your application becomes wildly popular.

GROWING HORIZONTALLY

Applications will often exceed the limit of resources available on a single machine. For some applications, this limit may be memory, and for others, the limit will be processor speed. Though adding more resources to the machine is an easy fix, there is a finite limit on how much can be added. Often it is better to *scale horizontally* by distributing the application over more than one physical machine.

XMPP applications can make use of a number of techniques to do this. What technique is appropriate depends on which resource is in contention and the nature of the specific application. Your application can grow horizontally in the following ways:

➤ Running multiple connection managers on different machines and load balancing between them

➤ Clustering XMPP servers to spread connections over multiple machines

➤ Running a single server component on several machines

➤ Using internal federation to spread the application over a network of XMPP servers

➤ Speaking the server-to-server protocol directly

Clever programmers will no doubt discover additional ways, but these constitute the current practices.

Multiple Connection Managers

The BOSH connection manager is an HTTP service, and like most HTTP services, is fairly easy to scale across multiple machines. If your application has many thousands of simultaneously connected users, you will probably need to spread their connections across several connection managers.

Running multiple connection managers is easy with standalone managers, but requires server support for clustering when using built-in managers. Once all the connection managers are running, you will want to load balance their use and provide a common end point for accessing them.

Great open source and commercial applications as well as specialized hardware are available that can load balance and aggregate HTTP services. Most large web sites already employ these tools for their normal web applications. Two open source tools built for these purposes are used as examples in this chapter: nginx and Haproxy.

Before you dive into the details, there is one more thing to note about load balancing BOSH connection managers; connection managers keep a small amount of state — the XMPP connection and its identifiers. When a user sends an HTTP request for the first time, the load balancer must pick a server to respond. For all later requests, the load balancer must continue to choose the same server or the connection may be interrupted. Fortunately, most load balancers are capable of tracking server assignments via special HTTP cookies because web applications with session support often need similar functionality.

Each product's configuration and setup procedures are unique, but many of the concepts described in the following examples are applicable to all of them.

nginx

nginx is a lightweight web server built for high performance and stability. Its great support for reverse HTTP proxies and load balancing make it a good fit for XMPP-based web applications. This section describes a basic load balancing setup for the standalone connection manager Punjab. See

Appendix B for more information on Punjab, standalone connection managers, and using nginx as a simple proxy.

You can find nginx at its web site, `http://nginx.net`.

First, you need to configure and set up Punjab on multiple machines, or run several instances on the same machine on different IPs or ports. For purposes of this example, it is assumed that Punjab is running on port 5280 on the following machines, and that the path to the service is `/xmpp-httpbind`:

➤ bosh-1.pemberley.lit

➤ bosh-2.pemberley.lit

➤ bosh-3.pemberley.lit

nginx will be configured to reverse proxy and load balance these three Punjab servers under the local path at `/xmpp-httpbind`.

Under the `http` section, you need to add an `upstream` configuration section, like the one here, to define the set of Punjab servers:

```
upstream punjab {
    ip_hash;
    server bosh-1.pemberley.lit:5280;
    server bosh-2.pemberley.lit:5280;
    server bosh-3.pemberley.lit:5280;
}
```

The `ip_hash` directive tells nginx to use a hash of the user's IP address to pick a server, guaranteeing that each request from that IP will be sent to the same server. Users will never accidentally get sent to a Punjab instance that does not have the user's state. You might notice that this is not quite true load balancing, but in many situations this hash-based approach is similarly effective.

Under the `server` section, you need to add a `location` configuration section to set up the reverse proxy. Instead of using the hostname of the proxied server, you instead use the previously set up upstream configuration named `punjab`:

```
location /xmpp-httpbind {
    proxy_pass http://punjab;
}
```

Now nginx will proxy an incoming request to `/xmpp-httpbind` to one of the three configured Punjab servers based on the hash of the user's IP address. Please note that adding or removing servers changes the hash function; users will likely experience a temporary disconnection if you reconfigure the server in this way.

That's all there is to it! Of course, nginx has many configuration options not covered here that can expand upon this basic example. Please see the nginx documentation at `http://wiki.nginx.org` for more information on nginx's configuration.

Haproxy

Haproxy is a high-performance, highly available load balancer for TCP and HTTP services. It is capable of supporting complex load balancing configurations, but here it is used in a basic configuration useful for BOSH connection managers.

You can find Haproxy at its web site, `http://haproxy.1wt.eu/`.

Just as with the nginx example, this example assumes the same three Punjab servers are available, all listening on port 5280, with the BOSH service accessible at the path `/xmpp-httpbind`. The servers are named bosh-1.pemberley.lit, bosh-2.pemberley.lit, and bosh-3.pemberley.lit.

First, in the `haproxy.cfg` file, you need to define a new `backend` listing the set of Punjab servers similar to the following:

```
backend punjab
    mode http
    balance leastconn
    cookie BOSHSRV insert indirect nocache
    server bosh-1 bosh-1.pemberley.lit:5280 cookie bosh-1
    server bosh-2 bosh-2.pemberley.lit:5280 cookie bosh-2
    server bosh-3 bosh-3.pemberley.lit:5280 cookie bosh-3
```

This section defines an HTTP backend called `punjab` with three servers. The balancing strategy, `leastconn`, is to choose the server with the least number of current connections. A cookie is used to make sure that each client continues to be served by the same Punjab server across multiple HTTP requests.

To use the new backend, you need to add some configuration to your relevant `frontend` configuration section. The following lines demonstrate such a configuration:

```
frontend www
    # normal config would be here
    option httpclose
    acl bosh path_beg /xmpp-httpbind
    use_backend punjab if bosh
```

The `httpclose` option is necessary because Haproxy does not support keep-alive mode; if it is omitted, Haproxy only processes the initial request, and this can cause some unexpected behavior. The `httpclose` option works around this by disabling keep-alive mode.

The other two lines tell Haproxy to use the `punjab` backend whenever the path begins with `/xmpp-httpbind`.

When Haproxy sees an `/xmpp-httpbind` path, it forwards the request to one of the three servers configured for the `punjab` backend. It inserts an HTTP cookie named BOSHSRV set to the identifier of the server, or if this cookie already exists, uses it to route the request to the correct server. Because Haproxy uses cookies to identify the servers instead of an IP hash, the configuration can be changed at will without affecting users.

More complex setups can be easily created with Haproxy. For example, each Punjab server can be limited to serving a specific number of connections, have custom timeouts set, and be continuously monitored for availability.

Please refer to the documentation for information on the specific configurations shown here or for information on more advanced uses. You can find the documentation at `http://haproxy.1wt.eu/download/1.3/doc/configuration.txt`.

Clustering XMPP Servers

Several XMPP servers support clustering. In a clustered configuration, several instances of the XMPP server provide services for a single XMPP domain. For example, the pemberley.lit server could resolve to a group of 10 clustered servers, but no matter which server was selected by a user, it would appear as pemberley.lit.

Each XMPP server has its own configuration requirements for clustering. In this section, you see an example of how to cluster an ejabberd server on two separate machines. You can obtain and learn more about ejabberd at `http://www.ejabberd.im`.

First, you need to install ejabberd on two separate machines. For this example, it is assumed that these machines are named xmpp-1.pemberley.lit and xmpp-2.pemberley.lit, and that both machines provide an XMPP service for the pemberley.lit domain. Please refer to the ejabberd documentation for basic installation instructions.

You must edit the `ejabberd.cfg` configuration file to configure both machines.

First, you must change the server's hostname to the correct domain; in this case it will be pemberley.lit. This should be the same on both xmpp-1.pemberley.lit and xmpp-2.pemberley.lit. Find the line similar to the following one, and change the domain to pemberley.lit:

```
{hosts, ["pemberley.lit"]}.
```

Next, you can make any other normal configuration changes, just as you normally would for a single server.

Now you can start the XMPP server on xmpp-1.pemberley.lit. Just run:

```
ejabberdctl start
```

You can check to see if the server started up correctly by running:

```
ejabberdctl status
```

After a few seconds, it should inform you that the node is started.

Once ejabberd is running, it creates an Erlang cookie file. You need to make sure that the Erlang cookie files on both machines match. ejabberd's Erlang cookie file is named `.erlang.cookie` and can be found along with ejabberd's other data files. On UNIX-like systems, including Mac OS X and GNU/Linux, it can usually be found in the `/var/lib/ejabberd` directory. Simply copy the cookie file from xmpp-1.pemberley.lit to the same location on xmpp-2.pemberley.lit.

Before you start up this second node, you must first initialize the cluster's database on this node. This step can be a little finicky depending on how you have named your ejabberd nodes. By default, ejabberd uses *short names*, but it can also use the fully qualified domain names if so configured. The command is slightly different for each case, and the one shown here is for the default setup.

To initialize the second node's database, run the following command:

```
erl -sname ejabberd@xmpp-2 -mnesia dir '"/var/lib/ejabberd"' \
    -mnesia extra_db_nodes "['ejabberd@xmpp-1']" -s mnesia
```

Be sure to use the correct quotes because they are very important, and the command won't work without the proper quoting. The backslash just continues the command on the next line; if you enter the entire command on one line, you can omit this character. You may also have to edit the node names and the path to the database if these are different on your system. Finally, if you are using fully qualified names, you'll want to change -sname to -name.

The previous command will leave you inside an Erlang command shell. You can verify that both nodes are connected to the database by typing the following command and pressing Enter:

```
mnesia:info().
```

You should see a line starting with "running db nodes" that includes your two ejabberd nodes.

If all has gone well, you can now copy the schema table to the new node. Type in the following command and press Enter:

```
mnesia:change_table_copy_type(schema, node(), disc_copies).
```

You can now exit the Erlang shell by typing:

```
q().
```

Your second ejabberd node is ready to be started. Start it the same way as the first node, with:

```
ejabberdctl start
```

If you want to run more than two nodes, you can repeat the instructions for the second node for all the additional nodes. Some people run ejabberd clusters spanning dozens of machines!

Note that if you are running the internal BOSH connection manager for ejabberd, you can use the same steps as in the previous section to load balance among them. If you want to load balance native XMPP connections, you can rely on DNS to round-robin requests by listing all available XMPP nodes in appropriate SRV records. You can even use Haproxy or another TCP load balancer solution to load balance the XMPP connections from a single endpoint.

Spreading Out Components

You learned a little about components in Chapter 1 when the different kinds of XMPP entities were described. All of the XMPP code in this book accesses the server as a client, but often XMPP services are written as server components. Several XMPP servers, including ejabberd, support load balancing components, offering yet another way to scale your applications.

The basic idea behind load balancing of components is that multiple components connect to the server with the same identity. For example, if the service is provided by library.pemberley.lit, each machine would run the component and connect as library.pemberley.lit.

In ejabberd's case, this load balancing is done by sending requests to each machine in a round-robin fashion. In a clustered setup, ejabberd first tries locally connected machines, followed by the remote ones. This load balancing strategy is not suited to all applications, but it is helpful in several cases. Currently, other strategies are not supported but should be easy to add by aspiring Erlang hackers.

You will need to consult your server's documentation to see if it supports load balancing of components and to see what strategies it employs. If your service can be written to take advantage of this, it will be able to scale very well.

Federating Internally

There is often no reason that every user or every component of an XMPP service must be located on the same server or domain. In these cases, you can forgo server clustering and turn to internal federation to achieve scale. Internally federated servers are just internal servers that talk to each other via the server-to-server protocol, just as public XMPP servers talk to each other.

Internal federation can even be combined with clustering. For example, a global XMPP service may have clusters in the U.S. and in Europe, each of which communicates with the other via regular server federation.

One advantage of federation over clustering is that there are no shared databases between the servers, so the achievable scale is far higher. There is practically no limit to how many XMPP servers (or e-mail, HTTP, or DNS servers) can exist and communicate with each other.

Often natural application boundaries exist at which to place the federation boundaries. Some services might use geography as a guide, and others might use IP hashes. If the service is the same at any location, any number of techniques can be used to place users at the fastest or most appropriate server.

Becoming a Server

There is no reason that XMPP servers must be the only things that speak the server-to-server protocol. Probably the most efficient way to scale an application is to bypass the server altogether and have your service speak the server-to-server protocol directly.

The server-to-server protocol is slightly more complicated than the client-to-server version, due to its reliance on TLS certificates or dialback authentication. Once the XMPP streams are set up, though, the same kinds of stanzas are sent back and forth.

If your XMPP service has little need for user accounts, rosters, or other traditional IM server features, you might be better off without a server. For example, an XMPP pubsub service might be unrelated to any particular server full of users, and such a pubsub service could be made directly addressable as a server.

There aren't yet a lot of libraries that make server-to-server protocol programming easier, but the situation is rapidly changing as more and more non–IM-related XMPP services spring up. This may soon become the way most XMPP services are exposed, in much the same way as web services have become their own HTTP servers as well.

GROWING VERTICALLY

Horizontal scalability is sometimes tough to achieve. Not only must you deal with your application's normal concerns, you must also keep in mind how the various machines involved will distribute the work and handle internal communication. If you don't plan ahead for such scalability, it can be difficult to retrofit your application. On the other hand, it is just a question of money to buy faster machines and a question of time and effort to optimize the application's code.

All applications can be profiled and timed to find slow operations. XMPP applications in particular have a few common places where performance problems appear, and this section focuses on those. The main areas to watch out for are communication latency, XML serialization, and HTML DOM operations.

Reducing Latency

All network applications must deal in some way with latency. The speed of an operation can be lightning fast, but if the time it takes to send the request to the server and receive the response is high, the user will still experience an irritating delay. Often, reducing latency provides enormous benefits to perceived application speed, so you should always aspire to make your application's latency as minimal as possible.

Latency can come from many places, but only a few are directly under your control as an application developer. The two biggest sources of latency in XMPP applications are initialization and setup of connections (and other resources) and overly large stanzas. Each of these can be handled in a number of ways depending on your application's particular needs.

Streamlining Connections and Setup

When XMPP applications start, they need to connect to a server. This process takes some time and involves a few rounds of requests and responses to complete. Once connected, applications often need to perform a set of initialization operations such as fetching the roster and joining chat rooms. When native XMPP connections are used, these processes are not as much of a problem, but over HTTP, the story is much different.

Any number of stanzas can be sent in one HTTP request to a connection manager, and the same is true for stanzas in responses. The nature of initialization stanzas is such that they must usually be sent and received sequentially, with the next stanza depending on the results of the previous one. If you assume 100 milliseconds of latency per request and response, a handful of initialization stanzas don't take long to add up to noticeable delays and annoyed users.

The first step to combating these problems is to parallelize as much as possible. If you can start several sequences simultaneously, fewer HTTP round trips will be needed to complete the initialization. If you have three initialization tasks that can be run in parallel, the number of round trips needed to complete all of them is equal to the number it takes to complete just the longest one. For example, if a group chat application joins rooms on startup, it should join every room at once, instead of serially. The end result will be much faster launch times for the application.

By default, Strophe automatically sends new stanzas as soon as you call the `send()` function. If your application is going to be sending a lot of stanzas in a short amount of time, this behavior is undesirable because it could result in using more HTTP round trips than is necessary. You could batch up stanzas in your code to send all at once, but this is hard to do if your initialization code is spread over several modules.

Strophe provides two functions that will help you optimize these areas of your application: `pause()` and `resume()`. After `pause()` is called for a connection, Strophe stops sending any data to the server until `resume()` is called. Optimizing the transmission of a large number of stanzas is as easy as pausing, doing all the individual calls to `send()`, and then resuming. The end result will be one large request to the server instead of many small ones.

You've already seen another helpful tool to reduce connection latency, the attached sessions described in Chapter 12. Because all of the initial set up of the connection happens over a native XMPP connection — often from a machine on the same network as the XMPP server — only one HTTP round trip is needed to start the connection. In addition to making the connection and authentication process faster, you can also put common initialization code in the server-side attachment service to make those operations faster as well. This can easily reduce multiple seconds of latency down to a mere instant.

Session attachment can't help once your application is already running, but the other techniques are equally applicable during other phases of your application's session. For example, a gaming client might need to make several requests to a central service as well as join a room and query initial state. The `pause()` and `resume()` functions combined with parallelization can make this happen as quickly as possible.

Of course, all these latency cost-saving measures can be combined in various ways. Choose the ones that are the most effective and appropriate for your particular application. Both Amazon and Google have done extensive research on the benefits of reducing latencies in page requests and found them to significantly impact their bottom lines. Your users will definitely appreciate your application's responsiveness.

Dealing with Large Stanzas

The XMPP protocol is built for exchanging small bits of information, and it is therefore no surprise that large stanzas can cause some problems. For the most part, it is easy to avoid large stanzas, but even when they can't be avoided, several tools can help mitigate their effect.

To understand why large stanzas can be a problem, remember that each XMPP session consists of two XMPP streams. Only one stanza at a time can be sent over a stream, and each stanza takes some time to transmit from the source to the destination. Any further stanzas that need to be sent must wait until the ones before them have been transmitted.

Normally, the stanzas are small, so each stanza must wait only a very short amount of time before it is actually transmitted. When a large stanza is sent, the transmission time can be quite large, and during this time, no other stanzas can be sent in the same direction.

Imagine playing a fast chess game over XMPP, and, in the middle of the game, right before you move, a giant avatar from one of your contacts is sent. Your move is sent to the server immediately, and your opponent instantly responds, but your client must now wait until the avatar is completely transmitted before you will see your opponent's move. Meanwhile, your move clock is ticking away precious seconds!

Two main methods exist for handling large stanzas: splitting them up into smaller stanzas and dealing with them out of band.

XMPP provides a number of ways to split a large amount of data over multiple, smaller stanzas. One such way is In-Band Bytestreams (XEP-0047), which break up a large payload into smaller chunks and send them in a series of `<iq>` or `<message>` stanzas. Once all the stanzas for the payload are received, the original data can be combined and processed. Unlike sending data in a large blob, chunking it over several stanzas allows for breaks where other stanzas can be sent as well, improving overall latency. In-Band Bytestreams work well for things like images and binary data.

Some XMPP stanzas consist of a long list of items or results. For example, a service discovery request to a busy pubsub system may return thousands of available nodes, resulting in a large, cumbersome stanza. For these types of stanzas, it is often better to return the set of results in pages. Results Set Management (XEP-0059) can be used to do this for arbitrary things, and Roster Versioning (XEP-0237) provides a similar solution specifically for rosters. These solutions aren't always built into every extension, but you can certainly add them to your own. Over time, I expect the XMPP community will apply a solution similar to these two across all extensions that may generate large stanzas.

Though XMPP may not be the best protocol for transferring large blocks of information, plenty of other protocols exist that handle this job with ease. Your application is free to use these other protocols to transfer large blobs of data out of band (OOB), outside of the XMPP connection.

The most common OOB technique for web-based XMPP applications is to use normal HTTP requests. For example, instead of transferring avatars or images over XMPP, the URLs of the data can be transmitted over XMPP and the actual data fetched via HTTP. The XMPP connection will retain the necessary low latencies, and the large pieces of data can be sent over a near-optimal transport. As an added bonus, the browser caches many requests, so multiple requests for the same data can be answered without wasting bandwidth on duplicate data.

The Jingle extensions (XEP-0166, XEP-0234, XEP-0247, and others) provide a very flexible framework for negotiating, establishing, and communicating over OOB connections. This technology was originally developed by Google for use in voice and video chat but has since been standardized and extended by the XMPP community to handle a wide variety of use cases.

If sufficient intermediary services exist, Jingle is capable of negotiating and facilitating connections even through NATs and firewalls. Jingle is also capable of negotiating in-band channels for those cases where no OOB channel is available. Although Jingle came from a need for multimedia transport negotiation and management, it is quickly becoming one of XMPP's most important tools, and extensions already exist for using Jingle for arbitrary file transfers and secure end-to-end communications.

Minimizing XML Serialization

Applications work with stanzas in a convenient data structure, and when ready for transmission, these data structures are serialized to XML bytes and sent over the network. Busy applications will be serializing a lot of XML data, and though it is not usually an expensive operation, it can become a critical factor in performance.

Aside from optimizing the XML serialization routines yourself, the only way to improve performance is to reduce the amount of serialization that is done. Applications can be structured to minimize serialization, but you must first know where it happens.

Every XMPP connection involves a minimum of two serialization steps. One entity must serialize XML to send to another, and the recipient must serialize any response it sends back.

For two clients on different servers, there are up to six serialization steps. First Darcy must serialize his stanzas to send them to the pemberley.lit server. His server may need to parse and serialize them to send them to the longbourn.lit server. The longbourn.lit server may need to serialize the stanza for transmission to Elizabeth's client. Finally, Elizabeth's response will take the reverse route. If both clients are using HTTP connection managers, there may even be more serialization occurring!

Some heavily optimized XMPP servers can route many stanzas without fully parsing them, thus avoiding re-serialization, and connection managers may use similar tricks to avoid unnecessary serialization as well. If serialization becomes a bottleneck for your application, you might consider using one of these existing, optimized implementations.

In some cases, your own application may be able to avoid serialization. For example, just like an optimized server, if you have access to the raw XML bytes and you only need to send a copy of a stanza, you can transmit the same raw bytes. Unfortunately, most interesting applications are not often resending copied stanzas.

There is, however, one instance where serialization can be more of an issue — components. XMPP server components communicate over an XMPP stream just like clients do, and because they are often both the endpoint and origin of communication, they cannot simply route pre-serialized stanzas around. Components are doomed to a life full of parsing and serialization.

The only way to eliminate this kind of serialization is to transmit the internal data structure representation of a stanza between the entities, but because the entities are often written in different programming languages by different people or teams, this is not usually a practical solution.

Server plug-ins do not have these kinds of serialization issues because they share data representations — and often the same memory or process — and have no need for serialization. Also, because they are part of the server itself, communication is usually done with function calls instead of TCP socket connections.

If you have a component that is bottlenecked on XML serialization, converting it to a server plug-in may be the most viable option.

In all cases, understanding where serialization is happening and at which points it is not strictly required is the first step to figuring out how to optimize this part of your application. Once you know where the extra serialization steps are, it is fairly straightforward to apply one of the preceding techniques to minimize it.

Optimizing DOM Operations

Dynamic web applications must do a lot of DOM operations. The application's user interface changes as new data or new user interactions are processed. Operations that manipulate the DOM are often among the most expensive.

You can use a few techniques to reduce or optimize your access and manipulation of the browser's DOM: batching operations, cloning, and limiting scope.

Batching Operations

If you've ever written any graphics code you might be familiar with double buffering. Instead of painting directly on the screen, a double-buffered graphics application paints on an off-screen buffer area. Once the painting is complete, the buffer is swapped with the on-screen buffer. This results in flicker-free frame changes.

Batching DOM operations is much the same as double buffering. Instead of manipulating the DOM one element at a time, you build up an updated part of a DOM tree off-screen, and then insert the entire part at once. Performance is gained because the browser does not have to render anything to the screen until your final structure is complete.

Another technique, also used extensively in computer graphics, is to update the user interface at regular intervals. Humans cannot perceive very small slices of time; any operation that completes fast enough is perceived as instantaneous. You can save up several intermediate updates over a small slice of time and then render them all at once at the end. The user will not be able to tell the difference, but the computer must do far fewer screen updates, which are expensive.

The following example may be helpful in illustrating both of these techniques. The on-screen roster in Chapter 6's Gab application is composed of a list of items, each of which is itself composed of several elements. When contacts are added or removed from the roster, the whole item is manipulated at once, as opposed to piece by piece, in order to manipulate the DOM efficiently. However, it is possible for many roster updates to happen nearly simultaneously. It would be much more efficient if Gab would accumulate roster changes in a batch and process them every 1/10th of a second. The user will not notice any significant decrease in responsiveness, but the browser will have to update the UI 10 times in a second at most, even if hundreds of changes per second are coming in.

Cloning Instead of Creating

Browsers can clone an already existing element much faster than they can create a similar element from scratch. By cloning and then changing template elements, you can optimize the insertion of new UI objects. You can also use cloning to facilitate batching up operations.

If your application needs to insert many similar kinds of elements that differ only in a few places, you can gain some efficiency by using template elements. You can include a template element in the HTML code or create one when your application starts. When you need to insert a similar element, you clone the template, make the necessary changes, and then insert the cloned element. jQuery provides the `clone()` function, which makes this operation easy.

You can also use cloning in conjunction with batching updates. First, clone the section of the UI that will be receiving the changes. Next, do all of your updates to this cloned element. When you're finished, you can replace the original element with the cloned one, exposing all your DOM manipulations at once.

Limiting the Scope of Operations

Many DOM operations are done on sets of elements, and before the operations can be done, the set of elements must be enumerated. By carefully choosing your selectors when using jQuery or similar libraries, you can limit the scope of the target element search. This can make a big difference; the code will only need to traverse a small set of elements to find the ones you want instead of traversing the entire document.

The easiest way to limit the scope is to use an element identifier as the first part of your selector. For example, if you want to manipulate all elements of class `roster-item` and these elements all happen to be descendants of an element with the `roster` id, you can use the selector `#roster .roster-item` instead of the less efficient `.roster-item`. The browser will only need to search through all descendants of the `roster` element instead of all elements in the entire document. For large documents, this can result in tremendous speed increases.

SUMMARY

The world may feel small, but it is filled with millions of potential users. You must take into account considerations of scale when your application needs to serve a large audience. Similarly, if your application is very resource intensive, you will often need to deploy it with special attention to optimization and scalability.

In this chapter, you learned about how to solve these kinds of deployment issues using techniques like:

- ➤ Scaling applications both horizontally and vertically
- ➤ Distributing HTTP connection managers
- ➤ Clustering XMPP servers
- ➤ Load balancing server components
- ➤ Internally federating servers
- ➤ Speaking the server-to-server protocol
- ➤ Minimizing latency in initialization
- ➤ Dealing with large stanzas
- ➤ Reducing XML serialization
- ➤ Optimizing DOM manipulations in browsers

In the next and final chapter, you will discover how the Strophe library is easily extendable by developers to add new functionality.

14

Writing Strophe Plug-ins

WHAT'S IN THIS CHAPTER?

➤ Using Strophe plug-ins

➤ Creating plug-ins

➤ Adding namespaces to Strophe

➤ Building a simple roster plug-in

The applications in this book were all written using Strophe's primitive functions to build and send XMPP stanzas. Developing the code this way provided valuable visibility into how the various extensions of XMPP work. In real applications, however, it is nice to develop some abstractions to reduce some of the grunt work. Strophe allows users to build and load plug-ins that extend its functionality so that such abstractions can be built by developers and used by applications.

As an example, recall that in Chapter 9 you built SketchCast, which broadcast drawing events to a pubsub node for subscribers to watch. The application's code created subscription stanzas, node creation stanzas, and configuration stanzas to accomplish its tasks. Imagine if there was a pubsub plug-in for Strophe that encapsulated this logic for you. Code using this plug-in might appear as follows:

```
SketchCast.connection.pubsub.create(
    SketchCast.node, SketchCast.created, SketchCast.create_error);

SketchCast.connection.pubsub.configure(
    SketchCast.node, {"max_items": 20},
    SketchCast.configured, SketchCast.configure_error);
```

This version of the code is no less correct, but much shorter and more clear. The details of how to build the various stanzas required for the operations are hidden behind the plug-in's interface, leaving you to think about your own application's logic rather than protocol details.

Several Strophe plug-ins are already available on the Strophe web site, and more are created by its users all the time. Before you start your next XMPP project, you might want to take a look at the available plug-ins to see if there is one that meets your application's needs. You should also feel free to contribute plug-ins to the community as well!

Plug-ins are a great way to create running code faster, by leveraging the work of others. They also enable you to modularize your own code, by separating application logic from the underlying protocol semantics. In this chapter, you see exactly how to use existing plug-ins and create ones of your own.

USING PLUG-INS

Using Strophe plug-ins is as easy as loading the plug-in code and then accessing the new functionality through a `Strophe.Connection` instance. Each plug-in automatically installs itself into the Strophe library when loaded and then becomes available as an attribute of the connection whenever a new connection is created.

Loading Plug-ins

Strophe plug-ins must be loaded after the Strophe library. The following HTML code loads the Strophe pubsub plug-in, included with the Strophe library, after the main Strophe code:

```
<script src='strophe.js'></script>
<script src='strophe.pubsub.js'></script>
```

By convention, plug-ins are named `strophe.plugin-name.js`. The plug-in injects itself into the Strophe library automatically once loaded (you see how this is done in the "Creating Plug-ins" section). If you are familiar with jQuery plug-ins, this should look very similar.

Accessing Plug-in Functionality

Once plug-ins are loaded, they become available to all `Strophe.Connection` object instances. If you load a plug-in from the file `strophe.myplugin.js`, the plug-in's interface will be accessible via the `myplugin` attribute on the connection object. If you load the Strophe pubsub as in the previous example, you would access it like this:

```
var connection = new Strophe.Connection(BOSH_URL);
connection.connect(. . .);
. . .
connection.pubsub.subscribe("pubsub.pemberly.lit", "latest_books",
                    function (iq) { . . . },
                    function (iq) { . . . });
```

Other pubsub plug-in functionality would be accessed the same way.

In addition to providing new functions, plug-ins can also add new namespaces to Strophe. These namespaces are accessible alongside the built-in ones found in the `Strophe.NS` object. For example, the Strophe pubsub plug-in adds many pubsub-related namespaces to Strophe, a few of which are:

➤ `Strophe.NS.PUBSUB`, which expands to `http://jabber.org/protocol/pubsub`

➤ `Strophe.NS.PUBSUB_OWNER`, which expands to `http://jabber.org/protocol/pubsub#owner`

➤ `Strophe.NS.PUBSUB_EVENT`, which expands to `http://jabber.org/protocol/pubsub#event`

These namespaces make it very convenient to build pubsub stanzas yourself if for some reason the plug-in doesn't provide the functionality you want directly. They will also save you some typing and some searching through the specifications.

Each plug-in provides different functions, but these functions are always accessible in the same way. If you want to learn more about a particular plug-in and the operations it provides, please see its documentation. Even if the plug-in is sparsely documented or not documented at all, the tools you have learned throughout this book should make it easy to understand all but the most complicated plug-ins. After all, most plug-ins are just convenience wrappers around common protocol operations.

Now that you know how to load and use plug-ins, you should read on to learn how to build your own!

BUILDING PLUG-INS

Plug-ins are created by making a prototype object that defines the plug-in's functionality and registering that prototype with the Strophe library. When a new Strophe connection is created, it creates a plug-in object from the plug-in prototype and calls the object's `init()` function to initialize the plug-in. After initialization, the plug-in is ready to be used by your application code.

The `init()` function also serves another purpose. Most plug-ins will need to send data over the XMPP connection and set up stanza handlers, and for these tasks, the plug-in needs access to a `Strophe.Connection` object. Strophe will pass the connection object as the first parameter to `init()`, and the plug-in can then save this reference for later use.

Another function common to most plug-ins is `statusChanged()`. Strophe calls each plug-in's `statusChanged()` function whenever the connection status changes. This is exactly the same as the connection callback you've seen in many of the previous chapters. This allows the plug-in to react to events like CONNECTED and DISCONNECTED. This function is optional, because some plug-ins only need to respond to direct invocation.

The example plug-in in Listing 14-1 is one of the smallest Strophe plug-ins you can make. Aside from the `init()` function discussed earlier, it also provides `online()` and `offline()` functions that change your presence.

LISTING 14-1: strophe.simple.js

```
Strophe.addConnectionPlugin('simple', {
    init: function (connection) {
        this.connection = connection;
    },

    online: function () {
        this.connection.send($pres());
    },

    offline: function () {
        this.connection.send($pres({type: "unavailable"}));
    }
});
```

Registering new Strophe plug-ins is accomplished via the `addConnectionPlugin()` function. This function takes the name of the plug-in and the plug-in prototype as arguments. These plug-ins are called connection plug-ins because they augment the `Strophe.Connection` object. In the future, Strophe may support other plug-in types that augment other parts of the library.

Finally, Strophe plug-ins can augment the namespaces available in the `Strophe.NS` object by using `.addNamespace()`. The following code adds service discovery namespaces to Strophe. The simple example plug-in has no new namespaces, but more complex plug-ins will often need to add to the namespaces for the convenience of the plug-in's users.

```
Strophe.addNamespace('DISCO_INFO', 'http://jabber.org/protocol/disco#info');
Strophe.addNamespace('DISCO_ITEMS', 'http://jabber.org/protocol/disco#items');
```

Users of the preceding example plug-in can write `connection.simple.online()` to send available presence and `connection.simple.offline()` to send unavailable presence instead of building the stanzas by hand. In this particular case, this doesn't save much effort, but as you soon see, more sophisticated plug-ins can make your XMPP programming tasks far simpler.

CREATING A ROSTER PLUG-IN

To really get a feel for what plug-ins can do, you will have to build one that has some non-trivial functionality. In this section, you develop a roster management plug-in, which abstracts away common roster operations and makes roster data available in a JavaScript-friendly data structure.

Managing the roster involves a few basic operations. First, you'll need to query the roster and store it. Then you'll need ways to add, edit, and delete roster items. Because other connection resources might also be making roster changes, you'll need to listen for those and update the roster accordingly. Finally, you will want to keep the status of your roster fresh as presence information comes in from your contacts.

Storing Contacts

Before starting on roster mutation operations, you should begin with how to store the roster's state in the plug-in. This will be the main interaction point between various pieces of the code.

Imagine that you've created an application that shows a user's roster in the user interface. To do this, your code could query the roster and add handlers for roster updates. When another piece of your application needs the roster data, you can either query for the roster again, which is inefficient, or have one part of the UI communicate with the other, which tightly couples the functionality. Instead of doing either of those things, it is better to put knowledge of the roster state in one place where the various parts of your application can interact with it.

Following is a sample roster expressed as a JavaScript literal; this same structure will be the basis of the roster state in your plug-in.

```
contacts = {
    "darcy@pemberley.lit": {
        name: "Darcy",
        resources: {
            "library":, {
                show: "away",
                status: "reading"
            }
        },
        subscription: "both",
        ask: "",
        groups: ["Family"]
    },
    "bingley@netherfield.lit": {
        name: "Charles",
        resources: {},
        subscription: "both",
        ask: "",
        groups: ["Friends"]
    }
};
```

The sample roster contains two contacts, Darcy and Bingley, who are online and offline, respectively. The `resources` attribute tells you which resources of the contacts are currently online along with their appropriate metadata; because Darcy has at least one resource, he is considered online, and because Bingley has none, he is considered offline.

The `name`, `subscription`, and `ask` properties of the contact and the `show` and `status` properties of the resource are named for the protocol attributes they represent. These attributes were covered in detail back in Chapter 6. The `show` and `status` attributes come from contacts' `<presence>` stanzas, and `name`, `subscription`, and `ask` are part of the user's roster state for a given contact.

We've simplified things slightly, however, with respect to the `show` and `status` attributes. When a contact's presence has no `<show>` element, they are considered online and available, so the `show` attribute is set to "available." Similarly, if the contact's presence has no `<status>` element, the `status` attribute is set to the empty string.

Finally, the `groups` attribute specifies which roster groups a contact belongs in.

It would be quite tedious for users of your plug-in to have to write code to enumerate the `resources` property to determine if a contact was online. You can make these programmers' lives easier by providing a utility method that computes this property based on the `resources` attribute's value:

```
online: function () {
    var result = false;
    for (var k in this.resources) {
        result = true;
        break;
    }
    return result;
}
```

code snippet strophe.roster.js

Now you have enough pieces to make a first outline of the plug-in code. The following version isn't very useful yet, but you will be extending it over the next sections. Add the following code to a new file called `strophe.roster.js`:

```
// Contact object
function Contact() {
    this.name = "";
    this.resources = {};
    this.subscription = "none";
    this.ask = "";
    this.groups = [];
}

Contact.prototype = {
    // compute whether user is online from their
    // list of resources
    online: function () {
        var result = false;
        for (var k in this.resources) {
            result = true;
            break;
        }
        return result;
    }
};

Strophe.addConnectionPlugin('roster', {
    init: function (connection) {
        this.connection = connection;
        this.contacts = {};

        Strophe.addNamespace('ROSTER', 'jabber:iq:roster');
    }
});
```

code snippet strophe.roster.js

Getting and Maintaining the Roster

You saw how to retrieve and deal with the roster in Chapter 6, and now you will put those skills to use again to populate the roster state in the plug-in. First, you must get an initial copy of the roster from the server once the connection is established. After that, each contact's information wi!¹ need to be updated as their presence changes. The plug-in must also trigger an event so that the user's code gets notified when new roster changes have been made.

In Chapter 6, you learned how to retrieve rosters from the server. The plug-in must do this every time the connection is established. After all, while a user is disconnected in one client, another client could have made changes. Also, when the plug-in is notified about disconnection, it needs to put the roster representation into an appropriate state.

The following code implements the `statusChanged()` function to handle these tasks for the `CONNECTED` and `DISCONNECTED` statuses. It also notifies any handlers for the `roster_changed` event that the roster has been updated. You should insert this into the plug-in's prototype after `init()`.

```
statusChanged: function (status) {
    if (status === Strophe.Status.CONNECTED) {
        this.contacts = {};

        // build and send initial roster query
        var roster_iq = $iq({type: "get"})
            .c('query', {xmlns: Strophe.NS.ROSTER});

        var that = this;
        this.connection.sendIQ(roster_iq, function (iq) {
            $(iq).find("item").each(function () {
                // build a new contact and add it to the roster
                var contact = new Contact();
                contact.name = $(this).attr('name') || "";
                contact.subscription = $(this).attr('subscription') ||
                    "none";
                contact.ask = $(this).attr('ask') || "";
                $(this).find("group").each(function () {
                    contact.groups.push(this.text());
                });
                that.contacts[$(this).attr('jid')] = contact;
            });

            // let user code know something happened
            $(document).trigger('roster_changed', that);
        });
    } else if (status === Strophe.Status.DISCONNECTED) {
        // set all users offline
        for (var contact in this.contacts) {
            this.contacts[contact].resources = {};
        }

        // notify user code
        $(document).trigger('roster_changed', this);
    }
}
```

code snippet strophe.roster.js

The plug-in will now keep track of the basic roster information, but it doesn't keep this information up to date as the roster changes or as contacts change their presence. You can solve the first issue by setting up stanza event handlers for IQ-set stanzas that contain roster updates from the server. The second issue can be solved by adding presence stanza handlers.

In Chapter 6, you discovered how to modify rosters by adding, updating, and deleting contacts. The server also notifies other connected resources about roster changes so that every client's state remains consistent. For example, if Darcy removes Wickham from his roster while connected on the resource `library`, his other resource, `drawing_room`, will be notified of the change. First, Darcy deletes Wickham from his roster:

```
<iq from='darcy@pemberley.lit/library'
    type='set'
    id='delete1'>
  <query xmlns='jabber:iq:roster'>
    <item jid='wickham@militia.lit' subscription='remove'/>
  </query>
</iq>
```

The server deletes Wickham and notifies all of Darcy's connected resources about the roster change. Darcy's `drawing_room` resource will receive:

```
<iq to='darcy@pemberley.lit/drawing_room'
    type='set'
    id='deleted1'>
  <query xmlns='jabber:iq:roster'>
    <item jid='wickham@militia.lit' subscription='remove'/>
  </query>
</iq>
```

Darcy's `library` resource will also receive the same update, even though it requested the change. The server will always notify all resources of roster state changes.

```
<iq to='darcy@pemberley.lit/library'
    type='set'
    id='deleted1'>
  <query xmlns='jabber:iq:roster'>
    <item jid='wickham@militia.lit' subscription='remove'/>
  </query>
</iq>
```

Both clients must acknowledge the IQ-set stanza with an IQ-result. At this point, each client will have the same view of the roster state.

You can extend `statusChanged()` to set up handlers for roster changes and add a new function to the plug-in prototype to handle these changes. A modified version of `statusChanged()` is shown in the following code, with the new lines highlighted, followed by the new `rosterChanged()` function. Because the server will always send a single change at a time, `rosterChanged()` only needs to handle one `<item/>` child.

```
statusChanged: function (status) {
    if (status === Strophe.Status.CONNECTED) {
        this.contacts = {};

        this.connection.addHandler(this.rosterChanged.bind(this),
                                   Strophe.NS.ROSTER, "iq", "set");

        // build and send initial roster query
        var roster_iq = $iq({type: "get"})
            .c('query', {xmlns: Strophe.NS.ROSTER});

        var that = this;
        this.connection.sendIQ(roster_iq, function (iq) {
            $(iq).find("item").each(function () {
                // build a new contact and add it to the roster
                var contact = new Contact();
                contact.name = $(this).attr('name') || "";
                contact.subscription = $(this).attr('subscription') ||
                    "none";
                contact.ask = $(this).attr('ask') || "";
                $(this).find("group").each(function () {
                    contact.groups.push(this.text());
                });
                that.contacts[$(this).attr('jid')] = contact;
            });

            // let user code know something happened
            $(document).trigger('roster_changed', that);
        });
    } else if (status === Strophe.Status.DISCONNECTED) {
        // set all users offline
        for (var contact in this.contacts) {
            this.contacts[contact].resources = {};
        }

        // notify user code
        $(document).trigger('roster_changed', this);
    }
},

rosterChanged: function (iq) {
    var item = $(iq).find('item');
    var jid = item.attr('jid');
    var subscription = item.attr('subscription') || "";

    if (subscription === "remove") {
        // removing contact from roster
        delete this.contacts[jid];
    } else if (subscription === "none") {
        // adding contact to roster
        var contact = new Contact();
        contact.name = item.attr('name') || "";
```

```
        item.find("group").each(function () {
            contact.groups.push(this.text());
        });
        this.contacts[jid] = contact;
    } else {
        // modifying contact on roster
        var contact = this.contacts[jid];
        contact.name = item.attr('name') || contact.name;
        contact.subscription = subscription || contact.subscription;
        contact.ask = item.attr('ask') || contact.ask;
        contact.groups = [];
        item.find("group").each(function () {
            contact.groups.push($(this).text());
        });
    }

    // acknowledge receipt
    this.connection.send($iq({type: "result", id: $(iq).attr('id')}));

    // notify user code of roster changes
    $(document).trigger("roster_changed", this);

    return true;
}
```

code snippet strophe.roster.js

With the roster updates handled, you can now move on to handling presence updates. You'll need to add a presence stanza handler to `statusChanged()` as well as a new function in the plug-in's proto-type, `presenceChanged()`. The `presenceChanged()` function just needs to add, modify, or delete the appropriate resource in the `resources` attribute for a contact based on the presence stanza information.

Add the following line just after the `addHandler()` line from the preceding version of `statusChanged()`:

```
this.connection.addHandler(this.presenceChanged.bind(this),
                           null, "presence");
```

code snippet strophe.roster.js

Now add the implementation of `presenceChanged()` to the prototype:

```
presenceChanged: function (presence) {
    var from = $(presence).attr("from");
    var jid = Strophe.getBareJidFromJid(from);
    var resource = Strophe.getResourceFromJid(from);
    var ptype = $(presence).attr("type") || "available";

    if (!this.contacts[jid] || ptype === "error") {
        // ignore presence updates from things not on the roster
        // as well as error presence
```

```
            return true;
        }

        if (ptype === "unavailable") {
            // remove resource, contact went offline
            delete this.contacts[jid].resources[resource];
        } else {
            // contact came online or changed status
            this.contacts[jid].resources[resource] = {
                show: $(presence).find("show").text() || "online",
                status: $(presence).find("status").text()
            };
        }

        // notify user code of roster changes
        $(document).trigger("roster_changed", this);
    }
```

code snippet strophe.roster.js

The plug-in will now maintain roster state over the lifetime of the connection. Plug-in users can access this information at any time with `connection.roster.contacts`. All that remains is to assist the developer with making roster changes.

Manipulating the Roster

In the previous section you handled notifications for the three roster manipulations: add, modify, and delete a contact. Here you implement the other side of this functionality by allowing the plug-in's users to change the roster with simple calls to `addContact()`, `deleteContact()`, and `modify-Contact()`. There are also two other times when the roster changes; contacts are added whenever a presence subscription is requested, and contacts are usually deleted whenever a user unsubscribes from a contact's presence. You'll make subscribing and unsubscribing just as easy as the other roster modifications with `subscribe()` and `unsubscribe()`.

The direct roster manipulation helpers are very simple. Because the plug-in already handles the change notifications, there is no need for your code to modify the `contacts` attribute at all. Once the server has processed the roster modification, it generates a change notification, and that notification will trigger the handlers you wrote that already do the appropriate modifications of the `contacts` attribute. You only need to send the appropriate IQ-sets to the server to initiate the chain of events. On top of that, roster item modification is exactly the same as addition, so you can reuse the same code!

All three functions are implemented in the following code. The code is very similar to the code you wrote in Chapter 6 to accomplish the same operations.

```
addContact: function (jid, name, groups) {
    var iq = $iq({type: "set"})
        .c("query", {xmlns: Strophe.NS.ROSTER})
        .c("item", {name: name || "", jid: jid});
    if (groups && groups.length > 0) {
```

```
            $.each(groups, function () {
                iq.c("group").t(this).up();
            });
        }
        this.connection.sendIQ(iq);
    },

    deleteContact: function (jid) {
        var iq = $iq({type: "set"})
            .c("query", {xmlns: Strophe.NS.ROSTER})
            .c("item", {jid: jid, subscription: "remove"});
        this.connection.sendIQ(iq);
    },

    modifyContact: function (jid, name, groups) {
        this.addContact(jid, name, groups);
    }
```

code snippet strophe.roster.js

Recall that subscribing and unsubscribing to someone's presence is a two-step process. For subscriptions, the client first adds a new contact, and then sends a presence subscription request. For unsubscribe requests, the client first sends the correct presence stanza, and then deletes the contact from the roster. The following code makes use of the roster manipulation functions you just wrote, and should be added to the plug-in prototype:

Available for download on Wrox.com

```
    subscribe: function (jid, name, groups) {
        this.addContact(jid, name, groups);

        var presence = $pres({to: jid, "type": "subscribe"});
        this.connection.send(presence);
    },

    unsubscribe: function (jid) {
        var presence = $pres({to: jid, "type": "unsubscribe"});
        this.connection.send(presence);

        this.deleteContact(jid);
    }
```

code snippet strophe.roster.js

Your shiny, new roster plug-in is now complete. It's time to see what it can do!

TAKING THE PLUG-IN FOR A SPIN

Strophe plug-ins are intended to make developers' lives easier than dealing with the messy details directly. Even the simple plug-in you developed in the previous section is surprisingly useful. To demonstrate this, you build a small mini-application that shows your current roster state and updates even as other resources are manipulating your contacts.

The HTML code and CSS styles for the RosterWatch application are shown in Listing 14-2 and Listing 14-3. There is nothing here that you haven't seen before. The main thing to notice in the HTML file is that the plug-in file `strophe.roster.js` is loaded as well as the Strophe library.

LISTING 14-2: rosterwatch.html

```html
<!DOCTYPE HTML PUBLIC "-//W3C//DTD HTML 4.01//EN"
        "http://www.w3.org/TR/html4/strict.dtd">
<html>
  <head>
    <meta http-equiv="Content-type" content="text/html;charset=UTF-8">
    <title>RosterWatch - Chapter 14</title>

    <link rel='stylesheet' href='http://ajax.googleapis.com/ajax/libs/jqueryu
i/1.7.2/themes/cupertino/jquery-ui.css'>
    <script src='http://ajax.googleapis.com/ajax/libs/jquery/1.3.2/jquery.js'>
</script>
    <script src='http://ajax.googleapis.com/ajax/libs/jqueryui/1.7.2/jquery-u
i.js'></script>
    <script src='scripts/strophe.js'></script>
    <script src='scripts/flXHR.js'></script>
    <script src='scripts/strophe.flxhr.js'></script>

    <script src='strophe.roster.js'></script>

    <link rel='stylesheet' type='text/css' href='rosterwatch.css'>
    <script src='rosterwatch.js'></script>
  </head>
  <body>
    <h1>RosterWatch</h1>

    <div class='toolbar'>
      <input id='disconnect' type='button' value='disconnect'
             disabled='disabled'>
    </div>

    <div id='roster'>
    </div>

    <!-- login dialog -->
    <div id='login_dialog' class='hidden'>
      <label>JID:</label><input type='text' id='jid'>
      <label>Password:</label><input type='password' id='password'>
    </div>
  </body>
</html>
```

LISTING 14-3: rosterwatch.css

```css
body {
    font-family: Helvetica;
}

h1 {
    text-align: center;
}

.toolbar {
    text-align: center;
}

#roster {
    width: 500px;
    margin: auto;
    border: solid 1px black;
}

.hidden {
    display: none;
}

.contact {
    padding: 10px;
}

.name {
    font-size: 150%;
    font-weight: bold;
}

.jid {
    font-size: 80%;
    font-style: italic;
}

.online {
    background-color: #7f7;
}

.away {
    background-color: #f77;
}

.offline {
    background-color: #777;
}
```

The actual JavaScript code for this application is quite simple and appears in Listing 14-4. Because all of the heavy lifting dealing with roster updates is handled by the plug-in, the code deals very little with XMPP except to make the connection and send initial presence. The roster_changed event handler just enumerates the roster contacts and writes out HTML, just like any modern, dynamic web application.

LISTING 14-4: rosterwatch.js

```js
RosterWatch = {
    connection: null
};

$(document).ready(function () {
    $('#login_dialog').dialog({
        autoOpen: true,
        draggable: false,
        model: true,
        title: 'Connect to XMPP',
        buttons: {
            "Connect": function () {
                $(document).trigger('connect', {
                    jid: $('#jid').val(),
                    password: $('#password').val()
                });

                $('#password').val('');
                $(this).dialog('close');
            }
        }
    });

    $('#disconnect').click(function () {
        $('#disconnect').attr('disabled', 'disabled');
        RosterWatch.connection.disconnect();
    });
});

$(document).bind('connect', function (ev, data) {
    var conn = new Strophe.Connection(
        'http://bosh.metajack.im:5280/xmpp-httpbind');

    conn.connect(data.jid, data.password, function (status) {
        if (status === Strophe.Status.CONNECTED) {
            $(document).trigger('connected');
        } else if (status === Strophe.Status.DISCONNECTED) {
            $(document).trigger('disconnected');
        }
    });

    RosterWatch.connection = conn;
});

$(document).bind('connected', function () {
    $('#disconnect').removeAttr('disabled');

    RosterWatch.connection.send($pres());
});

$(document).bind('disconnected', function () {
```

continues

LISTING 14-4 *(continued)*

```javascript
        RosterWatch.connection = null;

        $('#roster').empty();
        $('#login_dialog').dialog('open');
    });

    $(document).bind('roster_changed', function (ev, roster) {
        $('#roster').empty();

        var empty = true;
        $.each(roster.contacts, function (jid) {
            empty = false;

            var status = "offline";
            if (this.online()) {
                var away = true;
                for (var k in this.resources) {
                    if (this.resources[k].show === "online") {
                        away = false;
                    }
                }
                status = away ? "away": "online";
            }

            var html = [];
            html.push("<div class='contact " + status + "'>");

            html.push("<div class='name'>");
            html.push(this.name || jid);
            html.push("</div>");

            html.push("<div class='jid'>");
            html.push(jid);
            html.push("</div>");

            html.push("</div>");

            $('#roster').append(html.join(''));
        });

        if (empty) {
            $('#roster').append("<i>No contacts:(</i>");
        }
    });
```

The roster plug-in you created does an excellent job abstracting away the details of roster management, which is exactly what was intended.

Improving the Roster Plug-in

The roster plug-in you created is pretty simple, although it is still quite useful. Here are some ideas for improvements you can try:

➤ Send more detailed update information in the `roster_changed` event so that the user's code doesn't have to refresh the entire roster every time.

➤ Extend the plug-in to trigger more events for things like incoming presence subscriptions and contacts going on and offline.

➤ Add support for Personal Eventing Protocol (XEP-0163) and Entity Capabilities (XEP-0115) to get extended information, such as what music contacts are listening to.

SUMMARY

Plug-ins make developers' lives easier by abstracting away protocol details and letting developers reuse and build easily upon the work of others. The Strophe library provides a simple, yet highly effective plug-in system that allows its users to add advanced functionality. In this chapter you:

➤ Learned how to load and use Strophe plug-ins

➤ Discovered how to create your own plug-ins

➤ Created a roster management plug-in that made dealing with rosters, roster updates, and presence changes really easy

➤ Saw how easy application logic becomes when plug-ins are available to do the heavily lifting

It's been a long journey, but I hope an interesting and enjoyable one. You built nine applications, including several really sophisticated ones, and learned how to scale XMPP applications. You should now be well versed in the XMPP protocol and the Strophe library as well, and perhaps you've learned a few new JavaScript or jQuery tricks, too. Hopefully your head is now filled with wonderful ideas for great XMPP-powered applications. Good luck and happy hacking!

Getting Started with jQuery

For years JavaScript programmers have been dealing with the myriad idiosyncrasies of the DOM (Document Object Model) API. Many people created helper functions that abstracted particular operations so that they worked across all browsers, and a few of the best abstractions became polished enough to become generally useful for a wide range of applications. The jQuery library is a lightweight, cross-browser JavaScript library that replaces the ugly parts of the DOM API with a clever CSS selector-based API that makes quick work of most tasks.

jQuery is excellent for slicing and dicing HTML, but it also works very well on XML documents. Because XMPP stanzas are just XML document fragments, jQuery makes manipulating XMPP much easier than using the raw DOM APIs.

Strophe itself was partially inspired by the function chaining, use of callbacks, and plug-in architecture in jQuery, and so the two libraries fit together quite naturally.

If you haven't used or seen jQuery before, this appendix teaches you the basics and gives you the background you need to use jQuery effectively for your own XMPP applications. The jQuery library also provides many other useful functions for web programming, like AJAX requests and animations, but these are not covered here because they are not used in the book.

FINDING JQUERY

You can find the jQuery library on the Web at `http://jquery.com`. jQuery's web site also contains tutorials, reference documentation, examples, and a long list of third-party plug-ins that extend jQuery in interesting ways.

You can download the library to use in your own applications, or, as shown in Chapter 3, you can use the hosted version provided by Google as part of its AJAX Libraries API. The applications in this book use the Google-hosted version.

You can load jQuery by including a `<script>` element in your page like the one shown here:

```
<script src='http://ajax.googleapis.com/ajax/libs/jquery/1.3.2/jquery.js'>
</script>
```

In a production application, you may want to use the minified version of the library, which reduces to the size of the library to make your application's page load faster. The minified version is usually named `jquery.min.js` instead of `jquery.js`.

Once jQuery is loaded in your application, you access its functionality via the `$()` function. This funny looking function has a short name to save typing because it usually becomes one of the most used functions in an application.

JQUERY VERSUS DOM

Before you jump into the details of jQuery, take a look at the following example comparing DOM and jQuery. This example should give you a feeling for what jQuery code looks like and how it is different from using the DOM API directly.

The following code has a simple task. It finds all the `<p>` elements in the current page and changes their background color to a light red. First the DOM API version:

```
var p_elems = document.getElementsByTagName('p');
for (var i = 0; i < p_elems.length; i++) {
    p_elems[i].style.backgroundColor = '#faa';
}
```

Now the same action using jQuery:

```
$('p').css({backgroundColor: '#faa'});
```

The jQuery code is not only much shorter, but it is also much clearer. It selects a set of elements using CSS selector syntax and applies a new background color to all the matching elements.

The DOM code in the previous example works in all browsers, but jQuery really shines when the code uses some DOM functionality that is not consistent across all browsers. For the inconsistent DOM API functions, the jQuery code is just as short, but equivalent code without jQuery is generally filled with extra `if` statements for compability checks.

USING JQUERY

jQuery's design is simple, but powerful: find a set of elements and perform an operation on the resulting set.

Finding Elements

As you saw in the previous section, jQuery's `$()` function accepts an extended version of CSS selector syntax instead of using the DOM's `getElementById()` or `getElementsByTagName()`. This makes finding elements quick and easy. Once an initial selection has been made, jQuery contains helper functions to augment the selection if needed.

jQuery's `$()` function also accepts DOM elements instead of CSS selectors. The given DOM elements become the jQuery selection.

Selectors

Just like CSS, jQuery supports the following basic selectors:

➤   *anelement*: Selects elements with the name *anelement*

➤   *.aclass*: Selects elements that have the class *aclass*

➤   *#anid*: Selects the element with the unique ID *anid*

These selectors can be combined as in the selectors `p.error` and `input#textbox` to make more specific selectors. Multiple selectors can be separated by commas, and the resulting combined selector will find any element that matches any one of these selectors.

Selectors can also be made to find elements in a specific hierarchy by separating several selectors with spaces. For example, the selector `#chat p` finds any `<p>` element within the element identified by `chat`. More specific relationships can be specified with >, +, and -. The selector `div > p` finds only the `<p>` elements that are direct descendants of a `<div>` element. Using `h1 + p` only finds `<p>` elements that come immediately after an `<h1>` sibling, and similarly, `h1 - p` selects `<p>` elements that come immediately before an `<h1>` sibling.

Selectors can also be filtered. Adding `:first` or `:last` selects only the first or last of the elements that match the rest of the selector. The filters `:visible` and `:hidden` are similar, but restrict the selection to those elements that the user can or can't see on screen.

Finally, jQuery provides several filters for attributes. The main variants are `[anattr]`, which matches when the elements have an `anattr` attribute, and `[anattr='somevalue']`, which matches when the elements have the `anattr` attribute and its value equals `'somevalue'`.

See if you can determine what elements would match the following selectors:

➤   `p:first`

➤   `ul > li .name`

➤   `input[type='text'], input[type='password']`

Augmenting Selections

Once a selection is made, jQuery contains plenty of methods to refine it to just the elements you need. The most common of these are discussed here.

`filter()` picks out a subselection of elements from a given selection. If you have large selection of elements that needs a common manipulation performed, but a smaller subset that needs a second manipulation, you can use `filter()` after the first operation to narrow the selection and then perform the second manipulation.

`children()` filters the list for all immediate children of the matched elements. This is often used to match the first-level children of XMPP stanzas. For example, to get the `<error>` element out of a stanza, you could use `$(stanza).children('error')`.

`find()` looks for matching elements among the current selection's descendants. Because XMPP stanzas will generally start off with only the top-level element selected, `find()` is often used to select the interesting child elements from there.

`not()` removes the matching elements from the selection. This function is very useful for removing one or two stragglers from an otherwise perfect selection.

Acting on Elements

The operations that jQuery supports on selected elements include changing CSS properties, getting and setting the contents of each element or its attributes, and binding event handlers. jQuery also supports several functional programming-inspired methods like `each()` and `map()`, which allow easy iteration and function application over the entire selection. You are introduced to all these shortly.

Making Chains

Function call chaining also contributes to jQuery's accessibility and power. Chaining allows multiple operations to be performed on the same selection easily.

Most of jQuery's methods return the jQuery object itself along with its corresponding selection. This means that method calls on the object can be chained one after another.

The following code shows an example of a typical object's methods being called:

```
var obj = new SomeObject();
obj.foo();
obj.bar(2);
obj.baz('XMPP');
```

If each of `SomeObject`'s methods returned the object's instance, these methods could be chained. A chained invocation is shown here:

```
var obj = new SomeObject();
obj.foo().bar(2).baz('XMPP');
```

This may look a little peculiar if this is the first time you've seen such a construction. It turns out to be quite useful in practice with libraries that are designed for it, like jQuery. Strophe uses chaining to make building stanzas easier, as you can see in Chapter 3.

The following jQuery examples are understandable and quite readable even if you've never seen the library before:

```
$('p.error').css({backgroundColor: '#f00', fontHeight: '14pt'}).show();

$('#lists ul').append('<li>New item</li>').append('<li>Another new item</li>');
```

MANIPULATING ELEMENTS

Much of the work you will do with jQuery in this book relates to extracting data out of elements, adding new elements, or modifying existing elements. This section goes over the most common manipulations that jQuery supports and that are used throughout the book's applications.

Data Extraction

When dealing with XMPP stanzas, jQuery is used mainly to extract the interesting information out of the XML, much like a programmatic version of XPath.

`attr()` is used to get and set an element's attributes. To get an attribute, pass the attribute's name, and to set an attribute, pass both a name and the desired value. If the current jQuery selection contains more than one element, only the first element is affected when called as `attr(name)`; all elements are affected when called as `attr(name, value)`. See the following examples for the typical usage of `attr()`:

```
$(stanza).find('item').attr('jid'); // get the first item's jid attribute

// set the form's input elements to buttons
$('#someform input').attr('type', 'button');
```

`text()` and `html()` get or set the text or HTML contents of the element. Because Strophe's builders are used to construct most stanzas, this book most often uses these methods to retrieve values rather than set them.

```
var body = $(stanza).find('body').text(); // get the message body contents

$('#chat_input').text('Type your message here..'); // set the text box prompt
```

Styling Elements

Most dynamic web applications accomplish many UI tasks by manipulating the styles of various elements. Elements can be shown or hidden, change colors and size, or have their CSS classes manipulated programmatically. The following jQuery methods provide this behavior.

`show()` and `hide()` are somewhat obvious from their names. They change the visibility of all the selected elements. This is often used to make dialog boxes pop into view or to replace one tab's contents with another's.

`css()` can retrieve a specific CSS style from an element or change one or more of its style properties. The following code shows some typical uses of this method:

```
var c = $('#tab1').css('color'); // get the tab's font color
$('.username').css('background-color', '#fff'); // set a single css style
$('.errorMsg').css({fontSize: '150%', color: 'red'}); // change multiple styles at
once
```

Notice that the style's name can be written as `fontSize` or `'font-size'`. jQuery helpfully allows you to save typing the quotes and the dash.

`addClass()` and `removeClass()` change the CSS classes that are in effect for the selected elements. These provide a fast way to change lots of CSS styles at once, without having to specify them all individually.

Adding and Removing Elements

Showing and hiding elements works well for a lot of things, but sometimes you will have to add or remove elements completely from the DOM. For example, in Chapter 6's chat application, when roster items are received from the server, new items are added to the contact list.

You can add content with `append()` and `prepend()`, or with the previously mentioned `html()` function. Each of these functions just takes a string containing the new HTML to append, prepend, or replace.

`remove()` deletes the selected elements from the DOM completely. `empty()` removes all the child elements for each element in the selection, and it is often used to clear lists or whole `<div>`s.

Iterating over Selections

Applications will often need to perform some function over all the elements in a selection. In most popular languages, this is often done with the aid of a `for` or `while` loop, but jQuery allows you to do this easily by borrowing patterns from functional programming languages.

The jQuery object supports the `length` attribute, just like normal JavaScript arrays, and each element in the selection can be accessed with normal bracket notation for arrays. Using these properties, the following code follows the traditional iteration pattern to add contacts to a list:

```
var i;
var items = $(stanza).find('item');
for (i = 0; i < items.length; i++) {
    $('#contact_list').append('<li>' + $(items[i]).attr('jid') + '</li>');
}
```

This code finds all the `<item>` elements in an XMPP stanza and then extracts the `jid` attribute from each and uses this to add new elements to a contact list. Note that `items[i]` is wrapped by `$()` because it is a normal DOM element, not a jQuery selection; after calling `$()` on the element, it will be a normal jQuery selection of just the one element.

The same actions can be accomplished by using jQuery's `each()` method on the initial selection:

```
$(stanza).find('item').each(function () {
    $('#contact_list').append('<li>' + $(this).attr('jid') + '</li>');
});
```

`each()` takes a function as its argument, and that function performs the desired action for each item. Each time the function is called, the `this` variable references the current item of the iteration. Once again, because the item is a normal DOM element, to use the `attr()` method, it must first be wrapped by the `$()` function.

Notice that lots of unneeded things have been eliminated, such as the variable `i`, to leave a very readable bit of code.

`each()` can also be used on normal JavaScript arrays by using the global version of the method, accessed as a property of the global $ object:

```
var list = [1, 2, 3, 4, 5];
$.each(list, function () {
    $('body').append('called for item ' + this);
});
```

DEALING WITH EVENTS

Aside from dealing with DOM elements themselves, web applications must also handle and trigger events on the document and specific elements. The event models across two browsers can behave quite differently, but jQuery provides a consistent interface for events that makes using them simple.

Aside from the normal user interaction events like clicking a button or a page finishing loading, jQuery also provides support for custom events. Custom events can be used for all sorts of interesting things. You can have a piece of UI in your application trigger a `contact_added` event or turn a series of simple events into a composite event that has meaning in your particular application.

Custom events also provide an easy way to decouple your application's code. Instead of having one piece of code call another directly, it can instead fire an event that the other piece of code can listen for. If more pieces of the application need to be involved in the same bit of logic, they can simply listen and respond to the same event, instead of having to change the rest of the code to call the new function.

Custom events are handled exactly like normal DOM events; the only differences are that the event names are different and jQuery doesn't provide conveniently named helper functions for custom events.

Basic Event Methods

The basic event handling methods are `bind()` and `trigger()`. `bind()` is used to listen for events, and `trigger()` notifies listeners that an event has happened.

`bind()` accepts two parameters: an event name and a function that is executed when the event is triggered.

The following example code adds an event handler for the click event on a button:

```
$('#go_button').bind('click', function () {
    // do something here
});
```

Your code can trigger both custom events and normal DOM events with `trigger()`. The first argument to `trigger()` is the event's name, and the optional second argument is extra data that you can pass to the event's handlers.

```
$('#go_button').trigger('click'); // click the button programmatically

// trigger a custom event with some event specific data
$(document).trigger('contact_added', {jid: 'darcy@pemberley.lit'});
```

The handlers for normal events get passed a single argument, the event object. The `on_click()` handler here demonstrates this:

```
function on_click(ev) {
    // handler code
}
```

If `trigger()` is passed some data as its second parameter, this data will be passed along to the handler in the second parameter:

```
function on_new_contact(ev, data) {
    // add the new contact
}
```

Convenience Event Methods

To save typing and aid readability, jQuery supplies several convenience methods for working with common DOM events.

Most DOM events have a corresponding method in jQuery with the same name as the event. For example, the `click()` method triggers the `click` event. When these methods are invoked without arguments, the corresponding event is triggered, but when passed a function as the argument, they bind a new handler for the event. The example from the previous section for a button's `click` event handler can be rewritten as:

```
$('#go_button').click(function () {
    // do something here
});
```

The methods provided by jQuery include `keypress()`, `keyup()`, `keydown()`, `mouseup()`, `mousedown()`, `mousemove()`, `click()`, `load()`, and `ready()`.

The Document Ready Event

The document ready event is somewhat special. This event fires as soon as the DOM is available to be accessed and manipulated by JavaScript code. Most initialization and startup code for web applications is generally put in a handler for the document ready event.

To bind a handler to the document ready event, you can use either:

```
$(document).bind('ready', function () {
    // init code here
});
```

or:

```
$(document).ready(function () {
    // init code here
});
```

Because this construction is so common, jQuery also provides an even simpler shortcut. Just pass the handler directly to the `$()` function:

```
$(function () {
    // init code here
});
```

Many jQuery programmers seem to use the shortest construction, but this book uses `ready()` to make the code as easy to understand as possible. You will see other DOM events handled with their specially named methods as well, and custom events are managed with `bind()` and `trigger()`.

FURTHER READING

All jQuery methods are fully explained in the excellent reference documentation, which you can find at `http://docs.jquery.com`. The documentation wiki also contains pointers to numerous tutorials; you can find a list of these at `http://docs.jquery.com/Tutorials`.

jQuery also has a large community of programmers extending the library through plug-ins, much like the Strophe plug-ins discussed in Chapter 14. The jQuery UI plug-in used in this book is the most well known of these, and it provides rich user interface components for use in web applications. jQuery UI features used in this book are explained in the chapters where they appear. You can find more information on jQuery UI at `http://ui.jquery.com`, and the full list of jQuery plug-ins lives at `http://plugins.jquery.com`.

B
Setting Up a BOSH Connection Manager

Web browsers do not yet speak XMPP. In order to use XMPP in web applications, a middleman is needed that turns the stateless HTTP requests into stateful and long-lived XMPP connections. The details surrounding this process are called Bi-directional streams Over Synchronous HTTP (BOSH), and a server that provides this service is called a *connection manager*.

This chapter gives you the information you need to choose and install a BOSH connection manager for your XMPP applications. The applications in this book have all used a public BOSH connection manager provided by the author for testing purposes. If you plan to make your application widely available, you will probably want to set up your own.

Due to JavaScript's *same origin policy* (see the Same Origin Policy section of Chapter 3), direct communication with a connection manager is typically treated as a security violation. To circumvent this policy, the applications in this book have used a Flash library called flXHR to allow cross-domain requests. Alternatively, you can use a reverse proxy to make the connection manager appear to be part of your own web server.

The last section of this appendix shows you how to configure a reverse-proxied connection manager for the cases where using Flash is not possible or not desirable.

CHOOSING A CONNECTION MANAGER

Connection managers come in two main flavors: built-in to an XMPP server or standalone managers. Each type has its own advantages and disadvantages and, accordingly, may be more or less appropriate for your particular application.

Standalone Managers

The original connection managers were all standalone, because the XMPP server teams had not yet had time to integrate BOSH services into their systems. A standalone connection manager runs as a separate service or daemon, possibly on a machine far from any XMPP server.

Standalone managers can typically connect to any XMPP server reachable on the Internet. When a request comes in for an XMPP connection, the connection manager initiates a normal XMPP client connection to the desired server on behalf of the requesting party. This makes a standalone manager a great choice when the application's users already have XMPP accounts across a variety of different XMPP servers.

Because a standalone manager must maintain XMPP connections on behalf of users, there is some extra overhead to each connection. In addition to the normal TCP connection to the XMPP server, there will be two or more HTTP connections as well. This means that for every user of the connection manager at least three TCP sockets will be needed.

The benefit of this overhead is that standalone BOSH connection managers are often more easily scalable than the built-in ones. This is a result of the decoupling of the BOSH service from the rest of the XMPP server. Scaling a standalone connection manager is often achieved with the normal methods for scaling other HTTP services, but scaling a built-in manager relies on the scalability of the underlying XMPP server.

Built-In Managers

Most XMPP servers now come with built-in support for BOSH. These built-in connection managers are easy to set up; they generally require only a small change to the server's configuration to enable them. This means they are often a programmer's first stop when looking for a connection manager for their applications.

Unlike their standalone counterparts, built-in managers cannot establish XMPP connections to external servers, only the server they are running on. This makes them ideal for applications where all users have accounts on the server where the connection manager is located or where all users are connecting anonymously.

Built-in managers have low overhead because they are coupled to the XMPP server. There is no need for a TCP connection to the XMPP server, because the connection manager is running as a part of the server already. A built-in manager can convert the HTTP requests directly into internally routed packets without going through an extra network layer.

Another bit of efficiency gained by built-in managers is decreased serialization costs. Normally applications will store XML data in a specialized data structure that makes the data easy to manipulate and retrieve. When writing the XML to a socket for transmission to the server, this data structure must be serialized into actual XML. In high-performance situations, this serialization cost can be substantial. Standalone connection managers must often re-serialize the data they receive for transmission to the external XMPP server, but built-in managers can avoid this extra step.

Finally, built-in managers are well tested with their corresponding servers because they are developed as a unit. Standalone connection managers are generally tested against a wide variety of servers, but it is hard to beat the stability afforded by direct integration by the same team of programmers that write the XMPP server.

Connection Manager Trade-offs

Each connection manager has its own strengths and weaknesses.

Support for External Servers

Standalone connection managers can connect to any XMPP server reachable over the Internet, but built-in connection managers can only connect to the server that hosts them.

Setup and Configuration Complexity

Built-in servers are easy to set up because they require only a few configuration file changes to an existing XMPP server. Standalone servers, however, must be installed and configured on their own, making them slightly more complicated.

Scalability

Built-in servers can be much more efficient by saving extra serialization costs, but depend on the underlying server for their scalability. Standalone servers can usually be scaled similarly to any other web service, though they have slightly higher serialization cost.

No solution is perfect for all applications. The correct choice can only be made by careful consideration of the needs of your own applications.

PUNJAB: A STANDALONE MANAGER

If your application demands a standalone connection manager that can make connections to any XMPP server, Punjab can deliver. Punjab is a Python daemon written with the Twisted Python networking library. It is well tested and delivers high performance.

Getting Punjab

You can obtain Punjab from its web site at `http://code.stanziq.com/punjab`. It requires Python 2.5 or later, and Twisted Python 2.5 or later, although Twisted Python 8.1 or later is recommended.

Python is available from the Python web site at `http://www.python.org`. If you are running a Linux distribution or use Mac OS X, a suitable version of Python is probably already installed.

You can find Twisted Python at `http://www.twistedmatrix.com`. Linux users will probably find a version of Twisted Python in their distribution's package list, and Mac OS X users already get a copy preinstalled with the operating system.

Installation and Setup

Punjab can be installed in the familiar Python fashion by using `setup.py`. First, extract the compressed files in the distribution to a directory of your choice. Next, run the following command to install Punjab:

```
python setup.py install
```

Once installed, you can configure Punjab by creating a `.tac` file for it. A `.tac` file contains the application's configuration, and Twisted Python's `twistd` command uses this file when it launches Punjab.

The Punjab package comes with a default `punjab.tac` file, which configures Punjab to run on port 5280 with a BOSH URL of `/xmpp-httpbind`. This default configuration is usually good enough but feel free to change these settings if your application needs something different. The values you will want to change should be clear when you view the file.

Starting and Testing Punjab

Punjab is started by the `twistd` command. To start Punjab as a background process, or daemon, run the following command:

```
twistd -y punjab.tac
```

If you'd rather run Punjab in the foreground you can add the parameter `-n` to the command as shown here:

```
twistd -ny punjab.tac
```

Whichever way you choose, Punjab should start up normally and respond on port 5280 (or the port you chose in the configuration). If you are running Punjab on your local machine, you can visit `http://localhost:5280/xmpp-httpbind` to see if Punjab is working. If it is running on another host, use the host's normal domain name instead of `localhost`.

If Punjab is working correctly, you should see some variant of the following message when you visit the configured URL:

```
XEP-0124 - BOSH
```

Note that unless you are using the flXHR library with Strophe for cross-domain access, you will need to proxy Punjab into your web application's directory tree to comply with JavaScript's same origin policy.

EJABBERD AND MOD_HTTP_BIND: A BUILT-IN MANAGER

ejabberd is one of the most popular XMPP servers out there, and it should be no surprise that it comes with a BOSH connection manager to enable XMPP access over HTTP connections. If you are already running ejabberd as your XMPP server, it is very easy to enable BOSH support.

Obtaining mod_http_bind

ejabberd has included mod_http_bind along with its distribution files for some time, but if you happen to use a version that predates this practice, you can obtain mod_http_bind separately from the ejabberd modules page at `http://www.ejabberd.im/ejabberd-modules`.

If you need to get a copy of ejabberd itself or upgrade your older version, you can always find the latest code at `http://www.ejabberd.im`.

Configuring mod_http_bind

Modules in ejabberd are enabled in the `ejabberd.cfg` file. These files are actually full of actual Erlang syntax data structures, so they don't resemble most configuration files you might be used to. They are still easy to modify if you know what to watch out for.

The default `ejabberd.cfg` file has some web server options already enabled, so you only need to modify those slightly to add connection manager support.

Search through the `ejabberd.cfg` file until you find a section that looks similar to the following:

```
{listen,
 [
  {5222, ejabberd_c2s, [
```

This section of the configuration file handles the ports on which ejabberd will listen for connections. A few lines down, you should see a bit of configuration for port 5280:

```
{5280, ejabberd_http, [
                    http_poll,
                    web_admin
                    ]}
```

You will need to modify this section slightly to add support for `http_bind` instead of `http_poll`. Change the section so that it appears as shown here:

```
{5280, ejabberd_http, [
                    web_admin,
                    {request_handlers, [{["xmpp-httpbind"],
                                         mod_http_bind}}
                    ]}
```

If your configuration file did not already have a section for port 5280, you can easily add the preceding one to the file. Just make sure to put a comma after the last section of the listen block, and then add the new section. For example, see the following highlighted lines where a web section has been added to a listen block that did not previously contain one:

```
{listen,
 [

%% some sections omitted

{5269, ejabberd_s2s_in, [
```

```
                              {shaper, s2s_shaper},
                              {max_stanza_size, 131072}
                          ]},

  {5280, ejabberd_http, [
                          web_admin,
                          {request_handlers, [{["xmpp-httpbind"],
                                            mod_http_bind}}
                      ]}
  ]}.
```

Notice that a comma was added to the section for port 5269, and then a section for port 5280 was added including the new mod_http_bind section.

In addition to modifying the listen section, you must also add mod_http_bind to the modules section. Look for the modules section, which starts like this:

```
{modules
 [
  {mod_adhoc, []},
```

At the end of this section, just insert a line for mod_http_bind, making sure to put a comma at the end of the line preceding the new one:

```
  {mod_disco, []},
  {mod_roster, []},
  {mod_http_bind, []}
 ]}.
```

Once again, a comma was added to the line with mod_roster, and then the new line was added.

Restarting and Testing ejabberd

Once the configuration file is updated with mod_http_bind support, you can restart the ejabberd server by running:

```
ejabberdctl stop
ejabberdctl start
```

ejabberd should start normally, and you should be able to visit http://server.example.com:5280/xmpp-httpbind and see a message about BOSH support. Replace server.example.com with the correct hostname of your XMPP server.

You will also need to proxy this URL under the directory tree that serves your application unless you are using Strophe's flXHR plug-in for cross-domain request support.

PROXIES AND SECURITY POLICY

JavaScript code is subject to numerous restrictions when run inside a web browser. Among these is the same origin policy, which restricts JavaScript to making HTTP connections to the same server from which the application is loaded. If the `index.html` file for your application is served from example.com on port 80, the JavaScript code can only make requests to that same domain and port.

AJAX libraries like jQuery often have partial workarounds for this restriction, but these only help you if the requests you need to make are GETs and the remote server can return data in the special JSON-P format. Unfortunately, BOSH requests are done with HTTP POST, and because the data sent and received is XML, these workarounds won't help.

One solution to this problem is to use Flash's cross-domain abilities to make the HTTP connections, and this approach is used for the applications in this book via Strophe's flXHR plug-in. Another solution is to use a reverse proxy to make a URL local to the application's server proxy a remote BOSH service. To the JavaScript code, the requests are being made to the same server, but on the backend, the data is actually being sent by the web server to a remote service and then the responses are forwarded back to the requestor.

Cross-Domain Requests with Flash

Just like JavaScript, Flash has a strict security policy, but unlike JavaScript, it allows cross-domain requests to be sent to domains that permit such requests. Flash checks for this permission by reading a special configuration file at the target domain, `crossdomain.xml`.

The `crossdomain.xml` must reside in the root directory of the web site to which your application needs to make a cross-domain request. For example, if your application is hosted at `http://pemberley.lit` and it needs to access the connection manager at `http://longbourn.lit:5280/xmpp-httpbind`, then Flash will search the file `http://longbourn.lit:5280/crossdomain.xml` for permission to make the needed cross-domain requests. If a `crossdomain.xml` file is found and contains the appropriate configuration, the requests will be allowed.

To enable a BOSH connection manager to serve arbitrary Flash-based clients, it will need to serve up a permissive `crossdomain.xml` such as the one shown in Listing B-1. Note that this file allows cross-domain requests from *any* domain. If this liberal policy is not right for your application, you can use a more restrictive configuration. See `http://www.adobe.com/devnet/articles/crossdomain_policy_file_spec.html` to learn more about how to craft custom `crossdomain.xml` files.

LISTING B-1: crossdomain.xml

```
<!DOCTYPE cross-domain-policy SYSTEM
"http://www.macromedia.com/xml/dtds/cross-domain-policy.dtd">
<cross-domain-policy>
  <!--
        Cross domain policy file for allow everything.  If you need more
```

continues

```
        information on these, please see:
        http://www.adobe.com/devnet/articles/crossdomain_policy_file_spec.html
-->
 <site-control permitted-cross-domain-policies="all"/>
 <allow-access-from domain="*" />
 <allow-http-request-headers-from domain="*" headers="*" />
```

Serving crossdomain.xml with Punjab

Punjab's default `punjab.tac` configuration file includes support for serving static content. By default it makes the `html` subdirectory of the directory in which it runs accessible from HTTP.

To serve `crossdomain.xml`, just place the file in the `html` directory. You can verify that it is working by visiting `http://bosh.example.com:5280/crossdomain.xml` if your Punjab server is running at bosh.example.com on port 5280.

Serving crossdomain.xml with ejabberd

The ejabberd server also includes support for serving static content with its `mod_http_fileserver` module. You can enable this module and then add the appropriate request handler in ejabberd's configuration file.

First, add the following line within the `modules` section:

```
{mod_http_fileserver, [{docroot, "/path/to/html"}
                       {content_types, [{".xml", "text/xml"}]}]}
```

The `docroot` option provides a path where ejabberd will look for static files to serve. The `content_types` option just adds the appropriate `text/xml` content type to the list of known types. This is needed because ejabberd doesn't include this particular mapping by default.

Now that the module will be loaded, you must add a new request handler to tell ejabberd how and where to serve static files. Modify the `ejabberd_http` section inside the `listen` section of the configuration file to look like this:

```
{5280, ejabberd_http, [
                web_admin,
                {request_handlers, [{["xmpp-httpbind"],
                                     mod_http_bind},
                                    {[], mod_http_fileserver}]}
                ]}
```

The bolded line shows the new request handler, which serves the configured document root at the root of ejabberd's web service.

All that's left is for you to put the `crossdomain.xml` file in the document root. Once the file is in the right spot, you can check that everything is working by visiting `http://example.com:5280/cross-domain.xml`, replacing example.com with the name of your server.

Proxying BOSH

Proxies require the cooperation of a web server and some extra configuration. To make this book's material as simple as possible, the Flash plug-in was used, but sometimes the proxied solution is preferable. For example, the iPhone's web browser does not support Flash, so XMPP applications written for that platform will need to use proxied BOSH connection managers.

The examples in the next sections assume you already have a working BOSH connection manager set up. If you want to experiment with proxying BOSH services without having to set up a BOSH connection manager, you can use the BOSH service at `http://bosh.metajack.im:5280/xmpp-httpbind` for testing.

Configuring Apache to Proxy BOSH

The Apache HTTP server has long been one of the most popular choices for serving web pages and applications, and it has comprehensive proxy support via its mod_proxy module. If you use Apache for your web application, you can add a proxy for a BOSH connection manager.

You'll need to ensure the mod_proxy module is built or otherwise available, although it is often compiled and included by default.

First, you must allow access to the remote BOSH server. You can put the following `<Proxy>` section most anywhere, although it is often placed within the `<VirtualHost>` section or in the main `httpd.conf` configuration file.

```
<Proxy http://bosh.metajack.im:5280/xmpp-httpbind>
    Order allow,deny
    Allow from all
</Proxy>
```

The BOSH URL used here is `http://bosh.metajack.im:5280/xmpp-httpbind`, which can be used for testing, but you should substitute your own BOSH service URL.

Once the BOSH URL is allowed in proxy configurations, you can add the relevant `ProxyPass` and `ProxyPassReverse` lines:

```
ProxyPass /xmpp-httpbind http://bosh.metajack.im:5280/xmpp-httpbind
ProxyPassReverse /xmpp-httpbind http://bosh.metajack.im:5280/xmpp-httpbind
```

These two lines proxy the `/xmpp-httpbind` URL on the local server to the remote BOSH service URL.

Once Apache has been configured, you can restart the Apache server however you normally do so. You can check that the new configuration is working by visiting the `/xmpp-httpbind` URL on your Apache server; you should see some mention there of XEP-0124 or BOSH.

Configuring nginx to Proxy BOSH

nginx (pronounced "engine x") is a small and fast web server created by Igor Sysoev, and it is used by many of the busiest Internet startups due to its amazing performance. nginx also has great support for proxying resources, and this makes it an excellent choice for serving XMPP-enabled web applications.

Proxies are very easy to set up in nginx. You need only add a `location` block within the relevant `server` block. The following example adds the location `/xmpp-httpbind`, which proxies the BOSH service at `http://bosh.metajack.im:5280/xmpp-httpbind`:

```
server {
  listen 80;

  # more configuration..

  location /xmpp-httpbind {
      proxy_pass http://bosh.metajack.im:5280;
  }

  # more configuration..
}
```

Once the configuration is changed and the server restarted, you can test that the proxy setup is working by visiting the `/xmpp-httpbind` resource on your nginx server.

Using Tape for Local Development

If you're developing more than one XMPP application or if you are testing various versions of the same application, it can be a little tedious to keep changing web server configurations to proxy the correct BOSH service. To make this kind of development easy, the Tape program was created. Tape is a really simple instant web server.

Tape is generally run in a directory and serves up the files in that directory and its subdirectories over the Web. In addition to serving static files, it can also proxy arbitrary URLs under the local directory tree. This can be used to proxy BOSH services for use in your XMPP applications without having to set up and configure a traditional web server.

To get the most recent copy of Tape, you can visit `http://github.com/metajack/tape`. Like Punjab, described earlier in this appendix, Tape depends on the Twisted Python framework. It needs no special installation; just put the Tape file in `/usr/local/bin` on OS X or Linux and somewhere in your system path on Windows.

Change to the directory where your application is stored and launch Tape:

```
cd awesome_project
tape
```

By default, Tape serves files at `http://localhost:8273` (8273 spells out T-A-P-E on a phone number pad). You can easily tell Tape to proxy a BOSH service with the `-P` option on the command line:

```
tape -P /xmpp-httpbind=http://bosh.metajack.im:5280/xmpp-httpbind
```

If port 8273 is not to your liking, you can also change the port with the `-p` option:

```
tape -p 8000 -P /xmpp-httpbind=http://bosh.metajack.im:5280/xmpp-httpbind
```

To stop running Tape, simply press Ctrl+C or kill the process.

Tape also supports a simple configuration file that you can put in your XMPP application's directory. This file is named `.taperc`. The following `.taperc` example emulates the previous example using the `-p` and `-P` options:

```
[server]
port = 8000

[proxies]
/xmpp-httpbind = http://bosh.metajack.im:5280/xmpp-httpbind
```

Tape makes it easy to fire up an instant web server that proxies the correct URL. With a `.taperc` file in each XMPP application's directory, you can simply switch to the new project and type `tape`, and your application will be immediately available with the correct configuration.

Tape is also useful for serving the Flash-assisted version of Strophe because Flash's security policy requires that you compile the Flash code either for `file://` URL access or `http://` URL access. In order to use a Flash object with `http://` URLs, the Flash object will need to be served from an `http://` URL. If you don't already have a web server set up and ready to go, Tape makes a fine substitute during development.

MORE BOSH CONNECTION MANAGERS

More BOSH connection managers are available than the ones highlighted in this appendix. The following is a list of the other popular options and where you can find more information about them:

➤ Openfire, an XMPP server written in Java with BOSH support, `http://www.igniterealtime.org/projects/openfire/index.jsp`

➤ Tigase, another XMPP server written in Java with BOSH support, `http://www.tigase.org/`

➤ Prosody, a lightweight, easy-to-use XMPP server written in Lua, `http://prosody.im/`

➤ JabberHTTPBind, a Java servlet–based standalone connection manager, `http://blog.jwchat.org/jhb/`

➤ rhb, a standalone connection manager in Ruby, `http://rubyforge.org/projects/rhb/`

INDEX

-sname, 392
Socialcast, 25
Software Version, 81–82
  disco#info, 148
  XEPs, 95
some_global, 46
sortable(), jQuery UI, 123
spam, 4
<span>, 157
splice(), 261
SRV. *See* service records
SSL, 28
standalone connection managers, 430
  Punjab, 431–432
standards list, 35
stanzas, 4
  from, 10
  to, 10
  <body>, 69–70
  child, 54–55
  <error>, 17–18
  Hello, 53–57
  HTTP, 394
  id, 10–11
  <iq>, 15–17
  large size, 395–396
  matching, 57–58
  <message>, 13–15
  streams, 9
  Strophe.Builder, 54–56
  type, 10
  XMPP, 9–18
<start>, 273, 280, 334
  child, 282
  games, 306
  on_message(), 283
Start Game button, 334
start_collaboration(), 281–282
  chat, 285
  init(), 286–287
  update_pad(), 288
start-game(), <game-started>, 331
start_game(), 330
starting
  game status, 328
  start_game(), 330
startproject, 381
start_time(), 59
<state>, 273–274
state vector, 273–274
  operational transformation, 255
  <priority>, 273–274
statefulness, 29
statistics, 149

status, 405
  games, 328
<status>, 12
statusChanged(), 407–410
  addHandler(), 410
  Strophe, 403
StatusNet, 89
<stop>, 280
  <message>, 273
  on_message(), 283
stop_collaboration()
  chat, 285
  notify, 283
stop-waiting
  on_iq(), 320–321
  on_stop_waiting(), 321
<stop-waiting>, 304, 305
<stream:features>, 19
streams, 9, 19
<stream:stream>, 9, 19, 270
String, 96
stroke(), 227
Strophe, 25–27, 42, 403–404
  attach(), 379, 383
  authentication, 64
  connection managers, 48, 64
  Flash, 41
  flXHR, 41
  handlers, 40
  JavaScript, 32
  pause(), 395
  plug-ins, 43, 401–417
  rawInput(), 75
  resume(), 395
  RID, 379
  send(), 395
  SID, 379
  xmlInput(), 75
Strophe.Builder, 54–56, 74, 76
strophe.js, 42
Strophe.serialize(), 70, 72
<subject>, 191
submit, 208
subscribe, 13, 117
subscribe(), 411
<subscribe>, 216–218
subscribed, 119, 120
subscribed(), 231
subscribe_error(), 231
subscription, 405
  from, 120
  to, 111
  both, 111, 120
  pending, 217
  presence, 105
  pubsub nodes, 217